FROMMER'S
EasyGuide

TO

PRINCE EDWARD ISLAND, NOVA SCOTIA & NEW BRUNSWICK

By
Darcy Rhyno

Easy Guides are ✦ Quick To Read ✦ Light To Carry
✦ For Expert Advice ✦ In All Price Ranges

FrommerMedia LLC

Published by

FROMMER MEDIA LLC

Copyright © 2016 by Frommer Media LLC. All rights reserved. No part of this publication may be repro-
duced, stored in a retrieval system, or transmitted in any form or by any means, electronic, mechanical,
photocopying, recording, scanning or otherwise, except as permitted under Sections 107 or 108 of the
1976 United States Copyright Act, without the prior written permission of the Publisher. Requests to the
Publisher for permission should be addressed to support@frommermedia.com.

Frommer's is a registered trademark of Arthur Frommer. Frommer Media LLC is not associated with any
product or vendor mentioned in this book.

ISBN 978-1-62887-248-4 (paper), 978-1-62887-249-1 (ebk)

Editorial Director: Pauline Frommer
Editor: Pauline Frommer
Production Editor: Erin Geile
Cartographer: Roberta Stockwell
Cover Design: Howard Grossman

For information on our other products or services, see www.frommers.com.

Frommer Media LLC also publishes its books in a variety of electronic formats. Some content that
appears in print may not be available in electronic formats.

Manufactured in the United States of America

5 4 3 2 1

FROMMER'S STAR RATINGS SYSTEM

Every hotel, restaurant and attraction listed in this guide has been ranked for quality and value. Here's
what the stars mean:

★   Recommended
★★ Highly Recommended
★★★ A must! Don't miss!

AN IMPORTANT NOTE

The world is a dynamic place. Hotels change ownership, restaurants hike their prices, museums
alter their opening hours, and buses and trains change their routings. And all of this can occur
in the several months after our authors have visited, inspected, and written about these hotels,
restaurants, museums, and transportation services. Though we have made valiant efforts to keep
all our information fresh and up-to-date, some few changes can inevitably occur in the periods
before a revised edition of this guidebook is published. So please bear with us if a tiny number
of the details in this book have changed. Please also note that we have no responsibility or liabil-
ity for any inaccuracy or errors or omissions, or for inconvenience, loss, damage, or expenses suffered by anyone as a result of assertions in this guide.

CONTENTS

ABOUT THE AUTHOR

Darcy Rhyno is a storyteller first. The author of three books of fiction as well as plays for stage and radio, he infuses his travel writing with character of place. Born to a fishing family in a Nova Scotia fishing village, he is a trusted bank of knowledge when it comes to Canada's Maritime Provinces. His award-winning travel writing has appeared in publications such as *Canadian Geographic Travel*, *BBC Travel*, and *Dreamscapes*.

Darcy Rhyno lives in Little Harbour on Nova Scotia's South Shore.

ABOUT THE FROMMER'S TRAVEL GUIDES

For most of the past 50 years, Frommer's has been the leading series of travel guides in North America, accounting for as many as 24% of all guidebooks sold. I think I know why.

Though we hope our books are entertaining, we nevertheless deal with travel in a serious fashion. Our guidebooks have never looked on such journeys as a mere recreation, but as a far more important human function, a time of learning and introspection, an essential part of a civilized life. We stress the culture, lifestyle, history, and beliefs of the destinations we cover, and urge our readers to seek out people and new ideas as the chief rewards of travel.

We have never shied from controversy. We have, from the beginning, encouraged our authors to be intensely judgmental, critical—both pro and con—in their comments, and wholly independent. Our only clients are our readers, and we have triggered the ire of countless prominent sorts, from a tourist newspaper we called "practically worthless" (it unsuccessfully sued us) to the many rip-offs we've condemned.

And because we believe that travel should be available to everyone regardless of their incomes, we have always been cost-conscious at every level of expenditure. Though we have broadened our recommendations beyond the budget category, we insist that every lodging we include be sensibly priced. We use every form of media to assist our readers, and are particularly proud of our feisty daily website, the award-winning Frommers.com.

I have high hopes for the future of Frommer's. May these guidebooks, in all the years ahead, continue to reflect the joy of travel and the freedom that travel represents. May they always pursue a cost-conscious path, so that people of all incomes can enjoy the rewards of travel. And may they create, for both the traveler and the persons among whom we travel, a community of friends, where all human beings live in harmony and peace.

Arthur Frommer

THE BEST OF THE MARITIME PROVINCES

W ant to know where to find the most spectacular hike, the restaurant with the most creative kitchen, the best hole-in-the-wall pub for authentic folk music in the Maritimes? Read on. This chapter lays out the best Maritime destinations, activities, and experiences to make travel memories that will last a lifetime.

MARITIMES' best AUTHENTIC EXPERIENCES

o **Tapping Your Feet to Cape Breton Fiddle Music** (NS): Nothing says Cape Breton more than a fiddle tune expertly played by a seasoned Island musician at the **Red Shoe Pub** in Mabou, the heart of Celtic Cape Breton where impromptu jams occur regularly. See p. 242.

o **Tintamarre** (NB): For the first 2 weeks of August, the town of **Caraquet** explodes in celebration of the survival of Acadian culture. After much historical persecution, there is more than reason enough for this fortnight of fun to culminate in the *Tintamarre* on August 15, a local parade in which Acadians bang pots and pans, and generally make as much noise as possible as if to say, "We're still here!" See p. 159.

o **Walking onto a Wharf and Saying Hi** (Maritimes): The Maritimes are chock-a-block full of wharves with working fishing boats docked shoulder to shoulder. These are public places, and you should get out onto them to strike up a conversation with a fisherman (they're mostly men, but some women fish too). Start with "How's the season going?"

o **Weekly Ceilidhs** (PEI): Many small community halls in PEI hold weekly *ceilidhs,* or folk music jams, and they do it year-round. Ceilidhs aren't created for tourists, but visitors are warmly welcomed. Great music, lively dancing, and Maritime hospitality make them the best authentic experience bargain in PEI because admission is rarely more than C$5. See chapter 4.

o **Coffee at Timmy's** (Maritimes): It might seem strange to think that a stop at a chain coffee shop—Canada's largest—will provide an authentic experience, but Tim Hortons (nicknamed Timmy's) is where regular folks hang out in numbers, often for hours on end, chatting and telling stories, especially in small towns. To understand average Canadians, their lifestyle, and even their humor, stop at a Timmy's and strike up a conversation with a table of locals.

MARITIMES' best FREE THINGS TO DO

o **Going Public in Halifax** (NS): Of the many free things to do in Halifax, strolling the waterfront from Historic Properties all the way to the Museum of Immigration at **Pier 21** is a joy. I also recommend exploring the futuristic and fun **Halifax Central Library** and meandering through the Victorian-era **Halifax Public Gardens,** an oasis of serenity. See chapter 7.

o **Going to the Beach** (Maritimes): Dozens, perhaps hundreds of beaches await exploration in the Maritimes. Some, such as Cavendish in **Prince Edward Island National** Park and Kellys Beach in **Kouchibouguac National Park** in New Brunswick, are busy spots with amenities like change rooms and lifeguards. Others like Winging Point in the **Gabarus Wilderness Area** on Cape Breton's eastern coast are vast, wild, lonely places where you're unlikely to see another soul. See p. 59, 153, and 260.

o **Cycling Prince Edward Island** (PEI): This province sometimes seems like it was created specifically for bike touring. Villages are reasonably spaced apart, hills are virtually nonexistent, the coastal roads are picturesque in the extreme, and an island-wide bike path offers detours through marshes and quiet woodlands.

o **Driving the Cabot Trail** (NS): One of the world's most scenic drives, the 300km (186-mile) **Cabot Trail** loops around the mountainous northwestern tip of Nova Scotia, including Cape Breton Highlands National Park. Switchback roads reveal breathtaking vistas. See p. 235.

o **Hiking to Cape Split** (NS): The 16km (10-mile) hike on the **Cape Split Trail** through mature forest is lovely, but the real prize is at the end when you break from the trees into narrow meadows with 122m (400 ft.) drops on either side to the raging Bay of Fundy below. See p. 176.

MARITIMES' best OUTDOOR ADVENTURES

o **Biking the Cabot Trail** (NS): Not for the beginner, the long, strenuous loop around **Cape Breton Highlands National Park** is tough on the legs, but serious cyclists will come away with indelible memories. See p 265.

o **Birdwatching at the Maritimes' Wildest Place** (NB): Grand Manan is an isolated island in the Bay of Fundy, but it's just the jumping off point for **Sea Watch Tours** to see colonies of puffins, terns, and razorbills, as well as whales, dolphins, and seals on and around Machias Seal Island. See p. 114.

o **Hiking the Skyline Trail** (NS): Aptly named, the **Skyline Trail** in Cape Breton's Highlands National Park loops through moose-browsed shrubs and woods out to the edge of a cliff on a mountainside overlooking the sea and the dramatic, winding road that gets you there. See p. 265.

o **Hunting the Giant Bar Clam** (PEI): At least two outfitters get you to remote sandbars for unusual clam digging. With **By-the-Sea-Kayaking** in Victoria, a guide will lead you on a paddle of several kilometers to an off-shore sandbar you'd never know was just ankle deep beneath the waves; then return to make clam chowder at the dock. **Tranquility Cove Adventures** of Georgetown transports you by fishing boat to an uninhabited island for a clam dig and boil on the beach. See p. 85 and 47.

o **Sea Kayaking Rugged Coastline** (NS): The twisting, deeply indented coastline of Nova Scotia is custom-made for snooping around by sea kayak. Outfitters are scattered around the province—one of the best (and longest-operated) is Scott Cunningham of **Coastal Adventures** on the Eastern Shore, where you can explore 100 protected islands. See p. 171.

o **Seeing 10 Million Trees** (NB): The panoramic view from the peak of the highest mountain in the Maritimes, **Mount Carleton** (in the provincial park of the same name), includes an estimated 10 million trees, which makes a beautiful 10km (6 miles) hike all the more rewarding. See p. 162.

o **Biking the Confederation Trail** (PEI): The only Canadian province to complete its section of the country-wide **Confederation Trail** is PEI. Jump on for a section or ride the whole 470kms (292 miles) from one side of the island to the other to see pastoral landscapes, secluded woodlands, ocean vistas, and quiet villages. See p. 46.

MARITIMES' best RESTAURANTS

o **Burger Champion** (NS): Burgers so stacked, they come with a steak knife to cut into bite-sized pieces—that's the way they're built at **Coastal Waters Restaurant and Pub** in Ingonish. Their Coastal Ring Burger was featured on TV; it's a 6-ounce patty is topped with homemade smoky barbecue sauce and a giant onion ring. See p. 250.

o **Chef-Made Fish 'n' Chips** (NS): Fish and chips is a humble lunch, served as street food on newspaper in Britain. It's probably the most common menu item in the Maritimes, but in Lunenburg a chef has created an entire restaurant dedicated to its perfection called **The Fish Shack.** See p. 213.

o **Fireworks Feast:** (PEI): Sit down to a nine-course feast created in front of you on a custom-built, 25-foot-long fireplace (crammed with smokers, ovens, and rotisseries) as you chat up the cooks at **Inn at Bay Fortune** run by TV chef Michael Smith. See p. 80.

o **Local Star** (NB): Local food is what the Maritimes are all about, but no one is more imaginative or dedicated to it than Chef Chris Aerni at **Rossmount Inn** near St. Andrews. Goose tongue greens he gathered at the shore will be on the plate that very evening, alongside halibut caught by a local fisherman friend or a salad made with ingredients from Aerni's own garden. See p. 112.

o **Relax at Enrage** (NB): Perched over cliffs gouged by the world's highest tides in a small, white building next to a lighthouse—both humbled by the landscape—the **Cape House Restaurant** at Cape Enrage serves some of the best, most original dishes in the Maritimes. See p. 130.

o **Roadside French Pastries** (NS): From a tiny roadside stand next to a wildly colorful folk art gallery, the **Frog Pond Café** in Chéticamp on the spectacular Cabot Trail sells pastries and croissants that would make a *boulangerie* in France proud. See p. 244.

o **Traditional Lobster Supper** (PEI): Lobster suppers in community halls are a tradition around the Maritimes, but nowhere more so than in PEI, where someone got the bright idea in 1958 to offer **New Glasgow Lobster Suppers** to outsiders. Today, visitors sit down to whole steamed lobster and all the fixings, just like an Islander would. See p. 58.

o **Quick Change (Culinary) Artists** (NB): The name describes this dual-personality restaurant—**Urban Deli** and **Italian by Night.** No mere gimmick, these guys have studied Italian cooking and delicatessen foods in New York and Italy, so the menus are authentic and the food generous and delicious. See p. 125.

o **A Touch of Paris** (NB): Frederick, the waiter at **Windjammer Restaurant** in Moncton, has been tossing Caesar salads tableside for decades. He's old-school, formal, and charming with a thick French accent, and slavishly dedicated to his customers, who are guaranteed a culinary experience that could be taking place in Paris. See p. 137.

MARITIMES' best LODGINGS

o **Algonquin Resort** (NB): Tens of millions in renovations and closed 2 years to carry them out—that's what it took, but the stately, historic Algonquin Resort in St. Andrews is back, classier and more comfortable than ever. See p. 109.

o **Beachside Luxury From Another Era** (PEI): No TV, no phone, no radio—it's just you and miles of beach at the swank **Dalvay by the Sea** resort within the national park on PEI's north coast. See p. 62.

o **Best B&B** (NB): It's not just that you slip into the coziest of rooms at historic **Quartermain House** in Fredericton, it's that you wake up to one of the most delicious breakfast feasts you'll find anywhere, and that it's all delivered by a friendly, charming, and most attentive host. See p. 148.

- **Roomy Sites, Coastal Hikes** (NB): The roomy, wooded campsites at beautiful **New River Beach Provincial Park** would themselves make for a pleasant stay. But it's all the activities that make it one of the region's best campgrounds—long coastal hikes to secluded coves, lovely sandy beaches, games like volleyball, a big playground for kids, a good canteen. See p. 116.

- **Great George** (PEI): Within steps of where Canada was created, the historic Great George is a collection of row houses that pampers guests with swish rooms and chocolate chip cookies. See p. 68.

- **Greenside Vista** (NS): Through floor to ceiling windows, look out on the adjacent greens at **Cabot Cliffs**, one of the world's top golf courses, and beyond to the sea over which fabulous sunsets are guaranteed. See p. 238.

- **Modest Motel with Bragging Rights** (PEI): A motel with property enough for walking trails to the seashore is a rare bird; add super-comfortable rooms for very modest prices at **Clark's Sunny Isle Motel** near Summerside, and you've got a unique value. See p. 88.

- **Restful in the Woods** (NS): The contrast of opulence with the remote location in the peaceful forests of southern Nova Scotia—along with a fantastic dining room and lots of wilderness activities—has generated worldwide buzz for **Trout Point Lodge.** See p. 195.

- **Sleep in a Caboose** (NS): Your choice—sleep in the caboose, a boxcar, or in the Station Master's quarters at the **Train Station Inn,** a set of cozy lodgings within a retired train station. See p. 231.

MARITIMES' best NIGHTLIFE

- **Festivals, Festivals, Festivals** (Maritimes): One of the best ways to experience nightlife in pretty well any Maritime city or town is to arrive during a festival, and there are many. **Celtic Colours** is one of the best, filling the small halls and big concert venues of Cape Breton Island every October. See p. 236.

- **Parties of Historic Proportions** (NS): On the Halifax waterfront, the parties are legendary. Since the 18th century, sailors, laborers, and revelers have gathered in pubs like **The Lower Deck,** on the wharves, and in the alleys in what is now called Halifax Historic Properties for live music, drinking, and dancing. See p. 288.

- **Portside Party** (NB): The seasonal outdoor stage at the water's edge in downtown Saint John entertains folks at four shoulder-to-shoulder pubs like the **Saint John Ale House** that also happen to be some of the best places to eat in the Maritimes. See p. 124.

- **Pubs from Another Era** (PEI): In Olde Charlottetown, you might feel you've travelled through time and space to a 19th-century Irish or English street full of pubs like **Gahan House** and **Olde Dublin Pub** where local pints are on tap and the music is always playing. See p. 72.

o **Stargazing** (NB and NS): For nightlife of the quiet, contemplative kind, head to a Dark Sky Preserve; bring a blanket and gaze upward for great stargazing at three maritime national parks with official Dark Sky designation: **Fundy** and **Kouchibouguac** in New Brunswick, as well as **Kejimkujik** in Nova Scotia. See p. 126, 153, and 185.

o **Whiskey Heaven** (NB): Everything in Fredericton is within walking distance (or a short cab ride); thank goodness, because you'll want to sample more than one of the 100 single malt whiskeys on the menu at **Lunar Rogue,** once named "Greatest Whiskey Bar in the World" by *Whiskey* magazine. See p. 150.

THE MARITIME PROVINCES IN DEPTH

Canada's easternmost provinces can best be described as an eclectic mix of culture, history, nature, and geographic masterpieces, surrounded by mile after nautical mile of deep, gray-blue sea. You're never far from saltwater when traveling the three provinces known as the Maritimes: Nova Scotia, New Brunswick, and Prince Edward Island. Highways carry you alongside it, or to and from it, and most major cities cozy up to it.

This has been a fisherman's paradise since native Canadian times; abundant fish that thrive in icy waters rimming the region provided sustenance and income, and continue to do so today. The Bay of Fundy, Gulf of St. Lawrence, Atlantic Ocean, and the mighty rivers that flow into them influenced the pattern of settlement and provide the elements that hold such appeal for visitors today. The rich salmon-fishing rivers of New Brunswick; the whales of the Bay of Fundy, the glorious beaches of Prince Edward Island; the rugged, scenic vistas of Cape Breton; and the wide, protected bays of Nova Scotia's South Shore all translate into the foundation of a great vacation.

From the beginning, the Maritimes have been a challenging place to carve out a living. The abundance of natural bounty is offset by short summer growing seasons and long, storm-tossed winters. For travelers, those challenges become true benefits. Cooled by sea breezes, summers are appealing for those who suffer from the heat and humidity prevalent in other regions. Colder waters ensure an abundant year-round supply of delicious seafood—yes, they harvest in winter, sometimes through the ice. Topnotch chefs and cooks are drawn to this region, where the emphasis has long been on local ingredients and natural bounty; wineries and distillers are a growth industry, and people eagerly seek out new culinary experiences. Winter snows bring enthusiasts for snowmobiling, pond hockey, cross-country and downhill skiing, skating, and more, in pristine white landscapes. Spring and fall are especially appealing for nature lovers and photographers lured by migrating sea birds, whales, and seals, as well as wildflowers and autumn foliage; golfers looking for deals on world class courses will find much to like in these seasons.

The oft-touted friendliness of Maritimers reflects a high value placed on community. Indeed, you have to appreciate those who dug in and made the place their own. First Nations followed by English, Scottish, Irish, and French colonists, Black Loyalists, as well as other nationalities, created unique communities that have retained their culture to this day. Some have grown into cities rich with nightlife, dining, museums, and shopping in historic markets and modern malls. Others remain small and continue to live life based around activities like kitchen parties and community dinners or picnics.

Today the ocean is a major tourist draw. If ever a place were built for ecotourism and the quiet contemplation of nature, it's Eastern Canada. Wildlife-watching and deep-sea fishing are right up there with museum-hopping, toe-tapping music, scenic driving, and golf as top draws.

Tiring of megacities and life in the fast lane? Keening for a pie of locally harvested berries, a kayak in quiet waters, a private stretch of beach, or a spot of spontaneous fiddle music at the local pub? Well, then, this is the best place in North America. Kick off those shoes. They'll probably get wet anyway.

THE MARITIMES TODAY

NOVA SCOTIA   Canada's second-smallest province is almost entirely surrounded by the salt water that helped create a surprising variety of geological regions and three UNESCO World Heritage Sites—Joggins Fossil Cliffs, Grand Pré (the cultural heart of French Acadia), and the fishing town of Lunenburg. The capital, Halifax, has one of the best natural harbors in North America. As a result, the city became a financial and economic powerhouse back in the days of British colonialism and has never looked back. Modern Halifax, the region's largest city, is a transportation hub and center of industry and commerce. Culture and education, which came with European settlement, continue to affect city life today, with colleges and universities fostering a youthful, edgy element to entertainment, restaurants, and outdoor activities.

Beyond city limits, a number of distinctive regions are blessed with beaches, spectacular cliffs, ocean vistas, forests, and farmlands as well as fascinating history and culture. Music is a way of life on Cape Breton Island with its rich Scottish heritage and one of Canada's most spectacular national parks. The South Shore region, where German, Loyalist, and Acadian influences remain strong, embraces both the Atlantic Ocean and the Bay of Fundy. The isthmus between the Minas Basin and Northumberland Strait is world renowned for its rich fossil grounds and evidence of prehistoric times.

NEW BRUNSWICK   For many years, New Brunswick was referred to as a drive-through province that separated Nova Scotia, Prince Edward Island, and even Newfoundland from the rest of Canada and the United States. Smart tourists knew better and have been passing the message along. These days,

New Brunswick—with its beautiful Bay of Fundy, St. John River Valley, Acadian Peninsula, quaint villages, and Appalachian Mountains—is a destination of choice. Its cities are unique. Fredericton is a genteel place where history and culture can be tasted and sampled like fine wine. Saint John also reflects its past. As a seaport, it's always been a place to come ashore and enjoy great pubs, food, and entertainment. Today, it is a cruise-ship destination, and has primo nature parks and walking trails. Moncton capitalizes on its moniker, "Hub of the Maritimes," by offering big concerts and a variety of accommodations.

Culturally, New Brunswick is Canada's only officially bilingual province. With its population split between Anglophones and Francophones (a third of the province's residents speak French), and its heritage both proudly Acadian and proudly Anglophone, this province is a model for blending cultures. Head for the Tintamarre in Caraquet, a mid-August festival celebrating the Acadian national holiday, and you will feel as warm a welcome as at a typical Loyalist Thanksgiving dinner—in fact, New Brunswick is sometimes called the Loyalist Province, because so many United Empire Loyalists (Brits and Blacks still loyal to the crown) fleeing the United States after the American Revolution settled here.

PRINCE EDWARD ISLAND   This island soothes visitors' souls by offering places for quiet relaxation. An island of rolling hills, red soil, potato farms, and prolific wildflowers—plus healthy doses of fishing boats, golf, Acadian culture, and children's literature (you'll see what I mean)—PEI is the sort of place best explored via touring by car, RV, motorcycle, or bicycle (the ambitious can walk or cycle from tip to tip on quiet trails). The province's harborside capital city of Charlottetown is genuinely attractive, historic, and culturally diverse; this was the place where the deal consolidating Canada into one nation ("Confederation") was born, and it's still a little gem of a town.

The island has, somewhat remarkably, managed to retain the bucolic flavor of a century ago, and pockets of sprawl are still few and far apart. You can see signs of growth in the suburbs outside Charlottetown, and small developments here and there, but basically, the population of the province remains that of a large town. Much of the province is devoted to farming, fishing, arts, and tourism; a rural lifestyle prevails. Residents and visitors like it that way.

LOOKING BACK AT THE MARITIME PROVINCES

Here's a brief look at some history and trends that have shaped Eastern Canada.

Indigenous Peoples

Maritime Archaic Indians, primarily a hunting-and-fishing culture, populated parts of Atlantic Canada beginning some 7,500 years ago. These early natives relied chiefly on the sea for their food but eventually disappeared . . . why, nobody knows. Could it have been the long winters?

When Europeans discovered the region we now know as the Maritimes (Nova Scotia, New Brunswick, and Prince Edward Island) there were three Aboriginal groups: the Mi'kmaq, Maliseet, and Passamaquoddy, who have lived here for at least 500 generations. Part of the Algonquin linguistic family, these peoples lived a nomadic life of fishing, trapping, and hunting, changing camp locations several times each year to take advantage of seasonal fish runs, wildlife movements, and the like.

Today, more than 30,000 Mi'kmaq and Maliseet inhabit the region, adding to the cultural mix that is the Maritimes.

European Fishermen & British Loyalists

There are many theories about which Europeans were first to set foot in the Maritimes, but it is generally accepted that English explorer John Cabot visited in 1497. The Portuguese set up a small settlement in 1520, but left in 1523; apparently they didn't get along with the Mi'kmaq.

The French made the first significant attempts at establishing a new colony, though they failed time after time. Eventually, the Acadians managed to get a foothold and survive brutal winters with the help of dyke-building technology imported from France, and with the help of the Mi'kmaq, who allied with them against the British who were, at times, more brutal than the winters. They established a fur-trade monopoly through the Acadia Company and were determined to establish permanent settlement in the New World. In 1604, a party led by Samuel de Champlain built a fort on St. Croix Island up a river from Passamaquoddy Bay near St. Stephen, New Brunswick, but the site was unsuitable with few trees, no firewood or water, and harsh weather. Even worse, the native peoples were not interested in trade, just war. The French abandoned the settlement in the spring of 1605. The island is now a historic site.

Because of the difficult winters and a lack of experience surviving on this continent, the region's first permanent European settlement didn't come until 1605, when the Champlain group sailed across the Bay of Fundy and arrived at Port Royal—right across the river from present-day Annapolis Royal. Champlain called the lovely Annapolis Basin "one of the finest harbors that I have seen on all these coasts," and the strategic importance of that well-protected harbor was later proven during struggles for control of the region, when a series of forts was constructed on the low hills overlooking the water.

The settlement's impacts are still felt today. It was here that North America's first apple trees, grains, and dandelions were planted. As well, the Order of Good Cheer, the first social club, was established here.

Despite Revolutionary troubles brewing to the south, the eastern provinces were settling organically. Farmers and fishermen slowly began filtering in from Europe and the colonies to the south. The Louisbourg fortress was built. The mid-1750s saw an explosion of settlement along the South Shore, including the towns of Chester (by Brits), Mahone Bay (by Anglican devotees), and Lunenburg (by German, Swiss, and French fisherfolk and boatbuilders, who laid it out in a grid based on British planning policy, despite its hilly terrain).

And, of course, there was Halifax, whose well-shaped natural harbor attracted Europeans in 1749 when Colonel Edward Cornwallis established a military outpost here, violating an earlier treaty and sparking a war with First Nations people that spread to the Acadians.

The signing of the Treaty of Paris in 1783, which recognized the American right of separation from Mother England, exploded like a bombshell. This single piece of paper would have profound effects on the subsequent composition and history of the Maritimes.

For those in America whose sympathies (or livelihoods) lay with the British—including freed and escaped slaves of African descent—the treaty created an untenable situation: They were people without a country. But England still held Eastern Canada. The solution was obvious.

A huge wave of fearful British Loyalist settlers and their families began fleeing New England and New York City by ship, horse, and foot, washing up at little harbors like Shelburne, Nova Scotia (which became a wooden-boat-building stronghold—bigger, for a time, than both Montréal and Halifax). Before the arrival of the Loyalists, only about 5,000 peopled lived in the territory that would become New Brunswick, including indigenous peoples, uprooted Acadians, and first-generation settlers from Ireland, Great Britain, and New England. French settlers also ran for the eastern provinces. The Rustico region on the northern shore of PEI became one of the first in Canada to be permanently populated by the Acadians following the treaty's signing. Others were driven out violently by the British during the great expulsion of the Acadians starting in 1755.

An Industrial Age

Tensions grew with the Maritimes' sudden spike in population, but somehow the British retained their hold on Canada for nearly another century, though that too would eventually crumble. The eastern provinces' place in Canadian history was forever cemented in 1864 when Charlottetown hosted the conference that would eventually lead to the creation of Canada as a separate nation—an event that is still remembered and celebrated on PEI today. The deeper significance was clear, too: This was no longer some backwoods fishing hole. The Maritime Provinces, with their command of the sea and of the ship-building capacity to rule and harvest it, could be an engine of growth for the new nation.

And so it was. The second half of the 19th century was a time of incredible commerce and excitement for the Maritimes. No longer were they isolated fishing posts; railroads were added to ships for the export of fish to New York and Boston faster and fresher than ever. Boats could be built or fixed here, then sent anywhere in the world.

Demographics swung wildly as a consequence. Sydney, a working-class town, became northern Nova Scotia's industrial hub for decades, a legitimate rival to Halifax. Yet this northern heyday would be sadly short-lived, lasting only three generations or so. As the highway and the airplane took over as means of transportation on the continent, the shipbuilding centers supported by the mill towns and factories began to wane.

And then the Great Depression hit.

Modern Times: Tourism & Natural Resources

In the wake of the Great Depression and the larger changes happening in the world—new transport methods; wars; a growing taste for production, consumption, and fashion—the Maritimes were forced to scramble. Fortunately, the treasure that the land and sea and laidback, friendly culture provided was recognized and a tourism industry was born. While Americans began vacationing in the more temperate seaside towns of the north like St. Andrews and Chester, a concerted effort to attract tourists to more areas in the region began. Rather than cutting down all the trees, swaths of forest were preserved, and national and provincial parks were developed. Golf courses, roads, inns, and expansive resort hotels were built at a furious pace. The spectacular Cabot Trail, winding around Cape Breton Island, was paved in 1939, ushering in decades of wide-eyed tourists. Salmon fishing drew the rich and famous to New Brunswick's great rivers.

During the years since, the Maritimes have gradually moved ahead with the times. Natural resources sectors—specifically forestry, farming, mining, and fishing—remain the mainstays of the regional economy, just as they have for generations, though cultural industries, science, and media have grown significantly of late. The region's many protected natural harbors have also created important ports for oil, and similar products, imported from around the world to North America. Visitors continue coming for the unique charms of the eastern provinces; tourism income is still necessarily important.

There are subtle changes occurring. Second homes and cottages in the Maritimes are lately more valuable than before, and an uptick in new development by outsiders worries some longtime residents. Meanwhile, the provinces' most remote parts have not felt any economic kick from the past half-century of growth. For these locals, and for those moving here to work remotely via the Internet, the Maritimes remain an enduringly difficult place to eke out a living—yet they continue doing so, just as previous generations did, choosing lifestyle and community over the comforts and the faster pace of life in more populated areas of the country.

ARCHITECTURE

History is reflected in the buildings, particularly in towns like Yarmouth, where glamorous sea captains' homes reflect a prosperous era of seafaring; or Summerside, where skilled craftsmen put out of work at the end of the shipbuilding era turned their skills to building homes for those who made their fortunes farming silver fox for their fur—now known as "silver fox homes." The list of towns with unique architectural districts includes St. Andrews, NB, and Nova Scotia's Lunenburg, Wolfville, Shelburne, and more. Cities like Halifax, Saint John, Fredericton, and Charlottetown all have well-cared-for architectural districts, particularly on their waterfronts. Visitor information centers have maps of walking tours, and most have guided tours in the summer.

Those with an interest in architecture should factor visits to national historic sites and regional museums into their planning. Restorers and re-creators present the past with meticulous attention to detail.

THE MARITIMES IN POP CULTURE

Here's a "starter kit" of films, music, and literature that can prepare you for a rewarding visit to the Atlantic Provinces.

Books

Anne of Green Gables by L. M. Montgomery is a lovely evocation of 19th-century life on Prince Edward Island. Originally published in 1908, Montgomery's fictional, ever-sunny Anne is the island's most famous export, hands down; this cycle of children's novels about an adopted red-haired girl remains enormously popular worldwide, thanks to both Montgomery's portrait of quaint island life and Anne's irrepressible optimism and imagination. It's less well known that there is an entire series of *Anne* books; *Gables,* the original in the series, only takes Anne's life through age 16. The best "primer" for adult visitors, if you can locate it, is the Oxford University Press edition of *Anne of Green Gables.* It's annotated with biographical material from Montgomery's life: excerpts from the author's girlhood journals, colloquial explanations of cookery, directions to locations featured in the book, and the like.

The other PEI writer you must know about is **Milton Acorn,** the poet and playwright. It's was his first major collection of poetry, *I've Tasted My Blood* (1969) that earned him the affectionate nickname "the people's poet" (other writers created The People's Poet Award for Acorn when he was passed up for the major Governor General's Literary award, which he won in 1975 for *The Island Means Minago*). A carpenter by trade and an Islander to the core, Acorn's best writing illuminates everyday life on PEI, his poetry peopled with the working folks of Canada.

Three writers are essential to getting into the soul of New Brunswick. **David Adams Richards** is by far the most important English writer ever to pick up a pen in the province. His many award-winning novels of the hardscrabble lives of the people of the Miramichi constitute a body of work that has been compared to William Faulkner in the U.S. and Feodor Dostoyevsky of Russia. Start with his early Miramichi trilogy *Nights Below Station Street* (1988), *Evening Snow Will Bring Such Peace* (1990), and *For Those Who Hunt the Wounded Down* (1993).

His equivalent in French is the Acadian writer **Antonine Maillet,** the author the play *La Sagouine,* named for the cleaning lady who delivers the entire piece as a monologue and is now the subject of a small Acadian theme park near Caraquet. Like Richards, her characters were the ordinary people of New Brunswick's Acadian coast, and her themes universal. She wrote many novels and plays throughout her career, many of which won major awards, some of them in France where she was named an Officer of the Order of Arts and Letters in 1985.

Herb Curtis is New Brunswick's Mark Twain. The characters who populate his novels are every bit as deceptively ordinary as Richard's and Maillet's, but Curtis takes a humorous approach to his subjects, the most prominent of which is the way the simple lives of his Miramichi inhabitants change as American anglers come to fish salmon in the great river. His Brennen Siding trilogy gained international attention and nominations for major awards like the Commonwealth Prize.

So many great authors have come out of Nova Scotia, it's difficult to recommend just a few. Still, to help understand the people and the history of the province, and indeed the region, there are some essentials. Cape Breton writer **Allistair MacLeod** only wrote three books in his life, but they were all masterpieces that laid bare the hearts and lives of miners, fishermen, and subsistence farmers from the past and today.

While MacLeod's work at times leans toward nostalgia, the gritty realism of **Lynn Coady**'s novels is an unsentimental look into the lives of troubled Cape Breton characters who struggle with everything from alcoholism to mental illness, exacerbated by chronic unemployment and poverty. Her very first novel *Strange Heaven* (1998) won Canada's top literary prize, the Governor General's Award.

The lively, colorful poetry, plays, and novels of **George Elliott Clarke** are already considered national treasures; some of his material even spawned an opera. Clarke refers to his own work as Africadian for the way it explores the historic and contemporary lives of the descendents of African slaves amid the French Acadians of Nova Scotia and New Brunswick. His densely poetic novel *Whylah Falls* (1990) combines many voices to explore the life of a Black community in rural Nova Scotia.

Finally, for a deeper understanding of the Mi'kmaq people, look for a collection of the poetry and songs of **Rita Joe,** sometimes referred to as the Mi'kmaq poet laureate. Her most compelling work is actually her memoir, *Song of Rita Joe: Autobiography if a Mi'kmaq Poet* (1996), which includes poetry and photographs, and lays bare the many difficulties she faced in her life and the great things she nonetheless accomplished for herself and her people.

Films

Many films have been made in the Maritimes (sharp-eyed film buffs may recognize parts of Nova Scotia during their travels), but precious few have been made *about* them. Perhaps the best known is *Margaret's Museum* starring Helena Bonham Carter. It's based on a short novel famous in the Maritimes called *The Glace Bay Miners' Museum* by **Sheldon Currie,** a gripping love story of a young man and woman sucked into and eventually destroyed by life in a Cape Breton mining town. For those who don't mind a lot—and I mean a lot—of profanity, alcohol, and general idiocy in their humor, check out the smash hit TV series *Trailer Park Boys,* made and set in a Halifax trailer park.

Among recent award-winning films made here are *Titanic* and *The Shipping News.* Other films include *K-19* and *The Widowmaker.*

Music

It is often said that music ties together all of the Atlantic provinces. Nowhere is that more evident than at the East Coast Music Awards. This annual gathering demonstrates the diversity of both established and upcoming talent, be it traditional Celtic or Acadian, pop, blues, jazz, classical—the list just goes on. Homegrown music in the Maritimes leans toward Celtic-inflected folk, or pop music greatly influenced by that sound, but certainly isn't limited to it; over the past couple of decades, Halifax has turned out so much alternative pop music with bands like **Sloan,** it's become known as the Seattle of the east. Canada's original blues musician, **Dutch Mason,** known as "Prime Minister of the Blues," might hail from Truro, Nova Scotia.

Music from the region was entertaining the world as early as the 1930s, when **Hank Snow** of Nova Scotia burst on the scene. His first massive hit, "I'm Movin' On" was followed by "The Golden Rocket," "I Don't Hurt Anymore," "I've Been Everywhere," and "Hello Love." The country singer charted more than 70 singles. One of Elvis Presley's heroes, he's a member of the Country Music Hall of Fame and was a Grand Ole Opry staple for years. Today you can visit the Hank Snow Home Town Museum in Liverpool, Nova Scotia.

Another local country icon is **Stompin' Tom Conners.** Born in New Brunswick, he grew up on Prince Edward Island; his boot-stompin' style resulted in 20 albums and loyal fans across the nation. The great **Stan Rogers** and his Maritime-influenced folk music are feted at an annual Stan Rogers Festival, also known as StanFest, in Canso, Nova Scotia, which brings songwriters and 50 or more performers from around the world together with music fans. His songs "Northwest Passage" and "Barrett's Privateers" are extremely likely to be belted out in pubs when Maritimers gather and the beer flows free.

In 1966, "**The Men of the Deeps,**" coal miners from Cape Breton, formed and continue touring to this day. This world-renowned male choral ensemble was the first Canadian musical group to tour the People's Republic of China, and has toured most major cities in North America. Dressed in miners' coveralls and hard hats, these champions of miners around the world make an impressive statement when they enter a concert hall in total darkness, with their helmet lamps providing the only light.

With country and folk tunes like "Flying on Your Own" and "Working Man" topping the charts internationally, **Rita MacNeil**'s fame in Canada, the United Kingdom, and Australia led to her receiving the Order of Canada. MacNeil took her Cape Breton style to the world, but it was **John Allan Cameron** who showcased Nova Scotia's Celtic heritage to the mainstream. This ordained Catholic priest–turned–folk singer became known as "The Godfather of Celtic Music," who took Cape Breton music out of the kitchen and into the world. As did fiddler **Natalie MacMaster,** who thrills audiences in Europe and North America, performing with such greats as Paul Simon and Faith Hill. **The Rankin Family** of Cape Breton epitomizes much about the Maritime music scene. From a family of 12 who entertained the neighbors at local *ceilidhs,* these siblings have gone on to perform traditional jigs, reels, and Celtic folk songs with signature harmonies across Canada. Nova Scotia native **Sarah McLachlan** has made it big around the globe, thanks to haunting pop classics: *Fumbling Towards Ecstasy* features the single, "Possession"; *Surfacing* features "Sweet Surrender" and "Building a Mystery"; and the live record, *Mirrorball,* includes the gem, "I Will Remember You."

Arguably the best-known Maritime star, **Anne Murray,** was the first Canadian female solo singer to reach #1 on U.S. charts with her signature song, "Snowbird." The Nova Scotian crooner has sold over 54 million albums and won so many awards and accolades that they had to have a special museum, the Anne Murray Centre, built in Springhill to house them all. In 2011, *Billboard* magazine ranked her number 10 on their list of the 50 biggest AC (adult contemporary) artists of all time.

Music is part of life in the Maritimes, with festivals, concerts, and stage performances touching on every genre from blues to classical, Celtic to jazz. Search it out wherever you happen to be.

EATING & DRINKING

For generations, Eastern Canada has been known as the go-to place for great seafood; be it clams boiled up on the beach, deep-fried fish from a shack on the wharf, lobster from a community hall "supper," chowder at a festival, or a top-level chef's culinary masterpiece. As self-sufficient communities, Maritime towns have always placed great value on locally produced foods. The Culinary Institute of Canada in Charlottetown boasts gold-medal wins from Olympic and World competitions, as do many chefs from the region. Innovative restaurants are as common in small towns and rural areas as they are in cities.

Local Maritime specialties include:

BERRIES Blueberries, cranberries, raspberries, and strawberries top a long list of local fruits that burst with flavor. Fresh berry pies appear on most menus during their season, and farmers' markets are treasure troves for berry lovers. Natural blueberry and cranberry juices, as well as jams and jellies, are some of the region's best artisanal products.

FIDDLEHEADS & MUSHROOMS Spring greens like fiddlehead ferns and goose tongue grass are popular in New Brunswick and indicative of fresh wild harvests that include such delicacies as chanterelle mushrooms. Watch for them on seasonal menus at restaurants and at farmers' markets.

FISH & CHIPS Fish-and-chips shops certainly aren't unique to Eastern Canada, but they do the chippie proud. The most famous specialists are in the

Halifax area, the shoreline just to the south, and pretty well everywhere else along the Atlantic coast.

LOBSTER   Wherever you see inshore boats tied up to a wharf, a fresh lobster meal can't be far away. Among the most productive lobster fisheries are those around Shediac, New Brunswick and along Nova Scotia's entire Atlantic coast (see chapters 5 and 6), though the season varies from place to place.

North central Prince Edward Island is famous for its church-sponsored lobster suppers. The typical supper might include a lobster or two, steamed mussels, and strawberry shortcake. See chapter 4.

MUSSELS & OYSTERS   Some say you can't find better mussels or oysters anywhere in the world than those harvested in the shallow waters of Prince Edward Island. It's hard to argue with that sentiment, though some from New Brunswick and Nova Scotia are appearing beside them; restaurants from New York to Tokyo covet (and pay big bucks for) these prized PEI shellfish. In fact, PEI produces 45 million pounds a year. You can get them relatively cheap at local seafood outlets; sometimes you can even buy a bag off the docks.

RAPPIE PIE   The French enclave known as the Evangeline Trail is one of the best places in Canada to sample tried-and-true Acadian cooking. (The other great areas can be found around New Brunswick's Acadian shore.) Rappie pie, a staple of the Acadian family restaurant, has several variations, such as a rich potato stock–and–onion casserole topped with a pile of pork rinds (yup), and baked. Your body fat percentage *will* tick up after a meal.

SCALLOPS   The waters off Digby Neck (on the southwestern shore of Nova Scotia; see chapter 6) produce some of the choicest, most succulent scallops in the world. They're ubiquitous on menus of restaurants along the western shore of Nova Scotia, and show up in lots of fine kitchens around the rest of the region, too. A light sauté in butter brings out their rich flavor best.

SMOKED FISH   Here and there, particularly along the Atlantic shore of Nova Scotia and New Brunswick's Bay of Fundy, you'll come across the odd fish-smoking shack. That's not really surprising, given the huge supply of smoke-able fish just offshore. The most organized and commercialized operation is the J. Willy Krauch & Sons operation in the village of Tangier, Nova Scotia (see chapter 6). Krauch & Sons' "hot-smoked" herring is a classic.

WHISKEY   Deep in the highlands of Cape Breton, there's a distillery making lovely "Scotch" (which can't be called Scotch, due to appellation rules). So, single-malt whiskey then. It's still fantastic, crafted from the pure local water.

WINES, BEERS & SPIRITS   Each of the three provinces boasts a number of good artisan wineries, breweries, and distilleries that have a legion of awards to their credit. Wine production is concentrated and more advanced in Nova Scotia's Annapolis Valley, but there are winery tours and tastings in Nova Scotia and New Brunswick, too. Prince Edward Island is just starting out with three wineries, two distillers, and a few breweries.

WHEN TO GO

Weather

All the Atlantic Provinces lie within the **North Temperate Zone,** which means that they have weather much like New England in the United States. **Spring** is damp, cool, and short, though it can get warm as it eases into summer.

Summer's compact high season runs from mid-June to mid-September. That's when the great majority of travelers take to the road, enjoying the bright, clear days and warm temperatures. The average high is in the upper 70s°F (around 25°C) although in recent years, temperatures have been rising. Nights can become cool, even approaching light frost, by mid-September. These cool nights are what make summers so appealing—less daytime humidity and a good night's sleep make summer in the Maritimes a joy.

Be aware that there is no "typical" summer weather in Atlantic Canada. The only thing typical is change, and you're likely to experience balmy, sunny days as well as howling rainstorms—quite possibly on the same day. Travelers who come here prepared for an occasional downpour, both psychologically and equipment-wise, tend to be happier than those who expect all blue skies. That's because the weather in all three provinces is to a large degree affected by the ocean. This means frequent fogs, especially on the Fundy Coast of New Brunswick and the Atlantic Coast of Nova Scotia. The ocean also offers an unobstructed corridor for high winds, should a storm be making its way up the Eastern Seaboard.

The ocean does temper the climate: Prince Edward Island's summer tends to linger into fall, thanks to the warm, moderating influence of the Gulf of St. Lawrence, and you'll rarely experience a sultry hot, humid day in the Maritimes because of the natural air-conditioning action of the sea breezes.

Fall is a time of bright leaf colors but also rapidly cooling temperatures, especially at night, and much shorter daylight hours. Bring winter sweaters and a heavy coat. It is possible for the tail end of tropical storms or hurricanes to make their way up the Eastern Seaboard. If a storm is forecast, stay put. Your accommodations will be your best source of advice on riding out the storm.

Few travelers, with the exception of winter sports enthusiasts, tackle the Maritimes in the dead of **winter,** as frequent blustery storms sweep in. If you're one of those hardy souls who might, be aware that snow or ice storms are a very real possibility at any time during winter, and they can blow in suddenly; if you're driving, make sure your car is equipped with good snow tires and special antifreeze windshield wash (you can get it from any gas station). And drive cautiously: Outside the major urban areas, most of this region's high-speed arteries are two-lane roads without medians.

Always be aware that the weather can be vastly different throughout the three provinces, especially in winter. Check the weather report for where you are going, as well as where you are at the moment. And remember that folks here live by the saying, "Stay where you're at," should bad weather make travel unsafe. It is perfectly acceptable to be "storm stayed" rather than take risks.

Halifax Average Monthly Temperatures

	JAN	FEB	MAR	APR	MAY	JUNE	JULY	AUG	SEPT	OCT	NOV	DEC
HIGH(°F)	29	29	36	47	57	67	73	73	65	54	44	34
(°C)	–2	–2	2	8	14	19	22	23	18	12	7	1
LOW (°F)	14	14	22	32	41	50	57	57	50	40	32	20
(°C)	–10	–10	–6	0	5	10	14	14	10	4	0	–7

Holidays

The national holidays in Canada are celebrated from the Atlantic to the Pacific to the Arctic oceans; for the traveler, this means all government offices and banks will be closed at these times. (Shops generally close on national holidays.) **National holidays** here include New Year's Day, Good Friday, Easter Monday, Victoria Day (the third Mon in May), Canada Day (July 1; this is a biggie—expect fireworks), Labour Day (first Mon in Sept), Thanksgiving (mid-Oct), Remembrance Day (Nov 11), Christmas Day (Dec 25), and Boxing Day (Dec 26).

Locally observed **provincial holidays** include: Islander Day (third Mon in Feb on Prince Edward Island), a civic holiday (Aug 2) in Nova Scotia, and New Brunswick Day (the first Mon in Aug). Acadians observe their national holiday, Tintamarre, on August 15, usually with celebrations for up to 2 weeks prior to the grand day.

THE LAY OF THE LAND

When you're in the Maritimes, the rocks upon which you climb, sun yourself, and picnic are old—staggeringly old. Before arriving, then, it's a good idea to acquaint yourself with the natural history of the place. Armed with a little respect and appreciation for the landscape, travelers just might treat it more reverently—and help ensure that it remains for future generations to enjoy.

Rocky Road: Geology of the Landscape

The beginnings of Eastern Canada are about half-a-billion years old. You read right. At that time, deep wells of liquid rock known as magma were moving upward, exploding in underground volcanoes, then hardening—still underground, mind you—into granite-like rocks. Later, natural forces such as wind and water wore away and exposed the upper layers of these rocks. Their punishment was only beginning, however; soon enough (geologically speaking, that is), what is now eastern North America and most of Europe began to shove up against each other, slowly but inexorably. This "collision" (which was more like an *extremely* slow-motion car wreck) heated, squeezed, transformed, and thrust up the rocks that now form the backbone of the coastline. Ice ages came and went, but the rocks remained; the successive waves of great glaciation and retreat scratched up the stones, and the thick tongues of pressing ice cut deep notches out of them. Huge boulders were swept up and deposited by the ice in odd places; if you visit Peggy's Cove, Nova Scotia, you'll see what I mean. When the glaciers finally retreated for the last time, tens of thousands of years ago, the water melting from the huge ice sheet covering North America swelled the level of the Atlantic high enough to submerge formerly free-flowing river valleys and give the coastline, and places like Cape Breton, their distinctively rocky, knuckled faces. (At Prince Edward Island, the boulders left behind tons of silt and sand; that's what the island is, basically: a big sandbox.)

Simultaneously with the formation of the landscape came the flora and fauna. At places like Joggins and Parrsboro, Nova Scotia, you can see the fossils of life forms from the Coal Age some 300 million years ago right in the face of cliffs eroded by the Bay of Fundy. Much more recently, after the last ice age, more recognizable plants and animals returned; conifers such as spruce, pine, and fir trees and hardwoods like maple, birch, and beech grew, then died and decomposed to create soil. It was tough work: Most of Eastern Canada is a rocky, acidic place. Yet they persevered, and forests covered much of the coastal bedrock.

As the trees and flowers and fruits became reestablished, animals wandered back here, too—some now extinct (such as the mastodon) but some still thriving today in the fields, hills, and woods of the region. Of course, the forests are only a shadow of their former selves, the enormous old-growth trees cut for everything from ship's masts to lumber bound for Europe and the U.S. Similarly, the animal kingdom has changed dramatically since the arrival of Europeans. Gone, for example, are the herds of caribou that roamed the land and sea lions that lived along these shores. Introduced species like the white-tailed deer and the starling have taken their place.

Eastern Canada's unique position—it is near the warm Gulf Stream—also bequeathed it plenty of marine (and economic) life: The current passes over the high, shallow undersea plateau known as Georges Bank between New England and Nova Scotia, bringing an astonishing variety of microorganisms, and the marine life that follows, right to these provinces' doorsteps. Migrating whales make for a wonderful spectacle each year as they hunt the fish and plankton that thrive in these waters; seabirds travel similar passages, filling the wetlands, forests, and fields.

The waters once teemed with fish, but today, the once-coveted Atlantic salmon is in serious trouble, and the Northern cod that drew Europeans here in the first place is nearly commercially extinct. Instead, the ocean now seems to be an endless supply of lobster and crab, two fisheries that still thrive.

Then there are the coast's tidal pools and estuaries, that precarious zone where land and rock or marsh meet ocean; a closer look at these pools reveals an ever-changing world of seaweed, snails, barnacles, darting water bugs, clams, shellfish, mud-burrowing worms, and other creatures. Interestingly, the type of life you find changes in well-marked "bands" as you get closer to water; rocks that are always submerged contain one mixture of seaweed, shellfish, and marine organisms, while rocks that are exposed and then re-submerged each day by the tides have a different mix. It's fascinating to note how each particular organism has found its niche. Move it up or down a foot and it would perish.

What follows is only the barest sketch of some of the nature you'll find in Eastern Canada.

The Flora & Fauna
TREES & SHRUBS

BALSAM FIR   The best-smelling tree in the provinces must be the mighty balsam fir, whose tips are sometimes harvested to fabricate aromatic Christmas-tree wreaths and are farmed for Christmas trees. They're found in pockets of New Brunswick and Nova Scotia. It's sometimes hard to tell a fir from a spruce or hemlock, though the balsam's flat, paddle-like needles (white underneath) are unique—only a hemlock's are similar. Pull one off the twig to be sure; a fir's needle comes off clean, a hemlock's ragged. Still not sure you've got a fir tree on your hands? The long, glossy, almost purplish cones are absolutely distinctive. You can find tree farms around Lunenburg, Nova Scotia and other areas in the Maritimes.

LOWBUSH BLUEBERRY   Canada is the world's largest producer of wild blueberries, officially known as lowbush blueberries, cultivating nearly 40 million pounds annually. All three provinces support significant blueberry production; it's Nova Scotia's number one crop measured by acreage, export sales, and value. With shrubby, tea-like leaves and thick twigs, the plants lie low on exposed rocks on sunny hillsides, or sometimes crop up in shady woods; most of the year, the berries are inconspicuous and trail harmlessly underfoot. Come late summer, however, they're suddenly very popular—for bears as well as people. The wild berries ripen slowly in the sun (look behind and beneath leaves for the best bunches) and make for great eating off the bush, pancake baking, or jam making.

RED & SUGAR MAPLE   These two maple trees look vaguely alike when turning color in fall, but they're actually quite different, from the shapes of their leaves to the habitats they prefer. **Red maples** have skinny, gray trunks and like a swampy or wet area; often, several of the slim trunks grow together into a clump, and in fall the red maples' pointy leaves turn a brilliant scarlet color almost at once. **Sugar maples,** on the other hand, are stout-trunked trees with lovely, substantial leaves (marked with distinctive u-shaped notches), which autumn slowly changes to red and flame-orange. Sugar maples grow in or at the edges of mixed forests, often in combination with birch trees, oak trees, beech trees, and hemlocks. Their sap, of course, is collected and boiled down to make delicious maple syrup—big business in Eastern Canada.

RED & WHITE PINE   These pines grow in sandy soils. The **eastern white pine** is the familiar "King's pine" once prevalent throughout the northeast portions of North America; you can recognize it by its very long, strong needles that are always arranged five to a clump, like a hand's fingers. Its trunk was prized for the masts of ships of war in the 16th to 19th centuries. Countless huge pines were floated down Canadian rivers by lumberjacks. Sadly, old-growth white pines are virtually nonexistent today in many regions, but you can still find the tree throughout Eastern Canada. The less common **red pine** is distinguished by pairs of needles and a pitchy trunk. It grows on PEI (where it loves the sandy soil), and also in parts of New Brunswick and Nova Scotia.

LAND MAMMALS

BEAVER Often considered symbolic of Canada, beavers almost became extinct in the early 1900s due to a brisk world trade in beaver pelts and the rapid development of wetlands. Today the beaver's lodge-building, stick-chewing, and hibernating habits are well-known once again; you'll find them in streams, lakes, ponds, and often in wet areas beside the road. Beavers seem to think that man invented culverts as an aid to dam building.

BLACK BEAR Black bears live in Eastern Canada, though you're unlikely to see the shy creatures. The bears are mostly—emphasis on *mostly*—plant eaters and docile; they're the smallest of the North American bears and don't want trouble. Though they'll eat just about anything, these bears prefer easily reached foods on the woodland floor, such as berries, mushrooms, nuts . . . and campers' leftovers. (Suspend leftovers in a "bear bag" away from your tent if you're camping in bear territory.) Black bears fatten up in fall for a long winter hibernation that averages 6 months.

MOOSE Nothing says Canada like a moose, and the huge, skinny-legged, vegetarian moose is occasionally seen in the deep woods of Eastern Canada; in Nova Scotia, they're listed as a provincially endangered species, but both Cape Breton and New Brunswick hold a lottery dispensing hunting permits based on quotas determined annually. Moose are sometimes seen beside the road in New Brunswick and in Cape Breton, more rarely on mainland Nova Scotia. (But there are *no* moose—or even deer—on PEI.) The animal prefers deep woods, lakes, ponds, and marsh, and you can't miss it: The rack of antlers on the male, broad lineman-like shoulders, spindly but quick legs, and sheer bulk (it's as big as a truck) ensure you won't mistake it for anything else.

WHALES, DOLPHINS, PORPOISES & SEALS

DOLPHIN Two very similar-looking species of dolphin—the **Atlantic white-sided dolphin** and the **white-beaked dolphin**—come to the Atlantic coast of the eastern provinces. Cute and athletic, these dolphins also occasionally turn up on beaches, for the same reason as pilot whales: Large groups are occasionally stranded by the tides, resulting in major rescue efforts, since they will die if unable to get back to sea in time.

FINBACK WHALE A visitor to Eastern Canada's waters twice a year when migrating between polar and equatorial waters, the finback is the second largest of the world's whales. Finbacks are fast movers who spout up to 4m (13 ft.) above the surface and can be viewed from a mile away; even so, you will need a whale-watching excursion boat to see them. They often travel in pairs or groups of a half-dozen, leading to exciting sightings. Shipping and added fishing are having an impact on world populations; thus finbacks, a type of baleen whale, are protected under Canada's Species at Risk Act.

EYES ON THE road

Wildlife can be very dangerous for traffic on the highways of this region. Moose, deer, bears, and smaller mammals are so prevalent that busy highways, like the Trans-Canada, are fenced in some areas to keep the animals from the road. Drivers should always be diligent about watching the road ahead, particularly in spring and fall, at dawn and dusk. The more remote or wooded the area, the more careful you need to be. Road signs will warn of frequent animal crossings, so obey them and slow down. Remember, a collision with a moose can be fatal to drivers and/or passengers.

HARBOR PORPOISE   Quiet in behavior and habit, the porpoise is small and grey—their undersides are white. Just 1.5 to 2m (5–6 ft.) long, they can easily be seen from shore, particularly from Grand Manaan Island. Identified by their triangular dorsal fin and blunt snouts, they are sometimes referred to as a "puffing pig" because of the snuffling sounds made when they breathe. Though the year-round residents are not on the endangered list, porpoises are considered of "special concern" in Canada.

HARBOR SEAL   With beautiful, big round eyes, cat-like whiskers, and a look compared to a cocker spaniel, these seals often seem as curious about humans as we are about them. Common in all seasons in the Atlantic provinces, they are best seen by using a charter-boat service, as you're most likely to find them basking in the sun on rocks offshore. In a few places, the Irving Nature Park in Saint John and Charlottetown Harbour are two, their "haul-out" sites can be viewed from shore.

HUMPBACK WHALE   The gentle, gigantic humpback isn't often seen from shore in Eastern Canada, except in the Digby, Nova Scotia area. Whale-watch tours often find humpbacks, and if you see them, you'll never forget the sight: They are huge and jet-black, blow tremendous amounts of water when surfacing, and perform amazingly playful acrobatics above water. The males also sing haunting songs, sometimes for as long as 2 days at a time. Because of their tendency to come close to shore to feed, they were highly vulnerable to whale hunters—estimates are that more than 100,000 were killed by whalers throughout the modern whaling era. Though most whales are no longer hunted, the world's population of Humpbacks has shrunk to perhaps 18,000 whales, making them a threatened species.

MINKE WHALE   The smallest of the whales, the minke swims off the coast of Canada, usually moving in groups of two or three whales—but much larger groups collect in feeding areas and during certain seasons. They usually live at the surface. Sometimes curious, they may approach and congregate around boats, making this a whale you're quite likely to see while on a whale-watch tour. The minke is dark gray on top, the throat has grooves, and each black flipper fin is marked with a conspicuous white band.

NORTHERN RIGHT WHALE   So named because the slow-moving, easily harpooned giants were the "right whale" to hunt when whaling ships roamed the oceans, the Right Whale is now the world's most endangered whale. Easily recognized, the Right Whale has a huge head that takes up one third of its black body that can reach 18m (59 ft.). In front of the whale's blowhole grow crusty, light colored lumps (called *callosities*) in patterns particular to each individual. They have no dorsal fin. The population that visits the Bay of Fundy each year numbers only about 425, so seeing one on a boat tour off Digby or Grand Manan Island is a privilege few experience.

PILOT WHALE   These smallish whales swim up to 35kmph (22 mph), making successive leaps as they travel, much like dolphins. Since they often travel in groups which can reach the hundreds, sightings are exciting, if rare. Summer residents of the Gulf of St. Lawrence and Atlantic Ocean off Nova Scotia, they are sometimes spotted by whale-watching boats, particularly along the northeast coast of Cape Breton. Not a lot is known about these whales. Even though there are occasional mass strandings, populations remain healthy.

INVERTEBRATES
AMERICAN LOBSTER   Everyone knows the lobster by sight and taste; what few know is that it was once considered ugly, tasteless, and unfit to eat. They were once considered good for nothing but tossing on the garden as fertilizer. Today, lobster is one of Eastern Canada's major exports and a must-have for gourmands visiting the Maritimes. Lobsters are related to crabs, shrimp, and even spiders and insects (sorry to spoil your appetite); they feed by slowly scouring the ocean bottom in shallow, dark waters, locating food by smell (they see very poorly). The hard shell, which is periodically shed in order to grow larger, is the lobster's skeleton. A greenish-black or blue color when alive, it turns bright red only after the lobster is cooked.

BIRDS
BALD EAGLE   Yes, they're here in Atlantic Canada—year-round—and they breed here. Sightings are common, especially near coastal areas such as Cape Breton Island in Nova Scotia, or on Prince Edward Island in the spring. (Their endangered status means you shouldn't get too close, but if you keep your eyes peeled, watching the tops of trees and cliffs, you might just be lucky.) The bald eagle's black body, white head, and yellow bill make it almost impossible to confuse with any other bird. It was nearly wiped out in the 1970s, mainly due to environmental poisons such as DDT-based pesticides. However, the bird is making a comeback, particularly in the Maritimes.

DUCK   Between one and two dozen species of ducks and geese seasonally visit the lakes, ponds, and tidal zones of Eastern Canada every year, including—though hardly limited to—the **red-breasted merganser** and the **common eider.** Mergansers, characterized by very white sides and very red bills (in males) or reddish crests (in females), are more commonly spotted in winter months. So is the eider, which inhabits offshore islands and coastal waters rather than lakes; in winter, huge rafts of eiders float together on the ocean near shore. Males are marked with a sharp black-and-white pattern.

GREAT BLUE HERON   Everyone knows a great blue at once, by its prehistoric flapping wings, comb of feathers, and spindly legs. These magnificent hunters wade through tidal waters, fishing with lightning-fast strikes of its sharp beak, from May through around October. The smaller, stealthier green heron and yellow-crowned night heron are rare, but can be seen.

LOON   Two species of loon visit the region's lakes and tidal inlets, fishing for dinner. The **red-throated loon,** grayish with a red neck, is a spring passerthrough and very rare in summer or winter. The **common loon** is, indeed, much more common—it can be distinguished by a black band of white spots around the neck, as well as black-and-white stripes and dots—and can be found in Canada year-round, though it's most easily spotted in late spring and late fall. Its habit of swimming low in the water helps to distinguish the loon from other water birds. It summers on lakes and winters on open patches of ocean inlets, giving a distinctively mournful, almost laughing call. Both loons have been reduced in number by environmental changes such as acid rain and mercury.

PLOVER   Plovers inhabit and breed on beaches and in certain muddy tidal flats, so their habitat is precarious; a single human step can crush an entire generation of eggs. Three species of plover visit the Maritimes in numbers, in a few spots, while others are occasional visitors. The **lesser golden-plover** flocks here in August and September while passing through. The **semipalmated plover** is common on many beaches with its quite different brownish body and white breast. The plover most associated with the Maritimes is the **piping plover,** a species at risk, which is zealously protected during breeding season. If you see an area of beach barricaded off, don't venture forward; the fencing is to keep you away from their nests, which they build amid the pebbles and sand. Many other shorebirds and waders frequent tidal areas, such as the little **sanderling** that runs so quickly along the beach at the water's edge, its legs are just a flash.

SONGBIRD   There are literally dozens of species of songbirds that roost in open fields, forests, and dead snags—even in the rafters and bird boxes of houses. The region hosts a dozen or so distinct types of chirpy little **warblers,** each with unique and often liquid songs; a half-dozen **thrushes;** winter **wrens, swallows, sparrows, vireos, finches, creepers,** and **thrashers;** the whimsical **black-capped chickadee;** and occasionally lovely **bluebirds, cardinals,** and **tanagers,** among many other species.

STORM PETREL   The tiny storm petrel is a fascinating creature. These plucky little birds fly astonishing distances in winter, eating insects on the wing, only to return to the coast each spring like clockwork, usually in May. They spend an amazing 4 months incubating, hatching, and tending to their single, white eggs in nests eked out of rocks. **Wilson's storm petrels** sometimes follow behind offshore boats; the much less common **Leach's storm**

petrel restricts its visits and nests solely on far-offshore rocks and islands and is also mostly nocturnal, which further reduces the chances of seeing it. Both breed in summer, then head south for winter.

RESPONSIBLE TRAVEL

It would be a shame if what we find attractive about the Maritimes was harmed because people visited it too much, or in the wrong way—loved it to death, as it were. There are ways to help ensure this won't happen. Here's a primer on some current environmental issues in the region, plus some tips on traveling as "lightly" as possible.

Fisheries

Fisheries have been *the* hot-button issue in Eastern Canada for the last 500 years. This region depends upon fishing and shellfish harvesting more than any other industry for both its economic lifeblood and its identity. Yet the native fishing stocks are imperiled, thanks to centuries of rampant overfishing; the national and provincial governments have enacted a series of emergency rules preventing fishing of certain species.

Signing up for a fly-fishing or deep-sea fishing expedition isn't any different from joining a fishing crew, so don't feel guilty if you do. Just act responsibly. Don't fish for more than you need to eat. Catch and release (it is the law in some cases) if you're not planning to eat the fish. Do not throw any trash overboard. And don't use illegal fishing methods to coax out a bigger catch. (If you see your tour operator doing so, don't patronize them again. And you might think about writing a letter to the provincial authorities after you get home.)

Aquaculture has, to a degree, helped mitigate the drastic reductions in the harvesting of wild stocks. Mussels are a hugely successful farming venture on Prince Edward Island. Oysters and trout are among the other seafoods grown on fish farms. Salmon farming is controversial in the region because, some claim, the practice damages ocean habitat and endangers wild stocks. Educate yourself about the issue before deciding either to enjoy farmed salmon or to avoid it while you are in the Maritimes, because it appears on many menus.

Indigenous Culture

In Canada, they certainly don't refer to native peoples as "Indians," and they don't even call them "native Canadians"; they're referred to as members of the First Nation. There are First Nation reserves in all three Maritime Provinces.

However, reservations in Canada are not the same as those in the United States. There are few casinos here, no public religious ceremonies. There are some shops in places like Lennox Island on Prince Edward Island that carry native-made products. Individuals of the First Nations are also developing some attractions and programs that respectfully present their lifestyles, relationships with the land and sea, and traditions. The native peoples of Eastern Canada are proud of their heritage and valuable contributions to society. If you pass through or past a marked reserve, do so respectfully. Don't snap photos of signs, people, houses, or shops—it's just not cool. Instead, stop and shop or fill the gas tank and speak to the people you meet.

You can view indigenous art at many art galleries in Eastern Canada (at the Confederation Centre Art Gallery [p. 67] in Charlottetown or the Beaverbrook Art Gallery in Fredericton, to give just a couple of examples), and numerous museums throughout the region display artifacts from native settlements.

Staying Green

Yes, it's pretty hard to claim you're being "green" while you're staying in a resort hotel that pumps water into 300 rooms and also sprinkles it onto a golf course—or whose owners cleared off 20 acres of forest and marshlands to build it. But you can minimize your impact as a traveler in Eastern Canada. Here are just a few ways:

o **Stay in an accredited "green" hotel.** The **Hotel Association of Canada (HAC),** Canada's official hotel association, maintains a member-run "green" rating system called Green Key that assesses member hotels' practices, then assigns them a rating of two to five keys. Visit the organization's website (www.greenkeyglobal.com) for more information.

o **Play golf on an eco-friendly course.** Hundreds of courses in North America have been certified by the Audubon Society as wildlife sanctuaries, including about 80 in Canada. Of these, unfortunately, only three are located in Eastern Canada: **Bell Bay** in Baddeck, Nova Scotia on Cape Breton, **The Links at Crowbush** in PEI (p. 47), and the **Algonquin Golf Course** in St. Andrews, New Brunswick (p. 99).

o **Take public transit.** Every major city in this book operates some form of metropolitan bus system.

o **Ride a bike.** The parks of Eastern Canada are unusually tailor-made for great bicycle riding. What's better than getting in shape and burning calories while contributing exactly zero toxic emissions to the atmosphere? The following destinations provide superb cycling holidays: stretches of the **Cabot Trail** (p. 235) on Cape Breton Island (but watch carefully for touring cars); the outstandingly scenic **Fundy Trail Parkway** in New Brunswick (p. 100), which has a dedicated bike lane; and the **Confederation Trail** (p. 46), which stretches the entire length of Prince Edward Island—the best parts are in northeastern PEI, around the area of Mount Stewart.

o **Eat at restaurants that source locally.** The use of hyper-local or regional produce, meats, and fish—this is Atlantic Canada, after all—contributes to the local economy and cuts down on pollution by cutting out the freighters, trucks, planes, delivery vans, and refrigeration units required to ship and preserve foods over long distance. Luckily, numerous good restaurants in Eastern Canada now use this philosophy.

o **Stay on the trail.** Trails have boundaries for a reason: You're safer inside the trail (cliffs and handholds can crumble away in an instant), and sudden erosion is bad for a mountainside, because it creates a cascade effect: Each subsequent rain will wash more and more topsoil, forest litter, and nutrients off the hill, preventing future plant life from gaining a toehold (and hurting the animals who depend on those plants). Stay on-trail.

o **Don't collect.** Resist the urge to collect things from the sea or forest. Pulling sea creatures out of the ocean, prying fossils from cliffs, and yanking up flowers for your hotel room (or your kids' aquarium back home) is both gauche and prohibited; sometimes the penalties can be very steep, approaching those for a federal crime.

o **Save the whales.** Whale-watching is enduringly popular throughout the Maritime Provinces. Operators are conscientious, but lightly regulated; if you think your captain is heading too close in to the animals, speak up (nicely but firmly).

o **Get educated.** Finally, for more information on traveling green in general, check websites of groups such as **Tread Lightly** (www.treadlightly.org) and the **World Wildlife Federation** (wwf.panda.org).

SUGGESTED ITINERARIES

The eastern provinces of Canada are big, yet intimate. You can be a long way between major destinations only to find yourself suddenly overwhelmed with wonder when you happen upon a small wooden church, a wharf full of boats, sandy beach, or roadside market—and you end up staying longer than you intended. It happens often.

3

So here are two pieces of advice. First, leave a bit of flexibility in your itinerary; these provinces are full of unexpected surprises. Second, allow time for the long drives. Except when on Prince Edward Island, you'll log a few hours on the road to complete these tours. The provinces are big, and multilane highways rarely offer views. As much as you can, stick to the scenic routes—you'll be rewarded with lovely vistas, unique attractions, and encounters with friendly people.

The range of possible itineraries in Eastern Canada is practically endless. Even a month is not enough to see all of the Maritime Provinces, but these four itineraries taking you through the best of each province should get you started.

ISLANDS, TIDES & TIME: NEW BRUNSWICK'S FUNDY COAST

As the largest Maritime province, New Brunswick is impossible to see in a week. Although this itinerary can't cover all of the province's highlights, it offers a relaxed but eventful vacation along the Fundy coast, where the world's highest tides make for dramatic scenery in this ancient landscape. Assuming a border crossing at Calais, Maine, begin in St. Andrews. (If you plan to fly into Saint John and rent a car, see it first or last and move the itinerary around to suit your needs. From Moncton, reverse the itinerary.)

Day 1: St. Andrews

Check into your hotel and then take a stroll down the town's small main street, before spending a quiet couple of hours unwinding after the long drive in **Kingsbrae Gardens** (p. 108), named Canada's Garden of the Year in 2013. Dinner at **Rossmount Inn** (p. 112), one of New Brunswick's top restaurants, perfectly caps off the first day.

Day 2: St. Andrews & Grand Manan Island

Take a **whale-watching tour** on Passamaquoddy Bay in the morning, when winds are lowest. Lunch on the outdoor patio at **Station on King** (p. 111) before taking the half-hour drive to Blacks Harbour for the ferry to **Grand Manan Island** (p. 112). Although the trip will take the rest of the day, getting there is half the fun, as they say. You'll arrive when the **Swallowtail Lighthouse** near the terminal is set dramatically against the sunset. Have dinner at the **Inn at Whale Cove** (p. 115) where you'll find contemporary preparations of local delicacies in a rustic, peaceful setting.

From St. Andrews, take Rte. 127 to Route 1. Turn south at Rte. 176 to Blacks Harbour and the ferry terminal. The drive is 48km (30 miles).

Day 3: Grand Island & Saint John

Explore on foot the small craft shops around **North Head** where the ferry docks before renting a bike at **Adventure High** (p. 114) to ride to the **Seven Days' Work Trail** (p. 114), which follows the cliffs along the coast. Picnic on a dramatic bluff or a pebble beach next to fishing boats before cycling the island on the main road to **The Anchorage Provincial Park** (p. 115), where there's a nice beach and bird sanctuary to explore. After returning your bike, grab a bite to eat at one of the seafood restaurants near the terminal before catching the 7:15 ferry back to the mainland. Drive to **Saint John** for the night.

From Blacks Harbour, take the 70km (43-mile) drive along Rte. 176 to Rte. 1 and east to Saint John.

Day 4: Saint John

In the morning, hit the **Saint John City Market** (p. 119)—Canada's oldest continuous market—for fantastic breakfasts, coffee, and takeaway treats. Walk to the **New Brunswick Museum** (p. 119) to learn about the natural and human history of this province. Take a 2-hour cooking class at the **Urban Deli** (p. 125) before hooking up with **Go Fundy Events** (p. 120) for a kayak tour of part of the **Stonehammer Geopark** (p. 120) to work up an appetite for the dinner you helped prepare earlier. Drop into **Happinez Wine Bar** (p. 125) for a quiet nightcap or, for a raucous one, the outdoor patio at **Saint John Ale House** (p. 124, where there's an outdoor stage).

From Saint John, drive northeast on Rte. 1 to Springdale to pick up Rte. 114 southeast to Alma. The 132km (82 mile) trip takes about 1½ hours.

Day 5: Fundy National Park ★★

Saint John nightlife will probably keep you up late, so sleep in, then take the morning to get to **Fundy National Park** (p. 126). Stay in or near

New Brunswick's Fundy Coast in 1 Week

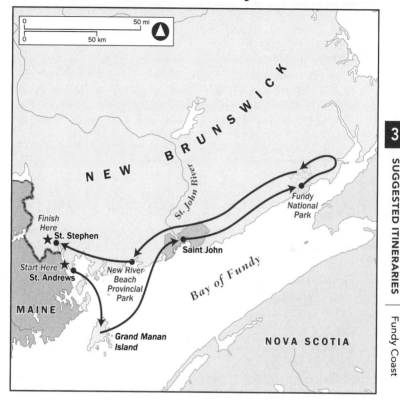

Alma (p. 131) for the next 2 nights because day trips from here are relatively short. Spend the afternoon on a nice hike in the park—**Third Vault Falls** (p. 128) comes with the reward of a waterfalls at the end and will take the afternoon. Dinner of homemade pasta at **An Octopus' Garden** (p. 133) will restore you; there's likely to be some evening entertainment here too.

Day 6: More of Fundy National Park

Make sure you get to **Hopewell Rocks** (p. 130) at low tide to walk the ocean floor among the columns of rock topped with trees and shrubs—they look like giant flowerpots. Depending on the tide, stop at **Cape Enrage** (p. 129, take Route 915 off 114) on the way there or the way back. Either way, time your drive to have a meal at the **Cape House Restaurant** (p. 130), one of New Brunswick's finest. Try the lobster tacos for starters.

Day 7: New River Beach Provincial Park & St. Stephen

It's a 3-hour drive back to the U.S. border, so your last day on the Fundy coast will include a lot of driving. About two hours in, have one last look at the mighty Bay of Fundy and stretch your legs at **New River Beach Provincial Park** (p. 116) 46km (29 miles) west of Saint John. The hiking trail here follows a forested coast along short cliffs and tiny beaches in isolated coves for spectacular views of the bay. At the border in St. Stephen, duck into **The Chocolate Museum** (p. 105) for a look at the history of the Ganong Brothers chocolate company that helped build this town, and pick up some hand-dipped chocolates for gifts or for the car.

From Alma, retrace your steps on Rte. 114 to Rte. 1, then stop at New River Beach, a total of 177km (110 miles). From there, take the 68km (42-mile) drive on Rte. 1 to St. Stephen.

PRINCE EDWARD ISLAND FOR FAMILIES

Let's be honest, kids get bored on long car rides—scenic drives are for adults. The best place in the Maritimes to get kids out of the car and doing things is PEI, where the drives are short and the kid-friendly activities plentiful.

Day 1: Victoria

Assuming you are arriving on the island late in the day after a long drive that ends with crossing the Confederation Bridge, follow Route 1 east 21km (13 miles) to Victoria, a lovely place to get this holiday started. This is a small, friendly village, so after checking in, walk the entire town—4 blocks—before heading to the wharf for a seafood dinner at **The Lobster Pub and Eatery** (p. 86). Stop at **Island Chocolates** (p. 85) on the way back for dessert and a look at how chocolates are made.

Day 2: Paddleboards, Ice Cream & Anne

In the morning, head down to **By-the-Sea-Kayaking** (p. 85) beside the wharf to rent stand-up paddleboards for everybody. After a quick lesson, paddle around the wharf and across the shallows where kids can look down to see crabs crawling through the seaweed. A couple of hours should work up appetites, so try the other wharf eatery, **Beachcomber's Restaurant** (p. 86), before hitting Route 1 toward **Charlottetown** (p. 63).

From Victoria, return to Route 1 and drive east 30km (19 miles) toward Charlottetown.

A short drive gets you to **Cows Ice Cream** factory (see p. 68); it's been called the best ice cream in Canada, so get the kids a cone, take the tour, and browse the shop full of funny cow-themed T-shirts.

After checking into your lodgings, walk around **Peake's Wharf** (p. 64) where kids are sure to find a shop that piques their interest. After dinner, take in the *Anne of Green Gables* musical at the **Confederation Centre for the Arts** (p. 67).

Prince Edward Island for Families

Gulf of St. Lawrence

From Charlottetown, drive north 20km (13 miles) to Brackley Beach on Route 2.

Day 3: Hit the Beach

Okay, it's time to let the kids run free. Head for **Prince Edward Island National Park** (see p. 59), which is a very long stretch of beaches less than half an hour away. Settle into a cottage or campground for the rest of the trip, then hit the beach to run, swim, build sandcastles, and generally kick back. Hot pizza at **Glasgow Glen Farm** (p. 56), where kids can watch the cheese that goes on their pie being made, will be a hit.

Day 4: Catch Your Own Dinner

On PEI's north shore, many boat-tour operators offer fishing trips. Book a 3-hour **deep-sea fishing tour** (p. 56) on a real fishing boat to catch mackerel. Your guides will clean the fish for the barbecue. Back at the Park, **bike one of the trails** (p. 61) to work up those appetites for your freshly caught meal.

Day 5: Anne's Land

It's only a 20-minute drive or 23km (14 miles) on Route 6 to Cavendish Beach and Anne's Land. The Anne attractions, like **Green Gables Heritage Place** (p. 51), will be of special interest if your family reads some of Lucy Maud Montgomery's books together before leaving home. For those who couldn't care less about "Anne," there's still plenty to do at small **theme parks:** go-kart racing, bumper boats, and small roller coasters. **Fish and chips** at any of the local shops will satisfy hungry kids.

Day 6: Butterflies & Jam

Spend the morning at the **PEI Preserve Company** (p. 56). Kids can watch jam being made through a window, then sample as many kinds as they want. There's a small park next to a quiet river to explore, but here's the real attraction—the owner has built a hothouse and filled it with tropical butterflies. For a change of beach scenery, spend the afternoon at Cavendish Beach for supervised swimming, miles of sand for playing, and gorgeous beachside trails to walk or bike.

From Brackley Beach, take Rte. 6 west then Rte. 251 west to Hunter River to pick up Rte. 2 into Summerside. The 53km (33-mile) trip is well under an hour. From Summerside, take Rte. 10 south 25km (15½ miles) to Gateway Village and the bridge.

Day 7: Preparing for Liftoff

To tear the kids away from the beach for the trip home, entice them with a look inside three military aircraft at **Air Force Heritage Park** (p. 86). Stop at the very good, unpretentious **Water Street Bakery and Deli** (p. 89) for lunch and treats for the road before heading to **Gateway Village** (p. 42) at the entrance to the bridge for souvenirs and gifts.

FROM LIGHTHOUSES TO CITY LIGHTS: THE NOVA SCOTIA LOOP

Nova Scotia can't be seen in a week, so you have to focus on certain regions. This itinerary excludes Cape Breton Island, which has its own itinerary (see p. 38). It also excludes the Eastern Shore, but only because it's out of the way when journeying from one Nova Scotia entry point to another. Begin in **Digby,** arrival point for the ferry from Saint John, New Brunswick. This itinerary includes the best mainland Nova Scotia has to offer: wilderness, culinary gems, lighthouses, natural and human history, fishing villages, vibrant city life, wine country, and the world's highest tides.

Day 1: Acadian Shore

When taking the ferry from New Brunswick to Digby, Nova Scotia, you'll pull into town around noon. Wait until you land to have lunch; Digby is the self-proclaimed scallop capital of the world, so poke around

Mainland Nova Scotia in 1 Week

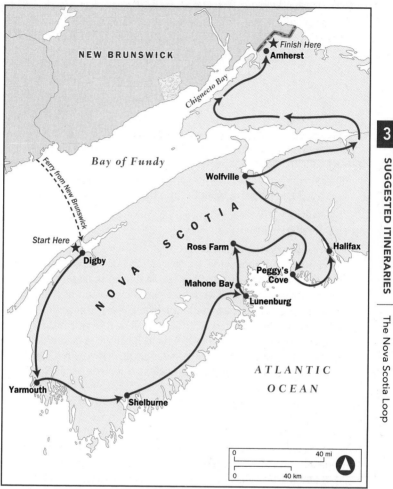

the wharves to see the fishing fleet and find a restaurant. They all serve scallops.

From Digby, turn south toward Yarmouth, but take coastal Route 1 at St. Bernard to see North America's largest wooden church, **St. Mary's** (see p. 192). This is a scenic coastal drive through Acadian villages and past several excellent beaches like **Mavillette** (p. 193) and **Port Maitland** (p. 193); stop at one to stretch your legs before continuing on with a side trip down Route 304 to the **Cape Forchu Lighthouse** (p. 195) just before entering **Yarmouth** (p. 194) for the night.

From Digby, turn south on Rte. 101 to Yarmouth. Hop over to Route 1 at St. Bernard and drive to Yarmouth, a trip of 108km (67 miles).

Day 2: Fishing Country

If you thought you saw a lot of fishing boats in Digby, you'll be bowled over by the size of the fleet along the South Shore. Meander east on Route 3, the "Lighthouse Route," into villages and towns like Wedgeport, the Pubnicos, Clark's Harbour, and Lockeport to see thousands of inshore fishing boats tied up at dozens of wharves. The drive will take a full day if you explore wharves, stop for lunch at **The Lobster Shack** (p. 198) in Barrington Passage (where a former fisherman cooks up award winning seafood), walk beaches like **Crescent Beach** (p. 204) in Lockeport, and walk around **Shelburne** (go into the **Dory Shop** to learn about the man who built 10,000 of the sturdy little boats, p. 202) before sitting down to dinner in the heart of the town's heritage district at **The Charlotte Lane Café** (p. 203), winner of Nova Scotia's Best Small Restaurant award.

From Yarmouth, continue east along Route 3, the Lighthouse Route, 150km (93 miles) as far as Lockeport.

Day 3: History & Shopping

The drive from Lockeport to Lunenburg and Mahone Bay on Highway 103 is dull, but necessary; you'll want lots of time in these two beautiful towns. Start in Lunenburg with the **Fisheries Museum of the Atlantic** (p. 209) which includes a tour aboard fishing boats. Sometimes, the legendary schooner, the *Bluenose* (p. 211, look on the back of a Canadian dime) is in port. Among the many options for lunch is fantastic fish and chips at **The Fish Shack** (p. 213). After lunch, drive out to **Blue Rocks** (p. 210) a picture-perfect little village at the end of a coastal road, before continuing on to Mahone Bay—the town of the iconic three waterfront churches—for shopping at the many artisans shops (see p. 215).

For dinner, try **Fleur de Sel** (p. 212) in Lunenburg, with food by arguably Nova Scotia's best chef (he's responsible for that fish and chips you had for lunch!) Check the online schedules at the following for evening entertainment: **The Chester Playhouse** (p. 218), and Mahone Bay's **Mug and Anchor Pub** (p. 216).

Take Hwy. 103 about 100km (62 miles) from Lockeport to Blockhouse to catch Rte. 324 to Lunenburg, Take Rte. 3 to Mahone Bay and Chester.

Day 4: Farmers & Fishermen

Spend the morning at the **Ross Farm Museum** (p. 214) 22km (14 miles) up Route 12 off Highway 103 from Mahone Bay; the farm operates as it did in the 19th century. Feed the animals, cook over an open hearth, make a horseshoe, go on a hayride.

In the afternoon, backtrack to Highway 103 and head for Exit 5 at Tantallon to find Route 333; about 24km (15 miles) along is **Peggy's Cove** (p. 199). There is no more iconic Nova Scotia location than this tiny fishing village balanced atop bare granite bedrock. From Peggy's Cove, continue on Route 333 to **Halifax** (chapter 7) for the night. If you still have energy, go to **Obladee Wine Bar** (p. 287) for a quiet tipple or **The Carleton** (p. 288) for live music, both in downtown.

Day 5: City Sites

Start the day in Halifax with a walk along the waterfront at Historic Properties, and make your way to the **Maritime Museum of the Atlantic** (p. 273). By the time you've gone through the new and surprisingly engaging **Canadian Museum of Immigration at Pier 21** (p. 273) at the end of the walk, you'll be ready for lunch. Next door at the **Seaport Farmers' Market**, you'll find many food stalls. In the afternoon, head up to the top of the hill to explore **Halifax Citadel National Historic Site** (p. 275) a large fortress that crowns the city. Then walk over to the adjacent **Halifax Public Gardens** (p. 277) to meander among Victorian gardens and feed the ducks. Walk down Spring Garden Road to the ultramodern **Halifax Central Library** (p. 277). Dinner is at **Chives Canadian Bistro** (p. 283) for casual fine dining or **The Stubborn Goat** (p. 284) for upscale pub food and many of the best craft beers in Nova Scotia. Lively nightlife at the **Economy Shoe Shop** (p. 287) or live music at **The Lower Deck** (p. 288) are good ways to end the evening.

From Halifax, take Hwy. 101 to Wolfville, a trip of about 91km (57 miles).

Day 6: Wine Country

Take Highway 101 to Wolfville in the morning for a tour of **Grand-Pré National Historic Site** (p. 176), a UNESCO World Heritage Site commemorating the contributions of French Acadians to this landscape and their persecution and expulsion by British forces in the 18th century. Stop at the excellent cafe and small coffee museum at **Just Us! Grand-Pré Coffee House** (p. 176) before beginning an afternoon of winery tours, the best of which can be found at **L'Acadie Vineyards, Gaspereau Vineyards, Grand Pre Winery,** and **Benjamin Bridge** (see p. 164). Dinner should be at **The Port Pub** (p. 180) a community-owned brewpub. Check the schedule at the **Al Whittle Theatre** (p. 175) or see if there's any live music at one of the local pubs.

From Wolfville, find Rte. 215 in Windsor to Truro. Take Hwy. 104 to Masstown, then Rte. 2 to Parrsboro. Rte. 209 leads to Joggins, and from there several roads go to Amherst. This is a long drive of 368km (230 miles).

Day 7: Ancient History

Hit the road early for Route 215, a scenic coastal drive to Truro. Briefly pick up Highway 104 as far as Masstown. This is the start of the Glooscap Trail toward Parrsboro on Route 2. Stop in Economy at **That Dutchman's Cheese Farm** (p. 172) to sample the outrageously good Gouda before going on to Parrsboro for lunch at **Black Rock Bistro** (p. 173). Start the afternoon at the **Fundy Geological Museum** (p. 172) to learn about Nova Scotia's ancient history as a tropical swamp where early amphibians and the first reptiles roamed 350 million years ago. Drive on to the **Joggins Fossil Centre** (p. 171) to explore cliffs eroded by the world's highest tides to expose fossilized trees and 200 other ancient species; it's a UNESCO World Heritage Site. End the day near Amherst at the New Brunswick border. The whole trip is about 5 hours in the car, and 3 or 4 hours at attractions—a long day, but most of the scenery is spectacular.

LANDSCAPE & FORTRESS: GIANTS OF CAPE BRETON ISLAND

Visiting Cape Breton Island puts you on one of the world's most eye-popping drives. The Cabot Trail hugs the mountainous coast of the rugged northern highlands, a fitting crown for land where Mother Nature did some of her best work, and Scottish and Acadian cultures create some of the best music you will ever hear. Consider taking this tour in the fall, when the trees are magnificent and the Celtic Colours International Festival—paying homage with music and feasting—takes place.

Day 1: Celtic Country

After crossing Canso Causeway, turn west onto Route 19, also known as the **Ceilidh Trail** (p. 237) for the Celtic music traditions along this coast. From a base between Port Hood and Inverness, designate a driver for a tour and tasting at **Glenora Distillery** (p. 239). Back in Mabou for the evening, drop in on a Celtic music jam at the **Red Shoe Pub** (p. 242) where folk music greats like The Rankins cut their teeth; you can grab dinner too.

Continue north on the Ceilidh Trail to Inverness.

Day 2: To Tee or Not to Tee

Inverness just became an important golfing town. If you're not a golfer, it is still worth a day here to stroll the boardwalk between the course and the beach, enjoy the beach itself, explore the adjacent wharf full of fishing boats, poke around town or drive as far as the Margarees for the scenery, and for craft and artisan shops. That would be your day if you are travelling with a golfer, who will (in fact, must) insist on heading straight for the new **Cabot Links and Cabot Cliffs** (p. 238), two of the world's top-rated golf courses. The best way to drag the golfer away is to book lodgings farther up the coast in Chéticamp.

Continue north until the Ceilidh Trail meets up with the Cabot Trail in Margaree Harbour. Choose the clockwise route toward Chéticamp.

Day 3: Arts & Nature

At Chéticamp, check out four nifty galleries: **Gallery La Bella Mona Lisa** (p. 243, whimsical, often funny artwork), **Elizabeth LeFort Gallery** and the **Hooked Rug Museum** (p. 243, in the same building, fabric arts) and **Sunset Folk Art Gallery** (p. 244). The last has brightly painted folk art spilling into the yard next to the **Frog Pond Café** (p. 244) where you can find Parisian-quality light lunches, pastries, and coffee. On the same road, enter **Cape Breton Highlands National Park** (p. 263), after

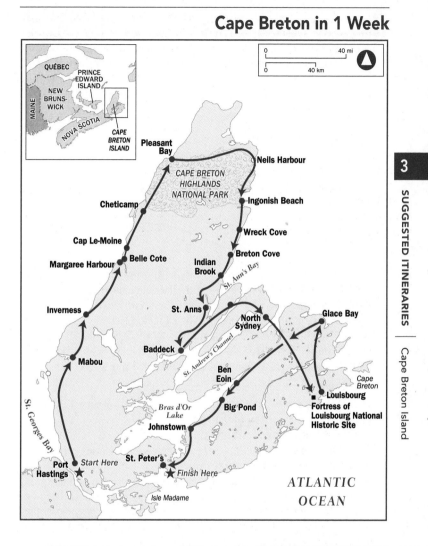

which the scenery gets increasingly dramatic. Spend the afternoon hiking the **Skyline Trail** (p. 265). Settle into **Pleasant Bay** for the evening.

Continue following the Cabot Trail to Ingonish.

Day 4: Whales, Walks & Burgers

Take a boat tour with **Capt. Mark's Whale and Seal Cruise** (p. 245) in the morning. From Pleasant Bay, re-enter the park for a drive to Cape North and a side trip to **Bay St. Lawrence** (p. 247) near the northern tip of Nova Scotia, for the spectacular scenery. Check in to your lodging in Ingonish before hiking the 4km (2½ miles) **Middle Head Trail** (p. 265) beyond **Keltic Lodge** for a look at both the lodge and the dramatic peninsula upon which it's built. For a leisurely evening, head to **Coastal Waters Restaurant and Pub** (p. 250) for incredible burgers and live entertainment.

Continue following the Cabot Trail to Baddeck. Note that the Cabot Trail joins the Trans-Canada Highway (Rte. 105) to go to Baddeck.

Day 5: The Bell of Baddeck

Leaving Ingonish in the morning, stop at the top of Cape Smokey just outside the park to walk some of the mountain-edge trail, then drive down the switchbacks to sea level where the road to Baddeck is filled with artisans' shops. Have lunch at **The Clucking Hen Café and Bakery** (p. 250). In the afternoon, check into Baddeck lodgings, then head to the **Alexander Graham Bell National Historic Site and Museum** (p. 253). Sign up for an evening boat tour with Amoeba Sailing Tours to see Bell's mansion near Baddeck, bald eagles, and a lighthouse.

From Baddeck, take Hwy. 105 (Trans-Canada) to Sydney Mines, where you pick up Rte. 125 around Sydney, then Rte. 22 on to Louisbourg.

Day 6: The Great Fortress

You're going to need a whole day at **Fortress Louisbourg** (p. 261)—North America's largest reconstruction project—and the drive takes well over an hour, so leave early. Once there you'll be treated to a day a day of exploration, re-enactments, and period dining experiences.

From Louisbourg, retrace your steps along Rte. 22 just past Albert Bridge to pick up Rte. 255 to Glace Bay. From there, get on Rte. 4 to St. Peters.

Day 7: Mines & Locks

Backtrack to Glace Bay to check out the **Cape Breton Miners Museum** (p. 260) where you can descend into a once-working mine. In the **Miners' Village** (p. 260) next door, tour humble homes where miners once lived and snoop about the company store. Head down Route 4 to Big Pond for afternoon tea at **Rita's Tea Room** (p. 258). Continue on to **St. Peter's** (p. 256) to watch boats navigate the locks into the Bras d'Or Lakes. The causeway back to the mainland is just 49km (30 miles) from here, so you can stay the night or keep going.

PRINCE EDWARD ISLAND

For Canada's smallest province, Prince Edward Island is rated highly for a surprising number of things. It's a top golfing and culinary destination, has the longest-running dinner theater and musical production in Canada, a literary character some travel halfway around the world to experience, and ice creams named Canada's best. Part of the reason for such success is repeat visitors who appreciate the getting-away-from-it-all feel of this gentle island, where life is simpler, the pace less harried, and the roads less traveled.

4

Sightseeing PEI's size is a bonus: Never far to anywhere, which makes for unhurried sightseeing. Beautiful **Charlottetown,** the "birthplace of Canada," brings history to life. **Prince Edward Island National Park** and the north shore region boast miles of red-sand beaches and dunes. A drive east reveals a beach where the sand sings, and a distillery making legal "shine." Up west, past **Summerside,** discover a reef you can walk on and a lighthouse to sleep in.

Eating & Drinking Sometimes it seems that PEI is one large farm surrounded by world-class fishing grounds. Evidence of the fishing and farming that stocks Island pantries is everywhere: fields of potatoes, mussel harvesting, and super-fresh ingredients at local farmers' markets. Add one chef made famous on TV, dozens of dedicated restaurateurs, a world famous oyster industry, Canada's best ice cream, and blend with the influence of the **Culinary Institute of Canada,** and you have a recipe for unique food encounters. For real foodies: **culinary boot camps,** the island-wide **Fall Flavours** (www.fallflavours.ca) culinary festival (which includes the **International Shellfish Festival**), and organized **culinary experiences** like cooking classes and chocolate making.

Arts & Culture Known worldwide as the birthplace of *Anne of Green Gables,* the story that brings 19th-century Prince Edward Island to life, the province rightly celebrates author Lucy Maud

Montgomery's contribution to world literature. Her success created an environment which fosters creativity: First-class music, handcrafts, art, photography, and live theater are showcased at venues like the **Confederation Centre of the Arts** and the **Dunes Studio Gallery,** *ceilidhs* (folk music jams, pronounced "KAY-lee"), markets, and artisans shops. But there's also an ever evolving mix of cultures on the island, starting with the presence of First Nations Mi'kmaq people, mostly concentrated on **Lennox Island,** and including centuries of settlement by **French Acadian, Scottish,** and **Irish immigrants.**

Relaxation   PEI's slow, relaxed pace is immediately obvious. Arriving feels like coming to the home we dream of: warm, welcoming, safe, and relaxed. Take relaxation how you wish—golf first-rate courses, cycle, walk tip to tip on **Confederation Trail,** laze on a beach serenaded by the surf, or go fishing. It's a perfect place to let children experience nature and relaxed play, and for all ages to learn to kayak, dig giant clams, or make chocolates. The peace and tranquillity that Montgomery treasured still inspires visitors to de-stress and appreciate what surrounds them.

EXPLORING PRINCE EDWARD ISLAND

PEI is, by far, Canada's smallest province—it's only about 280km (175 miles) long from tip to tip, and that keeps your transit down to a minimum. From one or two bases, you can easily explore the whole province in a week. However, traffic on island roads—slowed by farm tractors, shutterbugs, leisurely drivers, terrain, and odd twists and turns along the route—tends to be slower than you'd expect. So don't count on the sort of speedy travel common on a fast mainland four-lane. After all, one of the reasons people come here is to relax. Just kick back and enjoy the scenery.

In recent years, a number of PEI hotels and attractions have banded together to market a ton of different vacation packages that offer discounts ranging from moderate to generous. The provincial tourism department offers these deals online at www.tourismpei.com/about-the-island; click on "Packages & Deals."

Essentials

VISITOR INFORMATION   PEI has a Visitor Information Centre at each entry point to the province. Charlottetown boasts two, one at the airport (www.tourismpei.com; ⓒ **902/368-4489**) and another on the waterfront at 6 Prince Street (ⓒ **902/368-4444**) where cruise ships dock. People arriving via Confederation Bridge can exit directly to **Gateway Village** (ⓒ **902/437-8570**), as you come off the bridge. The Visitor's Centre is a worthwhile stop for gathering brochures and asking questions. There's also an exhibit about the building of the bridge. The Gateway features a number of retail shops, food, a liquor store, and a park to let the kids or dog stretch their legs. Be sure to check out **Shop and Play ★** (www.shopandplay.com; ⓒ **800/558-1908**), a fun store devoted to the production of Anne of Green Gables figurines (great

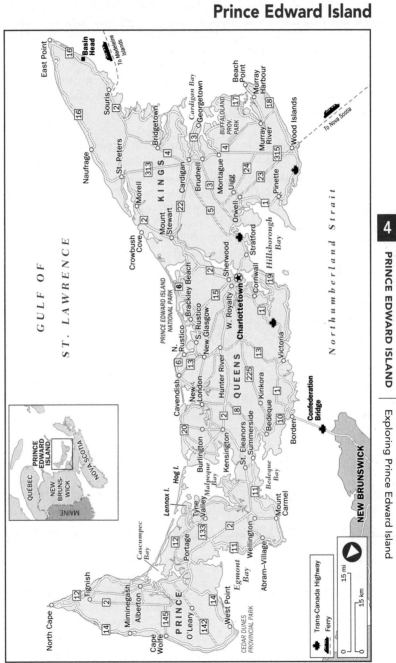

Prince Edward Island

GULF OF

ST. LAWRENCE

East Point

Basin Head

To Madeleine Islands

Souris

Naufrage

St. Peters

Bridgetown

Cardigan Bay

Georgetown

Beach Point

Murray Harbour

Wood Islands

To Nova Scotia

Morell

KINGS

Cardigan

Brudnell

Montague

Uigg

Murray River

Pinette

Crowbush Cove

Mount Stewart

Orwell

Sherwood

Stratford

Hillsborough Bay

Northumberland Strait

PRINCE EDWARD ISLAND NATIONAL PARK

Brackley Beach

N. Rustico

S. Rustico

New Glasgow

W. Royalty

Charlottetown

Cornwall

Cavendish

New London

Hunter River

QUEENS

Victoria

Kinkora

Bedeque

Borden

Confederation Bridge

Burlington

Kensington

St. Eleanors

Summerside

Bedeque Bay

Mount Carmel

Malpeque Bay

Hog I.

Lennox I.

Tyne Valley

Wellington

Abram-Village

Egmont Bay

Cascumpec Bay

Portage

Tignish

Mimingash

Alberton

O'Leary

PRINCE

West Point

Cape Wolfe

North Cape

CEDAR DUNES PROVINCIAL PARK

NEW BRUNSWICK

Trans-Canada Highway

Ferry

15 mi

15 km

QUÉBEC

NEW BRUNSWICK

MAINE

NOVA SCOTIA

PRINCE EDWARD ISLAND

BUFFALOLAND PROV. PARK

photo ops). If you are a photography buff, take the side road back toward the bridge, through Borden-Carleton; the little park at the lighthouse offers great view points. The road ends where the former ferry linking the island to the New Brunswick mainland used to dock year-round.

Visitor Information Centres at Wood Islands (✆ **902/962-7411**) and Souris (✆ **902/637-7030**) at 95 Main Street (both are open June–Sept) welcome those arriving by ferry. There are also welcome centers in Cavendish, on the Summerside waterfront, in St. Peters, and West Prince.

WHEN TO GO   PEI's peak tourism season is brief, running 8 to 9 weeks from **July through August.** If you plan to visit in June or September (lovely times to come), expect some restaurants and attractions to be closed. My advice? Check the listings in this book carefully for restaurant, hotel, and attraction opening seasons. If you like your vacation with a mix of rural and urban (it's more like large town in PEI) experiences, think about basing yourself in Charlottetown, from which you can make day trips around the island. If you prefer a beach or a countryside vacation, there is no shortage of very nice small resorts, cottages, campgrounds and other accommodations in the heart of PEI's best rural regions.

Getting There

If you're coming by car, as the vast majority do, you'll either arrive by ferry (see below) or drive onto the island via the big **Confederation Bridge** (www. confederationbridge.com; ✆ **888/437-6565** or 902/437-7300), which opened with great fanfare in 1997. The dramatic 13km (8-mile) bridge, the longest bridge in the world that crosses ice-covered water (in the winter), is open 24/7 and takes 10 to 12 minutes to cross. If the winds are high, check the website; it is occasionally shut down for bad weather. Alas, views are mostly obstructed by the concrete barriers that form the guardrails along both sides, unless you are high up in a van, truck, or RV.

The round-trip bridge toll is C$45.50 for passenger cars (more for vehicles with more than two axles; C$18.25 for motorcycles); the toll is collected when you leave the island, not when you enter it. Credit cards are accepted at the bridge plaza. **Cyclists and backpackers** can cross the bridge in the shuttle van provided, which charges C$4.25 per pedestrian or C$8.50 per cyclist.

SHUTTLES & BUSES   Even if you didn't bring wheels or rent any after arriving, you can get here via several long-distance shuttle, bus, or limo services. **PEI Express Shuttle** (www.peishuttle.com; ✆ **877/877-1771**), one of them, runs one van daily each way between Halifax, Halifax's airport, and Charlottetown. The ride takes about 5 hours from downtown Halifax (about 4 hr. from the airport, 3 from Truro where it makes a stop) and costs C$69 one-way for adults, C$65 for students and seniors, C$50 for children under age 12. **Maritime Bus** (www.maritimebus.com; ✆ **800/575-1807**) takes passengers from many locations in New Brunswick and Nova Scotia to several PEI points daily. The trip from Halifax, for example, takes about 4 hours and costs around C$70 one-way (adult). Check the website or call for details.

BY FERRY   For those arriving from Halifax, Cape Breton Island, or other points east, **Northumberland Ferries Limited** (www.ferries.ca; ✆ 877/762-7245) provides seasonal service between Caribou, Nova Scotia (just north of Pictou), and Woods Island, PEI. Ferries with a 220-car capacity run from May to mid-December. During peak season (May to mid-Dec), ferries depart each port approximately every 1½ to 2 hours throughout the day, with the last ferry departing as late as 8pm or 9:30pm in midsummer, depending on which direction you are traveling. The crossing takes about 75 minutes. Reserve ahead of time by calling or through the website. Early morning ferries tend to be less crowded. Fares are C$70 for a regular-size car (more for campers and RVs), plus C$18 per person (C$16 for seniors, free for kids 12 and under). There's a C$5 fuel surcharge, as well, and major credit cards are honored. *Tip:* This round-trip fare is only collected when leaving the island. If you take the ferry onto the island and drive off, you pay the cheaper bridge toll only; drive on and take the ferry off, and you pay the higher ferry toll only.

A second ferry run from Souris, PEI, takes automobiles to Îles de la Madeleine, Québec; however, you must return to PEI on the same ferry if traveling by car, because there is no other link to the mainland that takes vehicles.

BY AIR   The island's main airport, Charlottetown Airport (call sign YYG; www.flypei.com), is located within the city of Charlottetown, just minutes from downtown. In summer, you can get here from either the U.S. or Canada. **Air Canada** (www.aircanada.com; ✆ **888/422-7533**) and **WestJet** (www.westjet.com; ✆ **877/929-8646**) connect Charlottetown with Halifax, Ottawa, Montréal, and Toronto.

A taxi ride into Charlottetown from the airport costs a flat fee of C$14 single or C$11 for a shared cab. (Cabs also run to other parts of the island; rates are charged per kilometer.) There are also limousine firms and several chain auto-rental outfits in the terminal.

THE GREAT OUTDOORS

Prince Edward Island doesn't have much wildness to speak of. It's all about cultivated landscapes that have long ago been tamed by farmers. That doesn't mean you can't find outdoor adventures, though. Here are some places to start.

BICYCLING   There's no finer destination in Atlantic Canada for relaxed cycling than Prince Edward Island. The modest size of this island, the gentleness of the hills (the island's highest point is just 142m/466 ft. above sea level), and the loveliness of the landscapes all make for memorable biking trips. Although you won't find much rugged mountain biking here, you can find plenty of idyllic excursions, especially in the northern and eastern portions of the island. Don't get the idea that it is flat; with the exception of a couple of areas, the land is made up of gently rolling hills and vales. Just be sure to avoid the busy Trans-Canada Highway on the south coast, and main roads like Route 2. You'll find less traffic and superb backroads biking throughout the network of secondary routes.

There's also a very significant off-road bike trail here: the **Confederation Trail ★★★**, an impressive system of several hundred miles of pathway built along the former trackbed of an ill-fated railway. The main trail runs from Tignish (on the island's far northwestern shore) to Elmira (up in the northeastern corner), while good branch trails stretch right into downtown Charlottetown and touch on a number of towns mentioned in this chapter, such as Souris, Montague, and Georgetown. One spur even reaches all the way to the Confederation Bridge (see p. 44). The pathway is mostly covered in rolled stone dust, which makes for good traveling with either a mountain bike or hybrid. Services are slowly developing along this route, with more rental services and inns cropping up every year. Ask at tourist bureaus for updated information. Do remember the trail is also used by hikers and walkers (often with dogs), so be attentive.

The island has half a dozen bike rental and bike tour outfits, three of them in Charlottetown. The experts at **MacQueen's Island Tours & Bike Shop,** 430 Queen St. in Charlottetown (www.macqueens.com; ☏ **800/969-2822** or 902/368-2453), organize a range of bicycle tour packages with all-inclusive prices covering bike rentals, accommodations, route cards, maps, luggage transfers, and emergency road repair service. A customized 5- to 7-night tour of a section of the island for two might run C$1,286 to C$1,350 per person, double occupancy; group tours are cheaper. Bikes can be rented at the shop for C$40 per day and C$175 per week (kids' bikes are cheaper, touring bikes a bit more expensive). And, of course, they do all repairs. Gowheelin (www. gowheelinpei.com; ☏ **877/286-6532**) and Outer Limits Sports bike rentals (ols.ca/mystore/bike-rentals-pei; ☏ **902/569-5690**), both in Charlottetown, also rent bikes and offer tours for similar rates.

FISHING With 1,700km (1,100 miles) of coastline, inland rivers and streams, and more than 800 ponds, the island can be a fisherman's dream. If you're interested in deep-sea fishing, head to the north or east coasts, where you'll find plenty of fishing captains and outfitters happy to take you out on the big waves in search of tuna, mackerel, and others. The greatest concentrations of services are at the harbors of North Rustico and Covehead Bay. In North Rustico, at any given time, at least a half-dozen captains offer fishing trips, including **Aiden's Deep Sea Fishing Trips** (www.peifishing.com; ☏ **866/510-3474** or 902/963-3522). There's also **Salty Seas Deep Sea Fishing** (http://salty-seas-deep-sea-fishing.pei.xpei.ca; ☏ **902/672-3246**), about a 20-minute drive east of North Rustico at Covehead Harbour (within the national park). Rates range from about C$45 to C$100 for adults, less for children, for 2 to 3 hours or so, and most will clean and fillet fish to take home if you wish.

North Lake Harbour gives itself the moniker "Tuna Capital of the World" and is home to deep-sea charter vessels that will take you out in search of the giant bluefins, which can top 1,000 pounds. Whale, seal, and bird sightings can sweeten the experience. **Tony's Tuna Fishing ★★** (www.tonystunafish ing.com; ☏ **902/357-2207**) will take you on a private tuna charter July through

September for C$1,250 a day. Or you can go lobster fishing for C$150 in May or June, but be warned they will probably put you to work. **Top Notch Charters** ★★ (www.markscharters.com; ℂ **902/626-6689**) offers short fishing excursions, on-board lobster suppers, and tuna fishing charters out of Charlottetown. On the east coast, **Tranquility Cove Adventures** ★★ (www.tca pei.com; **902/969-7184**) runs fishing, clamming, and even starfish hunting excursions out of Georgetown.

Trout fishing attracts inland anglers, although, as always, the very best spots are a matter of local knowledge. A good place to start is the government website on recreational fishing (www.gov.pe.ca/forestry/angling) that contains all the regulations, license, and fee information, as well as a list of the many locations for trout fishing across the province. Among these, **Ben's Lake** in Bellevue (www.benslake.com; ℂ **902/838-2706**) offers catch-and-release fly-fishing and fee fishing by the pound on their 18-acre (7.2 hectare) lake. A top place to try fishing, Ben's has tackle for rent and a campground on-site.

GOLF PEI's reputation for golf has soared in recent years; *SCOREGolf* magazine twice named PEI the country's best golfing destination thanks to the variety and convenience of over 25 courses—and the LPGA success of Charlottetown native Lorie Kane. You can golf beside the ocean, within city limits, or in a pastoral setting—PEI has more golf courses per capita than any other province in Canada.

One of the best-regarded courses on the island is the **Links at Crowbush Cove** ★★★ (peisfinestgolf.com; ℂ **800/235-8909**). Sand dunes and persistent winds off the gulf add to the challenge at this course on the northeastern coast; greens fees run C$60 to C$100 per person. Another perennial favorite is the **Brudenell River Golf Course** ★★ (peisfinestgolf.com; ℂ **800/235-8909**), near Montague along the eastern shore at the Rodd Brudenell River Resort; in the late 1990s the course added a second 18-holer, **Dundarave** ★★ designed by Michael Hurdzan, and a double-ended driving range. Greens fees are C$40 to C$80 per person at both.

Golf Prince Edward Island (www.golfpei.ca; ℂ **866/465-3734**), a trade association, has a reservation system and info for all the courses.

SEA KAYAKING Little PEI packs in more than 1,200km (800 miles) of attractive coastline, most of it touched by relatively warm seawater, making for excellent sea kayaking. Paddlers can vary the scene from broad tidal inlets ringed with marsh to rusty-red cliffs sculpted by the wind to dunes topped with swaying waves of marram grass. Several operators rent kayaks and offer tours. On the north coast, **Outside Expeditions** (www.getoutside.com; ℂ **800/207-3899** or 902/963-3366) in North Rustico hosts half- and full-day excursions and clinics daily at the national park nearby and Brudenell River Provincial Park in eastern PEI. Rental rates vary from C$25 for an hour in a single to C$100 for a day in a tandem. On the southern coast, **By-the-Sea-Kayaking** ★★ (www.bytheseakayaking.ca; ℂ **877/879-2572** or 902/658-2572) in Victoria-by-the-Sea rents kayaks and stand-up paddle boards. Their

4

The Great Outdoors

tours include a unique clam digging adventure during which you paddle to an offshore sandbar, dig clams the size of your hand, and return to shore to make them into chowder.

SWIMMING   PEI's chief attraction is its beaches, which are generally excellent for swimming. You'll find them ringing the island, tucked in between dunes and crumbling cliffs. Generally speaking, the beaches along the Northumberland Strait, or south shore, have red sand and long shallows, while those along the Gulf of St. Lawrence in the north are less red, often backed by soaring dunes; these can be subject to rip tides, so stay in the shallows unless in an area with lifeguards. Thanks to the moderating influence of the Gulf of St. Lawrence, the water temperature is more humane here than elsewhere in Atlantic Canada. The most popular beaches (by far) are at **Prince Edward Island National Park** along the north shore, but you can easily find other local or provincial beaches with swell swimming by asking locals. Good choices include **Cedar Dunes Provincial Park** (on the island's southwestern coast), **Red Point Provincial Park, Basin Head Beach** (on its northeastern shore), and **Panmure Island Provincial Park** on the southeastern coast. **Basin Head,** on the eastern shore, is known as the "singing sands" because the sand squeaks when you walk on it.

QUEENS COUNTY

Queens County occupies the center of PEI. It's home to the island's largest city (**Charlottetown**), which is also the provincial capital, and hosts the greatest concentration of traveler services by far.

Cavendish on the north shore is the most tourist-oriented place in the province. Its became popular when visitors started arriving on pilgrimages to the home of Lucy Maud Montgomery and her fictional character Anne of Green Gables—as well as the glorious beaches of this coastal area. Today, attractions such as amusement parks, shops, golf courses, paintball, and water activities have been added to the mix. A visit to this area is a must, if you don't mind crowds and attractions that range from the spectacular to the tacky. Nearby villages are more serene and have their own quieter lures. **New Glasgow** boasts excellent restaurants, a preserve maker, and a toy shop, all located along River Clyde, known for its many geese and ducks, and the eagles that soar overhead. The fishing community of **North Rustico** is a charmer where visitors walk the wharfs and boardwalk, go deep-sea fishing, or trace Acadian roots dating back to 1790.

Two areas of Queens County merit their own sections within this chapter: **Charlottetown** on the south shore and **Prince Edward Island National Park** on the north shore.

Essentials

GETTING THERE   Three main routes travel east and west through the county. Route 1 in the south connects Charlottetown with the Confederation Bridge, and then Summerside. Route 2, the fastest way to travel east or west, runs through the center. Route 6, the main route along the county's northern reaches, involves a number of turns at intersections. Keep a sharp eye on the road signs or you'll lose the trail.

VISITOR INFORMATION The **Cavendish Visitor Information Centre** (© **902/963-7830**) is open year-round, daily from mid-June through mid-October, weekdays the rest of the year. It's located just north of the intersection of routes 13 and 6.

Cavendish

There are three things that make Cavendish a prime tourist destination: the Prince Edward Island National Park with its legendary long, sandy beaches; two top golf courses; and a huge dedication to fantasy. Cavendish is the home of the fictional redhead Anne of Green Gables, a beloved figure in Canadian literature (and, in fact, Anne is well known around the world, particularly in Japan where children use *Anne of Green Gables* to learn English). Fortunately for those who love and appreciate Anne and her creator, Lucy Maud Montgomery, important sites have been preserved and cared for, either by Parks Canada or descendants of the author. The enduring popularity of the novels attracts droves of tourists. It didn't take savvy entrepreneurs long to realize that the area could support amusement parks and shopping arcades, plus a surfeit of motels and "cottage courts," which are a popular option for families. The majority of what you want to find is conveniently located along the main road (Rte. 6).

As for "downtown" Cavendish, there's no discernible village center, just an intersection of roads and a tourist information center; everything is sprawled out along the approach roads. If you're on PEI to stroll quaint lanes and villages, rather than because of an interest in Anne, you're better off heading east to North Rustico or south to New Glasgow. If beaches, nature, walks in the woods, or quiet relaxation by the sea appeals, then turn north at any of the entrances to the national park. Check at the Interpretive Centre on the northwest corner of routes 6 and 13 to find out what is happening during your visit. If your kids enjoy amusements, buckle in for a day or two. This village has the most kid appeal of any community on the island, but don't expect a high-tech Disney-like experience or exciting nightlife.

EVERYTHING ANNE

I don't care if you're a grouchy guy or a novel-hater, if you're visiting Cavendish you'll be missing out on the fun if you don't prepare yourself by reading *Anne of Green Gables* first (it's an unusually engaging book, so it won't be a chore). The novel has inspired the longest-running musical theater in Canada, a television miniseries, movies, and spin-off fiction and nonfiction books. In fact, Anne has become so omnipresent and popular that a licensing authority was created in the 1990s to control the crush of Anne-related products popping up everywhere.

But if you don't want to take my advice about reading the book, here's a little background. In 1908, island native Lucy Maud Montgomery published

Anne of Green Gables, her very first book—and an instant success. The book is a fictional account of Anne Shirley, a precocious 11-year-old orphan who's mistakenly sent from Nova Scotia to the farm of dour Islanders Matthew and Marilla Cuthbert, who had requested an orphan *boy* to help with their farm chores. Anne's vivid imagination and outsized vocabulary get her into a series of increasingly more hilarious pickles, from which she generally emerges beloved by everyone who encounters her. It's a bright, somewhat bittersweet story that touched a serious nerve and became such a hit worldwide that it spawned a number of sequels. The book is still taught in many elementary schools in Japan, so throngs of Japanese tourists congregate in Cavendish each year to relive Anne's fictional life for a few days.

The nucleus of tourism in Cavendish is the preservation of all things Anne, as people come from around the world to pay homage and seek some of the magic. Even with the increased commercialism, there is a certain sweetness to both Anne's story and the bucolic landscape in which she lived. Except for a dozen or so attractions along Route 6, this area still looks more or less the same as it did during the era when Montgomery wrote the original book.

If you're a traveler who has never heard of Anne until this moment, or you're more interested in a holiday at the beach, locating fine foods, or taking scenic bike tours, head for nearby communities or the national park.

Anne of Green Gables Museum at Silver Bush ★ MUSEUM Lucy Maud Montgomery referred to this house—home to the Campbell family since 1776—as "the wonder castle of my childhood." The white-shingled two-story home belonged to her aunt and uncle, and her love for the place was so strong, she chose to marry in the parlor in 1911. Couples travel here from as far away as Japan to exchange vows just as Lucy Maud did in the house beside "the Lake of Shining Waters." The Campbell House is now the Anne of Green Gables Museum. Take a carriage ride like Anne did with Matthew down a country lane or just poke through photos, furniture, and personal effects of Montgomery that are kept in the museum.

4542 Rte. 20, Park Corner (about 6 miles north of intersection with Rte. 6). www.anne museum.com. ⓒ **800/665-2663** or 902/886-2884. Admission C$5.50 adults, C$2 children age 6–18. Carriage rides: Short (10 min.) C$5.50 adults, C$2 children; half-hour C$65 for up to 5 people; 1 hour C$95 for up to 5. May and Oct daily 11am–4pm; June and Sept daily 10am–4pm; July–Aug daily 9am–5pm.

Anne of Green Gables—The Musical ★★ PERFORMING ARTS For more than half a century, the story of Anne set to music has been entertaining visitors to the Confederation Centre in Charlottetown, easily making it the country's longest-running musical. The 2-hour, lively and professional production is usually staged in July and August up to four times a week, including Saturdays and some matinees. I'd say this is *the* Anne experience not to miss on the island.

Confederation Centre of the Arts, 145 Richmond St., Charlottetown. www.charlotte townfestival.com. ⓒ **800/565-0278** or 902/566-1267. July–Aug. Tickets C$25–C$79.

Avonlea Village ★ ATTRACTION This development of faux historic buildings opened in 1999, with the idea of creating the sort of a village center you might find in the Anne novels. (The actual Cavendish lacks anything remotely resembling a center, which makes sense because it's out in the middle of farmlands.) And, of course, the true goal is to entice paying tourists. The facility is on a big lot among amusement parks and motels, but several Anne-related buildings and artifacts are located at the site, including the actual one-room schoolhouse in which Montgomery taught (moved here from Belmont, about 48km/30 miles away) and a Presbyterian church she occasionally attended (moved from Long River). There's also a variety show, hayrides, staff in period dress, eateries, stores, excellent ice cream (it's a highlight), and candy. But for what it delivers, the attractions here are overpriced.

8779 Rte. 6, Cavendish. www.avonlea.ca. (𝒞 **902/963-3050.** Admission free. Musical performance C$7, pony ride C$5. Mid-June to mid-Sept daily 10am–8pm (Sept closes 5pm).

Cavendish Cemetery ★ CEMETERY It's easy to find in this old, scenic cemetery, the final resting place of Lucy Maud Montgomery. Follow the paving-stone path from the arched entrance to the stone marked with her married name, Lucy Maud Macdonald and the Rev. Ewan Macdonald, her husband. It's across from the Anne Shirley Motel.

Intersection of routes 13 and 6, Cavendish. Free admission. Open daily dawn–dusk.

Green Gables Heritage Place ★★ HISTORIC SITE The best place to start an "Anne tour" is at Green Gables itself, but this place somewhat disappoints, even if it is the closest thing we have to the "real" fictional Green Gables. (The author's birthplace or favorite home are equally authentic destinations.) The farmhouse here dates from the mid-19th century and belonged to cousins of Montgomery's grandfather; it is considered the chief inspiration for the Cuthbert farm in the books, and has since been furnished according to descriptions in the books. The home is operated by Parks Canada as part of the larger Lucy Maud Montgomery's Cavendish National Historic Site; as such, the parks department operates a helpful visitor center on the site where you can watch a short film about Montgomery, view a handful of exhibits, and explore the farm and trails. If you're a die-hard Anne fan, you'll no doubt delight in visiting settings where the literary characters ventured: Haunted Woods, Lover's Lane, and the like. But you'll need an active imagination to edit out the golf carts puttering through the scenery at an adjacent golf course and the busloads of tourists crowding through the house and moving, herdlike, down the outdoor pathways. Come very early or very late in the day to avoid the biggest crowds. For the most authentic Anne experience, make a pilgrimage to this former farm, the inspiration for the Green Gables of the Anne novels. (The author grew up nearby.)

8619 Rte. 6, Cavendish (just west of intersection with Rte. 13). www.pc.gc.ca/eng/lhn-nhs/pe/greengables/index.aspx. (𝒞 **902/963-7874.** Admission mid-June to late Aug, C$7.80 adults, C$6.55 seniors, C$3.90 children, C$20 families; rates discounted 25% May to mid-June and late Aug to Oct. May 1–Oct 31 daily 9am–5pm; Nov–Apr by appointment.

Lucy Maud Montgomery Birthplace ★ HISTORIC HOME   A few miles south of the Silver Bush Anne of Green Gables Museum is this simple white home, where the author was born in 1874. Today the house is once again decorated in the Victorian style of Montgomery's era, and it includes mementos like the author's wedding dress and scrapbook. Just like the (separately owned and operated) Silver Bush, this is historically authentic and worth an hour, but only for die-hard Anne fans.

Intersection of routes 6 and 20, New London. www.lmmontgomerybirthplace.ca. ✆ **902/886-2099** or 836-5502. Admission C$4 adults, C$1 children 6–12. Mid-May to mid-Oct daily 9am–5pm.

Site of Lucy Maud Montgomery's Cavendish Home at L. M. Montgomery's Cavendish National Historic Site ★ HISTORIC HOME "It is and ever must be hallowed ground to me." This is how Lucy Maud herself characterized her childhood home in Cavendish. Because of an illness her mother suffered, Lucy Maud was sent to live here with her grandparents as an infant. She stayed for over 20 years and wrote *Anne of Green Gables* and her other books at the home, which unfortunately is no longer standing. Visitors can roam the grounds and read interpretive signs and plaques about the property's literary history. There's a small gift shop on site.

Rte. 6. Cavendish (just east of Rte. 13 intersection). www.peisland.com/lmm. ✆ **902/963-2231.** Admission C$3 adults, C$1 children, C$12 families. Mid-May to Oct daily 9am–5pm (July–Aug 9am–6pm).

WHERE TO STAY

Cottage courts, properties that offer a number of cottages in one location, are common in and around Cavendish. Great for families, these cottages give kids room to play and adults room to relax. Costs can be similar to one good hotel room, while those with better amenities like pools, privacy, and beachfront will cost a bit more. Cavendish has lots of options ranging from bare basic to luxurious. While it's possible to book a cottage when you arrive, it's far better to book ahead so you get your choice. You'll find a listing of the options at **Tourism PEI** (www.tourismpei.com/pei-cottages) and at such sites as VRBO. com, Homeaway.com, and Flipkey.com

Cavendish Campground ★★   There is no way to get closer to the beach at PEI National Park than to camp at one of the two campgrounds—at Stanhope, and this one at Cavendish. The Cavendish campground is within steps of the ocean and several trails that take in miles of beach, marshes, and woodlands. While the sites are too close together, the location is spectacular and there's lots of room to hike, bike, walk, and otherwise stretch out. Serviced and unserviced sites are available for tents and RVs. If you arrive without any camping option, book one of six oTENTiks, a tent/cabin hybrid—a wood frame with canvas or thick plastic covering that allows for a wooden floor, doors, windows, and wooden bunks—Parks Canada has added to many campgrounds.

357 Graham's Lane, Cavendish. www.pc.gc.ca/eng/pn-np/pe/pei-ipe/index.aspx. ✆ **902/672-6350.** 304 sites. Open mid-June to mid-Sept. C$21–C$35. **Amenities:**

Beach, supervised swimming, trails, laundromat, showers, flush toilets, accessible bathrooms, kitchen shelters, playground, firewood, water.

Kindred Spirits Country Inn & Cottages ★★★ Loving care—and lots of wicker—has been put into this attractive, family-run inn, set right next to the Anne of Green Gables House. Though the rooms are modern, they have an old-fashioned charm to them, with hand-stenciled walls and floral-pattern quilts and drapes. Some bathrooms include Jacuzzi-style tubs. Breakfast is included in the rate and is downright splendiferous, a true feast that changes every morning. The grounds are serene and a delight to explore. In addition to the inn, the family runs two nicely equipped and decorated cottages.

46 Memory Lane, Cavendish. www.kindredspirits.ca. ℂ **800/461-1755** or 902/963-2434. 18 units. Economy rooms C$85–$170, suites $115–$260, honeymoon suite $150–$320. **Amenities:** Cooking facilities (some units), included breakfast and evening tea service, Wi-Fi (free)

The Resort at Cavendish Corner ★★ Every variety of accommodations but camping is available at this beachside resort: very simple motel units, a somewhat dated country inn, and best of all, cute-as-kittens cottages. The latter are more like small two-story homes than cottages, with fireplaces, Jacuzzis, and full kitchens, and are just lovely (go for those). When you're not in your cabin, you'll likely spend time at the pale yellow inn with wraparound veranda and porch swing, which dates from the 1850s (it has historical ties to Lucy Maud Montgomery); you might bump into one of the many Montgomery scholars who visit here every year. With some of PEI's best golfing, a 200-seat restaurant, shops, and, of course its beachside location, The Resort at Cavendish Corner offers good bang for the buck, er, loonie.

7600 Cawnpore Lane (off Rte. 6), Cavendish. www.resortatcavendishcorner.com. ℂ **877/963-2251** or 902/963-2251. 68 units C$60–C$95; 39 cottages C$105–C$252; 6 luxury C$195–C$298. Discounts for weekly cottage rentals. Closed mid-Oct to mid-May. **Amenities:** Golf, heated outdoor pools, playgrounds, exercise room, whirlpool tubs and large kitchen in luxury units, fireplace (some units), Wi-Fi (some units.)

WHERE TO EAT

Cavendish is well stocked with places offering hamburgers, fried clams, and the like, but there are some true originals in the mix. The **Café on the Clyde ★**, part of the Preserve Company (see p. 56) is a very busy place for breakfast, lunch, and tea.

Island Favorites ★★ SEAFOOD   Yes, it's a plain, counter-service joint, but the young owner goes out every morning to catch his own lobsters, and give credibility to the eatery's boast that it has the "best lobster roll on PEI." Make that four rolls, actually—Island Favorites has come up with four flavorful iterations, along with a mighty satisfying chowder, all quite affordable.

8989 Cavendish Rd, Cavendish. www.islandfavorites.net. ℂ **902/218-9449.** Lobster rolls $14, chowder $8.95, sandwiches from $5.95. Daily 11am–7pm.

The Mill Restaurant ★★ MEDITERRANEAN   The airy post-and-beam dining room, with its views of the lovely pond out front, may well be one of the most relaxing places for a meal in the Cavendish area. Food and service here is just as pampering. The latter is prepared by Chef Emily Wells, who brings her European upbringing (she's lived in England, Germany, and Switzerland) to the fresh seafood and produce of rural PEI. Those in the know order the Mediterranean chowder, a departure from the traditional creamy Maritime style: Fish and shellfish is presented in a rich tomato pesto broth and topped with roasted red pepper garlic *rouille.* But there are many stars on the menu, from the authentic Indian vegetable *jalfrezi* (a savory curry) to succulent stuffed chicken. The building and pond were once the location of a 19th-century mill.

5592 Rte. 13, New Glasgow. www.oldeglasgowmill.ca. © **902/964-3313.** Reservations recommended. Dinner C$18–C$28. Daily 5:30–9pm.

The Pearl ★★★ FUSION   The team at The Pearl have dubbed their grey-shingled restaurant "an eclectic eatery," an apt description for the creatively sourced, prepared, and presented dishes that change with season and availability. The menu is always surprising; ingredients from pickled apple blossoms to foraged wild mushrooms accent fresh mains of local seafood, pork, and chicken. For an idea of how eclectic The Pearl can be, imagine this dessert: wild PEI blueberry compote with bourbon caramel popcorn, and corn ice cream. The Pearl is a whimsical, delicious adventure every time.

7792 Cavendish Rd., North Rustico. www.pearleatery.com. © **902/963-2111.** Reservations recommended. Late May to mid-Sept, daily for dinner.

Piatto Pizzeria ★★ PIZZA   An improbable find in rural PEI, but welcome nonetheless, this Neapolitan wood-fired pizzeria serves up authentic Italian-style pies. Especially fun for the kids, diners can watch dough being tossed into the air, spread with fresh ingredients, and slid into the big oven next to sticks of burning hardwood. Italian coffee, ice-cold Italian Peroni (and many other beers), and Italian desserts complete the experience.

8779 Rte. 6, Avonlea Village, Cavendish. www.piattopizzeria.com/cavendish. © **902/360-0909.** Pizza C$12–C$19. Sun–Thurs 11:30am–8pm (Fri & Sat until 9pm).

North & South Rustico to Brackley Beach

A few miles east of Cavendish are the Rusticos, five in all: North Rustico, South Rustico, Rusticoville, Rustico Harbour, and Anglo Rustico. (Don't feel bad if you can't keep them straight.) They're a fun, relaxing place to head if you're seeking beaches, small harbors, and friendly locals.

This was one of the first Canadian regions to be populated by Acadians following the Treaty of Paris, and is the oldest Acadian presence on PEI dating from 1790. The Rusticos are attractive villages with far fewer tourist traps and auto traffic than Cavendish—which means they're much easier to explore by car or bike. Out of the hubbub, they're all still close enough to the national park *and* Anne's land, so they work well as a base. And the island's famous beaches are virtually at your doorstep.

North Rustico ★ clusters around a scenic harbor with views out toward Rustico Bay. Leave time for walking around, perusing deep-sea fishing opportunities (see below), and peeking into shops. The village curves around Rustico Bay to end at North Rustico Harbour, a sand spit with fishing wharves, summer cottages, a fisheries museum, and a couple of informal restaurants. A boardwalk follows the water's edge from town to harbor, a worthy destination for a quiet afternoon ramble or a picnic. Also, here is **Outside Expeditions** (www.getoutside.com; ✆ **800/207-3899** or 902/963-3366), one of PEI's best outfitters; they offer sea-kayaking excursions around the harbor and into surrounding areas (see "Sea Kayaking," earlier in this chapter, p. 47). If you need a book for the beach, stop at the excellent **Jem Books** (✆ **902/963-3802**) as you leave North Rustico at 6922 Route 6, open mid-May to early October.

To find **South Rustico** ★★, continue east on Route 6 to **Route 243** and ascend the low hill overlooking the bay. Here you'll find a handsome cluster of buildings that were once home to some of the most prosperous Acadian settlers. Among the structures is the sandstone **Farmers' Bank of Rustico Museum** ★ (www.farmersbank.ca; ✆ **902/963-3168**), beside St. Augustine's Parish Church (see below)—you can't miss it. A bank that's historic? In this case, yes. The bank was established with the help of a visionary local cleric, the Reverend Georges-Antoine Belcourt, in 1864 to help local farmers get their operations into the black. The Father and parishioners actually built the bank themselves, timber by timber, stone by stone. It operated for some 30 years and helped inspire the credit union movement in North America before it was, ironically, forced to shut down by legislative banking reforms. Open for tours from June through September, Monday through Saturday, 9:30am to 5:30pm, and Sundays 11am to 5pm (off season by request.) Admission costs C$6 per adult, C$4.50 per senior, C$3.50 per student, and C$12 per family.

Right next door to the bank, there are two more structures worth checking out. **Doucet House** ★, a sturdy log building of Acadian construction dating from 1772, was the home of Jean Doucet, who arrived in these parts on a type of inshore fishing boat called a "shallop." It's believed that this might be the oldest extant home on the entire island. The house was moved from its waterside location in 1999 and completely restored and furnished with period pieces. Its opening hours and admissions fees are the same as those for the Farmers' Bank; in fact, one ticket gets you into both.

Then there's the handsome **St. Augustine's Parish Church** (✆ **902/963-2246**) dating from 1838, with adjacent cemetery, next door at 2190 Church Road beside Route 243. If the church's door is open, enter and have a look around the graceful structure.

Brackley Beach ★ is the gateway to the eastern section of the main part of PEI's national park, and it has the fewest services of any town in these parts. It's best appreciated by those who prefer their beach vacations only lightly touched by civilization.

DEEP-SEA FISHING

PEI's north shore is home to the island's greatest concentration of deep-sea fishing boats. Starting at C$45 per person, you'll get about 3 hours' worth of time out on the open seas to fish for mackerel and cod. Don't worry about a lack of experience: All the necessary equipment is supplied, crewmembers are usually helpful as coaches, and some boat hands will even clean and fillet your catch for you to cook back at your cottage. (See "Fishing" on p. 46).

SHOPPING

Between Cavendish and Brackley Beach, you'll find a number of shops offering unique island crafts and products. Browsing is a good option on days when the weather doesn't lure you to the beach.

The Dunes Studio Gallery and Café ★★★ ARTS & CRAFTS   This architecturally striking modern gallery, on the road to the eastern section of PEI National Park, showcases works by international, Canadian, and island artisans and craftspeople. Housed on several open levels, the gallery features pottery (made by owner Peter Jansons—you'll often see him at work at his wheel creating elegant, unique items), furniture, lamps, woodworking, sculptures, and paintings, along with more affordable crafts, soaps and jewelry. The gallery is also home to serene gardens and an appealing **cafe** (see p. 58). The gallery is open daily from May through October, 9am to 6pm; the cafe daily from June through September. Rte. 15, Brackley Beach. www.dunesgallery.com. ✆ **902/672-2586** (gallery) or 672-1883 (cafe).

Gaudreau Fine Woodworking ★ ARTS & CRAFTS   Set beside Rustico Bay, this store sells woodworking by award-winning artisans. Items for sale might range from big, deep salad bowls to plates and elegant sushi trays. As a bonus, you can browse a wide selection of pottery from regional potters. Open early June to mid-October, 10am to 5pm. Rte. 6, South Rustico. www.wood magic.ca. ✆ **902/963-2273.**

Glasgow Glen Farm ★★ CHEESE   After watching a brief video about the making of Gouda, you'll see the equipment—sometimes in use—through a glass wall, then get down to the real business of tasting and buying the excellent cheeses produced here. If you don't feel like the usual aged Gouda, try a flavored variety with peppercorns, garlic, or herbs. The homemade breads and pizzas are very good as well. A short detour off Route 6, but well worth it. 190 Rte. 258, New Glasgow. www.glasgowglenfarm.ca. ✆ **902/963-2496.**

Prince Edward Island Preserve Co. ★★ FOOD   A variety of preserves are sold at this renovated butter factory in a lovely valley; abundant sampling is encouraged, and you can watch the preserve-making process through a glass window. Single jars of jam—black currant, raspberry and champagne jam, sour cherry marmalade—are, frankly, a little pricey, but so good most end up buying a few. The onsite **Café on the Clyde** serves hearty breakfasts, good lunches, and dinners. Intersection of routes 224 and 258 (just off Rte. 13), New Glasgow. www.preservecompany.com. ✆ **800/565-5267** or 902/964-4300.

WHERE TO STAY

In addition to the following, look at **Dalvay by the Sea ★★★** (described in the "Prince Edward Island National Park" section of this chapter on p. 62).

Barachois Inn ★★　Barachois hits all the notes a good B&B should. It's set in a 19th-century property (the mansard-roofed home won a restoration award back in the 1980s) and the decor prettily celebrates the Victorian era with fireplaces, sled- or four-poster canopy beds, and lovely wallpaper. Outside is elegant, too, thanks to a beautifully kept flower garden. Better yet, the expansive rooms have many modern comforts like air tubs in some, kitchenettes in others, and usable Wi-Fi throughout. Breakfast is made to order and quite good; and the devoted hosts make sure their guests have everything they need, whether it be free passes to the national park or towels for the beach.

2193 Church Rd., Rte. 243 (Hunter River R.R. 3), Rustico. www.barachoisinn.com. ℂ **800/963-2194.** 8 units. C$160–C$295. Rates include full breakfast. Open year-round **Amenities:** Sauna, fitness room, kitchenette (some units), Wi-Fi (free).

Shaw's Hotel ★★　As Canada's oldest family-operated inn, Shaw's was named a national historic site. Since 1860, the family has welcomed guests from around the world, particularly those from New England in Victorian times. A long walk down a quiet lane gets you to the national park beach from the historic hotel and cottages. Newer cottages range from one to four bedrooms for pretty well any size family and come with continental breakfast at the inn. Luxury chalets boast cozy fireplaces, full kitchens, and decks with barbecues (one to four bedrooms) ranging in looks from rustic to modern. The large property includes a playground that announces Shaw's kid-friendly approach; ask about hayrides, singsongs, and scavenger hunts. The bright, very good **dining room ★★**, with a view of Brackley Bay, serves Island-sourced produce and foraged ingredients for a menu that will seem both familiar and of high quality.

99 Apple Tree Rd. off Rte. 15, Brackley Beach. www.shawshotel.ca. ℂ **902/672-2022.** 15 hotel units, 10 cottages, 9 luxury chalets. C$110–C$160 double; C$145–C$230 suite; C$130–C$500 cottage for 2–8 people. Reduced rates for extended stays. Packages available. Closed mid-Oct to late May. **Amenities:** Restaurant, bar, children's program, fridge (some units), kitchenette (some units), no phone, Wi-Fi (free).

Stanhope Campground ★★　Like its sister campground in Cavendish, you can't get closer to the beach at PEI National Park than to camp here. Over a road from this campground is mile after mile of beach and dune, as well as a 10km (6.5 miles) multi-use trail for walkers, bikers, and skaters. There are fewer sites than at Cavendish, making the experience here less crowded and more private. Most sites are forested. Serviced and unserviced sites are available for every camping option, including a number of accessible sites; if you need one, ask about borrowing the beach wheelchair.

983 Gulf Shore Parkway, Brackley Beach. www.pc.gc.ca/eng/pn-np/pe/pei-ipe/index.aspx. ℂ **902/672-6350.** 130 sites. Open mid-July to early Sept. C$21–C$35. **Amenities:** Beach, supervised swimming, trails, laundromat, showers, flush toilets, accessible bathrooms, kitchen shelters, firewood, water.

PEI'S SEASONAL lobster suppers

If you have a must-do list for Prince Edward Island, the experience of an Island-style lobster supper should be on it. Lobster suppers have a long history here, beginning several decades ago as community suppers. The opening of lobster season was celebrated in community halls, church basements, or even outdoors. Not only did it mark the arrival of spring (the ice having departed from the harbors and fishing grounds), it also brought welcome income. As is the way with Islanders, they began using these events to raise funds for worthy projects or to support the church.

The logic behind the menu was simple. Local fishermen donated the lobster, farmers the potatoes and milk for chowder. Someone's cold cellar would provide cabbage and carrots for coleslaw. Strawberries were the first fruit of the season. Biscuits, bread, pies, and squares came from local housewives, along with their own pickles. Everyone pitched in.

Soon word spread. Townfolk wanted to go, as did savvy tourists. **New Glasgow Lobster Suppers** opened their doors in 1958 when the Junior Farmers Organization held a fundraiser. Twelve Junior Farmers turned it into a business in 1972, building ever bigger halls to accommodate the crowds. Meals include unlimited chowder, mussels, lobster, bread, desserts, and beverages. This institution is important to the community, providing employment in a region where jobs can be scarce.

These suppers still have the feel of the community events—informal, with lots of people chattering and having a good time. And the menu hasn't changed: Lobster is served at its best, fresh cooked, with a touch of the sea to keep it honest (hot or cold, your choice). The size of lobster you order will determine the price. Credit cards accepted. Expect to pay around C$40 each plus drinks. Two I recommend:

New Glasgow Lobster Suppers ★★ (www.peilobstersuppers.com; ℂ **902/964-2870**) is on Route 258 (just off Rte. 13), open daily from June through mid-October, 4 to 8:30pm. Lobster supper ranges from C$33 to C$65 per person, depending on lobster size. Alternatives include scallops, roast beef, ham, vegetarian, salmon, and chicken. There's a good kids' menu, and credit cards are accepted.

Fisherman's Wharf ★ (www.fishermanswharf.ca; ℂ **877/289-1010** or 902/963-2669) in North Rustico keeps their 60-foot salad bar well stocked, so if down-and-dirty eating is your goal, you will love it here. If you are on a budget or just want a taste of lobster, try a lobster roll.

Find other lobster supper locations at www.lobstersuppers.ca.

WHERE TO EAT

In addition to the selection below, consider the dining rooms at **Shaw's Hotel ★★** (see "Where to Stay," p. 57) and at **Dalvay by the Sea ★★★** (p. 62).

The Dunes Café ★★ CAFE   In the stylish surroundings of the Dunes Gallery (see "Shopping," p. 56) and gardens, the on-site cafe has become an attraction in its own right. And as with the gallery, there's an Asian presence; if you've traveled to Indonesia, you'll recognize *nasi goreng* (pork fried rice) on the menu, here served with fresh pineapple and spicy Asian sauce. There's also a Thai noodle salad with seasonal vegetables, as well as Island beef in coconut green curry. Back to PEI–inspired dishes, the cafe's lobster asparagus quiche is packed with Island lobster and served with fresh local greens. Desserts are equally original and the coffee excellent.

Rte. 15, Brackley Beach. www.dunesgallery.com. © **902/672-1883.** Lunch mains C$10–C$17; dinner entrees C$33–C$39. June–Oct daily 11:30am–9pm (July & Aug until 10pm).

Orwell ★★

In southeastern Queens County, the village of **Orwell** is a worthwhile historic detour off busy Route 1, about 32km (20 miles) east of Charlottetown. (Rte. 1 is the fast main road travelers drive to get from Charlottetown to Montague, the Murrays, Georgetown, or the Wood Islands ferry.) Both sites mentioned below are near each other on a side road; there are few landmarks other than simple signs directing you, so keep a sharp eye out for the corner and the turnoff.

Macphail Homestead ★★ HISTORIC SITE/NATURE   A few minutes' drive from the village is this handsome, white-shingled house, former home of Andrew Macphail. Macphail, born in this tiny village in 1864, gained renown as a doctor, pathologist, professor, writer, editor, and agricultural tinkerer; you learn a lot about his exceptional mind and career by walking through the house, which includes exhibits on his experiments in tobacco farming, his time as a medic in World War I, and his work as a medical scholar, as well as period furniture. There's also a tiny tea room which offers simple soup-and-sandwich type fare. But the real allure is a stroll across the green lawn and through the 57 hectares (140 acres) of forest called the Macphail Woods, laced by several **trails ★**. It's a project to bring back some of PEI's lost native Acadian forest.

www.macphailhomestead.ca. © **902/651-2789.** Free admission. Open daily from spring through fall, with shorter hours in the shoulder seasons.

Orwell Corner Historic Village ★★ HISTORIC SITE   One of the most aesthetically pleasing historic parks in the province, the village re-creates life as it might have been lived in a small island town of the 1890s. You can visit a general store, stop by a working blacksmith shop, say hi to a barn full of animals, wander through lush gardens, and have tea in the community hall. Look for regular events like folk music performances (often scheduled mid-week) and workhorse or artisan demonstrations.

www.orwellcorner.ca. © **902/651-8515.** Admission C$6 for adults, C$4.25 children 6 to 18, C$16 for families. July & Aug daily 9:30am–5pm, from 9:15am–4:45pm weekdays only until mid-Oct.

PRINCE EDWARD ISLAND NATIONAL PARK ★★

Located along PEI's sandy north central coast, Prince Edward Island National Park is big and small all at once. In total, the park encompasses just 40 skinny kilometers (25 miles) of sandy beaches and wind-sculpted dunes topped by marram grass, red-sandstone cliffs, salt marshes, and gentle inlets. Even what length it possesses is broached in several places by broad estuarine inlets that connect to harbors; as a result, you can't drive the entire park's length in one stretch, but rather must break away from the coastal road (and views) and backtrack inland.

You won't mind, though, because this is *the* reason many people come to the island. These empty beaches and lovely dunes define the park for a hefty percentage of PEI visitors. There's really little point in trying to tour the whole length of the park in 1 day. It's better to simply pick out one stretch of beach, stake a claim, and settle in and enjoy the gentle surroundings.

There's more to this national park than just beaches and dunes. Within its boundaries you can also find considerable woods and meadows, full of wildlife—you might spot red foxes (who den in the dunes), muskrats, mink, eagles, or osprey. In the marshes and tidal flats, great blue heron stalk their aquatic prey near sunset. And, where beach and dune meet, watch for the piping plover, a tiny, endangered beach bird that scratches its shallow, hard-to-spot nest right out of the beach sand. Walking trails and interpretive programs enrich a visit. Be sure to head to Greenwich at the far eastern reaches of the park, near St. Peters. There are fewer visitors here, and the interpretive center has very informative displays about the park's ecology and nature. The national park also administers the Green Gables house and grounds, but they're a bit of a drive from the beaches and a world apart from them, aesthetically speaking; see "Cavendish," earlier in this chapter, for details on "Anne's Land."

Essentials

GETTING THERE   From downtown Charlottetown, Route 15 (which passes the airport, then continues north) is the most direct route to central sections of the national park. To reach the lovely eastern sections and Dalvay by the Sea, you can also drive east on Route 2, then turn north on Route 6 at Bedford. Alternately, to reach the Cavendish (western) area and the attractive Rusticos most quickly, take Route 2 west to Hunter River, then turn north on Route 13. The entire drive from city to beach is only 30 or 40km (20 or 25 miles), yet it will take 45 minutes or more on the small roads, depending on traffic. Once you arrive at the park, if you want to drive its length and survey it more closely, enter at North Rustico and follow the Shore Road. Otherwise take Route 6 to the Cavendish entrances, which is sometimes heavy with traffic.

VISITOR INFORMATION   The **Cavendish Visitor Information Centre** (✆ **800/463-4734** or 902/963-7830), north of the intersection of routes 6 and 13, supplies information on the park's destinations and activities. It opens daily from mid-May through early September.

At the far eastern end of the park, past St. Peters, the modern **Greenwich Interpretation Centre** (✆ **902/961-2514**) is open daily in July and August from 10am to 6pm, June and September until 4pm.

FEES   The park is open year-round. Between June and early September, however, visitors must stop at one of the two tollhouses and pay entry fees. From July through September, the fees are C$7.80 adults, C$6.80 seniors, C$3.90 children ages 6 to 16, and C$19.60 per family; all these rates are discounted by 50% in June and September. Save money with seasonal passes if you plan to visit for more than 5 days.

Beaches

PEI National Park is home to two kinds of sandy beaches: popular, sometimes crowded strands with changing rooms, lifeguards, snack bars, and other amenities; and all the rest. Where you go depends on your temperament. If it's not a day at the beach without the aroma of other people's coconut tanning oil, head for Brackley Beach, Dalvay Beach, or Cavendish Beach. (The latter is within walking distance, about a kilometer through the fields of the Green Gables Historic Site and many amusements, thus making it good for families with kids; see "Cavendish" on p. 49 of this chapter for details on said attractions.)

Rip Currents

If the surf is up, or waves are breaking, you would be best advised to swim at beaches with a lifeguard. Rip currents form when waves breaking near the shoreline rush back out to sea through breaks in sandbars just offshore. It is easy for even the strongest swimmer to get pulled out to sea, so check out conditions and take appropriate care of yourself and your children. Never swim alone, and if caught in a rip tide, swim parallel to shore until the force subsides.

If you'd just as soon be left alone with the waves, sun, and sand, you need to head a bit farther afield—or just keep walking very far down the beaches from parking lots until you have left the crowds behind. Pick up a map of the national park, and look for ways to head away from the popular sites. A hint: "Fewer facilities" almost always translates to "far fewer people."

Hiking & Biking

For the true enthusiast, hiking is rather low-key in PEI National Park, especially when compared with the trails in Atlantic Canada's other national parks, but you can still find a number of pleasant strolls, with 14 trails to choose from. You won't find challenging grinds, or hard-to-navigate landscapes, but you will find what PEI is known for: gently rolling trails, scenic vistas, and very walkable trails. (Of course, there's also the beach, which is perfect for long, leisurely walks.)

The park maintains a total of 45km (28 miles) of trails, so there's plenty of room to roam. They have also added walking/bicycling lanes, separated from traffic by a grass verge, along paved roads throughout the park.

Among the most appealing is the **Homestead Trail ★**, which departs from the Cavendish campground. The trail offers both a 6.7km (4-mile) loop and an 8.8km (5.5-mile) loop and skirts wheat fields, woodlands, and estuaries, with frequent views of the distinctively bumpy dunes at the west end of the national park. Notably, mountain bikes are allowed on this trail, so it can become a relatively busy place on sunny days. If you are going into Green Gables (admission is charged in season), the two **short trails**—Balsam Hollow and Haunted Wood, each less than 2km (a mile)—are lovely but invariably crowded when buses are in the parking lot. **Cycling** the seaside roads in the park is sublime. Traffic is generally light, and it's easy to make frequent stops along the way to explore beaches, woodlands, or the marshy edges of inlets.

4

PRINCE EDWARD ISLAND | Prince Edward Island National Park

The two **shoreline roads** ★★ within the national park—between Dalvay and Rustico Island, and from Cavendish to North Rustico Harbour—are especially beautiful as sunset edges into twilight. As a bonus, there are snack bars located both at Brackley Beach and again at Covehead Bay. Both have bike lanes.

For mountain bikers, there's a trail just for you. At the end of Gulf Shore Way, there's a stacked, multi-use trail at **Robinson's Island** ★★. The 5km (3 mile) trail is open to hikers, but it was built with beginner and intermediate mountain bikers in mind; 11 technical challenges on spurs from the main trail include teeter totters and ramps.

For info on renting bikes in **Charlottetown,** see p. 46. You can also find hybrid and mountain bike rentals, for roughly the same rates, at **Dalvay Beach Bike Rentals** (🕿 **888/366-2955** or 902/672-2048). The facility is located at the venerable Dalvay by the Sea resort (see below).

Where to Stay & Eat

See also listings for "Cavendish" and "North & South Rustico to Brackley Beach," earlier in this chapter, for more choices in the vicinity of the park. Don't overlook Covehead Wharf, located on the Gulf Shore Highway between the Brackley and Stanhope park entrances. There is a deep-sea fishing and diving charter outfit here, as well as local fishing boats. And you cannot get fresher lobster than that found here—32 steps from boat to pound. Along with fresh oysters, mussels, and clams, buy it at the Fishmart to take with you (live or cooked) or better yet, order from **Richard's Fresh Seafood** ★ (www. richards freshseafood.com; 🕿 **902/672-3030**). The menu is all seafood: Fish and chips, lobster roll, scallop burger, steamed mussels.

Dalvay by the Sea ★★★ No TV, no radio, no phone; Dalvay by the Sea is a place to slow down, stroll the beach at sunset, and enjoy a leisurely dinner in sumptuous fashion. The Tudor-style inn with signature high, green gables; curved, enclosed veranda built on stone; and painted clapboard siding is a PEI landmark nestled in the sand dunes next to a large pond within the national park. Inside, the handcrafted wooden stairwell and varnished wooden walls harken back to a time of fine Craftsman homes and resorts. Comfortable sitting areas are gathered around a couple of massive fireplaces. The guest rooms feature four-poster beds and antiques, in keeping with the yesterday feel of the place. There are also eight cottages on the property. They have no cooking facilities, but all are three-bedroom units, half with one bathroom and half with two (there's a 2-night minimum stay in the cottages). **The MacMillan Dining Room** ★★★ is worthy of the setting, preparing local foods with flare and confidence; the menu changes regularly, but there's always sticky date pudding with toffee sauce, once featured in *Gourmet* magazine.

Rte. 6, Grand Tracadie. www.dalvaybythesea.com. 🕿 **888/366-2955** or 902/672-2048. 25 units and 8 cottages. June to late-Oct C$179 double, C$379–C$399 cottage. Closed late-Sept to May. **Amenities:** 2 dining rooms, bike rentals, canoeing/kayaking/paddleboating, lawn bowling, tennis court, fridge (cottages only), no TV or phone, Wi-Fi (free).

CHARLOTTETOWN ★★

It's not hard to figure out why PEI's earliest settlers situated the province's political and cultural capital where they did: It's on a point of land between two rivers and within a large, protected harbor. For ship captains plying the seas, this quiet harbor with ample anchorage and wharf space was a welcome sight. Of course, travelers rarely arrive by water these days (unless a cruise ship is in port), but Charlottetown's harborside location and compactness still translate into a lovely setting. This remains one of Atlantic Canada's most graceful cities.

Named for Queen Charlotte (wife of the infamous King George III), Charlottetown is home to only about 35,000 people, but counting its suburbs, that number almost doubles to about 65,000—that's nearly one of every two Islanders. To Canadians, the city is the home of Confederation; a conference held in 1864 led to the creation of the independent Dominion of Canada in 1867. (In a historic twist of fate, PEI itself actually declined to join the new confederation it spawned, until it relented in 1873 when promised a railroad and fixed link with the mainland.)

Today, the downtown has a relaxed feel to it, with its mixture of modern and Victorian commercial buildings, government and cultural centers, buttoned-up bureaucrats, students, and artists hanging out around town. Outside the business core, you'll find leafy streets and large, elegant homes dating from different eras (the most dramatic were built in the late 19th c.). Charlottetown is blessed with a number of pocket parks (or squares), which provide a quiet respite amid the gentle buzz. Big-box stores are concentrated at the northern entrance to the city; grocery and department stores (as well as malls, gas stations, and fast-food outlets) are located along Routes 1 and 2, but not in the historic downtown. Charlottetown is centrally located and a good base for exploring the rest of the island; only the western tip is too far for day-tripping. You can be touring Green Gables, relaxing on a north-shore beach, or teeing off at one of PEI's fine golf courses—all within 45 minutes of leaving Charlottetown. The capital has—by far—the island's best selection of inns and hotels, plus a fine assortment of restaurants. You can dine out every night for a week, and still be pleasantly surprised each time—no fried-fish capital, this. The establishment of the Culinary Institute of Canada ensures a high level of cuisine; students have brought home gold from the World Culinary Olympics—just a sampling of their many accolades.

The city itself can occupy a couple of days, especially if you like history or leisurely walks around old neighborhoods, waterfronts, or parks. Then of course there is the theater, a night at the races, boat tours, pub tours, nightlife, an excellent farmers' market, the sidewalk cafes on Victoria Row, and coffee shops. Be sure to take time to chat with the locals; they're a friendly bunch.

Essentials

GETTING THERE   Coming by car from the mainland and across the Confederation Bridge, Route 1 (the Trans-Canada Hwy.) makes more or less a straight shot east into downtown Charlottetown. From the Woods Island ferry, you also take Route 1 (the route begins at the ferry dock), except you go west.

Charlottetown Airport is just north of the city center. See the "By Air" section at the beginning of this chapter, p. 45, for airlines with links to PEI.

If you're coming from Montréal by VIA Rail train, disembark at Moncton and rent a car or take a **Maritime Bus** (www.maritimebus.com; ✆ **800/575-1807**) to Charlottetown; the cost is C$43 per adult for the trip, which takes about 3 hours. Do check ahead: Bus and train schedules don't always work together, so you may have a long wait. If you're coming from Halifax, **Advance Shuttle** (www.advanceshuttle.ca; ✆ **877/886-3322**) operates daily van trips from Halifax to Charlottetown. The trip takes 5 hours and costs C$69 one-way for adults, C$64 for students and seniors, C$50 for children 11 and under.

VISITOR INFORMATION The city's main Visitor Information Centre (www.discovercharlottetown.com; ✆ **902/368-7795**) is in a historic brick railroad building, now known as Founders' Hall. It's at the very end of Prince Street. (Brown question-mark signs help direct you there.) This place is loaded with helpful staffers, an interactive computer kiosk, a cafe, free Internet, and an ample supply of brochures; there's also a vacancy service to let you know where rooms are currently available around town. The center is open daily in July and August 8:30am to 7:30pm, with shorter hours in spring and fall.

Exploring Charlottetown

Charlottetown is a compact city that's easy to walk around. Focus on three areas: the waterfront, the downtown near Province House, and the parks and residential areas near Victoria Park. To begin, head to the **information center** (see above); parking is generally scarce downtown, but relatively abundant near the visitor center, both on the street and in free and paid lots. Be sure to ask for a map and free walking-tour brochures. **Peake's Wharf ★★** (www. discovercharlottetown.com, click on the "See & Do" button) is the heart of the waterfront; it's a collection of 20 boutiques and eateries that attract hordes in summer. The complex offers lobster on the wharf or live lobster to cook yourself, a couple of boat tours, and lots of shopping and dining options. **Free concerts,** featuring local folk musicians, take place afternoons and evenings (weather permitting) most of the summer. Next to the wharf is **Confederation Landing Park ★**, an open, modern park with a boardwalk along water's edge, with lush lawns and benches nicely situated for lazing about and letting the kids run. There's also a big marina where cruise ships tie up.

From the wharf, stroll up **Great George Street ★★★**, one of the best-looking streets in Eastern Canada with its leafy trees, perfectly scaled Georgian row houses, and stately churches. Designated as a National Historic District, this street is noteworthy because you are tracing the steps of the Fathers of Confederation who, in 1864, walked from the wharf to meetings at Province House, which led to the formation of Canada. Costumed reenactors

Charlottetown

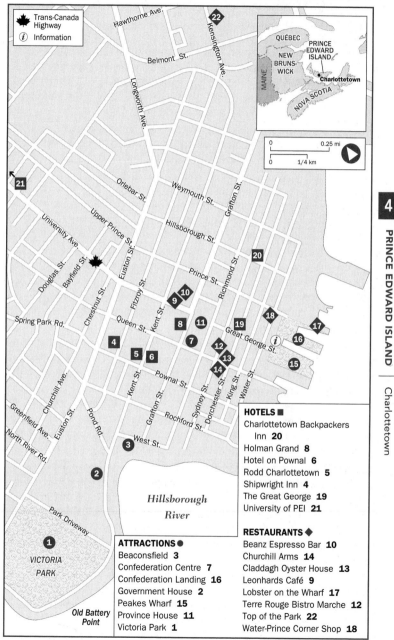

Trans-Canada Highway

i Information

QUÉBEC

MAINE

NEW BRUNS-WICK

PRINCE EDWARD ISLAND

Charlottetown

NOVA SCOTIA

0   0.25 mi

0   1/4 km

Hawthorne Ave.

Kensington Ave.

Belmont St.

Longworth Ave.

Orlebar St.

Weymouth St.

Grafton St.

Hillsborough St.

University Ave.

Upper Prince St.

Prince St.

Richmond St.

Douglas St.

Bayfield St.

Chestnut St.

Euston St.

Fitzroy St.

Kent St.

Spring Park Rd.

Queen St.

Great George St.

Churchill Ave.

Kent St.

Pownal St.

Water St.

Greenfield Ave.

Euston St.

Pond Rd.

Grafton St.

Sydney St.

Dorchester St.

King St.

Rochford St.

West St.

North River Rd.

Park Driveway

Hillsborough River

VICTORIA PARK

Old Battery Point

HOTELS ■
Charlottetown Backpackers Inn **20**
Holman Grand **8**
Hotel on Pownal **6**
Rodd Charlottetown **5**
Shipwright Inn **4**
The Great George **19**
University of PEI **21**

ATTRACTIONS ●
Beaconsfield **3**
Confederation Centre **7**
Confederation Landing **16**
Government House **2**
Peakes Wharf **15**
Province House **11**
Victoria Park **1**

RESTAURANTS ◆
Beanz Espresso Bar **10**
Churchill Arms **14**
Claddagh Oyster House **13**
Leonhards Café **9**
Lobster on the Wharf **17**
Terre Rouge Bistro Marche **12**
Top of the Park **22**
Water-Prince Corner Shop **18**

The **Port-la-Joye/Fort Amherst National Historic Site** (www.pc.gc.ca/eng/lhn-nhs/pe/amherst/index.aspx; *𝒞* **902/566-7050**) is easily seen across the harbor from Charlottetown; it's on the eastern side of the gut that takes shipping from the harbor out to Northumberland Strait. A 20km (12-mile) drive from Charlottetown, west on Route 1 to Cornwall, then south on Route 19 (part of the Red Sands Shore Drive), this site provides a panoramic view of Charlottetown and the harbor, and a lovely place for a walk or to fly kites. It's a self-guided site that's open year-round. A total of 5km (3 miles) of trails—all easy—wind through the property; interpretive panels along the way tell the history of this site, which goes back to 1720 as the location of early Acadian and British farms. This is a great place to view the city at night—fireworks on Canada Day (July 1) are awesome!

lead walking tours that bring history alive. At the top of Great George Street, stop into the **Province House,** then explore Victoria Row with its outdoor restaurants and entertainment. Visit **Confederation Centre Art Gallery** (see below), then explore downtown's shops and restaurants.

For a pleasant walk affording fine water views, head southwest on **Kent Street** (just north of the Confederation Mall). At 2 Kent St., you'll see **Beaconsfield ★** (www.peimuseum.com; *𝒞* **902/368-6603;** C$5 adults, C$4 students, C$14 families, free for children 12 and under; open daily 10am–4:30pm in summer, hours vary the rest of the year), a mansard-roofed mansion designed in 1877 by local architect William Harris for a prosperous shipbuilder. The architecture boasts an elegant mix of Georgian symmetry and Victorian exuberance, and rooms are furnished in high Victorian style. The home hosts lectures and events throughout the year.

From Beaconsfield, look for the boardwalk that follows the edge of the harbor for about a mile into **Victoria Park ★★**, a quiet place of ball fields, grassy picnic areas, and lovely paths through the woods. This walk along the water has unobstructed views of the harbor and the "gut" (also known as the channel between the cliffs) out to Northumberland Strait.

Along the way, look for the handsome **Government House ★★** (www.gov.pe.ca/olg/index.php?number=1022336; *𝒞* **902/368-5480;** open to public summers only, Mon–Fri 10am–4pm by guided tour), also known as Fanningbank. Built in 1834, this sturdy white-shingled residence with eight Doric columns is set back on a broad lawn. It's the official residence of the island's lieutenant governor, who serves as the Queen of England's personal representative to the province. The place probably looks familiar if you've been in Charlottetown for a few days: That famous photo of the Fathers of the Confederation you see around town was taken on the front portico. The cannons overlooking the water were placed there after an attack by Yankee privateers, who took a kidnapped resident back to George Washington, perhaps anticipating a ransom for their coffers.

Confederation Centre Art Gallery ★★ GALLERY   Inside the boxy, concrete building that dominates downtown is one of the Maritimes' largest art galleries. The permanent collection comprises some 16,500 pieces, including Robert Harris's iconic painting of the Fathers of Confederation. Changing exhibitions might range from a historic map of PEI and its influence on the establishment of Canada's smallest province, to solo exhibitions by contemporary artists. Spend an hour or more here if you appreciate art.

145 Richmond St. www.confederationcentre.com. ✆ **902/628-6142.** Mid-May to mid-Oct daily 9am–5pm; rest of the year Wed–Sat 11am–5pm, Sun 1–5pm.

Province House National Historic Site ★ HISTORIC SITE   PEI's seat of government is housed in the official legislative building and the location of the Charlottetown Conference in 1864 that led to the founding of Canada. It's now a National Historic Site and is undergoing a lengthy C$20 million restoration that could keep the building closed to the public until 2020. Built in 1847, the grand sandstone structure at the top of Great George Street—a National Historic Streetscape—sits on a parklike property at the edge of the treeless downtown. Outside the building in summer, actors in costume from the adjacent Confederation Centre play characters from PEI's history, perform skits, and interact with visitors, telling the story of confederation.

Intersection of Richmond and Great George sts.

Shopping

Charlottetown is full of shops and boutiques, but you have to seek them out. An artisan studio walking-tour map, available at Visitor Information Centres or brochure racks in many hotels, will help. If you're looking for malls and big-box stores, head up University Avenue to the outskirts of town. Otherwise, stick to downtown, starting at **Peake's Wharf** on the waterfront. While on the touristy side, the arts-and-crafts boutiques are nonetheless attractive, housed in small buildings reminiscent of wooden boat sheds. Among the standouts: **Amos Pewter ★★** (www.amospewter.com; ✆ **800/565-3369**) sells handmade jewelry, gifts, and home decor inspired by nature; the vibrant **My Little Stash ★★** (www.facebook.com/My-Little-Stash-448047195274952/photos_stream?ref=page_internal; ✆ **902/90-5533**) sells colorful jewelry, funky clothing, and retro hippie artwork; quality made-in-PEI stainless cookware is sold at factory outlet prices at **Paderno ★★** (www.paderno.com; ✆ **902/629-1500**). You'll also find casual dining, excellent ice cream, boat tours, and live entertainment here.

The **Confederation Court Mall ★** (www.confedcourtmall.com; ✆ **902/894-9505**), downtown right across from the Province House at 134 Kent St., is bigger, but more about chains than artisans. Come chiefly if you (or your kids) need a rainy-day shopping fix or a quick bite.

Anne of Green Gables Store ★ GIFTS   Find everything Anne, from dolls to stationery at this downtown branch of the main shop in Avonlea Village. Check out the chocolate shop next door—they might be hand-dipping.

110 Queen St. www.annestore.ca. ✆ **902/368-2663.**

The Bookman ★★ BOOKS Located across from the mall, this small shop has the city's best selection of new, used, and rare books, with a strong inventory of PEI and Canadian titles. 177 Queen St. www.bookmanpei.com. © **902/892-8872.**

Charlottetown Farmers' Market ★★★ FOOD There are now so many vendors of vegetables, meats, PEI cheese, baked goods, artisans, and ready-to-eat foods, that the market overflows into the parking lot, where barbecues and food stalls, flower hawkers and artists peddle their goods. It's quite the scene, and the prepared foods are so tasty, you might come for breakfast and stay on for lunch—there's great coffee, live entertainment, and lots of friendly chatter. The market is open Saturdays year-round and Wednesdays from mid-June to mid-October, 9am to 2pm. 100 Belvedere Ave. off University Ave. www.charlottetownfarmersmarket.weebly.com. © **902/626-3373.**

COWS ★★★ ICE CREAM Meet Canada's best ice cream, according to *Reader's Digest* and, well, me. I think you'll agree, too, after taking the factory tour and sampling such flavors as Wowie Cowie Coffee Toffee Crunch and Cotton Candy Bunny Tails. They also have a shop at Peake's Wharf and other island locations. 397 Capital Dr. www.cowscreamery.ca. © **800/565-2697.**

Northern Watters Knitwear ★★ CLOTHING This knit shop sells a diverse line of unusually well-made sweaters handcrafted right here on PEI. Knitters can buy yarn for passing time in the car. In addition, a range of crafts and wearable handiworks, like sheepskin slippers and mitts, soft mohair socks, and pewter jewelry, are on sale. 150 Richmond St. www.nwknitwear.com. © **800/565-9665** or 902/566-5850.

Where to Stay

If you're traveling on a tight budget, there are a number of moderately priced motels situated along the main access roads running into and out of town (namely, routes 1 and 2), and also out by the airport. These places are generally basic and clean but with few frills. The university and an international hostel (see below) provide inexpensive rooms, while fine downtown options are available for those after more luxurious accommodations.

EXPENSIVE

The Great George ★★★ From the outside, the Great George looks more like a string of well-kept heritage homes than the boutique hotel it is. Inside, the early 19th-century buildings are beautifully restored and remarkably welcoming. On the "We're glad you're here" side is complimentary wine or craft beer at happy hour, plus snacks, like warm cookies throughout the day. In terms of the rooms: No two units are alike. In one, you'll sleep in a four-poster bed, then walk across oriental carpets to a claw-foot tub. In another, a contemporary-looking mirror-backed king-size bed will dominate the bedroom, and a Jacuzzi framed by white-tile and marble column will do the same in the bathroom. Final perk: The hotel is set in the heart of the city's most historic district.

58 Great George St. www.thegreatgeorge.com. © **800/361-1118** or 902/892-0606. 54 units starting C$179–C$219 up to C$499–C$550. Rates include continental breakfast.

Open year-round. Packages available. Free parking. **Amenities:** Babysitting, concierge, elevator, fitness room, limited room service, kitchen (some units), Jacuzzi (some units), Wi-Fi (free).

The Holman Grand Hotel ★★

The Holman is indeed grand—it's the tallest building around, with a soaring seven-story central atrium at its heart and swank rooms (think shiny hardwood floors, cushy duvets over excellent mattresses, and walls of windows for light and views). We particularly like the spa-inspired bathrooms and the waterfall pool (your kids will like the latter, too). Underground walkways allow guests to hit the mall or see a play at the Confederation Centre without ever dressing for outside.

123 Grafton St. www.theholmangrand.com. ℭ **877/455-4726** or 902/367-7777. 68 rooms, 12 suites. Standard room C$164–C$275, suites C$205–C$355, penthouse C$439 per room or C$1500 entire suite. Valet parking (no parking on-site). **Amenities:** Restaurant, pool, hot tub, fitness room, spa, room service, Wi-Fi (free).

Shipwright Inn ★★★

A red brick path leads through quiet gardens to the door of the Victorian-era Shipwright Inn, built by a shipbuilder in 1865. Not surprisingly, rooms are nautically named—Captain's Quarters, Tiller Flat, Wheelhouse, Navigator's Retreat—but not overtly themed; there are no tacky knick-knacks. Rather, the emphasis is on comfort and elegance. Subdued period furniture reproduces Victorian comfort without being overly ornate. Our favorite room is "Quarterdeck": pine plank flooring, a hand-stenciled bedroom set with matching canopy. A private veranda, fireplace, and double air tub lend more than a touch of romance to this special room. Breakfasts of eggs benny, fruit tart pastries, and the like are delightful, as is afternoon tea with homemade lemonade and pastries, both prepared by Chef Shelby Spirak.

51 Fitzroy St. www.shipwrightinn.com. ℭ **888/306-9966** or 902/368-1905. 9 units. C$109–C$299 double. Rates include full breakfast. Free parking. **Amenities:** Dining room, fridge (most units), Jacuzzi (some units), kitchenette (some units), Wi-Fi (free).

MODERATE

Hotel on Pownal ★★

Take an aging, mid-city motel; completely renovate every unit; add a stylish, urban lobby, lounge, and breakfast room, and you've got the hotel on Pownal Street. The decor is subdued and comfortable with pillow-top mattresses and quiet color schemes. Most of the rooms have direct outdoor access, and the hotel is just a block or two away from the downtown core but surprisingly quiet nonetheless. Room types range from "petite doubles" with one double bed, to efficiency units with a queen bed, separate living room, and kitchenette.

146 Pownal St. www.thehotelonpownal.com. ℭ **800/268-6261** or 902/892-1217. 45 units. C$122–C$202 double. Rates include buffet breakfast. Free parking. **Amenities:** Kitchenette (one unit), Wi-Fi (free).

Rodd Charlottetown ★★

When was the last time you were handed an actual key for a hotel room? You'll get one at the handsome, 1931 brick Rodd which comes from the age of luxury railway hotels (just climbing the steps that pass between four pairs of 20-foot columns at the entry is a kick). Rooms can be small, but they have old-fashioned flourishes like heavy drapes and valances with matching bed skirts, plus new perks like very good mattresses. Kids will enjoy paddling about the small indoor pool while parents relax in the whirlpool. Particularly popular is the rooftop patio that overlooks Rochford Park (a small, treed park) and the harbor beyond. The hotel's **Chambers Restaurant ★★**, where kids eat free, is open daily for dinner and features prime rib and seafood. The hotel is also home to Canada's longest running dinner theater, the Feast Dinner Theatre, which entertains with a tightly produced evening of music, improv, and skits. The only downside here? Spotty Wi-Fi.

Kent and Pownal sts. www.roddvacations.com/rodd-charlottetown. ℂ **800/565-7633** or 902/894-7371. 115 units. C$115–C$269 double. Free parking. **Amenities:** Restaurant, bar, indoor pool, whirlpool, limited room service, sauna, Jacuzzi & propane fireplace (honeymoon suite only), Wi-Fi (free).

INEXPENSIVE

Charlottetown Backpackers Inn ★★   This international hostel is set in a typical Charlottetown home, painted grey with red shutters on a leafy residential street. Staff are extremely friendly and helpful and the inn is within walking distance of all the downtown attractions. Room options are many: female-only rooms, co-ed dorms, private rooms with TVs—some with en suite bathrooms. A well-equipped kitchen—in true PEI fashion, it comes with free potatoes—is shared by all guests, as is a lounge with computers, TV, and a cozy fireplace. There's even a recreation room with billiard table and a stack of vintage vinyl records to poke through. Out back, guests enjoy garden or cook on the barbecue.

60 Hillsborough St. www.charlottetownbackpackers.com. ℂ **902/367-5749** 6 units. Mid-Apr to mid-Oct C$29–C$80. Free parking. **Amenities:** Kitchen, fireplace, barbecue, recreation room, computer work station, local telephone access, bike rentals, Wi-Fi (free).

University of Prince Edward Island ★   Accommodations are basic here, but affordable, especially for solo travelers and for larger families of up to eight people. In Bernardine Hall, single rooms are furnished with a single bed, doubles with two single beds. Bathrooms are shared, as are kitchenettes and laundry facilities on each floor. Apartments are available in Blanchard Hall; they come with single beds, a full kitchen and cooking utensils, a living room with cable TV, and bathroom. The best units are new one- to three-bedroom suites in Andrew Hall, where the bedrooms are larger with double beds. One of the perks of renting at the university is access to the sports complex where the facilities are far beyond anything a hotel can offer.

550 University Ave. www.upei.ca/conference/accommodations. ℂ **902/566-0442** or 902/566-0952. 100+ units. May–Aug C$53–C$69 single/double; C$116 apartment; C$116–C$150 suites. Free parking. **Amenities:** Sports center, TV lounge, in-room TV (some units), kitchenette, laundry, bed linen and towel, local telephone access, Wi-Fi (free).

Where to Eat

For a quick pick-me-up while traversing the city, try **Beanz Espresso Bar & Café** at 138 Great George Street (www.beanzespressobar.com; ℂ **902/892-8797**), just a block from Province House. The espresso drinks are good, and they also sell pastries, sandwiches, soups, and other light items. Casual dining at waterside is found at **Lobster on the Wharf** at 2 Prince St. (www.lobsteron thewharf.com; ℂ **902/368-2888**). They're right on the water and have a menu that goes way beyond lobster to items like seafood charcuterie (scallop ceviche, medallions of smoked salmon, crostini, Island-made Gouda). Onsite is a seafood market so you can take home live lobster and other fresh seafood with you or have it shipped.

   Churchill Arms, a tiny eatery at 75 Queen St. (www.churchillarms.ca; ℂ **902/367-3450**) is known for British fare, like traditional curries and legendary fish and chips. The menu includes such unhealthy delights as chip butty and deep-fried Mars bars.

   On the east side of town, overlooking the Charlottetown Driving Park with horse track views from every table, **Top of the Park Restaurant** at 46 Kensington Rd. (www.redshores.ca; ℂ **877/620-4222** or 902/620-4264) offers lunch buffets Wednesday through Friday, dinner buffets Thursdays and Fridays, and weekend race day brunches. Placing bets from your table adds to the harness-racing fun.

Claddagh Oyster House ★★ SEAFOOD   If you're looking for the place the locals eat, you've found it. A modern take on an Irish pub, the Oyster House's menu excels at shellfish but reaches beyond, doing quite well by hazelnut-crusted rack of lamb or pan-roasted PEI halibut in brown butter. And if you *do* want shellfish, you've come to the right place, especially between 4pm and 6pm when happy hour drops the cost of oysters to just C$1 each. The chowder here is fab. Preparation and service are a notch above most other fish joints, with the bonus of live Irish music and a good selection of beers.

131 Sydney St. www.claddaghoysterhouse.com. ℂ **902/892-9661.** Reservations recommended. Main courses C$18–C$42. Mon–Sat 4–10pm.

Leonhard's Café & Restaurant ★★ CAFE & DELI   When Alexandra and Axel Leonhard of Germany arrived in Charlottetown for English lessons, they couldn't find the hearty bread they were used to, so they made their own, then started selling it. Today, they run one of the city's most beloved little restaurants for breakfast, lunch, and baked goods. Lunchtime sandwiches lean toward the European—the hearty *strammer max* is two slices of whole wheat rye bread topped with black forest ham and two sunny-side-up eggs. Breakfasts are Bavarian and so hearty you can go without lunch—an omelet filled with bacon, roasted potatoes, and onion satisfies and comes with a side salad. Gluten-free and lactose-free options are available. If you have no room for them here, take away some Florentines or chocolate croissants.

142 Great George St. www.leonhards.ca. ℂ **902/367-3621.** Lunches C$8–C$15. Mon–Sun 9am–5pm.

Terre Rouge Bistro Marche ★★★ BISTRO As Charlottetown's hot-test restaurant, Terre Rouge is consistently packed, so make a reservation. It's hip, it's trendy, sure, but its food is also deeply satisfying. That may be because all of the meats are cured in-house, the veggies are likely to have been pulled from the ground that morning, and the fish snatched from the sea that day, too. Signature dishes include the charcuterie plate, the bone marrow, mussels in scrumptious wine sauce, and crispy pork *torchon*. The food can be paired with a robust local craft beer. The adjacent market is stocked with mostly house-made or Island-sourced—with some imported—hard-to-find goodies like artisanal cheeses, preserves, pastries, and charcuterie.

72 Queen St. www.terrerougepei.com. © **902/892-4032.** Reservations recommended. Main courses C$18–C$38. Tues–Sun 5–9pm.

Water-Prince Corner Shop ★★ SEAFOOD Located in what was once the community's general store, the big blue peak-roofed building is a little bit of history and a lot of good casual food. You'll find the usual seafood chowder, fish and chips, steamed mussels, and lobster dinners, but all as fresh as possible and well made in a home-cooking, nothin' fancy, generous por-tions way. The placemats have instructions for cracking open your lobster. Dine inside or on the patio. Located a block from the waterfront, their location is announced by a Maritime comic touch—rubber boots are mounted upside down on a blue box at the corner, as if the fisherman in them is stuffed inside.

141 Water St. www.waterprincelobster.ca. © **902/368-3212.** Reservations recom-mended. Lunch and dinner C$9–C$30. May–Oct.

Charlottetown After Dark

One good resource for planning evening adventures is *The Buzz* (www.buzz on.com), a free monthly newspaper that details ongoing and special events around the island with an emphasis on Charlottetown. It's widely available; look for it in visitor centers, bars, and restaurants.

Pubs and eateries spill onto sidewalk patios at **Victoria Row** ★, a small section of Richmond Street beside the Confederation Centre that is blocked off to traffic in summer. Things get lively when musicians show up, which happens regularly. A local favorite is **Fishbones** ★ (www.fishbones.ca; © **902/628-6569**), an oyster bar and seafood grill with good live music at 136 Richmond St.

Olde Charlottetown, as the heritage district is called, is a great spot for those who enjoy pubs. **Gahan House Pub** ★ (126 Sydney St.; www.gahan. ca; © **902/626-2337**) was PEI's first microbrewery. It serves solid pub food (fish and chips are served in a bag) plus a full range of brews to sample. They do tours of the brewery for C$10.

For live Celtic music and lobster and roast-beef dinners, head for the **Olde Dublin Pub**, above the Claddagh Oyster House (see previous page) at 131 Sydney St. (www.oldedublinpub.com; © **902/892-6992**).

On the waterfront at 23 Queen St., the **Merchantman Pub** ★★ (www. merchantman.ca; ✆ **902/892-9150**) offers a more upscale menu than the usual pub fare—think lobster bruschetta, crab cakes, walnut-coated scallops.

Upstreet Craft Brewing ★★ (www.upstreetcraftbrewing.com; ✆ **902/894-0543**) is a few blocks removed from downtown at 41 Allen St. off University Avenue, but the beer is the best on the island, and it's open noon until midnight. There's usually a quality food truck parked outside. They make an excellent Czech-style pilsner called Commons and a tasty light beer called Rhuby Social, a rhubarb strawberry wheat beer.

For high culture, always check first with the **Confederation Centre of the Arts** ★★ (www.charlottetownfestival.com; ✆ **800/565-0278** or 902/566-1267), where the stage bustles with dramatic and musical activity throughout the year. The musical *Anne of Green Gables,* a perennial favorite, is performed here throughout the summer—but so are concerts, plays, and other performances. The **Guild** ★ (www.theguildpei.com; ✆ **866/774-0717** or 902/620-3333), a black-box theater at 111 Queen St., showcases emerging and professional artists and is a hotbed of fundraising events, giving it a unique community feel. Music, comedy, theater, dance: It's always affordable. Finally, the art-house **City Cinema** ★, at 64 King St. (www.citycinema.net; ✆ **902/368-3669**), has an excellent lineup of domestic and foreign films; typically, there's a choice of two films each evening.

KINGS COUNTY

After visits to Charlottetown and the island's north shore area, Kings County comes as a bit of a surprise. It's tranquil and uncluttered, more rustic rural. The landscapes feature woodlots alternating with corn, grain, and potato fields and superb water views. Although locals play up this county's two largest commercial centers—**Souris** and **Montague**—keep in mind that each of these coastal hamlets has a population of less than 2,000. So don't arrive here expecting attractions to entertain you; you'll have to do that yourself. Long drives in the country, with occasional stops for eats or to snap photos or a walk on one of many beaches, are as rewarding in a car as on a bicycle. For the best scenery, follow the **Points East Coastal Drive** ★★ (www.pointseastcoastal drive.com; ✆ **902/961-3540**), a 475km (298-mile) coastal route that hits most of the highlights. You can pick up a free map and brochure, which details the route that circles the eastern end of the island at any Visitor Information Centre or just follow the signs.

One way to enjoy the route is to plot your course for a *spirited* tour. Kings County is home to the province's award-winning wineries and two distilleries. **Rossignol Estate Winery** ★ on Route 4 (www.rossignolwinery.com; ✆ **902/962-4193**) at 11147 Shore Rd. in Murray River offers a panoramic view of Northumberland Strait; the winery has a wide array of table and fruit wines, as well as liqueurs and an art gallery. Rossignol's strength is fruit wines like Blackberry Mead. For grape wines, **Matos Winery** ★★ at (www.matoswinery.com; ✆ **902/675-9463**) is a better choice. Jaimie and Heather Matos—originally from the Azores off Portugal—have won an armload of awards at larger competitions recently, and continue to improve wines like Gamay Noir and chardonnay made from grapes best suited to the Maritime climate. In Murray River at 2404 Gladstone Rd., **Newman Estate Winery** ★ (www.newman estatewinery.com; ⓒ **902/962-4223**) is just starting out, but their white wine blends from estate grapes look promising. **Myriad View Artisan Distillery** ★ at 1336 Route 2 in Rollo Bay (www.straitshine.com; ⓒ **902/687-1281**) is creating a glimpse into the days of prohibition by producing "Strait Shine" collected straight from the still. It's something that doesn't happen anywhere else. The distillery produces other spirits like rum, gin, and vodka. Free tours are available, and donations go to the local hospital. Up on the north shore, at 9984 Hermanville on Route 16, **Prince Edward Distillery** ★★ (www.princeedwarddistillery.com; ⓒ **877/510-9669** or 902/687-2586) has won international gold and silver medals for its potato vodka, plain and flavored. Take a tour to learn more about the art of craft distilling. They also make wild blueberry vodka and gins. Remember that drivers can't sample and drive; PEI has tough drinking and driving laws.

If you're a **lighthouse** buff, there are several you won't want to miss. Each has a unique story to tell, wonderful scenery, and its own magic. Top of the list are **Wood Islands Lighthouse** ★★ (www.woodislandslighthouse.com; ⓒ **902/962-3110**) and **East Point Lighthouse** ★★ (www.eastpointlighthouse. com; ⓒ **902/357-2106**). The museums here are full of fascinating flotsam and jetsam (literally, for the things that wash up after shipwrecks and otherwise are displayed) and the shops offer local arts, crafts, and memorabilia. At Wood Islands, learn about rum-running, phantom ships, ice boats, and much more. At East Point, there's a reasonable cafe for small bites to enjoy outside at a picnic table.

Note that if you're heading to Kings County from Charlottetown, you may pass right through **Orwell** (p. 59) and its historic sites en route.

Essentials

GETTING THERE   Several of the Island's main roads, including Highways 1, 2, 3, and 4, connect Kings County with Charlottetown. So it's easy to get here; get out a map, plot a route, and point your car east. If you're coming from Nova Scotia, the **Woods Island** ferry docks up on the southern coast. See "Exploring Prince Edward Island," p. 42, for more information.

VISITOR INFORMATION   There's a provincial Visitor Information Centre at 95 Main St. in Souris (which is also Rte. 2; ⓒ **902/687-7030**), open daily from June through September. There's another VIC at the head of pretty St. Peters Bay, on Route 2 at the intersection of routes 313 and 16 (ⓒ **902/961-3540**); this info center, which borders the lovely Confederation Trail, opens daily mid-May through mid-October. Yet another is located where Route 1 meets Route 4, just after you roll off the ferry at Wood Islands (ⓒ **800/463-4734** or 902/962-7411) also open mid-May through mid-October.

Wood Islands to Murray Harbour & Murray River ★

Assuming you are starting your eastern tour from Charlottetown on Route 1, you'll soon find yourself tempted to leave the main road to explore treasures like the 1845 **Point Prim Lighthouse** ★ (www.pointprimlighthouse.com; ℰ **902/659-2768**), the only round, brick lighthouse on the island, now a historic site (open daily July to mid-Sept, 10am–6pm). Follow Route 1 to the ferry terminal, turning left just before the compound, to get to the **Wood Islands Lighthouse and Interpretive Museum** (see above). A great little park here provides a photo-op of ferries and the shoreline of Northumberland Strait.

Leaving Wood Islands, watch for Route 4 and turn east. This beautiful drive takes you 9km (5½ miles) on Route 4 to **Rossignol Estate Winery** (see above). Bearing right on Route 18, watch for the signs to **Cape Bear Lighthouse & Museum** ★ (www.capebearlighthouse.com; ℰ **902/962-2469**; admission C$4/adults, C$2.50/seniors and children 6–15, and C$8/families; open June–Sept 10am–6pm). Built in 1881 on a (crumbling) cliff on the island's southeastern-most tip, it was one of Marconi's wireless stations—and the one where an operator first heard the *Titanic*'s desperate SOS calls. The lighthouse was later used to track German U-boats during World War II. A **small seasonal museum** ★ documents the station, which is no longer here, and it includes audio from Thomas Bartlett, the man who received the *Titanic* call. You can also climb about 40 steps to get a great view of the red-sand beaches and cliffs off the point. Continue on to **Beach Point** ★ beach, a quiet stretch of sand especially good for families with kids. When the tide is out, there's room to roam and tide pools aplenty.

As you drive, watch for the tight lines of buoys in the coastal waterways: The island's famous blue mussels are cultivated in the rivers here in mesh "socks" suspended underwater by ropes attached to those buoys, then shipped out to fine kitchens around the island and worldwide.

EXPLORING THE MURRAYS

Route 18 will take you to the Murrays. These two small and tidy villages offer little in the way of drama but lots of repose. **Murray River** has several natural attractions beyond the views. One short **interpretive trail,** about half a kilometer (.35 mile) long, skirts the local golf course; another trail takes you through a grove of tall, ancient pine trees on the east side of McLure's Pond, the island's largest body of fresh water.

Young children enjoy corny **Kings Castle Provincial Park** (ℰ **902/962-7422**), an old-fashioned kiddy park of the sort that was popular in the 1950s and 1960s. Set on the shores of the Murray River (with swimming at a small beach) it features life-size depictions of storybook characters scattered about the fields and woodlands and an array of playground equipment. It's open daily from 9am to 9pm from June through mid-September; admission is free. The park is on Route 348, about 3km (2 miles) east of Murray River on the south river bank.

A short drive from Murray River, along the north bank of the river (take Rte. 17), is remote, empty **Poverty Point Beach** ★. Dunes back this long strand of eastward-facing beach. You park at the end of the road and walk along the beach watching for bird life. Swimming is problematic; the beach is pebbly at low tide, and currents can be troublesome. But it's certainly quiet: You might not see another soul, even in summer, on the entire strand.

A few miles north is **Panmure Island** ★ and its **provincial park** ★ (www. tourismpei.com/provincial-park/panmure-island; ⓒ **902/838-0668**), open from early June through the middle of September; it's one of PEI's most popular beaches outside the national park. There's a small campground (see below in "Where to Stay") if you'd like to stay overnight or longer. This island is connected to the mainland via a sand-dune isthmus; the contrast between the white sands (on the ocean side) and the red beach of the inner cove is striking. It's a lovely spot, with swimming on the ocean side (lifeguards in summer); bathrooms and changing rooms; a viewing tower; and views northward to a striking little **lighthouse** ★. *Note:* If you see a lot of broken seashells on the road, drive with care. Seagulls drop clams and such from high in the air, to break open dinner. The largest can puncture a tire.

There's also the small but surprisingly attractive 9-hole **Eagles View Golf Course** ★★ (www.eaglesviewgolf.com; ⓒ **866/962-4433** or 902/962-4433); a 1,000 foot boardwalk across the river links two parts of the course. If you're here at the end of July, don't miss the **Murray River Fisheries Festival** ★, a very local fest of dory-rowing competitions, log-rolling, and a parade.

WHERE TO STAY

Ocean Acres Cottages ★★   This row of five new log cottages are situated along a rural road between Murray River and Murray Harbour on grassy grounds next to a quiet inlet. Though built a little too close together and on the small side, the cottages are comfortable and well-equipped. The living room, dining room, and fully stocked kitchen are in a single room with knotty pine walls and hardwood floors. The two bedrooms are furnished with attractive wooden Craftsman beds and chest of drawers. Outside, a very small veranda with picnic table and barbecue overlooks roomy grounds with lots of opportunity for activities; there's a heated outdoor pool, a fitness center, access to the Confederation Trail, and kayaking in the bay. Take note that there's a 3-night minimum stay in summer and 2 nights in May, June, and September.

247 Fox River Rd., Murray Harbour. www.oceanacres.ca. ⓒ **888/966-2326** or 902/962-3913. 5 units (double occupancy) C$120–C$140 nightly, C$840–C$980 weekly. Closed Nov–Apr. **Amenities:** Pool, kayaks, Wi-Fi (free).

Panmure Island Provincial Park ★★   A long curve of sand links Panmure Island to PEI's eastern shore. A lighthouse on the island, the beach, and a grassy lot on the mainland behind the beach where the campsite is located make up the park. Some of the sites have hookups. Water views are everywhere, and the beach is just steps away. Dunes back the beach, and in front a series of sandbars makes for safe swimming conditions and warmer water temperatures.

350 Panmure Island Rd., Rte. 347, Gaspereaux. www.tourismpei.com/provincial-park/panmure-island. ✆ **902/838-0668.** 43 sites. C$26–C$32. **Amenities:** Restaurant, supervised beach (July & Aug), laundromat, showers, kitchen shelter.

Montague

Montague may be the Kings County region's main commercial hub, but it's a hub in pretty low gear: compact and attractive, with a handsome business district on a pair of flanking hills sloping down to a bridge across the Montague River. Shipbuilding was the economic mainstay in the 19th century; today, though, fishing, dairy, and farming are the primary local endeavors. Montague has a lovely little waterfront on the river where you can enjoy refreshments overlooking the marina. In 2014, the town launched a major public art project; the result is what amounts to an **outdoor gallery ★★** of murals and sculptures. Next to the bridge over the river near the marina, you'll see three giant black cormorants, each in a different stance atop a 15-foot pole. On the other side of the river from the cormorant sculptures is a cooperative art gallery called **Artists on Main ★★** (www.artisansonmain.wordpress.com; ✆ **902/361-3081**). Inside, you'll find the work of painters, rug hookers, quilters, and many more. Usually, an artist is at work while others take their turn tending the bright, new shop full of fine arts and high-quality crafts.

EXPLORING THE OUTDOORS

East of Montague at Three Rivers, the **Roma National Historic Site ★** (www.roma3rivers.com; ✆ **902/838-3413**) brings to life the story of a French merchant who, in 1732, established an international trading post. You'll find lively interpretive events, a heritage garden, a set of reproductions of period buildings, and an old-fashioned lunch of baked beans and fishcakes which comes with bread baked in Roma's outdoor oven. Buy a loaf to go—it's delicious. The park is open daily late June to late September, 11am to 5pm. Admission is C$5 adult, C$3 for children 6 to 17 (younger children free), and C$15 for a family.

Southeast of Montague (en route to Murray River) is **Buffaloland Park ★** (✆ **902/652-8950**), home to a small herd of buffalo. A gift from the province of Alberta, the magnificent animals number about two dozen. Walk down the fenced-in corridor and ascend the platform for the best view. Often they're hunkered down at the far end of the meadow, but be patient; they sometimes wander closer. The park is right off Route 4, about 6km (4 miles) outside town; watch for signs. Like so many PEI parks, it's free.

A bit north of Buffaloland on Route 4, between routes 216 and 317, is the **Harvey Moore Wildlife Management Area ★**, a delightful place for a stroll. A privately owned park named for the naturalist who created this sanctuary in 1949, its centerpiece is a 45-minute trail that loops around a pond and through varied forest and across fields. Watch for waterfowl (with which Moore had an unusually close rapport) such as black ducks, blue-winged teal, ring-necked ducks, pintails, and plenty of Canada geese. Open during daylight hours June to mid-September. Once again, admission is free.

Brudenell River Provincial Park ★★★ (www.tourismpei.com/provin cial-park/brudenell-river; ✆ **800/463-4734**) is one of the province's best parks and the largest in eastern PEI. You'll find two well-regarded championship golf courses, an executive course, a resort (see "Where to Stay," below), tennis, lawn bowling, a playground, a campground, and nature trails. There are also interpretive programs for kids and adults. You can ride horses and rent canoes, kayaks, and jet skis from private operators within the park, which is open daily from mid-May through early October, and is free to enter. To reach it, head north of Montague on Route 4, then east on Route 3 to the park signs.

WHERE TO STAY

Brudenell River Provincial Park Campground ★★
If you like tons of activities for young and old with your camping, this is your pick. From horseback riding to golf, from swimming in the pool to kayaking, there's enough to keep the whole family busy for a week. Those in tents and in RVs are equally welcome but kept far enough apart so as not to disturb each other. You'll find the campsites on wide, grassy areas and tucked into woods that reach to the river—the woods add privacy and keep things quiet. Be warned: The showers and bathrooms are small and in need of upgrading, but if you can forgive this drawback, there's a lot here to reward a stay.

283 Brudenell Island Blvd., Rte. 3, Georgetown Royalty. www.tourismpei.com/search/ en/OperatorDetails/op_id/2183. ✆ **877/445-4938** or 902/652-8966. 95 sites. C$26–C$32. Mid-May to late Sept. **Amenities:** 2 golf courses, laundromat, showers, trails, kitchen shelter, outdoor supervised pool, playground, children's activities, marina access (extra cost).

Rodd Brudenell River Resort ★★
Adjacent to the campground, the resort's many rooms and suites overlook either the river or one of the two best golf courses on the island—**Brudenell River** and **Dundarave ★★**. The king suites feature four-poster beds, corner Jacuzzis, and wraparound patios. Sixteen two-bedroom cottages with cathedral ceilings are fully loaded, each with kitchen, fireplace, Jacuzzi, bar, and deck with barbecue. Guests have access to indoor and outdoor pools with bar, as well as a spa, a restaurant, and a bistro. Bonus: Kids 10 and under eat for free . . . and golf for free as well (ages 18 and under.)

Rte. 3, Cardigan. www.roddvacations.com/rodd-brudenell-river. ✆ **800/565-7633** or 902/652-2332. 181 units. C$123–C$269 double; C$195–C$475 cottage and housekeeping suite. Packages available. Closed mid-Oct to mid-May. Pets allowed (C$10 per pet per night). **Amenities:** 2 restaurants, bar, canoe/kayak/bike rentals, children's center, 2 golf courses, fitness center, Jacuzzi, indoor and outdoor pools, sauna, spa, 2 tennis courts, fridge (some units), kitchenette (some units), Wi-Fi (free).

WHERE TO EAT

Although it doesn't seem so when you drive into Montague, there are some terrific little eateries here during the summer. **Famous Peppers ★** (www. fpeppers.websites.ca/Montague.page; ✆ **902/361-6161**) is a vibrant little pizzeria at 3 Rink St. with a long list of pies, including The Spud Islander—topped with potato slices and flavored with caramelized onion and bacon—only on PEI. At 500 Main St., **The Lady's Slipper Café ★★** (www.facebook.com/Ladysslippercafe; ✆ **902/838-7088**) serves up surprisingly creative burgers and sandwiches (like the Cuban and the Philly steak), as well as skip-lunch (huge) breakfasts. The Hawaiian-jerk BBQ burger is topped with grilled pineapple, Cajun sauce, and cheese—super flavorful.

Windows on the Water Café ★★ SEAFOOD   If the weather is suitable, the outdoor patio overlooking the river is one of the most scenic places to dine on PEI. The views compliment the food, which is served in generous portions and made from all fresh ingredients. I'd especially recommend the cheesy haddock bake and lobster quiche; seared scallops atop a mandarin salad are a good pick for those looking for a lighter meal. Although the emphasis is on PEI seafood, the menu is large with loads of alternatives—pasta, crepes, wraps, steaks, stir fry. Desserts are topnotch, from the down-home bread pudding with brown sugar sauce to the more uptown raspberry swirl cheesecake.

106 Sackville St., Montague. www.windowswater.ca. ✆ **902/838-2080.** Reservations recommended. Main courses C$13–C$15 at lunch, C$22–C$30 at dinner. Mid-May to Sept daily 11:30am–closing. Closed Oct to mid-May.

Souris & Northeast PEI ★★

Some 40km (25 miles) northeast of Montague—take Route 4 north out of town, merge with Route 2, and keep going east—is the little town of **Souris,** an active fishing town attractively set on a gentle hill overlooking its harbor and a lovely beach. Yet things weren't always so great here. Souris (pronounced Soo-*ree*) is actually French for "mice"—the town owes its name to its frustrated early settlers, who were beset by waves of voracious field mice that repeatedly destroyed their food crops. Today, the mice are (mostly) gone, and the townspeople have long relied on the sea rather than the land for a living.

In addition to its own little charms, Souris is the departure and arrival port for the car ferry to the **Magdalen Islands** (actually part of Québec; see box on p. 81 for ferry details). It also makes a good central base for exploring northeastern PEI, a place that's remote, less populated, and more greenly forested than the rest of PEI, where farming prevails. Because a spur of the **Confederation Trail** ends in Souris, this is a good spot from which to launch a bike excursion of the area. You can ride to the main trunk trail, then turn northeast and continue to land's end at the East Point Lighthouse.

EXPLORING THE AREA

Several good beaches can be found ringing this wedge-shaped peninsula that points toward Nova Scotia's Cape Breton Island. In addition to **Souris Beach ★**, which you cross heading east on Route 2 to enter town, **Red Point Provincial Park ★★** (www.tourismpei.com/provincial-park/red-point; ✆ **902/357-3075**) lies about 13km (8 miles) northeast of Souris, on Route 16. Open from June through mid-September, it offers a handsome beach and supervised swimming, along with a **campground** that's popular with families (see "Where to Stay," below).

Farther along Route 16, there's another inviting beach at **Basin Head,** which features **"singing sands"** ★ that allegedly sing (actually, they squeak) when you walk on them. The dunes are especially nice. Access is via the **Basin Head Fisheries Museum** ★ (www.peimuseum.com; ✆ **902/357-7233;** C$4adults, C$3.50/students, C$12/families; daily July and Aug 9:30am–4:45pm; weekdays June and Sept at the same times) a provincially operated museum that offers insight into the history of inshore fishing with small wooden boats and a cannery to tour. Check the website for its kid's programming.

At the island's far eastern tip is the aptly named **East Point Lighthouse** ★★ (www.eastpointlighthouse.com; ✆ **902/357-2106;** C$3/adults, C$2/seniors and students, C$1/children, C$8/families; open late May to early Oct). You can simply enjoy the dramatic setting with the octagonal, shingled lighthouse and light-keepers cottage overlooking the sometimes turbulent meeting of the tides; or take a tour of the lighthouse from June through early September. Ask for your East Point ribbon while you're here; if you also made it to the North Cape Lighthouse on PEI's western shore, you'll receive a certificate saying you've traveled the island tip-to-tip. There's also a craft shop on-site selling jewelry, soap, sand paintings, local books and music, and other island goods.

WHERE TO STAY & DINE

Evergreen Café & Wellness Studio ★★ CAFE   It's all about healthy eating at the Evergreen. Much of the menu is build-your-own style: Design a smoothie or a juice combo with your favorite berries and fruit or choose from a long list of ingredients for your wrap (and the wrap itself—spinach pesto or tomato basil). The same approach is taken with pizza, salad, quesadillas, and panini. This is an Internet cafe, so lingering is welcomed. There's also a shop full of health products like vitamins, herbal remedies, and teas.

95 Main St. Souris. www.evergreencafeandwellness.com. ✆ **902/743-3330.** Pizza C$8–C$17, sandwiches C$6.50–C$8. Mon–Tues 10:30am–5pm, Wed–Fri until 6pm.

Inn at Bay Fortune ★★★   Not just an inn, not just a restaurant—foodies book a stay at this inn so that they can have the complete Chef Michael Smith *experience.* Smith is one of Canada's most acclaimed chefs, with TV shows (some taped here), nine cookbooks, and a flair for making meals an event—and that's what guests get. Called the "Fireworks Feast," the nightly, multi-course meal starts with cocktails, moves on to an oyster bar in the "old kitchen" (local oysters are often topped with a scrumptious play on the Bloody Mary) and then shifts to several communal tables where guests watch the cooking action and interact with the chefs, all of whom seem as if they're having as much fun as the diners. The food is revelatory and changes nightly, but could include a salad with 30 types of greens, or smoked lobster, or rutabaga fried in duck fat. *Tip:* The square table has the best view of all the activity in the kitchen.

Most guests then bed down for the night at the cozy inn, a series of cedar-shingled sections, including rounded towers, set across the street from the bay.

AN EXCURSION TO THE magdalen islands

The **Magdalen Islands (Les Îsles de la Madeleine),** a 5-hour ferry ride north of PEI, are half a dozen low-lying islands linked to each other by sand spits. Around 13,000 people live here—95% are Francophone—in peaceful fishing villages and farming communities; the red-sand cliffs look like PEI, but the farmhouses, wharves, cows, boats, and accents are reminiscent of the Atlantic coast of France. (The Magdalens are actually part of Québec, even though they're closer to PEI.) The islands boast nearly 320km (200 miles) of uncrowded beaches, and urban Montréalers in search of leisure time love the place. The islands are also famous for their persistent winds, which seemingly never cease blowing; great for windsurfing and kite flying over the long, protected lagoons between beaches. When the weather isn't fit for beaches, there are lots of cafes, bars, cultural events, and culinary experiences like cooking classes and visits to a smokehouse or a cheesemaker.

Advance planning is necessary for a trip to the islands, because the summertime demand for accommodations far outstrips supply. Head to www.tourismei lesdelamadeleine.com/en for a list of lodgings.

Ferry service from Souris to Cap-aux-Meules is provided by the **Coopérative de Transport Maritime** (www.traversi erctma.ca/en; ✆ **888/986-3278** or 418/986-3278), also known as the CTMA. The seven-deck ferry holds 95 cars and 400 passengers. The boats sail as many as 11 times weekly in summer; the schedule is reduced to as few as 3 times weekly in the off season, so check a schedule online before arriving on PEI.

One-way rates during high season (mid-June to mid-Sept) are C$51 per adult, C$41 per senior, and C$26 per child age 5 to 12, plus C$95 for a normal-size automobile (more for vans and campers). **Tip:** Those rates plunge by about 40% outside of the 3 peak months.

Built by a playwright and an actress in 1910, the inn became the location for *The Inn Chef,* just one of the TV cooking shows created by and starring Chef Smith. Walkways wind through perennial flower gardens to the 17 rooms and suites furnished with sturdy antiques and modern amenities like flatscreen TVs and new gas fireplaces. It's not super-luxe, but the digs feel warm and welcoming—like you're staying at the home of a favorite aunt (the one with good taste). Most swank are the tower suites, which have living rooms and a small balcony overlooking the gardens and the bay beyond. Breakfast is included in the nightly cost, and such activities as a stretch and meditation class, guided beach walks, and in-room massage are available.

758 Rte. 310 (turn south off Rte. 2 about 5 miles west of Souris), Bay Fortune. www.innat bayfortune.com. ✆ **888/687-3745** or 902/687-3745. 17 units. C$150–C$400 doubles & suites. Dinner is C$80. Room rates include gourmet breakfast. Closed mid-Oct to mid-May. **Amenities:** Restaurant, fireplace (most units), Jacuzzi (some units), no phone, Wi-Fi (free).

Red Point Provincial Park ★   Camping here is in an open field, so it can be windy, but sunrises over the water are spectacular. The beach is wide and the waters relatively calm, making it a good place for children to play and splash about safely. Keeping families in mind, management offers lots of children's activities and special events in summer; kids will be thrilled when they spot the ferry between Souris and the Magdalene Islands passing just off shore.

249 Red Point Park Rd., Rte. 16, Red Point. www.tourismpei.com/provincial-park/red-point. ℰ **877/445-4938** or 902/357-3075. 120 sites. C$26–C$35. Early June to late Sept. **Amenities:** Beach with supervised swimming, kitchen shelter, laundromat, playground.

East Point to Mount Stewart

The easternmost sector of Kings County attracts fewer tourists, but it's worth visiting this region—the pastoral landscapes are sublime, and the best vistas are found off the main roads. It's also an area blessed with a number of appealing bike routes and what might be the island's top golf course. Route 16 follows the coast from Souris to East Point and then along the north coast to **St. Peters Bay ★**. Although this north coast has few prominent natural landmarks—it's mostly just a nice drive through wooded areas interrupted by fields and farms with glimpses of the ocean—there are a few stops of interest.

The **Prince Edward Distillery ★** (www.princeedwarddistillery.com; ℰ **877/510-9669** or 902/687-2586) at 9984 Route 16 is owned by two women who left the southern U.S. for the quiet lifestyle they discovered on a trip to PEI. Roadside on Route 16, the artisanal distillery makes potato vodka, one version flavored with wild blueberries.

St. Peters Bay ★ is a narrow and attractive inlet that twists eastward from the coast. This is also the real PEI: full-service filling stations that look like they could be straight out of the Midwestern U.S. in the 1950s; folks fishing from bridges; a quiet lobster fishery; and wildflowers such as bold purple lupines far outnumbering cows, cars, and people.

A collection of shops next to the bridge at the head of the bay called **St. Peters Landing ★** (www.stpeterslanding.ca) is worth a look; enjoy an ice cream or a coffee, pick up some fresh fish, or browse gift shops. The **Turret Bell ★** (www.turretbell.com; ℰ **902/739-3008**) is a great spot to find a book or local island music. Artisans run a pewter shop, **St. Peters Bay Craft and Giftware ★** (www.facebook.com/St-Peters-Bay-Craft-Giftware-131113680286995/?fref=nf; ℰ **902/961-3223**) nearby at 15465 Northside Rd., where you can even learn to pour your own piece of pewter.

EXPLORING THE AREA

From the village, follow Route 313 along the north shore of St. Peter's Bay to its tip and you'll come to the **Greenwich Dunes ★**, a stunning area of uniquely wind-carved migrating sand dunes capped with grasses. This region was slated for vacation-home development until 1997, when it was acquired (and thus saved) by Parks Canada, which added it as an extension to **Prince Edward Island National Park.** The grey-shingled **Interpretation Centre ★★** (www.pc.gc.ca/eng/pn-np/pe/pei-ipe/activ/activ-menu/centre-interpretation.aspx; ℰ **902/961-2514;** open June–Sept; admission C$7.80/ adult, C$6.80/senior, C$2.90/child) has all the information you need to enhance your visit, and it's fun for the kids—along with multimedia exhibits, there are games like the Shorebird Challenge and the Dune Plant Quiz. There's an extensive trail system, including a floating boardwalk. A supervised (July and Aug) beach with facilities and observation tower is nearby.

The cute little town of **Mount Stewart** (on Rte. 2, just over the county line in Queens County) is located near the confluence of several spurs of the **Confederation Trail,** the excellent island-wide recreation trail described earlier (see "The Great Outdoors," p. 45). The Mount Stewart area is home to some of the best-maintained eastern segments of this trail, one section of which crosses the river for great views.

Drop in to the **Hillsborough River Eco-Centre ★★** at 104 Main St. (www.pointseastcoastaldrive.com, click "Things to Do"; ℂ **902/676-2050** or 676-2881) and ask about the best viewing area for eagles and other wildlife, as well as the history of this Canadian Heritage River. There's a nice boardwalk.

WHERE TO EAT & STAY

In addition to the dining facilities at Crowbush and Trailside (below), Mount Stewart has a couple of small but trendy eateries. At **The Thoughtful Squash ★** at 324 Main St. (www.facebook.com/thoughtfulsquash/info?tab=overview; ℂ **902/394-3626**) you can take out a couple of lobster samosas (a large, triangular eggroll with potato and lobster flavored with curry) or sit down to a bowl of squash soup with red pepper and herbs. If you have the nerve, try lobster cheesecake, but not for dessert. It's a savory, rather rich treat served with greens, avocado, and tomato.

Rodd Crowbush Golf & Beach Resort ★★★   You can't get much better than this comfortable resort that comes with one of the island's finest golf courses (often ranked #1) and a gorgeous stretch of beach with a shuttle service to get there. The inn itself has rooms and suites overlooking the course and the bay, many with king beds and some with balconies. The one-bedroom housekeeping cottages with kitchenettes are built for romance; they come with a propane fireplace and a heart-shaped, two-person Jacuzzi (plus a patio and barbecue). The two-bedroom units are ideal for families with a more complete kitchen, fireplace, an upper floor, and a deck with barbecue. **David's ★★,** the hotel's dining room (serving three meals daily), serves such winning dishes as aged island rib-eye, island lamb, and a juicy brined chicken breast with apple sauce. The main dining room is complemented by an adjacent lounge and the clubhouse grill at the golf course; kids 10 and under eat free from the kid's menu at all of them. Kids 18 and under can play a free round of golf, too.

632 Rte. 350, Morell. www.roddvacations.com. ℂ **800/565-7633** or 902/961-5600. 81 units. C$123–C$331 double, C$209–C$475 cottages. Packages available. Closed late Oct to mid-May. **Amenities:** 2 restaurants, lounge, golf course, fitness center, Jacuzzi, indoor pool, spa, outdoor whirlpool, 2 tennis courts, laundromat, Wi-Fi (free).

Trailside Café and Inn ★★   Across from the Hillsborough River Eco Center in Mount Stewart is the smart little Trailside, offering rooms and a cafe. It's a cheery place with a cafe space that can be set up for evening entertainment, often featuring some of the best singer-songwriters in the Maritimes. The menu is a simple one, but varied and made with fresh, local ingredients—charcuterie, thin-crust pizza, hearty burgers, fishcakes. The mac and cheese is made with a flavorful blend of island Gouda, smoked bacon, tomatoes, and green onions. The rooms are relaxed and pleasant—a homemade quilt, hooked rug kind of place. The owners also rent a three-bedroom cottage.

109 Main St., Mount Stewart. www.trailside.ca. © **902/394-3626.** 3 units. C$89. Lunch mains C$8–C$22. Closed Dec–Mar.

PRINCE COUNTY

Prince County encompasses the western end of PEI, and offers a mixture of lush agricultural landscapes, rugged coastline, and unpopulated sandy beaches. Generally speaking, this region is a working-farm, working-harbors kind of place. In other words: Real people live and work here.

Within this landscape, you can find pockets of charm, such as the village of **Victoria-by-the-Sea** on the south coast (at the county line) and in **Tyne Valley** near the north coast, which is vaguely reminiscent of a Cotswold hamlet. Two of the province's tourism icons, **West Point Lighthouse** and **North Cape** complex, are located "up west" and the province's second city, **Summerside** resides on the narrow isthmus between **Malpeque** and **Bedeque Bays.** These two bays are among of the best in the world for harvesting oysters.

In addition, the **Confederation Trail** (described in "The Great Outdoors," p. 46) offers quiet access to the rolling countryside throughout much of northwestern Prince County. As well, several provincial parks here rank among the best on the island.

Essentials

GETTING THERE   From Confederation Bridge, take Route 1A to connect with Route 2 west, the main highway connecting Prince County with the rest of the island. Route 2 goes right up the middle to North Cape and is the fast way to get to the western tip. A better route if you have time is to pick up the North Cape Coastal Drive in Summerside and follow it around the coast for a spectacular loop (about 350km/218 miles).

VISITOR INFORMATION   The best source of travel information for the county is **Gateway Village** (© **902/437-8570**) at the end of the Confederation Bridge, described in the introduction to this chapter (see "Essentials," p. 42). It's open daily, year-round. There is also a **Visitor Information Centre** (© **877/734-2382** or 902/888-8364) on Summerside's waterfront open daily in summer, weekdays otherwise.

Victoria-by-the-Sea ★★

The picture postcard perfect village of **Victoria-by-the-Sea**—often shortened to Victoria—is surrounded by farmers' fields on one side and the Northumberland Strait on the other. Located a short detour off Route 1, between the Confederation Bridge and Charlottetown, it's a tiny, scenic few blocks that has attracted a clutch of artists, boutique owners, restaurateurs, and craftspeople. The couple of blocks that is the village is perfect for strolling—parking is near the wharf that's crowded with shops and off the streets, keeping the narrow lanes free for foot traffic.

Wander these short, shady streets while admiring the architecture, much of which is in an elemental, farmhouse style or dotted with elaborate Victorian homes. The village, which was first settled in 1767, has escaped the creeping sprawl that has plagued so many otherwise attractive places. The entire village consists of a grand total of 4 square blocks that probably looked almost the same (except for the cars puttering through) a century or more ago.

EXPLORING VICTORIA

The **Victoria Seaport Lighthouse Museum** is located inside the shingled, square **lighthouse** ★ near the town parking lot. (You can't miss it.) You'll find a rustic local history museum with an assortment of artifacts from the past century or so, like navigational aids and kerosene lamps. It's open daily in summer 10am to 5pm; admission is by donation.

In the middle of town is the well-regarded **Victoria Playhouse** ★ (www. victoriaplayhouse.com; ℂ 800/925-2025 or 902/658-2025). Built in 1913 as a community hall, the building has a unique raked stage (it drops 17cm/7 inches over 6m/21 ft. to create the illusion of space), four beautiful stained-glass lamps, and a proscenium arch—pretty unusual for a community hall. It's hard to say which is more fun: the quality of the performances or the fun-night-out air of a professional play being staged in a small village with little else going on. Monday-night concerts offer up everything from traditional folk to Latin jazz. Most tickets are C$32 adults, C$30 seniors, and C$20 students, though a few performances are priced higher; matinees cost about C$25.

Among the dozen or so businesses in the village, the most intriguing is **Island Chocolates** (www.islandchocolates.ca; ℂ **902/658-2320**), where delicious Belgian-style chocolates are made. The shop is open daily 9am to 6pm. There's nothing more relaxing than sitting on the garden patio next to the sidewalk with a hot chocolate on a sunny morning.

With a little hunting, you can also find artisans, eateries, and the small, day-use **Bonshaw Provincial Park** ★ (ℂ **902/859-8790**) with a playground, an antiques shop, and a lobster outlet (great for a picnic in the park). **By-the-Sea-Kayaking** ★★ (www.bytheseakayaking.ca; ℂ **877/879-2572** or 902/658-2572) rents kayaks, stand-up paddle boards, and bicycles. Their tours include a unique clam-digging adventure during which you paddle to an offshore sandbar, dig clams the size of your hand, and return to shore to make them into chowder.

WHERE TO STAY

Orient Hotel Bed & Breakfast ★★   Since 1900, The Orient has offered a restful room in a quiet location at the end of Main Street for travelers. Not that the look of it is quiet: It's painted a bright yellow and features a wide veranda, furnished with a rainbow of colorful Adirondack chairs and flower boxes. In the cozy rooms, patchwork quilts match both the warm pastel hues of the walls and the patchwork of fields visible out the windows—yellow canola, mauve potato blossoms, green pasture. Hot breakfast in the morning, served in the charming Victorian dining room, comes with muffins, eggs, and homemade preserves.

34 Main St. www.theorienthotel.com. ⓒ**800/565-6743** or 902/658-2503. 7 units. C$80–C$164 double and suite. Rates include full breakfast. Packages available. Off-street parking. **Amenities:** Wi-Fi (free).

WHERE TO EAT

In addition to **Beachcomber's Restaurant ★** (ⓒ **902/658-2556**) and **The Lobster Pub and Eatery ★** (ⓒ **902/658-2722**), both on the wharf, here's another option.

Landmark Café ★CAFE   Once the town's general store and post office, the cafe sits across the street from the Victoria Playhouse, making it a popular dining location on nights when folks come to town for entertainment. The ever-present lobster roll is well made, as are dishes like the tasty and filling seafood bake in tarragon cream sauce. There's a patio for fine-weather dining and a good wine list.

12 Main St. www.landmarkcafe.ca. ⓒ **902/658-2286.** Reservations recommended. Main courses C$15–C$29. June–Sept daily 11:30am–2:45pm and 5pm–close.

Summerside ★★

Prince Edward Island's second city is more of a small industrial center than Charlottetown, which is anchored by its government offices and universities. There are not many visible signs of the aerospace and other industries that employ many, at the same time, Summerside lacks the busy city vibe of Charlottetown. Still, there is much to recommend it, starting with green spaces. Summerside has a fantastic waterfront boardwalk called the **Baywalk ★★**, stretching 6.5km (4 miles) alongside Bedeque Bay, and overlooking Indian Head Lighthouse. Another, the **Rotary Park Trail ★★**, is possibly the most used in the city; it's a 26 hectare (64 acres) park with a 4.8 km (3-mile) trail for cycling and walking. Add to the mix the **College of Piping and Celtic Performing Arts,** lots of high-quality year-round entertainment at **Harbourfront Theatre,** free live music along the waterfront, numerous museums, and harness racing, and you have a reason to linger for a few days.

EXPLORING SUMMERSIDE & AREA

The city waterfront is best explored by following Water Street from the east, right through the town. A number of eateries are located along the way, as is a continuous walking trail alongside the water. The majority of shopping is found on Granville Street, which also takes you to Route 2.

Slemon Park off Route 2 is a former military base, now home to businesses that take advantage of the airport. Here, at the former Canadian Forces Base Summerside, is **Air Force Heritage Park ★** (www.airforceparkpei.ca), home to three historical aircraft along with interpretive displays. Admission is free

Head out in the morning, following Route 20 northeast of Summerside, until you get to the hamlet of Indian River. Watch for signs to **St. Mary's Church** at 1374 Hamilton Road, home to the **Indian River Festival** ★★★ (www.indianriverfestival.com; ✆ 866/856-3733 or 902/836-3733), a summer-long presentation of classical, jazz, world music, choral, and Maritime music. This rural church, known for its architecture and acoustics, attracts world-class musicians to play, and sometimes record. Construction of a handsome new outdoor pavilion adds a pre-show gathering place. As you continue driving east on Route 20, note the body of water to the west. This is **Malpeque Bay,** where the famous Malpeque oysters were first found. Long considered a delicacy, they are now "farmed" in these same waters and make their way to eager diners around the world. Walk on the beach at Cabot Park just off Route 20, or continue on Route 20 to Park Corner for the **Anne of Green Gables Museum** (p. 50). Book a carriage ride, which takes you around the Lake of Shining Waters and to a beautiful beach. Continue on Route 20 to Route 6, turn right and you'll end up at the **Shipwright's Café** (p. 88) to dine before taking in a concert at St. Mary's Church. You did make reservations, right? A late night refreshment at **Brothers 2** (below) or the **Loyalist Lakeview Resort** (p. 88) in Summerside will suitably close a great day.

4

and it's always open. On Route 2, the **Acadian Museum** (23 Main Dr., Miscouche; www.peimuseum.com; ✆ 902/432-2880) is a great introduction to the Acadian region that lies to the west. Learn about the 300-year Acadian presence here, stroll their Heritage Trail, or access their genealogy resources. Admission is C$5.25 adult, C$3.50 student, and C$14.25 family. It's open year-round (9:30am–7pm daily July–Aug; 9:30am–5pm Mon–Fri and 1–4pm Sun Sept–June).

SUMMERSIDE AFTER DARK

In the summer months, Summerside has lots to offer in the evenings. Along with a number of pubs and eateries that offer entertainment, the city boasts surprisingly good stage performances. The **Harbourfront Theatre** ★★ (www.harbourfronttheatre.com; ✆ 800/708-6505 or 902/888-2500) at 124 Harbour Dr. on the waterfront is a 520-seat theater with year-round productions. **Credit Union Place** ★ (www.cupevents.ca; ✆ 902/432-1234) at 511 Notre Dame St. hosts sporting events and whatever high-demand performers come to town (Elton John once performed here). For even more rousing entertainment, head for the **College of Piping and Celtic Performing Arts of Canada** ★★ (www.collegeofpiping.com; ✆ 877/224-7473 [BAG-PIPE] or 902-436-5377), located at 618 Water St., the only year-round institution of its kind in North America. Their summer stage production, *Highland Storm*, is an exhilarating presentation of highland dance, bagpipers, drummers, and step dancers. The **Feast Dinner Theatre** (www.brothers2.ca; ✆ 902/436-7674), at **Brothers 2,** a restaurant, pub, and dinner theater at 618 Water St., began here in 1979 and has been running every summer since, making it Canada's longest-running dinner theater. Shows change each season, but the entertainment value is high with a tightly produced evening of music, improv, and skits.

WHERE TO STAY

As you enter Summerside along Water Street, there are a number of mom-and-pop motels that are clean and moderately priced—good value for the dollar.

Clark's Sunny Isle Motel ★★★   A couple of miles east of downtown, Sunny Isle is one of those surprisingly swell little properties, a motel in a nice setting with well-kept grounds and gardens, and rooms, though small, are very well cared for, all at reasonable rates. Many rooms are recently renovated with new furniture, bedding, flooring, and soundproofing. Rooms in back look out over the gardens; rooms in front have private decks. Across parklike lawns on an 8-hectare (20-acre) property, there's a new cedar gazebo among large shade trees and a trail to the beach beyond.

720 Water St. E. (Rte. 11). www.sunnyislemotel.com. ℭ **877/682-6824** or 902/436-5665. 21 units. C$55–C$86. Free parking. **Amenities:** Large grounds, gardens, gazebo, trails, beach, private deck (some units), Wi-Fi (free).

Loyalist Lakeview Resort Summerside ★★   Overlooking the waterfront and within easy walking distance of attractions, this modern inn certainly has location going for it. A wide range of rooms and relatively affordable prices, plus amenities like the pool and exercise room, also recommend it. Standard rooms (many with views of the harbor) are clean and comfortable, if narrow and simply furnished, available with queen or king beds, and whirlpool tubs. The most luxurious feature a four-poster bed with lacy canopy. The Confederation Trail passes right outside the door, ideal for walkers and bicyclists.

195 Heather Moyse Dr. 80 rooms. www.lakeviewhotels.com. ℭ **877/355-3500** or 902/436-3333. C$99–C$199 double. **Amenities:** Restaurant, lounge, exercise room, indoor pool, sauna, whirlpool tub (some units), electric fireplace (some units), Wi-Fi (free).

WHERE TO EAT

The Shipwright's Café ★★ CONTEMPORARY CANADIAN   In the PEI tradition of garden- and boat-to-table, Chef Calvin Burt—he earned his cooking chops as a teenager helping prepare lobster suppers for busloads of tourists—planted a large vegetable garden at this restored farmhouse, and he sources fish, beef, and lamb from island producers. With all these good, fresh building blocks, he creates dishes like PEI paella with lobster, mussels, scallops, shrimp; and salmon with aioli garden vegetables and crusty garlic bread. If you're staying in a cottage nearby and don't feel like cooking, Shipwright's will pack you a dinner to go.

11869 Rte. 6 (at junction of Rte. 233), Margate. www.shipwrightspei.com. ℭ **902/836-3403.** Reservations recommended. Lunch items C$15–C$25; dinner entrees C$27–C$45. June–Sept daily 11:30am–3:30pm and 5 until closing. Closed Oct–May.

Water Street Bakery & Deli ★★ BAKERY & CAFE   More than a bakery, the Water Street specializes in hearty take-out food with an Acadian accent. Along with fresh breads, pastries, and desserts, there's *rapure,* a traditional Acadian meat-and-potato pie. More mains include well-made pizza, soups, sandwiches, casseroles, fish cakes, and more.

605 Water St. ⓒ **902/436-5055.** Sandwiches C$5–C$9 Weekdays 7am–6pm (Sat 8am–6pm). Closed Sunday.

Tyne Valley ★

Although the village is tiny, there is much to admire in this area: verdant barley and potato fields surrounding gingerbread-like homes, plus azure inlets nosing in on the view from the long distance. (Those inlets are the arms of the bay, world-famous for its succulent oysters.) A former 19th-century shipbuilding center, Tyne Valley now attracts artisans and others in search of the slow lane; the gorgeous scenery is a bonus. A handful of good restaurants, inns, and shops cater to summer travelers.

EXPLORING TYNE VALLEY

Just north of the village on Route 12 is lovely **Green Park Provincial Park** ★★ (www.tourismpei.com/provincial-park/green-park; ⓒ **902/831-2021**), open from mid-June through mid-September. Once the site of an active shipyard, this 80-hectare (219-acre) park is now a lush riverside destination with emerald lawns and leafy trees. It still has the feel of that turn-of-the-20th-century estate. In the heart of the park is the extravagant 1865 gingerbread mansion built by James Yeo, a merchant, shipbuilder, and landowner who in his time was the island's wealthiest and most powerful man.

The historic Yeo House and the **Green Park Shipbuilding Museum** ★ (www.peimuseum.com; ⓒ **902/368-6600**), open June through September, are now the park's centerpieces. Get a glimpse into the prosperous lives of shipbuilders during the golden age of PEI shipbuilding. The museum and house are open daily in July and August, 9am to 5pm (same hours on weekdays in June). Admission is C$5 adults, C$3.50 students, C$14 families.

The history and current culture of the island's 400 First Nations Mi'kmaq people is reviewed via artifacts and photographs at the 526-hectare (1,300-acre) **Lennox Island Cultural Centre** ★★ (www.lennoxisland.com/attractions; ⓒ **902/831-2476**), 8 Eagle Feather Trail. Stacked-loop nature trails with interpretive signs lead through forests and along scenic shores for hikes of 3 to 10km (around 2 to 6 miles). On the website is a list of summer events like powwows.

WHERE TO STAY

Green Park Provincial Park ★★   The wooded sites in this 89-hectare (219-acre) riverside park, a boot-shaped peninsula in Malpeque Bay, are quiet, except when the place fills up for a summer music festival. Behind the campsites, there's a large field with a stage where occasional concerts are held. Stands of white birch separate many of the sites, some of which are equipped with three-way hookups. Those with tents can enjoy wooded riverfront sites. Primitive camp cabins are also available. These are the grounds for the historic Yeo House and the shipbuilding museum (see above), so in addition to the usual campground activities, kids can explore these to pass the time.

364 Green Park Rd., Port Hill. www.greenparkcampground.com. © **902/831-2021.** 80 sites, 12 cabins. C$25–C$45. Mid-June to mid-Sept. **Amenities:** Museum, nature trail, playground, activity center, river beach, recreation and interpretation programs, laundromat, kitchen shelter, showers, store.

WHERE TO EAT

The Doctor's Inn ★★ CONTEMPORARY CANADIAN When a chef can select the best produce from his own 2-acre organic garden, the kitchen has an easy time of it. Or so you'd think after dining at this 1860s country home-turned restaurant. Meals start with sensational salads, a preview for mains that range from Arctic char to veal prepared on a wood stove in the old-fashioned kitchen. Homemade bread and desserts come out of the same highly experienced kitchen. *Note:* Management insists that guests make reservations at least 24 hours in advance.

Rte. 167 (at junction with Rte. 12). www.peisland.com/doctorsinn. © **902/831-3057.** 4-course meal about C$65.

Tignish Area ★★

The road west, Route 12, takes travelers through Alberton, the only town in the region; take a short side trip down Route 152 to the picturesque fishing village of Northport. **Northport Pier** ★ (www.northportpier.ca; © **902/853-4900**) is home to shops, a restaurant, an interpretation center, and a good-size fishing fleet. A great blue heron rookery means you are sure to find the great birds posing for photos in the shallows near the lighthouse. The **Sea Rescue Interpretive Centre** ★ (www.northportpier.ca/searescue.asp) offers insight into the lives of fishermen from the past, early settlement, disasters and heroics, shipwrecks and lighthouses. It's open daily, and admission is free.

Legend has it that the first European to visit the island came ashore at Kildare Capes in 1534 and recorded it as being "the fairest land 'tis possible to see!" **Jacques Cartier Provincial Park** ★ (www.tourismpei.com/provincial-park/jacques-cartier; © **877/445-4938** or 902/853-8632), named for that French explorer, is certainly pretty and offers camping, a handsome beach with supervised swimming, nature walks, and children's games during the summer.

Continue on Route 12 to Tignish, home to one of the largest fleets of inshore fishing vessels in Atlantic Canada, and mile "0" of the Confederation Trail. The wharf at Tignish Run is a great place to take pictures and soak up atmosphere. Depending on the time of year you visit, you may be able to watch crates of lobster, or giant bluefin tuna being off-loaded. In Tignish proper, **St. Simon & St. Jude Catholic Church** ★, the largest in PEI, is home to one of only four surviving Louis Mitchell Tracker pipe organs in the world; the 19th-century Québec resident, who studied pipe organ construction in England, built organs respected for their craftsmanship in Montréal, Québec,

Chicago, and many smaller locations. The convent next door has been turned into the **Tignish Heritage Inn and Gardens** (see "Where to Stay" below). Stroll the quiet grounds and visit the church. Consider checking in before moving on to North Cape, where Mother Nature will lure you to linger past sunset.

It's just a short drive to North Cape, past Sea Cow Pond. The skyline ahead will be dominated by huge sweeping blades outlined against the sky. You have arrived at the Energy Institute of Canada and the **North Cape Wind Farm.** This test facility has been a leader in developing wind energy and now has an interpretive display to tell you all about it. It's part of the North Cape complex (www.northcape.ca; ✆ **902/882-2991**), which houses a restaurant, gift shop, and historical information about shipwrecks, ghost ships, storms, and natural history. Black Marsh Nature Trail will take you back to nature.

North Cape is famous for the natural wonders found here. At low tide you can walk out to sea, atop the longest natural rock reef in North America: About 2.4km (1½ miles) long, it is the dividing point between the Gulf of St. Lawrence and Northumberland Strait. As the tide moves in, their waters merge over the reef. It's a great place for seal watching; seabirds and bank swallows soar and the tide pools are great for checking out sea life.

WHERE TO STAY

Tignish Heritage Inn & Gardens ★★   Does PEI have a more serene inn than this former convent? Built in 1868, the restored heritage property was the parish convent for St. Simon and St. Jude Church. It offers 17 simple units on the four stories of the brick building but all have a grace to them, thanks to high ceilings, hardwood floors, and old wood trim. Homemade quilts adorn antique wooden beds. A stay here includes use of a kitchen. The large, quiet gardens make for enjoyable strolls.

206 Maple St., Tignish. www.tignishheritageinn.ca. ✆ **877/882-2491** or 902/882-2491, 17 units. C$90–C$145 double. Open year-round. **Amenities:** Continental breakfast included, gardens, laundry, kitchen, bike rental, Wi-Fi (free).

Jacques Cartier Provincial Park ★★   A wide beach on the Gulf of St. Lawrence near the possible landing location of explorer Jacques Cartier is the attraction at this campground. The park holds a celebration of Cartier's discovery every year in July. Kids can play all day on the beach and swim with a lifeguard on hand while parents relax with a good book. Organized recreation and interpretation activities and program add to the experience for the kids.

Route 12, Kildare Capes. www.tourismpei.com/provincial-park/jacques-cartier. ✆ **877/445-4938** or 902/853-8632. 75 sites. C$26–C$35. Open mid-June to mid-Sep. **Amenities:** Beach, supervised swimming, recreation and interpretation programs, playground, laundromat, kitchen shelter.

WHERE TO EAT

Wind & Reef Restaurant ★★ SEAFOOD   Lunch in the middle of a wind farm (surrounded by giant windmills) is as much about the views as it is about the food. And if it's a windy day, you've struck gold, what with the whirring and low tide exposing the large natural reef rock (see above). As for the food: The menu is all PEI, with offerings like lobster omelets and potato biscuits. Seafood chowder, pan-fried haddock, PEI oysters on the half shell, and the Lighthouse Keepers Platter are all made with the freshest of fish. Portions are generous and the prices reasonable.

North end of Rte. 12, North Cape. www.northcape.ca. © **902/882-3535.** Main courses C$13–C$30. May–Oct daily 12am–9pm.

Tignish to West Point

The southern shore, Route 14, from Tignish back toward Summerside takes you to **Skinner's Pond,** home to spectacular dunes and legendary singer Stompin' Tom Connors, one of Canada's favorite country musicians. If you like a little whimsy in your art—colorful parrots with lobster-claw-shaped beaks, 6-foot-long fishing lures, both carved from single pieces of wood—detour onto Route 151 to **Back Roads Folk Art** (www.backroadfolkart. blogspot.ca; © **902/853-3644**) at 1176 Centerline Road in Lauretta. *The Guinness Book of World Records* affirms their possession of the world's largest egg beater. Resident artist Kerras Jeffery will make you smile, even laugh out loud, with his whimsical creations. He makes some very nice rustic reproduction furniture, as well.

Backtrack to Route 14. Your next stop is West Point, the home of the black-and-white-striped lighthouse that so often represents Prince Edward Island in promotional material. **West Point Lighthouse Inn ★★** (see listing below) is one of a kind: a preserved lighthouse, housing a museum and an inn. A short walk or drive past **Cedar Dunes Provincial Park** takes you to the West Point waterfront, where there's a campground (see listing below) and the West Point Lighthouse restaurant, **Sandals** (159 Cedar Dunes Park Rd.; © **902/859-1674**), which serves up a delightful meal to enjoy while you overlook the marina, working fishing village, the shore, and sea. Interpretive walking trails, boardwalk, and miles of beautiful beach make West Point a very worthwhile place to stop and explore.

After lingering for a day or two, continue to follow the North Cape Coastal Drive. It will take you to the town of O'Leary for a couple of hours at the **PEI Potato Museum ★★** located on Dewar Lane (www.peipotatomuseum.com; © **800/565-3457** or 902/859-2039). Spuds are a big thing here, and the museum claims to have the largest collection of potato-related artifacts in the world (Look! There's a giant potato at the entrance!). Inside, eat the best French fries ever, see surprisingly engaging exhibits on the lowly spud and many pieces of antique farming and potato-processing equipment, make potato fudge, and head out to a working farm where a potato farmer will take you on a tour of the fields. There is also a natty quilt shop in town, the **Quilt Gallery and Fabric, Crafts and More,** at 534 Main St. (www.quiltgallery pei.com; © **800/859-2606** or 902/859-1888).

The final leg of the North Cape Coastal Drive is through the region known as Evangeline. Culturally rich, this community's artisans, festivals, and traditional foods celebrate their Acadian heritage. And just to prove they are creative, one of the chief attractions is a house made of bottles. The **Bottle Houses** (www.bottlehouses.com; ✆ **902/854-2987**) at 6891 Rte. 11 in Cap-Egmont are life-size buildings created from 25,000 recycled bottles. Described as "symphonies of light and color," they have been featured by Ripley's Believe It or Not!

WHERE TO STAY

Cedar Dunes Provincial Park Campground ★★

The most dramatic location on PEI's southwestern coast is the setting for this excellent campground. (The island's iconic black-and-white-striped West Point Lighthouse and museum is on these grounds, and the dunes are as big and beautiful as the sunsets.) The beach here is very wide, providing endless room for sandcastle construction. And the view of the opposite shore in New Brunswick is as close as it gets, other than at the Confederation Bridge; West Point is known as the place Mi'kmaq once landed on a regular basis as they crossed the Northumberland Strait in their large, seagoing canoes. The swimming in these relatively warm waters is supervised in summer, and there's a nice nature trail through a wooded area. Campsites are in open areas with small groves of trees, and the services can be counted on as they can in all PEI provincial campgrounds: clean showers and changing rooms, a kitchen shelter for preparing meals in poor weather, areas for games like volleyball. Book early to get a treed site if you're in a tent. Watch out for poison ivy.

364 Cedar Dunes Park Rd., West Point. www.tourismpei.com/provincial-park/cedar-dunes. ✆ **877/445-4938** or 902/859-8785. 70 sites. C$26–C$35. Open mid-June to late-Sept. **Amenities:** Beach, lifeguard and recreation services in summer, nature trail, playground, laundromat, shower, kitchen shelter.

West Point Lighthouse Inn ★★

There's only one lighthouse guests can sleep inside in all of Canada, and it's in West Point, PEI. But beyond that once-in-a-lifetime lure, this is a darn nice place to stay on its own terms. The mattresses are excellent, lace curtains shade the windows, and the prettily furnished rooms all have shiny hardwood floors. And when you walk out on the deck at night, the sky is a magnificent carpet of stars. Pssst: Some people think this place is haunted, but the ghost is a friendly one.

364 Cedar Dunes Park Rd., West Point. www.westpointharmony.ca. ✆ **800/764-6854** or 902/859-3605. 13 rooms. C$155–C$175 double. Open June–Sept. **Amenities:** Continental breakfast included, Wi-Fi in all but one unit (free).

NEW BRUNSWICK

As rich in natural beauty as it is in culture, New Brunswick offers new and unexpected adventures to visitors. There is much to explore: two distinct coastal regions, interior wilderness, mighty rivers, peaceful farmlands, refined cities, sleepy towns, neat villages, the world's highest tides, and encounters with nature that are truly special; prepare for a vacation of discovery in Canada's most underrated East Coast province.

5

Sightseeing Tremendous diversity sets the tone: Cliffs and islands sculpted by wind and sea dominate the **Bay of Fundy,** beaches and dunes line the eastern coast, and river valleys run through the interior. Renowned scenic drives tie them all together. Little equals the views you get from a boat tour, the top of Mount Carleton, the side of a cliff as you rappel down, or a lighthouse at lands' end. If you crave the arts, heritage, and urban life, you'll find three distinct urban locations to explore: **Fredericton, Saint John,** and **Moncton** each have something unique to offer.

Eating & Drinking The culinary arts in New Brunswick are advancing by leaps and bounds. You'll find no shortage of talented chefs, all working to bring the natural abundance of this land and the sea to the table. Seafood is the headliner, thanks to coastal waters that yield salmon, lobster, oysters, clams, and more. Rich harvests from the land appear in both traditional and nouveau cuisine. Foraged fiddlehead ferns—the curly symbol adorning road signs—along with European style fromageries and a promising new wine industry are some of the exciting culinary discoveries that await.

Nature The province's most recognizable natural wonder, the **Bay of Fundy,** Canada's only finalist (one of two in North America) in the New 7 Wonders of Nature worldwide campaign, is home to the highest tides in the world, and is a rich feeding ground for marine mammals, including a dozen species of whale. Three impressive river systems (the **St. John, Miramichi,** and **Restigouche**) and the Appalachian mountain range are rich in wildlife. Experience ancient geology in **Stonehammer Geopark** around Saint John, among other places.

History   The original inhabitants—the Mi'kmaq, Malecite, and Passama-quoddy Nations—were followed by French Acadian, English, Scottish, and Irish settlers. These cultures are celebrated today through festivals, concerts, heritage sites, museums, and attractions in Canada's only officially bilingual province. Communities reflect their distinct heritage: **Caraquet** is pure Acadian, **St. Andrews** is English Loyalist; **Edmundston** celebrates Madawaska, **Miramichi** its Irish. Visitors can relive history at **King's Landing** and **Acadian Village** historic sites, learn heritage crafts or trades, master traditional cooking, or learn about history and nature through educational adventures.

EXPLORING NEW BRUNSWICK

New Brunswick is too often dismissed as an obstacle, the Canadian province between the traveler and a great destination like PEI or Nova Scotia. This was never true, but given the ways both culture and tourism have developed over the past couple of decades, such a sentiment means that some may miss out on the many and varied pleasures of travelling this great region.

To fully enjoy New Brunswick, get off the highways and onto the secondary roads, linger in communities large and small, get out into the wilderness and onto the water, and seek out the many fantastic new culinary and cultural experiences that await.

Those who want to shop at Canada's oldest continuing farmers' market, wander a historic downtown full of wonderful architecture; learn about the province at an excellent museum; and dine at a growing number of affordable, gourmet restaurants should swing through **Saint John.** A lovely country drive will take you to **Fredericton,** New Brunswick's capital city and university hub for riverfront parks, great food, and exciting festivals. Those interested in French Acadian culture or sandy beaches, on the other hand, can concentrate on the **Gulf of St. Lawrence** for traditional Acadian cuisine with a contemporary twist, a chance to experience the pride of a resurgent culture, and the warmest waters adjacent to the longest beaches in the Maritimes.

If you're drawn to rugged beauty, plan to focus mostly on the **Fundy Coast** where the world's highest tides have carved rocky cliffs and twice daily expose the ocean floor for exploring. This part of the coastline actually feels a lot more remote and northerly than the more densely settled (and tamer) northeastern coast. Take at least a day to detour through Fundy National Park to see **Cape Enrage** and **Hopewell Rocks**—two of Eastern Canada's most dramatic attractions. If nothing else, you'll be able to tell your friends that New Brunswick should never again be written off on any tour of Eastern Canada.

Essentials

VISITOR INFORMATION   New Brunswick publishes a great website for visitors (www.tourismnewbrunswick.ca; ℭ **800/561-0123**) and staffs seven official visitor information centers. More than 50 cities, towns, and villages also have their own municipal information centers. A complete listing of locations and phone numbers for these centers can be found on the website, or via the toll-free number. Look for "?" direction signs on the highway and in communities to lead you to these centers. Phone numbers and addresses for the appropriate visitor information centers are provided in each section of this chapter.

GETTING THERE

BY CAR & FERRY The Trans-Canada Highway bisects the province, entering from Québec at St. Jacques. It follows the St. John River Valley before veering through Moncton and exiting into Nova Scotia. The entire distance is about 530km (329 miles).

ENTERING FROM THE U.S. The fastest route from New York City or New England to New Brunswick is the Maine Turnpike (a toll road). Take the turnpike north to Bangor, Maine, then slice east on Route 9 to connect to Route 1. Continue to Calais, Maine, which is just across the river from **St. Stephen,** New Brunswick.

A more scenic variation is to drive across a bridge onto **Campobello Island** from Lubec, Maine (see the "Passamaquoddy Bay" section, p. 101), then take a ferry to Deer Island, drive the length of the island, and board a second ferry to the mainland.

Those headed to **Fredericton** or **Moncton** can speed their trips somewhat by following the Maine Turnpike to its conclusion, then continuing north on I-95 all the way to Houlton, Maine, and beyond; you'll connect with the Trans-Canada after crossing the border.

Bay Ferries (www.nfl-bay.com; ⓒ **877/762-7245**) operates the ferry MV *Fundy Rose* that links **Saint John** with Digby, Nova Scotia. The ferry sails year-round, with one to two crossings daily (travel time: 2½ hours) each way. The peak-season (June–Oct) one-way fares are C$45 for adults, C$35 for seniors and students, C$30 for children ages 6 to 13, free for children 5 and under, and C$90 and up per vehicle, plus a C$20 fuel surcharge; fares are cheaper during the rest of the year. Also, discounts are available on round-trips completed within 30 days, so be sure to buy a round-trip ticket if you'll return the same way you came. Reservations are advised.

BY AIR The province's main airports are at Fredericton (the provincial capital), Saint John, and Moncton, all of which are chiefly served by **Air Canada** (www.aircanada.com; ⓒ **888/247-2262**) which also flies to Bathurst. At each you'll find major car-rental companies. **United** (www.united.com; ⓒ **800/864-8331**) also flies nonstop from Newark, New Jersey's Liberty International Airport to Moncton and Fredericton, while **WestJet** (www.westjet.com; ⓒ **888/937-8538**) flies into and out of Moncton and Fredericton. **Porter Airlines** (www.flyporter.com; ⓒ **888/619-8622** or 416/619-8622) offers flights from Moncton to several Canadian and U.S. cities, usually connecting through Ottawa or Toronto City Airport.

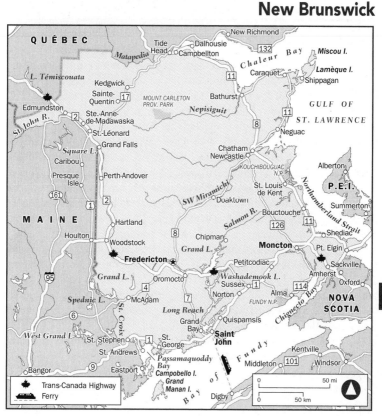

BY TRAIN **VIA Rail** (www.viarail.ca; *©* **888/842-7245**) offers train service through the province between Halifax and Montréal 3 days a week on Wednesday, Friday, and Sunday year-round. The train stops in many stations along the route. Check the VIA Rail website for more details

BY CRUISE SHIP Oceana, Princess, Carnival, Crystal, and many other cruise lines call on Saint John. See the city's tourism website www.cruise saintjohn.com for a complete list and links to cruise-booking sites.

THE GREAT OUTDOORS

Readers who really want to see the wild should think about visiting the outdoor center at **Cape Enrage** (see the "Fundy National Park" section later in this chapter), where one can canoe, rappel, rock-climb, zip-line and/or kayak—all in the same dramatic coastal setting.

BACKPACKING Among the best destinations for a backcountry hike in this province are **Mount Carleton Provincial Park** (p. 100) and **Fundy**

National Park (p. 126), both of which maintain backcountry campsites for visitors. The two landscapes are quite different to hike through—see the appropriate sections for more information on each park, then take your pick.

BICYCLING   The islands and peninsulas of **Passamaquoddy Bay** lend themselves nicely to cruising in the slow lane—especially **Campobello Island** (p. 101), which also has good dirt roads for mountain biking. **Grand Manan** (p. 112) holds lots of appeal for cyclists, too, even if the main road (Rte. 776) has some rather narrow shoulders and pretty quick local drivers. Some of the best coastal biking is around **Fundy National Park**—especially the back roads to Cape Enrage—and the **Fundy Trail Parkway,** an 11km (7-mile) multi-use trail that hugs the coast of Fundy Bay. Along the Acadian Coast, **Kouchibouguac National Park** has limited but unusually nice biking trails through mixed terrain (rentals of bikes and all-terrain wheelchairs are available right in the park). A lovely network of trails run beside the St. John River in Fredericton, connecting the historic downtown to the countryside, and even across the river on a former railway bridge that now caters to pedestrians and bicyclists. Several trails (South Riverfront, Salamanca, and Old Train Bridge) join up to create a 5.4km (3.6 miles) multi-use trail. A few blocks north, the North Riverfront Trail adds another 5.6km (3.5 miles). The province is in the process of developing over 2,000km (1,240 miles) of multipurpose trails that link to Québec, Nova Scotia and through Maine to the Appalachian Trail. Much of it will become part of the ambitious Trans Canada Trail.

Mountain bikers would be well advised to check out St. Andrews and Sugar Loaf Provincial Park near Campbellton (p. 161).

BIRDWATCHING   **Grand Manan** is the province's most notable destination for birders, right on the Atlantic flyway. (The great John James Audubon lodged here while studying and drawing bird life more than 150 years ago.) Over the course of a typical year, as many as 275 species can be observed on the island; September is often the best month for sightings. Boat tours from Grand Manan can also take you farther out to **Machias Seal Island,** with its colonies of puffins, Arctic terns, and razorbills. It's fun to swap information and stories with other birders, too; during the ferry ride, look for excitable folks with binoculars and floppy hats dashing from one side of the boat to the other.

Campobello Island's mixed terrain attracts a good array of birds, including the sharp-shinned hawk, common eider, and black guillemot. Ask for a checklist and map at the visitor center. The lower St. John River is a birder's paradise, and the folks here have produced a free guide, "The Birding Route," that details exactly how to get to the best viewing areas. It's online at www.discover thepassage.com. Download it or pick up a paper copy at any Visitor Information Centre. Shorebird enthusiasts also flock to **Shepody Bay National Wildlife Area,** which maintains preserves in the mudflats between **Alma** (near the entrance to Fundy National Park) and Hopewell Cape. There's good birding in the marshes around **Sackville,** near the Nova Scotia border. For a complete list of the best birding spots, search for "birdwatching" on the tourism website.

The Great Outdoors

NEW BRUNSWICK

CANOEING & KAYAKING New Brunswick has some 3,500km (2,175 miles) of inland waterways, plus countless lakes and protected bays. Canoeists and kayakers can find everything from glass-smooth waters to daunting rapids. Several guides and tour operators can help you plan your trip; their contact info is available at www.tourismnewbrunswick.ca (select canoeing from the Activities). Kouchibouguac National Park offers the rewarding **Voyageur Canoe Adventure** (© 506/876-2443) that goes out weekday mornings, at 8:30am mid-June to mid-September for just C$30 per person, for a morning with grey seals, Common Terns (the largest single-species colony in Canada is here), and learning about the Mi'kmaq way of life. More experienced canoeists looking for a longer expedition have any number of options from the **St. Croix River** along the U.S. border to the mighty **Miramichi** and its branches or many portions of the **St. John River.** Experienced **sea kayakers** have endless coastal options, but it would be wise to go with a guide, especially on the Fundy coast where the extreme tides can cause unpredictable dangers. See "Sea Kayaking" below for the most recommended guides.

FISHING The **Miramichi River** has long attracted anglers eager to catch wily Atlantic salmon. Some experts consider it to be among the best salmon rivers on the planet. There are strict laws regarding river fishing of the salmon: The fish must be caught using flies, not hooks, and nonresidents must hire a licensed guide. (There's an exemption from this rule during Fish New Brunswick Days in early June, when you don't need to use a guide but still need a license; check ahead with your lodging if you are interested.) For other freshwater species, including bass, as well as open-ocean saltwater angling, the rules are less restrictive. Get up to date on the rules and regulations at www.gnb.ca/naturalresources.

GOLF With over 40 courses to choose from (visit www.golfnb.ca for a list), New Brunswick is a world-class destination for a golfing vacation. In St. Andrews, the **Algonquin Hotel**'s redesigned golf course is a beaut—more than 100 years old, it was retouched by Donald Ross's plans in the 1920s, then rethought and expanded in the late 1990s—easily ranking among Eastern Canada's top 10. The course features newer inland holes (the front 9), in addition to original seaside holes that become increasingly spectacular as you approach the point of land separating New Brunswick from Maine. All 18 of them are challenging, so bring your "A" game. Service and upkeep are impeccable, and there's both a snack bar on premises and a roving club car with sandwiches and drinks. Greens fees are C$35 to C$85 for 18 holes (carts extra). Lessons are offered, and there's a short-game practice area with a huge putting green in addition to the usual driving range. Call © **506/529-8168** or go to www.fairmontgolf.com/algonquin for tee times and other details. In Fredericton, lovely **Kingswood** (www.kingswoodpark.ca/golf; © **800/423-5969** or 506/443-3333)—located inside a family entertainment park—was named by Vacay.ca as one of New Brunswick's top five courses, and one of the "Best Places to Play" by *Golf Digest.* It features 27 holes, a par-3 course,

The Great Outdoors

and a double-ended driving range. A round of 18 holes costs C$59 to C$89, with twilight discounts.

HIKING   The province's highest point is on top of **Mount Carleton Provincial Park** (_ℭ_ **506/235-0793**), in the center of a vast area of woodlands far from all major population centers. Several demanding hikes in the park yield glorious views. The park is open daily from mid-May to mid-October. Depending on whether or not you're camping, you'll pay between C$5 and C$75 per day. You get there either by following Route 17 from **Campbellton** or taking various local roads (routes 105, 108, and then 385, to be specific) from the border crossing at Limestone, Maine. This should take less than 3 hours from either Campbellton or Caribou, Maine. There's also superb hiking at **Fundy National Park,** with a mix of coastal and woodland hikes on well-marked trails. The multi-use, 11km (7-mile) **Fundy Trail Parkway ★★** has terrific views of the coast and is wheelchair-accessible. **Grand Manan ★** is also a good destination for independent-minded hikers who enjoy the challenge of _finding_ the trail as much as they enjoy hiking itself. The province is developing over 2,000km (1,240miles) of multipurpose trails that link to Québec, Nova Scotia, and Maine, so trail hiking will become increasingly easy to access.

Hiking Trails of New Brunswick, by Canada's hiking expert Michael Haynes, is an invaluable resource for hikers (www.gooselane.com; _ℭ_ **888/926-8377**).

SEA KAYAKING   The huge tides that make kayaking so fascinating along the **Bay of Fundy** also make it exceptionally dangerous—even the strongest kayakers are no match for these fierce ebb tides if they're in the wrong place. Fortunately, a number of skilled sea-kayaking guides work the province. Stay safe and use them.

Among the most extraordinary places to explore in New Brunswick is **Hopewell Rocks,** where the coast is sculpted by tides and time into stone pinnacles and arches. At high tide, there are sea caves and narrow channels to explore. **Baymount Outdoor Adventure** (www.baymountadventures.com; _ℭ_ **877/601-2660**), run by the Faulkners in Hillsborough, offers 90-minute sea-kayak tours of Hopewell Rocks from June through early September for C$59 adults, C$49 children, or C$199 per family. (They also run mountain biking and hiking tours.)

Other good kayak outfitters along the coast include **FreshAir Adventure** (www.freshairadventure.com; _ℭ_ **800/545-0020** or 506/887-2249) in Alma (near Fundy National Park) and Bruce Smith's **Seascape Kayak Tours** (www.seascapekayaktours.com; _ℭ_ **866/747-1884** or 506/747-1884) down in Deer Island (with an amazingly international staff).

SWIMMING   Parts of New Brunswick offer surprisingly good ocean swimming. The water is much warmer (and the terrain more forgiving) along the Gulf of St. Lawrence than it is in the often frigid, mostly rocky Bay of Fundy. In fact, random testing has shown temperatures can reach 25°C (77°F), validating claims that these waters are warmer than any other salt water north of Virginia. The best beaches are mostly along the "Acadian Coast," especially near the town of **Shediac** and within **Kouchibouguac National Park.** But **New River Beach** on the Fundy coast south of Saint John is also a standout location, with a campground and hiking trails nearby.

WHALE-WATCHING The **Bay of Fundy** is rich with plankton and schools of herring, and therefore rich with whales. Some 12 types of whales can be spotted in the bay, including finback, minke, humpback, and the endangered right whale. Whale-watching expeditions sail throughout the summer from various wharves and ports, including Campobello Island, Deer Island, Grand Manan, St. Andrews, and St. George. Any visitor information center can point you in the right direction; the province's website and travel guide also lists lots of tours, which typically cost around C$40 to C$60 for 2 to 4 hours of whale-watching.

PASSAMAQUODDY BAY

The **Passamaquoddy Bay** region is often the point of entry for those arriving over land from the United States. The deep, island-studded bay is wracked by massive tides that produce currents powerful enough to stymie even the sturdiest fishing boats. It's a place of deep fogs; spruce-clad islands; bald eagles; quirky communities; grand summer colonies; and a peninsula that boasts five-star inns, excellent dining, a stately turn-of-the-20th-century resort, great camping, charming B&Bs, and economical digs for tight budgets.

Campobello Island ★★

Campobello is a compact island (about 16km/10 miles long and 5km/3 miles wide) at the mouth of Passamaquoddy Bay. It is connected by a graceful modern bridge to Lubec, Maine, and by a series of small ferries from Canada. This is an ideal quick trip into Canada if you're already in Downeast Maine; from Bar Harbor it's about a 2½-hour drive—into another world that feels more relaxed and distinctly Canadian.

Campobello has been home to both working fishermen and wealthy families over the years, who have coexisted quite amicably. (Locals approved when the summer folks wanted to build a golf course, for example—because it gave them a nice place to graze their sheep.) Today, the island is a mix of elegant summer mansions and simpler local homes.

Campobello offers excellent shoreline **walks ★** at **Roosevelt Campobello International Park** (see below) and **Herring Cove Provincial Park** (www.campobello. com/herring.html; © **506/752-7010**), which opens from late May until mid-September and in other

Don't Forget Your Passport

Remember that passports will be required, as you are crossing international borders if choosing the Lubec route.

marked locations. The landscapes are extraordinarily diverse. On some trails you'll enjoy a shoreline tableau of white houses and church spires across the channel in Lubec and Eastport; 10 minutes later you'll be walking along a wild, rocky coast pummeled by surging waves. In the air above you may see bald eagles and osprey. Herring Cove's thousand or so acres include a mile-long beach that's perfect for a slow stroll in the fog, camping (see "Where to Stay & Eat" below), and a good golf course with a pro shop. Look for whales, porpoises, and seals from observation decks at Ragged Point or Liberty Point.

ESSENTIALS

GETTING THERE   Campobello Island is accessible year-round from the United States. From Route 1 in Whiting, Maine, take Route 189 to Lubec, then cross the free **FDR International Bridge** from the mainland onto Campobello.

In summer only, there's a second fun option, although it will cost you. From **St. George** on the Canadian mainland, drive down Route 172 to the dock at **L'Etete.** Board the **provincial ferry** that runs year-round (operates on the half-hour 6:30am, 7:40am, 8am, and on the hour until 10pm) to **Deer Island**'s northern tip. Then drive the length of that island to Cummings Cove—it's only about 24km (15 miles or a 20-min. drive)—and board the small ferry to Campobello. This second ferry is operated by **East Coast Ferries** (www.eastcoast ferries.nb.ca; ℭ **877/747-2159** or 506/747-2159) from mid-June through September, running every half hour from 8:30am to 6:30pm. The ride takes about a half-hour. The fare is C$16 for a car and driver, plus C$4 for each additional passenger and a small fuel surcharge (currently C$4). You can later retrace your steps for another C$16, or just drive on across the border into Maine. Remember: These ferry times are in local Atlantic time, 1 hour ahead of Eastern Standard Time.

VISITOR INFORMATION   The Campobello Welcome Center, 44 Rte. 774, Welshpool (ℭ **506/752-7043**), is on the right side just after you cross the bridge from Lubec. It's usually open July and August 9am to 7pm; from late May to June and from September to early October, it's open 9am to 6pm.

ROOSEVELT CAMPOBELLO INTERNATIONAL PARK ★★

As the name suggests, Roosevelt Campobello International Park (www.fdr. net; ℭ **877/851-6663** or 506/752-2922) is as much about Franklin Delano Roosevelt as it is the scenery. FDR's experiences here shaped him into the impressive world leader he ultimately became. From the age of 1, this is where the U.S. President and his family vacationed, drawn by the cool air and restorative powers of these lands and the surrounding sea. As President, his policies toward Canada, and his approach to both international cooperation and to Native Americans, were likely shaped by his early associations with the fishermen and the Passamaquoddy Indians he came to know—and respect here. Many think his policies concerning natural resources, too, were likely "seeded" by his time spent outdoors in the area. An excellent short film at the visitor center will introduce you to that history, as will a tour of the family mansion, painted the same red it's always been. Afterward, take a stroll along the 16km (10 miles) of scenic coastal walking trails.

The park is run by a commission with representatives from both the U.S. and Canada—the only such arrangement in North America.

The park's visitor center closes late-November until mid-May, but the extensive grounds and parklands remain open year-round sunrise to sunset; maps, walk suggestions, and info on birdwatching, bog life, geology, and more are available at the visitor center and its website. From mid-May to mid-October, the center and cottage are open daily from 10am to 6pm. For the rest of October, the visitor center closes an hour earlier and the cottage is closed. The last tour leaves 15 minutes before closing.

WHERE TO STAY & EAT

There's camping next to a lovely mile-long sand-and-pebble beach and a nine-hole golf course at **Herring Cove Provincial Park ★** (© **506/752-7010**). Nightly fees at the 88 sites range from C$25 (for a simple site) to C$39 (for a rustic shelter to somewhat protect you from the elements), with discounts for seniors. And if you're looking for a place to check your e-mail, re-caffeinate, and perhaps get a light bite to eat (excellent house-made pastries and sandwiches), **Jocie's Porch ★★** (724 Rte. 774, Welshpool www.jociesporch.com; © **506752-9816**) should do the trick. There are few more pleasant places to mooch off free Wi-Fi than the porch here, with its swings and Adirondack chairs overlooking the water.

Campobello Whale Watch Motel ★ It doesn't get more old-school motel than this, but sometimes that's just fine. Especially when the owners are as gracious, helpful, and obsessively tidy as the two here are; and the digs are conveniently located. Unexpected extras include airy, large rooms stocked with more than enough towels and extra hangers, plus microwaves, coffee makers, and a little deck you can sit out on and enjoy your cup of joe. A darn nice place.

935 Rte. 774, Welshpool. www.campobellowhalewatchmotel.ca. © **506/752-2008.** 8 units. C$109 double. **Amenities:** Microwaves, coffee makers, Wi-Fi (free).

Fireside Restaurant ★ Since 1964, the Fireside has been feeding hungry hikers and other visitors to the island with a good, basic menu of burgers, pasta, and grilled dishes. Best on the menu: the shepherd's pie made with lamb and peaches, and creamed corn topped with garlic mashed potatoes.

610 Rte. 774. www.fdr.net. © **506/752-6055.** Main courses C$18–C$28. Late-May to mid-Oct Mon–Wed noon–5pm, Thurs–Sat noon–9pm.

Owen House, A Country Inn & Gallery ★★ Admiral William Fitzwilliam Owen was given the island by royal decree in 1769, and his family ruled it like a feudal estate for over a century. The seat of power was this historic home, built in 1835, and it still has more than a touch of nobility (though the floors now slope). Rooms, both common rooms and bedrooms, are decorated with antiques—a sprightly rocking horse, four-poster beds (with excellent and new mattresses), spinning wheels, ship portraits—all off-set by riotously colorful period wallpapers. The house itself is set on beautifully landscaped (and forested) headlands. A gut-bustingly big, tasty breakfast is included in the nightly cost. *Note:* Only four rooms have private bathrooms, and they tend to go first, so book early if that's important to you.

11 Welshpool St., Welshpool. www.owenhouse.ca. ℂ **506/752-2977.** 9 units, 4 with shared bathroom. C$104–C$210 double. Rates include full breakfast. **Amenities:** Wi-Fi (free).

St. Stephen

St. Stephen is the Canadian gateway for many travelers arriving from the United States. It's directly across the tidal St. Croix River from Calais, Maine. The two towns enjoy a friendly relationship—in 1812, the people of St. Stephen loaned Calais enough gunpowder to celebrate the 4th of July, even though the United States and what was then a British colony were technically at war. Downtown St. Stephen is a handy pit stop—and the smell of chocolate (as you'll read below) entices many visitors into a longer stay.

A second border crossing located just outside the town of Calais and St. Stephen avoids passing through either town. If you are in a hurry, this crossing is a better choice, steering you directly onto a multilane highway heading east toward Saint John. However, you'll miss the charm of the border towns.

ESSENTIALS

VISITOR INFORMATION The Provincial Visitor Information Centre (ℂ **506/466-7390**) is open daily from 9am to 7pm in summer (mid-June to Labour Day), 9am to 6pm during the shoulder seasons (mid-May to early Oct). It's in the old train station at Milltown Boulevard and King Street, about a mile from Canadian Customs—turn right after crossing the border (follow signs toward St. Andrews and Saint John), watching for the information center at the stoplight where the road turns left.

EXPLORING ST. STEPHEN

While the lumber industry and wood trades built this town and are responsible for those handsome brick-and-stone buildings along the main street, today St. Stephen is Canada's "Chocolate Town"—and for good reason (see below). After all the sweet samplings, if you feel the need to work off the calories, there is a lovely Riverfront Walking Trail between downtown buildings and the river. You might spot a bald eagle as you hike. Just out of town, the **Ganong Nature Park** ★ (www.ganongnaturepark.org) has even more walking trails, a spectacular coastline, and huge tide swings that expose the ocean floor twice daily. It is located at 350 Todd's Point Rd. in Charlotte County, about 10km (6 miles) out of town.

You can learn more about the region's history near the visitor center (see above) at the **Charlotte County Museum** ★, 443 Milltown Blvd. (www.charlottecountymuseum.ca; ℂ **506/466-3295**), set in a handsome mansard-roofed home. Besides information about the chocolate factory—who knew Ganong invented both the chocolate bar and the heart-shaped candy box?—you can learn about the city's formerly impressive cotton mill (which was the second-largest in Canada in its heyday) and soap factory. Admission is just C$2. It's open June through August only, Monday to Saturday 10am to 4pm.

In 1604 and 1605, 79 men suffered through winter on this tiny, now-uninhabited island in the Saint Croix River, creating the first "capital of l'Acadie" and leading to an enduring French presence in what we now call Canada. Today, the site is considered the first European colony in all of North America and is the only international historic site in the United States Park Service. In the 18th century, it became known as "Bone Island" when erosion exposed 23 gravesites. Analysis proved the cause of death was scurvy for most of those buried here. The island again made history during the War of 1812 when officers from the United States and Britain met here, as the land was considered "neutral territory." **Saint Croix Island International Historic Site,** as it's called, is in Bayside about 24km (15 miles) from St. Stephen. To get there from St. Stephen on Route 1, take exit 25 onto Route 127 toward St. Andrews.

The Chocolate Museum ★ MUSEUM   Chocolate built modern-day St. Stephen's. It all started in 1873 when the Ganong family (a group of brothers, actually) began selling chocolate from their general store. From there an empire was built, employing up to 700 workers by the 1930s. Take the **Heritage Chocolate Walking Tour** (June–Aug, Mon–Sat, 10am and 2pm) to learn more about the homes and other buildings that chocolate built. Today, chocolates and candy are manufactured in a plant on the outskirts of town. Alas, the working factory doesn't give tours, but the museum downtown is housed in one of the company's original factories, so you'll get a feeling for the roots of the enterprise. And a taste of those bygone days: In one section, behind glass, workers hand-dip chocolates (you can then buy them in the store out front). The museum is a surprisingly engaging place, with exhibits of vintage chocolate boxes that look like art pieces today; the Ganongs were the first to sell chocolates for Valentine's Day in heart-shaped boxes. This enterprising family (still the owners today) was also the first, in 1910, to think of wrapping chocolate pieces in foil, thus inventing the modern chocolate bar!

73 Milltown Blvd. www.chocolatemuseum.ca. ✆ **506/466-7848.** Admission C$10 adults, C$8.50 students and seniors, free children 5 and under, C$30 families. Downtown tour plus museum C$15 adult, C$14 seniors, free children 5 and under, C$40 families. July–Aug Mon–Sat 9am–6pm, Sun 11am–3pm; June Mon–Sat 10am–4pm, Sun 11am–3pm; May and Sept Mon–Fri 10am–4pm, Sat 11am–3pm; Oct–Nov, Mar–Apr Mon–Fri 10am–4pm.

St. Andrews ★★

St. Andrews—or St. Andrews-by-the-Sea as it's sometimes called—traces its roots back to the United Empire Loyalists. After the American Revolution, New Englanders who supported the British needed a new life. They moved first to seaside Castine, Maine, which they thought was safely on British soil. But it wasn't; the St. Croix River was later determined to be the true border between Canada and the United States. Forced to uproot once more, these Loyalists

5

NEW BRUNSWICK | Passamaquoddy Bay

dismantled their homes, loaded the pieces aboard ships, and rebuilt them on the welcoming peninsula of St. Andrews (not so far away from Castine, by water). Some of these remarkably resilient saltbox houses *still* stand in the town today.

The community emerged as a fashionable summer resort in the 19th century, when many of Canada's affluent built homes and gathered here annually. The Tudor-style Algonquin Hotel was built in 1889 on a small rise overlooking the town and quickly became the area's social hub and defining landmark.

St. Andrews is situated at the tip of a long, wedge-shaped peninsula. Thanks to its location off the beaten track, the community hasn't been spoiled by modern development. Walking the wide, shady streets—especially around the Algonquin—takes one back to a simpler time, as do century-old homes in the town. A number of appealing boutiques, shops, and interesting eateries are spread along Water Street and adjoining streets on the town's shoreline, and it's easy to grab a whale-watching or boat tour at the wharf. I definitely recommend this town if you're seeking an easy dip into New Brunswick. Don't miss the weekly farmers' market, held Thursday mornings May to September 8:30am to 1pm at the corner of King and Water Streets.

ESSENTIALS

GETTING THERE   St. Andrews is located at the apex of Route 127, which dips southward from Route 1 between St. Stephen and St. George. It's an easy drive north from **St. Stephen** or south from **Saint John** (but more scenic coming from Saint John); the turnoff is well marked from both directions.

VISITOR INFORMATION   St. Andrews' seasonal **Welcome Centre** (www.standrewsbythesea.ca; $\textcircled{C}$ **506/529-3556**) is located at 24 Reed Ave., on your left as you enter the village. The center opens daily from May through October; the rest of the year, the Welcome Centre is closed.

EXPLORING ST. ANDREWS

Pick up a helpful, free town map at the Welcome Centre and set off. Many of the private dwellings in St. Andrews feature plaques with information on their origins—look for them especially on the sides of the town's saltbox-style homes. The village's compact and handsome downtown flanks **Water Street,** the long commercial street paralleling the bay. You'll find understated commercial architecture here, much of it from the turn of the 20th century, in a variety of styles. Allow an hour or so for browsing through the boutiques and art galleries. There's also a mix of restaurants and inns.

Single Track Alert

If you are a mountain biking fan, you've come to the right place. **Off Kilter Bike** (www.offkilterbike.com; $\textcircled{C}$ **506/466-8388**) organizes tours and rentals. From sea floor to mountaintop, Off Kilter offers 2-hour sightseeing tours, day trips, overnights, and multiday trips, including rides on nearby islands like Grand Manan.

Two blocks inland on King Street, get a dose of local history at the **Ross Memorial Museum** ★, 188 Montague St. (www.rossmemorialmuseum.ca; ✆ **506/529-5124**). Though they never lived here, choosing instead to spend their time over a 40-year period at what is now the **Rossmount Inn ★★★** (see p. 112), American reverend Henry Phipps Ross and his wife Sarah Juliette Ross traveled the world and this house, built in 1824, became an elegant storage place for their eclectic and intriguing collection of art, furniture, carpets. The museum is open June through mid-October, Monday through Saturday from 10am to 4:30pm; and in July and August only, Sundays 1 to 4:30pm. Admission is by donation—leave a few dollars. Just uphill from the museum, at the head of King Street, is the growing **Kingsbrae Garden ★★** (see below).

Toward the western end of Water Street, you'll come to Joe's Point Road at the foot of Harriet Street. The stout wooden **blockhouse** that sits just off the water behind low, grass-covered earthworks was built by townspeople during the War of 1812, when the colonials anticipated a U.S. attack (which never came). This structure is almost all that remains of the scattered fortifications created around town during that war—there are cannons here from a different era—but it's in excellent shape, with artifacts placed so it appears the soldiers might have just ducked out for some sun. It has great views of the bay and, at low tide, the expansive flats where clam diggers sometimes drive their trucks far out on the ocean floor. The fortification is administered to visitors as the **Blockhouse National Historic Site ★** (✆ **888/773-8888**). It's open June through August; the entry fee is a mere C90¢ per person, half that for youth. Across the street from the blockhouse sit peaceful lawns and gardens, established in 1967 to mark the centenary of Canadian Confederation. **Centennial Park** has nice views of the bay and is a pleasant spot for a picnic.

At the other end of Water Street, headed east from downtown, is the open space of **Indian Point** and a local campground. Now the views of the bay become even more panoramic, and they're especially dramatic at sunrise. The water is swimmable, but frigid. Better to beachcomb. You might turn up worn, rounded pieces of flint and coral on the shoreline. It's imported—early traders loaded up their holds with flint from England and coral from the Caribbean to serve as ballast during the long crossings. When they arrived, they simply dumped the rocks overboard, and today they still churn up from the deep.

For a more protected swimming spot, wander down **Acadia Drive,** which runs downhill behind the Algonquin Hotel. You'll come to popular **Katy's Cove,** where floating docks form a sort of natural saltwater swimming pool along a lovely inlet. You'll find swimming lessons by certified lifeguards, beach volleyball, barbecue, sand sculpting, a playground, and a sense of ease. There's a small fee to swim and use the playground.

Fundy Discovery Aquarium ★ AQUARIUM The new aquarium on the grounds of the **Huntsman Marine Science Centre** is a welcome distraction for visitors, especially beloved by kids (who can watch colorful seahorses at feeding time, get splashed by rambunctious salmon, and say hello to Loki and Snorkel, a couple of very active harbor seals). Children and adults alike can test their yuckiness thresholds by probing strange creatures like skates, sea urchins, and hermit crabs in the large touch tank.

1 Lower Campus Road (from Reed Street, turn left 1.8km/approx. 1 mile onto Marine Science Drive). www.huntsmanmarine.ca. ☏ **506/529-1200.** Admission C$14 adults, C$12 senior, C$9.75 children 4-17 years-old, free children under 4. Open daily May–Oct 10am–5pm.

Kingsbrae Garden ★★ GARDEN   Possibly the best all-around activity in St. Andrews is a visit to this 11-hectare (27-acre) horticultural garden. Opened in 1998 on the grounds of several former estates, Kingsbrae has won many awards, including Canadian Garden of the Year in 2013 and one of the "Top Five North American Gardens Worth Traveling For" at the International Garden Tourism Conference in 2011. It hosts the Canadian Sculpture Competition, so there is always temporary and permanent art to discover among the gardens. Its designers incorporated existing hedges and trees as they developed theme gardens where every turn reveals new vistas. Almost 2,000 varieties of trees, some extremely rare, are among the 50,000 perennials. Notable features include a day-lily collection, extensive rose garden, cedar maze, fully functional Dutch windmill, animals, duck ponds, and a children's garden with an elaborate Victorian-mansion playhouse. The **Garden Café** has a patio with lovely views over the lawns to the bay below. There's a gift shop, art gallery, and plant center on the premises. Croquet and bocce ball are ready for anyone to play. Anyone who has a hard time walking the 11 hectares (27 acres) can book a personal, motorized golf cart tour. Those with a horticultural bent should plan to spend a few hours here, strolling, marveling and enjoying.

220 King St. www.kingsbraegarden.com. ☏ **506/529-3335.** Admission C$16 adults, C$12 students and seniors, C$38 families, free for children 6 and under. Gardens open mid-May to mid-Oct daily 9am–8pm; cafe, mid-May to mid-Oct daily 10am–5pm. Closed mid-Oct to mid-May.

Ministers Island Historic Site/Covenhoven ★★ HISTORIC SITE The trip to 200-hectare (500-acre) Ministers Island is part of the adventure, as it requires driving across the ocean floor which can only be done at low tide (so schedules are strict here). A guide escorts you and others in your cars across the sandbar road to Covenhoven, an 1890s sandstone mansion. Fifty rooms (17 bedrooms), some, like the grand drawing room, as big as modern homes, wait to be explored. This, the summer home of Sir William Van Horne, the visionary president of Canadian Pacific Railway, is now a protected Provincial Historic Site which reveals his ingenuity, and the wealth he had to indulge his passions. Stroll to the circular stone bathhouse and tidal swimming pool, or the innovative windmill, gigantic livestock barn and creamery. When Van Horne was stuck working in Montréal, he shipped dairy products from the creamery and vegetables from the greenhouse to himself daily—by rail, of course. (He extended the rail line here.)

At the end of Bar Rd. off Rte. 127 (northeast of St. Andrews), Chamcook. www.ministers island.net. ☏ **506/529-5081.** Admission C$10, free for children under 8. Open mid-May to Oct. Tours are available by calling ahead.

Passamaquoddy Bay

NEW BRUNSWICK

BOAT TOURS

The docks of St. Andrews are an excellent spot from which to launch an exploration of Passamaquoddy Bay, which is very much alive, biologically speaking. That means you'll very likely see a combination of whales, porpoises, seals, and bald eagles, no matter what tour you select. All 2- to 3-hour tours generally run the same price: C$55 to C$60 per adult, less for children. Reservations are strongly advised. Your selection really comes down to the type of vessel and experience you prefer.

Quoddy Link Marine ★ (www.quoddylinkmarine.com; © **877/688-2600** or 506/529-2600) offers seasonal (late-June to late-Oct) whale-watch tours, one to three times daily on a 17m (56-foot) power catamaran, and the tour includes seafood snacks and use of binoculars with an on-board touch tank; the tours take 2½ to 3 hours. Two-hour tours in search of wildlife aboard 7m (24-ft.) rigid-hull Zodiacs are offered by **Fundy Tide Runners** ★ (www.fundytiderunners.com; © **506/529-4481**). Flotation suits (provided) are a must as the boats cruise through the West Isles archipelago to the whale feeding grounds. This outfitter opens May through October.

For a more traditional experience, sign up for a trip aboard the 22m (72-ft.) square-rigged cutter the *Jolly Breeze of St. Andrews* ★ with **Tall Ship Whale Watching** ★ (www.jollybreeze.com; © **866/529-8116** or 506/529-8116). The outfit offers three 3½-hour sails a day from mid-June through mid-October. Complimentary breakfast or soup is included. A flat-fee deal for families of four (or more) is also offered. Watch for whales, seals, dolphins, and eagles—all have been sighted from the sailboat's deck.

Bruce Smith's **excellent Seascape Kayak Tours** ★ (www.seascapekayaktours.com; © **866/747-1884** or 506/747-1884) outfit on nearby Deer Island (see "Getting There," in the Campobello Island section, p. 102) offers a quieter up-close and personal view of the bay's natural wonders. Seascape's talented international staff leads kayak trips lasting from 2 hours (C$65 per adult) to a full day (C$150) through the islands and bays of the Campobello/Deer Isle/St. Andrews area; you might see whales, seals, porpoises, and/or eagles. Snacks are provided, and no prior kayaking experience is required.

WHERE TO STAY

As a top destination in New Brunswick, there is no shortage of accommodations in all price ranges and types in St. Andrews. From harbor-side inns and motels to campgrounds and resorts, the selection is substantial.

Algonquin Resort ★★★   Under new management and with tens of millions in recent renovations, the rooms at The Algonquin are now as contemporary as you'll find in St. Andrews. New bathrooms with walk-in glass showers, comfortable furnishings—including pillow-top mattresses—and decorative tile floors have brought this exquisite 1889 Tudor-style resort into the 21st century. Historic photos throughout recall a long history as the retreat and playground of the wealthy. Second-story rooms open to spacious balconies. Corner suites with separate bedrooms and living rooms feel like small apartments. Nearby is an outstanding seaside golf course (see "Golf," p. 99). On site are tennis courts, a spa, an outdoor pool, and an indoor pool where the kids can careen through a tube slide. Guests gather in the evening at outdoor firepits on the lawn in front of the resort. "Anyplace Dining" (waiters will deliver your order anywhere on the property) is one of my favorite perks at The Algonquin—what could be more posh than appetizers and a drink in the shade of the front veranda? **Braxton's Restaurant and Bar** ★ (off the main lobby) is good, but not as creative as it should be for a resort of this caliber. A light lunch can also be had at the **Clubhouse Grill** ★ on the resort's golf course.

184 Adolphus St. www.algonquinresort.com. ℰ **855/529-8693** or 506/529-8823. 234 units. Rooms start at C$229. Valet parking is C$25 daily. Small cats and dogs C$35 per night. **Amenities:** Restaurant, bar, complimentary touring bikes, concierge, golf course, Jacuzzi, outdoor and indoor heated pools, fitness studio, spa, 2 tennis courts, Wi-Fi (free).

Kingsbrae Arms Relais & Châteaux ★★★

Pack something really flattering to wear, because this place looks like it was ripped from the pages of *Town & Country* magazine—and it would be a pity to spoil the illusion. An 1897 manor house built by jade merchants, some rooms overlook the award-winning Kingsbrae Garden (see p. 108), others the sea beyond. Not that you'll need to stare out the windows for eye-candy: it will be all around you, from the perfectly chosen framed prints, to the handsomely patterned armchairs, to the gas fireplaces framed by historic mantelpieces. Even the bathrooms feel regal, thanks to their marble accents. And all of this swank isn't just for adults: a slightly more down-to-earth family wing is on two floors and accommodates up to ten. Children and pets are welcome here and with limits in other rooms, kids 12 and older throughout. In the communal dining room, the chef focuses on specialties from the kitchen garden and nearby sea for an oft-changed five-course dinner.

219 King St. www.kingsbrae.com. ℰ **506/529-1897.** 8 units. C$319–C$649. Packages and meal plans available. **Amenities:** Dining room, garden, Jacuzzi (some rooms), Wi-Fi (free).

Kiwanis Oceanfront Camping ★

It's rare to have access to a campground so close to a town center, so this little gem nestled next to the bay within walking distance of all that St. Andrews has to offer is especially welcome to RVers and campers. Be aware, you're trading proximity to town for wilderness—there is little in the way of trees. The washrooms, showers, and other buildings here are accessible for those with mobility issues.

550 Water St. www.kiwanisoceanfrontcamping.com. ℰ **877/393-7070** or 506/529-3439. RV with full hookups (oceanfront) C$44 night; tents (unserviced) C$31. **Amenities:** Washrooms, laundry, playground.

Picket Fence Motel ★

This little roadside motel is affordable, clean, and quite friendly (bend-over backward service) making it a good choice for budget travelers who want dignified lodgings, but don't need frills. It's the kind of place where you can sit out in front of your room and meet other travelers, and it's within walking distance of St. Andrews' village center.

102 Reed Ave. www.picketfencenb.com ✆ **506/529-8985.** 17 units. Queen and double-bedded rooms C$80–C$110. One efficiency unit with a small kitchen. **Amenities:** Wi-Fi (free).

Seaside Beach Resort ★★ Several establishments along the waterfront offer reasonable accommodations, but the Seaside is the roomiest and boasts the nicest grounds. In fact, the only thing separating the Seaside from the bay, the pier, and the shoreline is a lovely boardwalk. That means the views are stellar, as is the location close to downtown streets, making this collection of cedar shingle–clad cabins and cottages (along with some apartment units) a real winner. All units have beachy-feeling pine board interiors—floor, walls, and ceiling—and are furnished with sturdy, if not fashion-forward, sofas, tables, and chairs. Each is equipped with surprisingly modern kitchens or kitchenettes. Open year-round; leashed dogs welcome.

339 Water St. www.seaside.nb.ca. ✆ **800/506-8677** or 506/529-3846. 24 units. Rates range from C$105–C$250. Two and three-night minimum stays for some units. **Amenities:** TV, fridge, kitchenette, Wi-Fi (free).

WHERE TO EAT

Too much food on Main Street in St. Andrews is of the deep fried variety, but there are alternatives and some real gems. Locals swear by the **Gables,** 143 Water St. (✆ **506/529-3440**), a waterside spot where you can relax and nosh on seafood, lobster, or burgers. It isn't fancy, but it's friendly. For tip top coffee and dessert, and the best chance of a conversation, head for **Honeybeans Coffee, Tea and Treats** (157 Water St.; ✆ **506/529-4888**). For the finest breakfast in town—and fresh, light lunches—try the new **Station on King** (49 King St.; www.thestationonking.com; ✆ **506/529-4949**).

Europa ★★ CONTINENTAL In an intriguing yellow building that once housed a movie theater and dance hall, Bavarian husband-and-wife transplants Markus and Simone Ritter whip up French-, Swiss-, and Austrian-accented cuisine for a 35-seat room. Starters could run to a colorful bell pepper soup; smoked salmon with rösti and capers; or scallops seared in Mornay sauce and baked with cheese (a house specialty). Main courses usually include several versions of schnitzel (grilled pork or veal steak) with different fillings, toppings, and sauces; duck à l'orange; and haddock in lemon butter or champagne sauce. The wine list is surprisingly strong. All in all, a lovely slice of Europe—just as the name promises.

48 King St. www.europainn.com. ✆ **877/938-7672** or 506/529-3818. Reservations recommended. Main courses C$23–C$28. Apr to New Year's Eve daily 5:30–9pm. Closed Jan–Mar.

Niger Reef Teahouse ★ CANADIAN Life seems unusually pleasant when you're sitting out on the porch of this 1926 chapter house (of the Imperial Orders of the Daughters of the Empire) watching all of the tidal action on the Bay of Fundy, and eating some of the fruits of that bay. The fish chowder here is particularly satisfying, especially if you pair a cup with their signature potato tart, which blends potatoes with cheddar and bacon, a genius combination for a baked good. Not feeling fancy? The burgers (veggie or lamb) are mighty tasty, as is the pesto pizza.

1 Joe's Point Rd. www.nigerreefteahouse.com. ✆ **506/529-8005.** Main courses C$10–C$20. May–Oct 11am–3pm only, June–Sept 11am–9pm.

Rossmount Inn ★★★ CONTEMPORARY CANADIAN   Chef Chris Aerni has made the Rossmount into a culinary landmark that food lovers from far and wide seek out. And so they should. When a chef is dedicated enough to forage for edible goose tongue greens (from the marsh), grow dozens of types of herbs in the restaurant garden, and handpick fish and meat from local producers, he rightly earns a reputation as one of the best in the country. Dinners here are constantly changing and are artfully presented, in a civilized room with tables spread widely enough for quiet conversation—or perhaps a proposal. Yes, it's that special of a place.

4599 Rte. 127. www.rossmountinn.com. ✆ **506/529-3351.** Reservations required. Main courses C$18–C$38. Mid-Apr to New Year's Eve daily 6–9:30pm. Closed Jan to mid-Apr.

GRAND MANAN ISLAND ★★

Grand Manan is the main island of an archipelago at the mouth of the Bay of Fundy not far from the U.S. border. Geologically rugged, profoundly peaceful, and indisputably remote, the handsome island of 2,500 year-round residents is 34km (21 miles) long by 18km (11 miles) wide, and just a 90-minute ferry ride from the port of Blacks Harbour, southeast of St. George. The small population lives along the eastern shore with most of the services in and around North Head where the ferry lands. The west coast is wild and windswept. This is a much-prized destination for adventurous travelers, often a highlight of their vacation. Nature lovers, whale-watchers, and those who seek solitude will relish the rough-hewn charm of these islands.

Grand Manan is a special favorite of serious birders on a quest to see some of the 300 or so species of birds that either nest here or stop during migration. From bald eagles to puffins to sandpipers, birds abound on the marshes, cliffs, and sky. You're practically guaranteed to see something you've never seen before. John James Audubon and Winslow Homer came here to paint; Pulitzer Prize–winning author Willa Cather kept a cottage here, which you can rent. This unique island continues to attract artists, photographers, and others who seek out special places.

Essentials

GETTING THERE   Grand Manan is reached from Blacks Harbour on the Canadian mainland via frequent ferry service. **Coastal Transport car ferries** (www.coastaltransport.ca; ✆ **855/882-1978** or 506/642-0520) depart from the mainland and the island every 2 hours between 7:30am and 5:30pm (and at 9pm) from mid-June to mid-Sept, four times daily the rest of the year. Two ferries run in summer, one the rest of the year. The GM Adventure and the GMV offer simple food like hearty breakfasts and chowders in their on-board restaurants, a children's play area, arcade, lounge, and observation decks for taking in the scenery and watching for whales. The ferry does not sail on Christmas or New Year's Day. The round-trip fare is C$12 per adult, C$5.95 per child age 5 to 12, and C$36 per car. Boarding the ferry on the mainland is free; you buy tickets when you leave the island. In summer, book early and arrive at the terminal early.

GETTING AROUND Most of the services on the island including are crowded into the community of North Head. In fact, it's possible to leave your car on the mainland, walk onto the ferry, and walk off in North Head and up the street to your reserved accommodations. A rented bike will get you around and to services like a grocery store and banks, located mid island.

VISITOR INFORMATION The island's Visitor Information Centre (www. grandmanannb.com; ℰ **888/525-1655** or 506/662-3442) is located in the business center in North Head across from Surfside Motel. Many local businesses have visitor information. Ask for the map that lists most accommodations, restaurants, gift shops and activities.

Exploring the Island

Start exploring before you even land. As you come abreast of the island aboard the ferry, head for the starboard (right) side: You'll soon see the so-called **Seven Days' Work** in the rocky cliffs of Whale's Cove, a spot where seven layers of hardened lava and sill (intrusive igneous rock) have come together to create a sort of geological Dagwood sandwich.

Once on the island, a deeper understanding of that topography can be garnered at the **Grand Manan Museum ★** (www.grandmananmuseum.ca; ℰ **506/662-3524**) at 1141 Rte. 776 in Grand Harbour; its geology exhibit teaches visitors what to look for as they roam around the island. The museum also houses an impressive lighthouse lens from the Gannet Rock Lighthouse, plus a collection of items that have washed up from shipwrecks. The museum is open from June to September, Monday through Friday 9am to 5pm; it's also open Saturdays (same hours) in July and August. Admission is C$5 for adults, C$3 for seniors and students, and free for children 12 and under.

While Grand Manan is about as quiet as it gets, you can find even more silence and solitude by driving to **White Head Island,** population 190 on a good day. To get there, drive to Ingalls Head (follow Ingalls Head Rd. from Grand Harbour) and catch a free ferry to the island. You walk along the shore to a lighthouse guarding the passage between Battle Beach and Sandy Cove. The ferry holds nine cars and sails year-round, several times per day during the summer.

BIKING & KAYAKING

The relatively flat and compact island is perfect for cycling; the only stretches to avoid are some fast, less scenic segments of Route 776. Any of the side roads offer superb biking, and the paved cross-island road to **Dark Harbour** is especially nice; when you get there, you'll find a scenic little harbor with a few cabins, dories, and salmon pens. This route is wild and hilly for a stretch, but then offers a memorably scenic coast down to the ocean on the island's western side as your reward.

Bike rentals are available at **Adventure High ★** (www.adventurehigh.com; *C* **800/732-5492** or 506/662-3563) at 83 Rte. 776 in **North Head,** not far from the ferry. The outfitter also offers sea kayak tours around the island, for those who prefer to get a rarely seen, whale's-eye view of the impressive cliffs. Bikes rent for C$25 per day, C$18 for a half-day. Kayak tours run from C$25 to C$45 for a 2-hour sunset tour to C$55 to C$110 for a full day's excursion.

HIKING

Numerous hiking trails lace Grand Manan, particularly around the coast, with several overland routes crossing the island. The degree of difficulty varies, from easy strolls along boardwalks to more challenging terrain for experienced hikers. Don't hesitate to ask at your inn or the visitor information center about trail access, or good places to walk. The Grand Manan Tourism Association publishes a trail guide, *Heritage Trails and Footpaths of Grand Manan,* which can be purchased on the island. Also check out www.grandmanannb.ca or visit Grand Manan Hikers on Facebook for a trail map of the island, which has 18 trails along shoreline, cliff side, and beach.

The most accessible clusters of trails on Grand Manan are at the island's northern and southern tips. An easy and rewarding start is the short walk out to the dramatic setting of **Swallowtail Lighthouse ★★**, the one rounded by the ferry as it enters port. Head up Route 776 to the end, where you can park and walk a short bridge to the lighthouse trail. Head north up Whistle Road to Whistle Beach, and you'll find both the **Northwestern Coastal Trail ★** and the **Seven Days' Work Trail ★**, both of which follow the rocky shoreline. Near the low lighthouse and towering radio antennae at Southwest Head, trails radiate out along cliffs topped with scrappy trees. The views are remarkable. Just be sure to watch your step.

WHALE-WATCHING & BOAT TOURS

A fine way to experience island ecology is to head offshore. Several outfitters offer complete nature tours, providing a nice sampling of the world above and beneath the sea. On an excursion you might see minke, finback, humpback, or even endangered right whales, along with exotic birds including puffins and phalaropes. **Sea Watch Tours ★** (www.seawatchtours.com; *C* **877/662-8552** or 506/662-8552), run by Peter and Kenda Wilcox, operates a series of excursions from spring through September—including birdwatching tours to remote Machias Seal Island—with whale sightings guaranteed or your money back, aboard a 13m (43-ft.) vessel with canopy. Rates run C$65 to C$113 for adults and C$45 to C$55 per child 12 or younger. **Whales-n-Sails Adventures ★** (www.whales-n-sails.com; *C* **888/994-4044** or 506/662-1999) offers the double attraction of sailing offshore to spot whales. Adults pay C$70, children 12 and under C$50. Find them on the North Head wharf.

Where to Stay

Choose from a couple dozen accommodation options on the island. The **Anchorage Provincial Park ★** (*②* **506/662-7022**) has about 100 campsites scattered about forest and field, available mid-May through late-September. There's a small beach and a hiking trail on the property, and it's well situated for exploring the southern part of the island. It's very popular midsummer; call before you board the ferry to ask about campsite availability. Sites are C$24 to C$35, some with hookups for RVs, others better suited for a simple tent— including some involving crude shelters to help you fend off the weather.

Inn at Whale Cove Cottages ★★   A tree-lined lane leads to an open field where cottages are spread out for privacy, and to take advantage of the fabulous view of the cove and the cliffs on the far side. These 4 hectares (10 acres), the beach below, and the cove are as peaceful and picturesque as you'll find on Grand Manan. Innkeeper and chef Laura Buckley, who trained in Toronto, maintains that peaceful, secluded feel by quietly operating these five cottages as if each one belonged to the occupant, and by running a small dining room in the farmhouse (dating to 1816) as if the meals there were prepared just for you, which, in fact, is mostly the case. It's easy to see why the early-20th-century Pulitzer Prize–winning author Willa Cather built her own cottage here, the one that is now most in demand. The three rooms of the inn itself are furnished with simple antiques. Dinners in the **dining room ★★** are served nightly from mid-June through mid-October, weekends only in May and early June.

26 Whale Cove Cottage Rd., North Head. www.whalecovecottages.ca. *②* **506/662-3181.** 9 units. C$135–C$180 double; C$1,000–C$1,200 per week cottage. Rates include full breakfast. All but 1 unit closed Nov–Apr. Dogs welcome in most, C$10 per day. **Amenities:** Dining room, laundry, Jacuzzi (1 unit), TV (2 units), kitchenette (3 units), Wi-Fi (free).

Marathon Inn ★   This big, rambling old hotel, built by a sea captain over a century ago, sits on the hill overlooking North Head. Finding your room feels like wandering through an Escher sketch the way the stairs wind and the floors slope. It's a creaky old building with lots of character, antique furnishings, and contemporary bathrooms. Be prepared to be pampered at breakfast with large helpings of delicious home cooking, like plate-size wild-blueberry pancakes. The lane to the inn is a little hard to find; the entrance is just past the old post office, a brick building on the right heading out of North Head.

19 Marathon Ln., North Head. www.marathoninn.com. *②* **888/660-8488** or 506/662-8488. C$89–C$139 double. Rates include full breakfast. **Amenities:** Lounge, BBQs, laundry, free long-distance calling in North America, heated pool, Wi-Fi (free).

Where to Eat

Options for dining out aren't exactly extravagant on Grand Manan, but there are a few good choices among the many simple restaurants that serve mostly fried foods. Owner and chef Laura Buckley at **Inn at Whale Cove Cottages ★** (see "Where to Stay," above) incorporates fresh local ingredients into the meals she prepares, and it pays off in grub that tastes like it was cooked to

A complete CAMPING EXPERIENCE

One of New Brunswick's best campgrounds is next to a popular beach about 58km (36 miles) east of St. Andrews, about halfway to Saint John, but the attractiveness of **New River Beach Provincial Park ★★★** to locals and travelers alike doesn't stop at sand, surf, and sun. The 99 campsites here are tidy and roomy. Many are equipped with electrical hookups. Kids love this place for the beach, but also for the playground, outdoor volleyball courts, and canteen. The big bonus for lovers of the outdoors is the adjacent hiking area that follows the shoreline past several picturesque coves with isolated beaches and short cliffs to a point with great views of the bay. New River is a great place to spend a day at the beach and enjoy a hike or to settle in for a week.

76 New River Beach Rd. (Take exit 69 off Highway 1 to Highway 175.) http://parcsnbparks.ca. ℂ **506/755-4046.** Reservations required. Rates C$5–C$75 for daily pass to campsite fee. Mid-May to mid-Sept, 8am–10pm. Closed mid-Sept to mid-May.

order (which it almost always is). **Shorecrest Lodge ★** (www.shorecrest lodge.com; ℂ **506/662-3216**) in North Head, another local inn, has a country-style dining room with fireplace and hardwood floors, and serves a choice of one fish and one meat entree each evening. You must make a reservation before 4pm. You'll also encounter a few other family restaurants and grocers along the main road. The seasonal, summer-only **North Head Bakery ★** (ℂ **506/662-8862**) on Route 776 has been using traditional baking methods and whole grains since 1990. Breads made here daily include baguettes, boules, and other French traditional loaves. Some of the pastries, however, disappoint (when they're made with canned fillings rather than fresh ingredients). The bakery is on the main road, on the left as you're heading south from the ferry. It's open late April to mid-October (Tues–Sat 6:30am–9:30pm).

If you're here on Saturday morning between late June and early September, check out the weekly **farmers' market** in North Head.

SAINT JOHN ★★

Don't be put off by the industrial edges of New Brunswick's largest city. Once you get past the few factory smokestacks, the overbuilt overpasses and the busy docks that reduce pedestrian harbor access, you'll find a surprisingly rich array of natural attractions, and a small but charming "uptown" with more than its fair share of great restaurants. **Rockwood Park** boasts 13 lakes, a campground, and golf course; **Harbour Passage**, a series of interconnected waterfront park and heritage sites, links past and present; the **Reversing Rapids** (once oversold as the Reversing Falls) provides opportunity for thrill seekers. In fact, Saint John is at the center of **Stonehammer Geopark,** North America's first global geopark: a UNESCO site that has exceptional geological heritage.

Down at the harbor, cruise ships almost outnumber cargo vessels, bringing a festive air downtown. Ironically, this waterfront area is known locally as

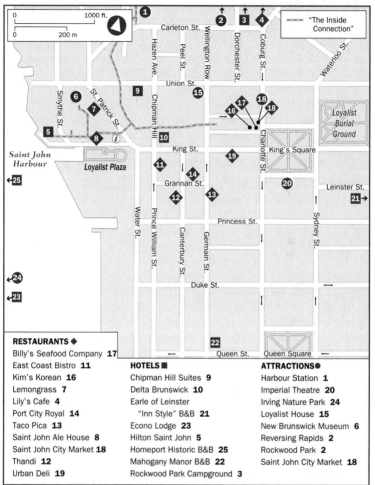

RESTAURANTS ◆

Billy's Seafood Company **17**
East Coast Bistro **11**
Kim's Korean **16**
Lemongrass **7**
Lily's Cafe **4**
Port City Royal **14**
Taco Pica **13**
Saint John Ale House **8**
Saint John City Market **18**
Thandi **12**
Urban Deli **19**

HOTELS ■

Chipman Hill Suites **9**
Delta Brunswick **10**
Earle of Leinster
    "Inn Style" B&B **21**
Econo Lodge **23**
Hilton Saint John **5**
Homeport Historic B&B **25**
Mahogany Manor B&B **22**
Rockwood Park Campground **3**

ATTRACTIONS●

Harbour Station **1**
Imperial Theatre **20**
Irving Nature Park **24**
Loyalist House **15**
New Brunswick Museum **6**
Reversing Rapids **2**
Rockwood Park **2**
Saint John City Market **18**

"Uptown Saint John." Shopping, dining, artisans, entertainment, and history all come together at or near **Market Square.** And throughout the steep streets in the brick-clad uptown area, more often than not fog rolls in off the Bay of Fundy, lending the city a mysterious air and even a softness. As one vendor at the wonderful **Saint John City Market** (the oldest continuous farmers market in Canada) told me, "The fog here is like kissing the clouds."

An eclectic mix of old and new is found throughout the city. Impressive mansions tucked into the side streets reflect the timber barons and shipping magnates of the past. Yet the modern city is full of life: Streets often bustle with skateboarders, merchants, carousers, out-for-the-weekenders, and local old-timers casing the public market for bargains. Here the St. John River empties into the Bay of Fundy (except when the tide is coming in) on the Fundy Coastal Drive, 90 minutes from the U.S. border, and linked by ferry to Nova Scotia.

GETTING THERE   Saint John is located on Route 1. It's 106km (66 miles) from the U.S. border at St. Stephen and 427km (265 miles) around the bend from Halifax. Reach downtown by taking exit 122 or 123 off Route 1.

A year-round **ferry service** connects Saint John with Digby, Nova Scotia. For more details, see "Exploring New Brunswick" at the beginning of this chapter. Saint John's **airport,** coded YSJ (www.saintjohnairport.com; ☎ 506/638-5555), has regular flights to and from Montréal, Toronto, and Halifax on **Air Canada** (www.aircanada.com; ☎ 888/247-2262). There are auto-rental kiosks in the terminal, and a taxi ride into the city costs about C$30.

VISITOR INFORMATION   Saint John (www.discoversaintjohn.com) has three Visitor Information Centres (VICs).

The VIC on **Route 1 West** (☎ 506/658-2940) is open Victoria Day Weekend (mid-May) and closes at Thanksgiving (early Oct). Arriving from the west, look for the contemporary triangular building near the Route 1 off-ramp. You'll find a trove of information and brochures here.

Upon arrival in the downtown or if you're visiting off-season, look for the **City Hall Visitor Information Centre** (☎ 866/463-8639 or 506/658-2855) in the Shoppes of City Hall on the pedestrian walkway connecting Brunswick Square and Market Square. It's open daily 9am to 7pm in July and August; 9am to 6pm late May to June and September to early October; open Monday to Saturday 9am to 5pm the rest of the year.

There's also a seasonal VIC (open mid-May to early Oct), the **Reversing Rapids Information Centre** (☎ 506/658-2937). It overlooks the popular rapids (see "Outdoor Pursuits," p. 120) on Route 100, which is also labeled on maps as Bridge Road. Get there from Route 1 by taking exit 119 or 119B.

Exploring Saint John

If the weather's good, begin by wandering around the **waterfront.** Discover Saint John has published a brochure with three historical walking tours, a map, and plenty of history and architectural trivia. If you have time for only one walk, architecture buffs should go on **"Prince William's Walk,"** an hour-long, self-guided tour of the city's impressive commercial buildings. There's a second brochure called **"Art in Public Places,"** which includes information on John Hooper's wonderfully whimsical, brightly painted wooden figures. You can obtain tour brochures at the Visitor Information Centers.

Wherever you ramble, be sure to drop by the **Saint John City Market ★★** (detailed below) and the **Old Burial Ground ★** (across from King's Square); the latter is a good place to rest for a spell. The ancient cemetery dates from 1784, but it was renovated quite recently—note the beaver pond. When the Irving family empire—the Irvings own the pulp mill, the oil refinery, and a whole lot more in this province—refurbished the cemetery in 1995, they installed this monument, comparing their employees (a good number of the local residents) to hard-working beavers.

If you have a car, you'll also want to visit at least two of the city's tremendous **nature preserves** ★★, described below in the section "Outdoor Pursuits." I can't tell you how surprising it is to find so much lovely, varied green space in the middle of a city, especially a small and (on the surface) industrial one like Saint John.

An elaborate network of underground passageways and overhead pedestrian walkways links up many of the city's malls, hotels, restaurants, and attractions. The whole thing has been dubbed the **Inside Connection** ★, and despite the silly name it's worth a look. In places, it gives the illusion of a whole different underground city—the central mall is three floors high.

Loyalist House ★ HISTORIC HOME   It must have been the commanding view of the harbor that inspired the Merritts, a family of wealthy Loyalists who fled from New York, to build this Georgian mansion in 1817 atop a chunk of jutting bedrock at the zenith of the hill in downtown Saint John. Inside, you'll find attractive antiques; most furnished the original house and have never left. The family took great care to steam-fit doors to the curved stairway, decorate with intricate carvings, and endow their home with the finest furniture available at the time. Tours last 30 to 45 minutes.

120 Union St. www.loyalisthouse.com. ℂ **506/652-3590.** C$5 adults, C$2 children, C$7 families. July to mid-Sept daily 10am–5pm (last admission 4:45pm); mid-May to June Mon–Fri 10am–5pm; Sept–Apr by appointment only.

New Brunswick Museum ★★ MUSEUM   The imposing-looking New Brunswick Museum is a must-stop for anyone seriously curious about this province's natural or cultural history. Collections are displayed on three open floors, an exhaustive mixture of traditional artifacts and quirky objects. Exhibits include a massive section of ship's frame; wonderful geological exhibits; and even life-sized skeletons and reproductions of seals, dolphins, and a humongous North Atlantic right whale named Delilah. Her bones and a life-size model based on them hang next to each other, and the effect is so impressive, it might put a cramp in your neck. Allow at least 4 hours to enjoy the eclectic, uncommonly well-displayed exhibits here.

1 Market Sq. www.nbm-mnb.ca. ℂ **888/268-9595** or 506/643-2300. Admission mid-May to mid-Oct C$8 adults, C$6 seniors, C$4.50 students and children, C$17 families; Nov to mid-May C$7 adults, C$5.50 seniors, C$4 students and children, C$15 families. Mon–Fri 9am–5pm (Thurs until 9pm); Sat 10am–5pm; Sun noon–5pm.

Saint John City Market ★★   Operating since 1785—it's Canada's oldest continuous farmers' market—the market's stately iron-and-glass structure lends the place a European flavor and looks about the same as it did when it was built in 1876. (The handsome iron gates at either end have been in place since 1880.) The building follows the slope of the steep hill, so the roof (resembling the hull of an inverted ship) is higher at one end than the other. For a complete history lesson, and a look at a ledger dating back more than a century, stop by the **Slocum and Ferris,** a popular eatery that has operated in the same location in three different centuries, and chat with owner Dave Forestell. The market bustles with vendors hawking meat, fresh seafood, cheeses, flowers, baked goods, and bountiful fresh produce. You can even sample *dulse,* a snack of dried seaweed from the Bay of Fundy. A number of vendors offer meals to go, and there's seating in an enclosed terrace on the south side. At lunchtime, you'll line up shoulder to shoulder with uptown workers.

47 Charlotte St. (facing King's Square). www.sjcitymarket.ca. © **506/658-2820.** Mon–Fri 7:30am–6pm; Sat 7:30am–5pm. Closed Sun and holidays.

Outdoor Pursuits

Just after construction workers found a 500-million-year-old rock formation called the Hinge in 2010, the United Nations named **Stonehammer Geopark ★★** North America's first UNESCO-recognized geopark. Saint John lies in the heart of the swath of land along the Bay of Fundy that is recognized for a range of natural attributes, geoscientific significance, and beauty. Supporters and tour operators have created outdoor activities like geocaching, guided kayak and hiking tours, and winter activities like snowshoeing to help visitors experience Stonehammer's attributes. Find them in brochures available at visitor centers and on line at www.stonehammergeopark.com.

Several local companies offer tour services: **Go Fundy Events ★** (www. gofundyevents.com; © **866/672-0770**) is run by a team of experienced and knowledgeable guides who exhibit an intense dedication to their city and to Stonehammer. Find others listed in the Saint John Visitor Guide available at most New Brunswick visitor centers.

Irving Nature Park ★★ Thanks to the Irving family's oil and forestry empire, Saint John is surrounded by industry. But it's thanks to the same empire that you can escape that industry, at least at the Irving Nature Park at the west end of the city across the river. On a dramatic 243-hectare (600-acre) coastal peninsula, Irving has built boardwalks and trails to provide access to forest, marsh, and shore where upwards of 240 species of birds spend at least part of their lives. From the observation tower on the "Squirrel Trail" you might see clouds of migrating sandpipers gorging on small sea creatures on the mud flats before migrating south on a 4-day flight. In mid-June and mid-October, the seals can be so thick on the rocks that they have been described as "a great gray noisy carpet." Check the website or call ahead to ask about the park's excellent program of tours and events.

Sand Cove Rd. www.jdirving.com. © **506/653-7367.** Take exit 119A off Rte. 1, then follow Bleury St. to Sand Cove Rd. and continue to the end. Free admission and tours. Daily May to mid-Sept 8am–8pm. Mid-Sept to mid-Oct 8am–6pm.

Reversing Rapids ★   Just west of downtown, the Reversing Rapids, formerly known as the Reversing Falls (locals went with the more accurate name), is located within an impressive rocky gorge, a natural phenomenon that has been turned into a tourism site. The rapids here reverse because of huge local tides battling against the St. John River's flow; rapids, small waterfalls, and big, slurping whirlpools flow one way up through the gorge during the incoming tide, then reverse during the opposite tide. It's dramatic, but it is in a busy part of the city next to highways and across from a paper mill with smokestacks, which will spoil it for some. There are several ways to observe the falls. You can scramble down wooden steps to a park at river's edge, or climb atop a rooftop viewing platform, both for free. You can cross the river to **Fallsview Park** (go left on Douglas Ave., then left again on Fallsview Ave.) and get a water-level view. The adventurous can take a zip-line tour with **Saint John Adventures** (www.saintjohnadventures.ca; ☏ **877/634-9477** or 506/634-9477), which offers an amazing view of the falls from six towers (five zip lines). Allow about 90 minutes and about C$70 for adults; students and seniors get a discount. Prices vary per season. Participants must weigh between 70 and 270 pounds.

Rte. 100. www.discoversaintjohn.com/places/reversing-rapids. ☏ **506/658-2937.** Free admission to viewing platform. Early June to mid-Oct daylight hours, but best at low or high tide. Call for tidal schedule or find them in the Saint John Visitor Guide available at most Visitor Information Centres in the province.

Rockwood Park ★★   This is the park where most locals head for recreation and relaxation. Those out for a stroll or a run hit the network of trails through these 890 hectares (2,200 acres) of lovely urban preserve, which take in lakes, forests, and rocky hills. There's swimming at sandy beaches, horseback riding, mountain biking, rock climbing, golf at a pretty 18-hole municipal golf course (☏ **506/634-0090;** greens fees C$25–C$40), a campground, gardens, minigolf, and the small Cherry Creek Zoo with several dozen species of exotic animals, including six species of monkeys on the endangered species list. In short, there's something for everyone in the family. Boat rentals include canoes and kayaks. **Lily's Café** ★ in the new Hatheway Pavilion at Lily Lake, supplies food on the go. The park, located just 5 minutes' drive north of downtown, gets especially popular on weekends.

Lake Dr. S. ☏ **506/658-2883.** Free admission to park; Cherry Creek Zoo C$11 adults, C$8.50 senior and youth 13-17; C$5.50 children 3–12; free for children 2 and under; C$27 family; various fees for equipment rental and golf. Daily 10am–8:30pm.

Where to Stay
EXPENSIVE
Delta Brunswick ★   On par with the Hilton, the Delta sits atop the Brunswick Square mall next door. While it's not right on the water like the Hilton, its sightlines are pretty much the same, especially in the frequent fog. Some rooms are in need of updating, but many others have already been renovated and the rest are on the way. **Mix Resto Bar** provides the in-hotel

dining, a contemporary space with a water view. It's open daily 6:30am to midnight.

39 King St. www.deltahotels.com. © **800/335-8233** or 506/648-198. 254 units. C$119 double to C$178 Signature Club. Self-parking C$16 per night (free Fri & Sat). Pets allowed. **Amenities:** Restaurant, concierge, fitness room, indoor pool, 24-hr. room service, Wi-Fi (free).

Hilton Saint John ★   This 12-story waterfront hotel was built in 1984, and has all the amenities you'd expect from an upscale chain hotel: you're trading personality and charm for dependability. Oh, and the best location in the city, overlooking the harbor yet also just steps from the rest of downtown by street or indoor walkway. Windows in all guest rooms open, allowing in the sea breeze, and the business center is well stocked. This Hilton is connected to the city's convention center, so it attracts large groups of conventioneers; ask whether anything's scheduled before you book if you don't want to be overwhelmed. The onsite **York Bistro Pub** serves good food until midnight, though not of the creativeness and quality of the best nearby restaurants.

1 Market Sq. www3.hilton.com. © **800/561-8282** in Canada, 800/445-8667 in the U.S., or 506/693-8484. 197 units. C$139–C$239 double. Self-parking C$18 per night. Pets allowed. **Amenities:** Restaurant, concierge, fitness room, indoor pool, 24-hr. room service, Wi-Fi (free).

Homeport Historic Bed & Breakfast ★★   An architectural oddity, these two conjoined Italianate homes, built by a prominent shipbuilding family, sit high atop a rocky ridge north of Route 1, overlooking downtown and the harbor. Built around 1858, the Homeport is one of southern New Brunswick's best options for an overnight if you're a fan of old houses. Of the ten units, the Veranda Room is among the most spacious, with fine harbor views, walls decorated with steel engravings, floors of hand-cut pine, and locally made antique furniture. The Harbour Master Suite has a four-poster bed and small sitting room good for those traveling with a child or two. Communal breakfasts are served around a long heritage table in the dining room.

80 Douglas Ave. (take exit 121 or 123 to Main St.). www.homeport.nb.ca. © **888/678-7678** or 506/672-7255. 10 units. C$109–C$175 double and suite. Rates include full hot breakfast. Free parking. **Amenities:** Fridge (1 unit), kitchenette (1 unit), Wi-Fi (free).

MODERATE

Chipman Hill Suites ★★★   We were really pleased to find this unusual "hybrid" lodging, which mixes the helpful amenities of a long-stay apartment (useable kitchens or kitchenette, laundry facilities on site, sufficient room to spread out) with the character and looks of a classic inn. The handsomely restored and appointed suites are in a set of historic buildings on the hill at the edge of "uptown" Saint John, within steps of the big hotels, restaurants and shops. And they're so comfortable and reasonably priced, many are filled with long-term renters. Service, too, is unusually gracious and helpful. A find!

76 Union St. www.chipmanhill.com. © **877/859-3919** or 506/693-1171. 10 units. C$79–C$139 double. **Amenities:** Laundry, kitchenettes, Jacuzzis (in some units), Wi-Fi (free).

Earle of Leinster "Inn Style" Bed & Breakfast ★ Fronting the street, The Earl is a handsome Victorian row house in a working-class neighborhood not far from King's Square. It feels like a small European hotel. The Fitzgerald and Lord Edward rooms in the main house are the most historic, with high ceilings and regal furniture. Out back, the carriage house feels more like a dated motel, though a second-floor loft is quite spacious and some units resemble minisuites with microwave ovens and more elbow room. Bathrooms, while private, are on the small side.

96 Leinster St. www.earleofleinster.com. ℃ **506/650-3896.** 12 units. C$74–C$160 double. Rates include full hot breakfast. Free parking. **Amenities:** Wi-Fi (free).

Mahogany Manor Bed & Breakfast ★★ Not many years ago, this stately 1902 merchant's home had fallen into a desperate state. Chopped up as apartments and let go, it needed major renovations to restore it to its former glory. That renovation happened, and today, the common areas of the home look downright elegant, their shiny wood floor covered with handsome area rugs and well-curated antiques; guest rooms are as evocative, done up in bold colors or happy florals and furnished with mix of comfortable antiques and antique reproductions. Although it sits at the heart of Saint John's uptown area, around the corner from Queen's Square, this end of the street is quiet. One room on the first floor is wheelchair accessible. Owners Carl and Jim give a very warm welcome to everyone—gay or straight, old or young—and present a grand breakfast each morning.

220 Germain St. www.sjnow.com/mm. ℃ **800/796-7755** or 506/636-8000. 5 units. C$110–C$120 double. Rates include full hot breakfast. Free parking. **Amenities:** Wi-Fi (free).

INEXPENSIVE

Econo Lodge Inn & Suites ★ Great views from a hillside over fields and woodland to the Bay of Fundy are the nicest perk at this budget motel to the south of town. Rooms are simple, but very clean, and the suites are equipped with kitchenettes for basic food preparation—there's a microwave, but not stove. The highway passes by below, but it is far enough away that it won't interfere with sleep.

1441 Manawagonish Rd. www.choicehotels.ca. ℃ **800/4-CHOICE** [424-6423] or 506/635-8700. 30 units. C$79–C$179 double. Rates include breakfast buffet. Free parking. **Amenities:** Fridge and microwave (some units), Wi-Fi (free).

Rockwood Park Campground ★ If you pitch your tent at Rockwood Park, you'll literally be camping in town, just a short drive over the highway from the city center. The 201 sites sit between the highway and rail yard on one side and a wooded area with trails to lakes and access to a large playground, a zoo, and an 18-hole golf course on the other. Car and train noise can be uncomfortable, if you're in a tent, but in an RV, it's not as much of an issue. If you need hookups, you'll have to settle for a site in what resembles a parking lot, but the convenience of the location and proximity to wooded trails, lakes, and other attractions make it worth the stay.

142 Lake Dr. S. www.rockwoodparkcampground.com. ℃ **506/652-4050.** 201 sites. C$28–C$38 double. **Amenities:** Playground, walking trails.

Where to Eat

For lunch, don't overlook Saint John's **city market** (see p. 119)—grab a light meal and some fresh juice, then eat it at one of the onsite tables, in the alley atrium or right on King's Square.

As for dinner, frankly, Saint John has undergone such a sudden and extensive culinary revolution, it's impossible to highlight all the deserving eateries here. Below are a few absolute standouts, especially for showing off local, fresh ingredients, but any number of runners up are well worth a try. For example, there's **Billy's Seafood Company** ★ (www.billysseafood.com; 𝄐 888/933-3474 or 506/672-3474) right at the Saint John City Market for a lobster roll, fish and chips, or seafood chowder. At Rockwood Park, **Lily's Café** ★ (www.lilylake.ca/lilyscafe.html; 𝄐 **506/693-5033**) is a treat when you're on a relaxing lakeside outing, with the sun on the patio in summer and the cozy fireplace in cooler weather. The menu gives a nod to North America's first geopark with items like "Cambrian crustacean chowder" and "chocolate maple lava cake." **Port City Royal** ★ (www.portcityroyal.com; 𝄐 **506/631-3714**) serves food so fresh and local, the menu changes daily; the minimalist setting matches the tiny but outstanding menu items, like the lobster mint roll I devoured on my last visit. For delicious Latin American flavors a few steps off King Street, head for **Taco Pica** ★ (www.tacopica.ca; 𝄐 **506/633-8492**) which is both a restaurant and what the Guatemalan staff call a worker cooperative.

Other ethnic restaurants worth checking out include **Lemongrass** for Thai at 1 Market Sq. (www.lemongrasssaintjohn.com; 𝄐 **506/657-8424**), **Thandi Restaurant** for East Indian fare at 33 Canterbury St. (www.singhdining.com/thandi; 𝄐 **506/648-2377**), and **Kim's Korean Food** at 47 Charlotte St. (𝄐 **506/642-1040**).

East Coast Bistro ★★ CONTEMPORARY CANADIAN   The food and the drink menus here are both familiar and creative. By which I mean the chefs make smart use of local ingredients, but with a twist; the ubiquitous Fundy scallops are presented here seared with apple cider–braised pork belly and classic haddock is floated in a fennel cream broth and topped with pesto, to name just two examples. And not only is the food local, everything is made from scratch, from the bread to the aioli. This place is popular, so make a reservation at least the day before.

60 Prince William St. www.eastcoastbistro.com. 𝄐 **506/696-3278.** Main courses C$19–C$26. Mon 11am–3pm; Tues–Thurs 11am–9pm; Fri–Sat 11am–10pm.

Saint John Ale House ★★ GASTRO PUB   The name implies pub—indeed, the craft beer selection here is the best in the city, with brews from across the Maritimes, and the nightlife scene attracts crowds of young revelers. But the food is also surprisingly good. Chef Jesse Vergen is among the best in Canada and goes out of his way to find locally sourced foods you can't get anywhere else. His smoked mackerel and barbecued eel are packed with flavor. The country ham and certain cuts of beef are dry aged for several years before serving. There's an unforgettable rib-eye steak, but it'll set you back C$43; luckily, there's a lot more worth exploring on the menu for a lot less.

1 Market Sq. www.saintjohnalehouse.com. ℰ **506/667-2337.** Main courses C$17–C$43. Sun–Thurs 11am–11pm; Fri–Sat 11–12am.

Urban Deli and Italian by Night ★★★ ITALIAN DELI   If Saint John weren't flush with great restaurants, this one would be all you'd need, a lunch bar by day and a classic Italian restaurant by night. The 30 or so deli sandwiches here are inspired by the Reubens, clubs, and other bready treats of Montréal, New Orleans, and New York City. The Food Network's *You Gotta Eat Here* featured their muffuletta, and for good reason: The layers of smoked turkey, corned beef, and ham are melted together with aged white cheddar and the added zip of olive tapenade. Even the hungriest will have trouble finding the end of this 6-inch stack. Dining here in the evening usually involves a leisurely tour through five or six courses at a private table or the central communal table (hey, you'll meet new friends!). Cooking classes here are also quite popular.

69 King St. www.urbandeli.ca and www.italianbynight.com. ℰ **506/652-3354.** Reservations recommended. Urban Deli main courses C$9–C$14; open Mon–Sat 11:30am–3pm. Italian by Night main courses C$10–C$29; open Wed–Sat starting 5pm.

Saint John After Dark

The **Imperial Theatre** ★★ (ℰ **506/674-4100,** or 800/323-7469 from Maine and the Maritimes) on King's Square not only presents topnotch performances, it is, to quote the Toronto *Globe and Mail,* the "most beautifully restored theatre in Canada." It opened in 1913 and hosted such luminaries as Edgar Bergen, Al Jolson, and Walter Pidgeon (the latter a Saint John native). Driven out of business by movie houses, it served for a time as a Pentecostal church and was threatened with demolition. That's when concerned citizens stepped in. The Imperial reopened in 1994, and has since hosted a wide range of performances, from Broadway road shows to local theater productions and music concerts. See the theater's website at www.imperialtheatre.nb.ca for performance schedules.

If you're looking to catch a big-time recording act passing through town, head for **Harbour Station** ★ (www.harbourstation.ca; ℰ **506/657-1234,** or 800/267-2800 from Maine or the Maritimes) at 99 Station St. The acts here run the gamut—your stay in town might coincide with anyone from Mötley Crüe to WWE wrestling and pre-season hockey.

The rest of Saint John's nightlife revolves around the city's seemingly unending selection of **pubs,** most featuring live music and concentrated in the downtown district. Among the best is the brewpub **Big Tide Brewing** ★ at 47 Princess St. (ℰ **506/214-3311**), where you'll find an excellent selection of beers brewed on site; a complete, if uninspired, pub menu; and a lively, friendly atmosphere. For a quiet evening where the chance of meeting new friends is improved among fine wines and in an intimate setting, try **Happinez Wine Bar** ★ (ℰ **506/634-7340**) at 42 Princess St.

A Road Trip to the Fundy Trail Parkway

Fundy Trail Parkway ★★   Less than an hour's drive from downtown Saint John, the amazing Fundy Trail Parkway is almost unknown outside New Brunswick. This ambitious multi-use trail will eventually extend for 48km (30 miles) and link up with the Trans Canada Trail. As we go to press, the parkway consists of hiking and biking trails paralleled by about 11km (7 miles) of paved road for low speed automobile touring, showing off the spectacular local bays and cliffs. The trail is wide and easy to hike or bike, with wheelchair-accessible pullouts that have spectacular coastal views. Side trails lead to various beaches, some of which can only be reached at low tide. You can also catch a free shuttle (with paid admission) that stops at nine parking lots. The trail is expected to be completed in 2018. The interpretive center has interesting displays, but the real thing is much better. Ask about step-on guides, day adventures, box lunches (you'll find a number of picnic tables and water stations along the Parkway), and interpretive programs.

If you want to stay overnight on the trail, you can. The **Hearst Lodge ★** (© **866/386-3987**), built by the newspaper magnate, is a rustic cabin about a 1-hour (3km/2-mile) hike off the trail. Open in summer.

Serious hikers can pick up the Fundy Footpath, a challenging 41km (25-mile) wilderness trail; it crosses one of the last remaining coastal wilderness areas between Florida and Labrador. Plan for 4 days, with primitive campsites and challenging terrain. No permit is required; however, you must register and obtain maps at the Interpretive Centre in Big Salmon River (C$20, C$23 if mailed to you). You can hike in the off season but will have an additional 10km (6 miles) to get to the gate.

Rte. 111 (at St. Martins) 229 Main St. www.fundytrailparkway.com. © **866/386-3987** or 506/833-2019. Day pass C$6 adult, C$5 senior, C$4 child 12 and under, C$22 family. Mid-May to mid-Oct daily. Open Mid-May to mid-June and mid-Sept to mid-Oct 9am–5pm; mid-June to mid-Aug 8am–8pm; mid-Aug to mid-Sept 9am–7pm. Take Rte. 111 east; entrance is 10km (6¼ miles) east of St. Martins (watch for signs). Leashed dogs allowed.

FUNDY NATIONAL PARK ★★

The **Fundy Coast** (btw. Saint John and Alma) is for the most part wild, remote, and unpopulated. It's crisscrossed by few roads other than the Fundy Drive, making it difficult to explore deeply—unless you happen to have a boat with you, which I'm guessing you don't. The best access is at **Fundy National Park,** a gem of a destination that's hugely popular in summer with travelers of an outdoors bent. Because the town of Alma is a long walk or short drive over the bridge from the park entrance and one of the main campgrounds, amenities are immediately available. Families often settle in to a campground for a week or so, filling their days with activities in and around the park such as hiking, sea kayaking, biking, and splashing around in a seaside pool. There are also a slew of organized activities and interpretive programs. These include outdoor theater presentations and concerts, guided paddles, bike hikes, forays to catch and count eels, fossil walks, even photo safaris. For kids there are bedtime stories and evenings gathered around the campfire, or looking for night birds, bats, and bugs. Pick up a schedule as you enter the park.

Nearby there are also some lovely drives, plus an innovative adventure center within an hours' drive of the park at **Cape Enrage.** You can even vary your adventuring according to the weather: If a muffling fog moves in and smothers the coastline (and it might), head inland for a hike to a waterfall through lush forest. If it's a day of brilliant sunshine, on the other hand, venture along the rocky shores by foot, bike, or boat, and bring a camera.

Essentials

GETTING THERE   Route 114 runs through the center of Fundy National Park. If you're coming from the west, follow the prominent national park signs just east of **Sussex.** If you're coming from Prince Edward Island or Nova Scotia, head southward on Route 114 from Moncton.

VISITOR INFORMATION   The park's main **Visitor Centre** (© **506/887-6000**) is located just inside the **Alma** (eastern) entrance to the park. The stone building is open late June to early September from 8am to 9:45pm; mid-May to June and early September to mid-October 9am to 4:45pm. You can watch a video presentation, peruse a handful of exhibits on wildlife and tides, and shop at the nicely stocked nature bookstore.

The small town of **Alma** also maintains a seasonal information center at 8584 Main St. (© **506/887-6127**), open from late spring through September.

FEES   Park entry fees are charged from mid-May to mid-October. The fee is C$7.80 adults, C$6.80 seniors, C$3.90 children ages 6 to 16, and C$20 families. Seasonal and annual passes are also available.

Exploring Fundy National Park

Most national park activities are centered around the Alma (eastern) side of the park, where the park entrance has a manicured air, as if part of a landed estate. Here you'll find stone walls, well-tended lawns, and attractive landscaping, along with a golf course, amphitheater, lawn bowling, and tennis.

Also in this area is a **heated saltwater pool,** set near the bay with a sweeping ocean view. There's a lifeguard on duty, and it's a popular destination for families. The pool is open from late June through early September 11am to 6:45pm.

Kayaks and canoes can be rented at Bennett Lake from Sinc's Boats for C$11 an hour for a single kayak and C$17 for a double. Other available activities include geocaching, fishing, golfing, lawn bowling or tennis. Sea kayaking tours are a great way to get an up-close look at the marine environment here—but you want expert help when kayaking the world's highest tides. **FreshAir Adventure** (www.freshairadventure.com; © **800/545-0020** or 506/887-2249) at 16 Fundy View Dr. in Alma offers tours that range from 2 hours to several days. The half-day tours explore marsh and coastline (C$59–C$69 per person, C$209 family, including snack); the full-day adventure includes a hot meal and 6 hours of exploring the wild shores (C$95–C$117 per person, C$375 family). Ask about their multi-day tours.

Birders are always pleased to learn that some 250-plus species have been sighted within park boundaries, and almost half of them breed here. Notably, the endangered peregrine falcon has been reintroduced to the bay's steep cliffs.

HIKING

The park maintains miles and miles of scenic trails for hikers and walkers, with good signage and stairs where necessary. These range from a 20-minute loop to a 4-hour trek, and pass through varied terrain. The trails are arranged such that several can be linked into a full 48km (30-mile) backpacker's loop, dubbed the **Fundy Circuit ★★** (which typically requires 3–5 nights camping in the backcountry; pre-registration is required, so check in at the visitor center if you're serious about doing it).

Among the most accessible hikes is the **Dickson Falls ★★** with a short route of 1km (under a mile) and a slightly longer one of 1.5km (1 mile). Many steps lead to a mossy, cool ravine and a boardwalk up to the waterfall. Interpretive signs educate about the special ecosystem in and around the brook, like the flying squirrels that dig up mushrooms and spread the spores which in turn grow into new mushrooms that provide nutrients for the trees.

The **Third Vault Falls Trail ★★** is an 8km (5-mile), in-and-back hike that takes you to the park's highest waterfall (it's about 14m/46 ft. high). The trail is largely a flat stroll through leafy woodlands—until you begin a steady descent into a mossy gorge. You round a corner and the waterfall appears before you.

All the park's trails are covered in the trail guide you receive when you pay your entry fee at the gatehouse.

BIKING

The roads east of Alma offer superb bicycling terrain, at least if you get off busy Route 114 and are in good shape. Especially appealing is **Route 915 ★** from Riverside-Albert to Alma; combined with a detour to Cape Enrage, it makes for lovely touring. Along this scenic road you'll pedal through rolling farmland and scattered settlements, past vistas of salt marshes (as well as the wonderfully named Ha Ha Cemetery). The hills here look low, but they get steep in spots and require a serious grind at times. Route 915 runs for about 27km (17 miles) in all; the detour to Cape Enrage adds about 13km (8 miles).

Also note that the park allows **mountain biking** on seven trails: Marven Lake, Whitetail, Black Horse, Black Hole, Bennett Brook (to the top of Point Wolfe valley), East Branch (must take right-hand side trail only, and return from river on same path), and Maple Grove. These first two trails are *steep;* be prepared.

The nearest bike shop is 26km (16 miles) away at 5970 King St., Riverside-Albert. **Crooked Creek Adventures** (www.crookedcreekadventures.com; ✆ **506/882-2918**) rents mountain bikes for C$12 per hour, C$35 half day,

C$45 full day. They also rent boats and offer packages. Open mid-May to October 10am to 6pm, weekends only in spring and fall (closed Tues and Wed in summer).

CAMPING

The national park maintains three drive-in campgrounds and about 15 back-country sites. The two main campgrounds are near the Alma entrance. **Head-quarters Campground ★★** is within walking distance of Alma, the saltwater pool, and numerous other attractions. Since it is near the bay, this campground tends to be cool and subject to fogs. **Chignecto North Campground ★★** is higher on the hillside, sunnier, and warmer. You can hike down to Alma on an attractive hiking trail in 1 to 2 hours. Both campgrounds have hookups for RVs, flush toilets, and showers, and both can be reserved in advance online (www.pccamping.ca; © **877/737-3783**); sites cost C$16 to C$115 per night, depending on services offered; the higher-end fees are for the rentals of yurts and oTENTiks, rustic fixed accommodations with bunks, stoves, and solar lights. Sites 1 and 2 have the best views. Rates drop in the shoulder seasons.

The **Point Wolfe** and **Wolfe Lake** campgrounds lack RV hookups and are slightly more primitive, but they are the preferred destinations for campers seeking a quieter camping experience. Rates at Point Wolfe, where showers and flush toilets are available, are about C$25 and it too can be reserved online via Canada's national parks campground website at www.pccamping.ca. Wolfe Lake lacks showers and has only pit toilets—thus a night there costs only about C$16. Call the park directly to reserve.

Backcountry sites are scattered throughout the park, with only one located directly on the coast (at the confluence of the coast and Goose River). Ask at the visitor centers for more information or to reserve a site (mandatory). Back-country camping fees are about C$10 per person per night.

Before leaving the park, check the tide tables. Your visits to the next two sites are best made at low tide, or ideally, arrive at high tide and stay until it is totally out—or vice versa so you can experience both.

Road Trip to Cape Enrage ★★

Cape Enrage is a blustery and bold cape that juts out into Chignecto Bay. It costs C$5 for adults, C$4.50 seniors and, C$4 children 5 to 17 and students to enter the grounds and cluster of buildings at the end. Children under 5 admitted free. There you'll find very friendly staff and volunteers, lots of places to explore and walk (including the sea bottom next to Fossil Beach when the 15m/50-ft. tides are out), great views from platforms, a gift shop, and a top-notch restaurant. The Cape Enrage Interpretive Centre is open from mid-May to mid-October.

Cape Enrage Adventures ★   Cape Enrage Adventures traces its roots to 1993, when a group of high school teachers and students from Moncton decided to arrest the decay of the cape's historic lighthouse, which had been abandoned a few years earlier. They put together a plan to restore the light and keeper's quarters and establish an adventure center. And it worked. Today, with the help of experts in rock climbing, rappelling, and local history, you can indulge in a day of adventure; appointments are needed for rappelling and rock climbing. Part of what makes the program so notable is its flexibility. You can pick and choose from day adventures, which are scheduled throughout the summer, as though from a menu. Prices vary; you might pay about C$90 per person for a 2-hour rock-climbing or rappelling workshop. There's zip-lining at a cost of about C$45 for two runs. They have packages and group discounts. For more information about the program, contact **Cape Enrage Adventures** (www.capenrage.ca; ℂ **888/423-5454** or 506/887-2273).

The **Cape House Restaurant** ★★★ (ℂ **506/887-2275**) boasts a surprisingly upscale menu for this remote a location. A trio of lobster tacos (topped with caviar and candied lemon peel!) is artistically presented and the flavors are perfectly balanced. And that's just an appetizer. The mains are just as remarkable, particularly the flash-seared scallops paired with hand-rolled honey gnocchi flavored with roasted garlic and shaved Gouda. For all this, prices are surprisingly affordable. And you get entertainment with your meal: Out the window or from the deck, you may see zip-liners speeding by.

650 Cape Enrage Rd. www.capeenrage.ca. ℂ **506/887-2275.** Restaurant main courses C$16–C$27. Daily mid-May to mid-June 10am–5pm; mid-June to mid-Aug 11am–8pm; mid-Aug to early Sept 10am–6pm; early Sept to mid-Oct 1am–5pm.

Road Trip to the Hopewell Rocks

There's no better place in Canada to witness the extraordinary power of ocean tides than at the **Hopewell Rocks** ★★★ (www.thehopewellrocks.ca; ℂ **877/734-3429**), located about 40km (25 miles) northeast of Fundy National Park on Route 114. Think of it as a natural sculpture garden. At low tide (the best time to visit), a couple dozen eroded columns as high as 15m (50 ft.) stand on the ocean floor like Easter Island statues, and you can walk right out among them. (They're sometimes called the "flowerpots," on account of the trees and plants that still flourish on the narrowing summits.) A few hours later, the huge Bay of Fundy tide creeps half way up these quirky formations. As the shuttle driver will tell you, everyone comes away smiling.

The drive from Alma to Hopewell is one of the most scenic in New Brunswick, with low mountains, pastures, marshes, lovely little villages, covered bridges, and the Bay of Fundy. When you arrive, park at the visitor center and restaurant. Sign up for a tour or just walk down to the shore. (There's also a shuttle service that runs from the interpretive center to the rocks for C$2.) Signboards fill you in on the natural history of the rocks. If you've come at low tide, you can descend the steel staircase to the sea floor and admire these wondrous free-standing rock sculptures, chiseled by waves and tides. Even the **visitor center** is a pleasant place to spend some time. It not only has intriguing exhibits (look for the satellite photos of the area, and a time-lapse video of the tides) but the cafeteria-style restaurant has terrific views from its floor-to-ceiling windows and serves simple food. The park charges an entry fee of C$9 adults, C$7.75 students and seniors, C$6.75 children ages 5 to 18, and C$24 families. It's open daily mid-May to mid-June, 9am to 5pm, then 8am to 8pm from mid-June until mid-August (mid-Aug to early Sept 9am to 7pm), and from 9am to 5pm from September until it closes in mid-October. Note that the site can get crowded at peak times, which is understandable given its uniqueness and beauty, but that might not jive with your idea of peace and quiet. If you arrive at the top half of the tide, consider a sea-kayak tour around the islands and caves. **Baymount Outdoor Adventures ★** (www.baymount adventures.com; ℂ **877/601-2660** or 506/734-2660) runs 90-minute kayak tours of Hopewell Rocks from June through early September for C$59 per adult, C$49 per child, or C$199 per family. A "Walk on the Ocean Floor" tour provides before- and after-the-tide photo-ops. Caving tours of nearby caverns are also offered by this family outfit; contact them for details.

Where to Stay

The village of Alma just across the river has all the services you'll need for a stay in the park and day trips to Cape Enrage and Hopewell Rocks. There's a grocery store, gas station, post office, and even the **Tipsy Tails Bar & Grill ★** (ℂ **506/887-2190**) with a patio overlooking the wharf and bay. It's open until 10pm. Check out the wharf at low tide to see fishing boats resting on the ocean floor. The short main drag is lined with accommodations and restaurants. Most of the latter serve up standard seafood preparations.

Broadleaf Guest Ranch ★★ The two-bedroom cottages at this homey, family-operated ranch are a great choice for families or couples traveling together, particularly those with an interest in horses: The ranch offers rides of varying duration; cattle checks; even some basic spa packages. (Think of it as a dude ranch without the snakes.) Cottages here sport full kitchens, small sitting areas with gas stoves, homey knotty pine walls, and lovely sweeping views of the 607-hectare (1,500-acre) ranch property and bay. While un-fancy, staying here is like sinking into a favorite chair: comforting. If you ever want to travel with a very large group, there's a luxury chalet that sleeps up to 26

Mary's Point

On your way to Hopewell Rocks, take the loop road around Mary's Point. The coastal nature preserves are a stopover for migrating sea birds whose flight displays can be spectacular. At 255 Mary's Point Rd., the widow of Lars Larsen, one of Canada's premier wildlife artists, continues to operate **Studio on the Marsh** (www.studioonthemarsh.com; ℂ **506/882-2917**). Larsen's work and that of other fine artists is available at this lovely little gallery.

people at $1,000 a night. Home-cooking is dished up in a large, cafeteria-style dining area.

5526 Rte. 114, Hopewell Hill. www.broadleafranch.com. ℭ **800/226-5405** or 506/882-2349. Fax 506/882-2075. 7 units. Cottages C$150–C$200. Pets welcome for an extra C$25 a night. Packages available. **Amenities:** Restaurant, spa, horseback riding, watersports equipment, kitchenette (some units), no phone, Wi-Fi (free in office or restaurant).

Fundy Highlands Inn and Chalets ★

It seems odd to find an independently run motel, inn, and cottages complex situated inside a National Park, but they were here first. Not far from the park's own campgrounds, you'll find 24 open-concept cottages with pine interiors, kitchenettes, and roomy decks with spectacular views. The grounds are suitably lovely, with rose gardens and grand views from a hillside. If the chalets are all taken, ask about the adjacent **Fundy Park Motel ★** with 20 very basic rooms (they only have bunkbeds!) for C$75 to C$130 each; all of the motel rooms have kitchenettes, and second-floor rooms have a veranda.

8714 Rte. 114, Fundy National Park. www.fundyhighlandchalets.com. ℭ **888/883-8639** or 506/887-2930. 24 units. Cottages C$75–C$130. Packages available. **Amenities:** Playground, kitchenette, Wi-Fi (free).

Parkland Village Inn ★

You can't get any closer to the ocean in Alma than the grounds of the Parkland, where beach, wharf, and town are all steps away. It's an old-fashioned seaside hotel with updated rooms and suites with huge windows to enjoy views of either the bay or of the hills. Some have balconies while others have access to a veranda. You can easily walk to the park from here. A dining room, the **Tides ★** specializes in seafood and enjoys the same views of wharf, beach, and Bay of Fundy as the rooms.

8601 Main St. (Rte. 114), Alma, www.parklandvillageinn.com. ℭ **866/668-4337** or 506/887-2313. 10 rooms, 2 suites. C$95–C$120 double; C$100–C$160 suites. Open May–Oct. **Amenities:** Restaurant, parking, no phone, Wi-Fi (free).

Vista Ridge ★

Simple cabins are set amid birch and pines very near the park's eastern entrance, on a pretty little site overlooking a beach and the headlands of the park. The cottages are updated with satellite televisions, electric fireplaces, and full kitchens in all units. These three-bedroom cottages are small and basically furnished, but they do have lots of exposed wood and good kitchen appliances; bring food to prepare your own meals. There's an RV campground on-site, too—call the owners for more details if you're seeking a scenic place to park a big rig.

41 Foster Rd., Alma. www.fundyparkchalets.com. ℭ **877/887-2808** or 506/887-2808. 29 cabins. C$125 cabin. Pets accepted (C$10 per pet). **Amenities:** Full kitchen, no phone, no Wi-Fi.

Where to Eat

Amid the scattering of seafood takeout and lobster shops in and around the park, one good pick is **Butland's ★** (www.fundylobster.com; ℭ **506/887-2190**) at 8607 Main St. in Alma beside the town wharf. They sell locally caught crustaceans, scallops, and smoked salmon you can cook yourself. The most upbeat of the seafood eateries is the beachside eat in/takeout seafood shack at called **Alma Lobster Shop** ★ at 36 Shore Lane (www.thankfultoo.com/alma; ✆ **506/887-1987**), where you can find a good lobster roll. There's also a bakery in Alma, **Kelly's Bake Shop** ★ at 8587 Main St. (✆ **506/887-2460**). They serve big, locally famous sticky buns. My favorite restaurant in Alma is **An Octopus' Garden Café** ★ at 8561 Main St. (✆ **506/887-1020**) just beyond the cluster of other restaurants. The house-made pasta here is prepared in a variety of classic styles. There's good craft beer on tap and a corner of the cafe is set up for musicians who perform here regularly.

MONCTON

Moncton makes a claim that it's the crossroads of the Maritimes, and it hasn't been bashful about using this lucky geographic position to promote itself as a regional business hub. As a result, the majority of downtown's hotels and restaurants here cater to people in suits, rather than leisure travelers, at least on the weekdays. But there is some life here; take a walk down Main Street from Foundry Street as far as Assomption Boulevard and you'll see a number of nightlife and dining spots. And if you're travelling with kids, Moncton offers a number of child-oriented amusements. A concentration of family-friendly attractions, including **Magnetic Hill** ★ (see "Exploring Moncton," below), offer entertaining—if somewhat pricey and over-hyped—ways to fill an idle afternoon.

Essentials

GETTING THERE Moncton is at the crossroads of several major routes through New Brunswick, including Route 2 (the Trans-Canada Hwy.) and Route 15.

Moncton's small **international airport** (www.gmia.ca) on Aviation Avenue in Dieppe, is about 11km (7 miles, or 10 min.) from downtown Moncton via Route 132; you basically head straight out Main Street (which becomes Champlain St.) to Dieppe and follow the airport signs. (From the airport, take Rue Champlain straight into town.) **Air Canada** (www.aircanada.com; ✆ **888/247-2262**) has long served the city, and Canadian carrier **WestJet** (www.westjet.com; ✆ **888/937-8538**) now also connects Moncton with Toronto and other points in Canada. **Porter Airlines** (www.flyporter.com; ✆ **888/619-8622**) flies to and from Toronto via Ottawa, Ontario daily. At last count, there were four international-chain car rental agencies at the airport.

The **VIA Rail** (www.viarail.com; ✆ **888/842-7245**) *Ocean* train from Montréal to Halifax stops in Moncton 3 days a week. Moncton's station is located off Main Street, behind Highfield Square.

VISITOR INFORMATION There's a downtown visitor information center located centrally in **Bore Park,** just off Main Street at 10 Bendview Court (www.tourism.moncton.ca; ✆ **800/363-4558** or 506/853-3540), open daily from mid-May through September.

Exploring Moncton

Moncton's downtown is easily explored on foot—if you can find parking. (Look for lots a block just north and south of Main St.) **Downtown Moncton, Inc.** publishes a nicely designed "Historic Walking Tour" brochure that touches upon some of the most significant buildings; ask for it at the visitor center. They have also developed some really good walking trails and have more than 2,000 acres of parkland for outdoor lovers. The most active stretch of Main Street is the section between City Hall and the train underpass: an accumulation of cafes, hotels, restaurants and shops. On Saturdays, check out the nice farmers' market just 1 block off Main. For nightlife, head for Robinson Street just off Main, where bars and nightclubs rub shoulders. The 800-seat, 1920s-vaudeville-era **Capitol Theatre** ★★ (www.capitol.nb.ca; ℂ **506/856-4379**) is right here too at 811 Main St. for cultural entertainment. There's also quite a mix of architectural styles here, the earliest examples of which testify to Moncton's former prosperity and prominence as a regional center of commerce. **Exploring by bike** is a good idea, especially if you go pedaling along **Riverfront Park** or through the 121 hectares (300 acres) of popular **Centennial Park.** Centennial Park is also home to **Treego** ★ (www. treegomoncton.com; ℂ **877/707-4646**) aerial adventure courses designed for use by all ages (C$33 adults, C$28 ages 16 and under).

Magic Mountain Water Park ★   At Atlantic Canada's largest water park, adjacent to novelty attraction Magnetic Hill (see below), kids can entertain themselves for hours. While the big kids zoom down the giant Kamikaze, where daredevils can reach speeds of up to 60kmph (40 mph), more timid water lovers will enjoy the wave pools and eight tamer slides. Really little kids will like the Splashpad, a more passive attraction that sprays water in four directions. There's also mini-golf on site.

2875 Mountain Rd. (Trans-Canada Hwy., exit 488). www.magicmountain.ca.ℂ **506/857-9283.** Admission C$29 adults full day, C$16–C$22 children under 4 ft. tall (children under age 3 free), C$10 seniors over 60, C$97 families. Afternoon tickets (enter after 3pm) about 30% lower. July to late Aug daily 10am–7pm; mid-June to end of June and late Aug to early Sept daily 10am–6pm.

Magnetic Hill ★   Locals discovered in the 19th century that any object capable of rolling, like wagons and barrels, seemed to defy the law of gravity on this little stretch of road by rolling uphill. When cars came along, folks would cut the engine at the bottom of a short stretch of downhill and gasp in amazement as they seemed to roll uphill. By the 1950s, this optical illusion was such an attraction, it boasted the biggest souvenir shop in the Maritimes. Today it's not much more than a dated novelty, though if there are young children in the car, they'll enjoy the short-lived mystery of rolling uphill backward in the car. Adjacent attractions will hold their interest longer. Wharf Village (souvenir shops and snack bars designed to look like a seaside village); a popular zoo, video arcades, driving ranges, and the like, as well as the Magic Mountain water park (see above). Despite—maybe because of—its

Saint John is located at the mouth of the river that was known as the "road to Canada." It dissects the province north to the French-speaking Republic of Madawaska, a region near the Québec border with a unique heritage, customs, and dialect. The St. John River Heritage Corridor has four regions: Lower River Passage, Capital, River Valley, and Madawaska. If you enjoy exploring roads less traveled, without completely entering the wilderness, consider exploring this great river and the communities that surround it. I recommend, especially, the often-overlooked area north of Fredericton. The road to **Edmundston** takes you past several worthwhile stops: **Kings Landing Heritage Village** (see p. 144); the town of **Nakawic,** home to the world's largest

axe; **Hartland,** home of the world's longest covered bridge and the **Covered Bridge Potato Chips** factory—you'll find their bags of chips in stores across the region—beside the Trans-Canada Highway where you can season your own freshly cooked chips; **Florenceville-Bristol,** French Fry Capital of the World with a natty potato museum; **Grand Falls,** with its gorge and waterfall, where you can ride the zip line for a bird's-eye view, hike and climb to the "Wells in the Rocks," or take a lazy ride on a pontoon boat. Edmundston itself has a fine botanical garden. This region surrounded by the Appalachian Mountains is the heart of Madawaska. For other activities in the Heritage Corridor, read on.

5

NEW BRUNSWICK | Moncton

utter cheesiness, the complex of activities is a decent stop for families. It's located in Moncton's northwest outskirts.

Mountain Rd. (Trans-Canada Hwy., exit 488). © **506/389-5980.** Admission Magnetic Hill C$5 per car, free if the gate is open and unstaffed; Magnetic Hill Zoo C$15 adults, C$13 seniors and children 12–18, C$11 children 4–11, C$44 families in summer, cheaper off season. Mid-June to mid-Sept daily 9am–7pm; hours vary in spring and fall—check the website or call. Closed Jan–Apr.

Where to Stay

In addition to the properties listed below, a surplus of inexpensive and mid-priced chain hotels have set up shop near the complex of services around Magnetic Hill along Mountain Road. They include the **Comfort Inn ★** 2495 Mountain Rd. (© **800/228-5150** or 506/384-3175); **Country Inn & Suites ★** 2475 Mountain Rd. (© **800/596-2375** or 506/852-7000); and **Holiday Inn Express ★** also just off the exit at 2515 Mountain Rd. (© **506/384-1050**). Expect a low of just under C$100 to a high just over C$200, though they tend toward the lower end of that range. To get here from the Trans-Canada Highway, take exit 450.

Delta Beauséjour ★★   In many ways, the Delta is the center of Moncton. Not only is it at the very heart of the busy dining and nightlife area, it also opens onto one of the few green spaces on Main Street. Comfortable rooms are appointed in usual business-hotel style; a third-floor indoor pool offers year-round swimming, and a pleasant outdoor deck overlooks the distant marshes of the Petitcodiac River. Riverfront Park, behind the hotel, is a great place for a run or leisurely stroll. In addition to the elegant **Windjammer** ★★★ restaurant (dinner only; see below), the hotel also has **Triiio** (a restaurant/lounge serving three meals a day), a cafeteria space open all day, and a lounge on the eighth floor.

750 Main St. www.deltahotels.com. © **888/351-7666** or 506/854-4344. 310 A/C units. C$119–C$399 double. Rates include continental breakfast. **Amenities:** 3 restaurants, bar, babysitting, fitness center, indoor heated pool, 24-hr. room service, Wi-Fi (free).

Midtown Motel and Suites ★   For an inexpensive, clean alternative handy to downtown, this tidy little property is the answer. It's a motel, so don't expect luxury, but it's comfortable and spotlessly clean, with an attentive staff. You might consider the second floor to avoid the noise in first-floor rooms from people walking above. Suites include fully equipped kitchens, Jacuzzi tubs, and king-size beds. Others have kitchenettes, and all come with air-conditioning.

61 Weldon St. www.midtownms.ca. © **800/463-1999** or 506/388-5000. 22 A/C units. C$80–C$153. Free parking. **Amenities:** Kitchens or kitchenettes, on-site laundry, Wi-Fi (free).

Residence Inn by Marriott ★★   From studios to two-bedroom suites, many of the rooms in this new downtown hotel across the street from City Hall come with fully equipped kitchenettes. While the rates are higher than in other nearby hotels, there are savings to be had if you like to cook for yourself. A hot breakfast is included in the room rate. The rooms are modern with the usual amenities of a big chain hotel. There's a pool with a hot tub and a fitness room.

600 Main St. www.marriott.com. © **506/854-7100**. 133 A/C units. C$149–C$450. **Amenities:** Indoor pool, whirlpool, fitness room, free hot breakfast, kitchenettes in suites, Wi-Fi (free).

Where to Eat

As with most cities in the Maritimes, Moncton is in the middle of a culinary renaissance. Virtually all the storefronts along Main Street on either side of the Delta Beauséjour Hotel are eateries of some type. Others can be found within a block of the main drag, along with a few on St. George Street. Luckily for the traveler, it's hard to find one that will disappoint. From ethnic to pub fare, from lunch counters to night spots, the variety is impressive. Here are the standouts.

Calactus ★★ VEGETARIAN BISTRO   Make a reservation if you plan to dine at this popular local cafe; even on a weekday evening, the aromas from the kitchen wafting down St. George Street pull in an overflow crowd. The menu is a mix of Mexican, Italian, Mediterranean, and Indian dishes, all made with a flavor-first approach.

125 Church St. at St. George St. www.calactus.ca. © **506/388-4833.** Mains C$11–C$17. Daily 11am–10pm.

Tide and Boar Bistro ★★ GASTROPUB   Located at the very heart of downtown, the Tide and Boar is a hybrid of bistro and pub with an emphasis on homemade. You'll find in-house versions of everything from bacon to

A road trip TO SACKVILLE

On a road trip southeast of Moncton to Sackville and the Nova Scotia border, you'll see some mighty beautiful country. Take Route 106 (country) or Route 2 (multilane) south 28km (18 miles) from Moncton to Memramcook. The **Lefebvre National Historic Site** ★ (www.pc.gc.ca/lhn-nhs/nb/lefebvre/index.aspx; 🕾 **506/758-9808**) will interest history buffs, especially those keen on understanding the rebirth of l'Acadie after the great expulsion of 1755. Continue on 106 through Dorchester and into Sackville, a small university town with a happy vibe. You are in a fabulous area for birdwatching. In August, a diversion on Route 935 to **Johnson's Mills** could reward with tens of thousands of migrating sandpipers who stop here to feed during summer migration. The **Johnson's Mills Shorebird Reserve Interpretive Centre** ★★ (🕾 **506/379-6347**) is open in July and August.

Return to Sackville and park at the **Visitor Information Centre** (www.sackville.com; 🕾 **506/364-4967**) at the end of Mallard Drive. From there, you can stroll the 55-acre **Sackville Waterfowl Park** ★★ into town where you can enjoy a nice lunch at any of several good cafes around the intersection of Main and Bridge Streets including **Cranewood Bakery** ★ ((🕾 **506/939-3133**), **Pickles European Deli** ★ (🕾 **506/939-3354**), **Black Duck Café** ★ ((🕾 **506/536-8084**) and **Bridge Street Café** ★ ((🕾 **506/536-4428**). Boardwalks take you through a gorgeous birch grove out over the wetlands of the waterfowl park where more than 150 species of birds and about 200 species of plants have been recorded. Guided tours are available May to August, or take a self-guided tour with the information available at the Visitor Information Centre. Just 10 minutes down Route 2, you'll find the **Fortress Beausejour-Fort Cumberland National Historic Site** ★★ at 111 Fort Beausejour Rd. in Aulac (www.pc.gc.ca/lhn-nhs/nb/beausejour/index.aspx; 🕾 **506/364-5080**). Kids will love clambering over the grassy ramparts of the fort that played a pivotal role in the struggle for North America. Adults may be more interested in the site's museum (open July and Aug) or the spectacular view of the head of Fundy Bay. As the crow flies, you are about 60km (37 miles) from Moncton, so your day isn't spent driving, but rather exploring and enjoying.

ketchup. Their smoker runs year-round out back, and they are as popular at breakfast as at dinner. "The Burger" says everything you need to know about this affordable, casual eatery. House-ground local beef brisket chuck is served with bacon on a brioche bun with tomato, pickle, caramelized onion, and aged cheddar for $15.

700 Main St. www.tideandboar.com. 🕾 **506/857-9118.** Lunch C$10–C$19; dinner C$13–C$22. Mon–Wed 11am–12am; Thurs–Fri 11am–2am; Sun 12pm–12am.

The Windjammer ★★★ STEAK AND SEAFOOD The Windjammer is a Canadian classic, an unlikely slice of authentic France in a small Maritime city. Chef Stefan Müller and his team have served VIPs ranging from the Queen of England to visiting celebrities. Its signature is the "100 Mile Table," offering four courses of local seasonal ingredients, including in-season tomatoes and herbs from the rooftop garden where bees produce honey. The meal might include half a dozen of New Brunswick's finest oysters, mildly briny and delicately sweet Beau Soleil; and such star mains as the finest cuts of Blue Dot PEI beef and Australian Wagyu, bison, New Zealand rack of lamb or Atlantic lobster. Ask to be assigned to the waiter Frederick's table—one of the most charming men in the Maritimes (think: Maurice Chevalier)

750 Main St. (inside the Delta Beauséjour). www.windjammermoncton.com. ⓒ **506/877-7137.** Reservations recommended. Main courses C$22–C$140. Tues–Sat 5:30–10pm.

FREDERICTON

In contrast to New Brunswick's coastal working-class cities—Saint John and Miramichi—and its commercial center in and around Moncton, the riverside capital of Fredericton is home to both government and university communities. Nestled along the shores of the mighty St. John River, this small city feels more like a big town. The handsome heritage buildings, broad streets, and wide sidewalks give the city an airy, clean feeling.

Lower Fredericton, along the river, is considered the downtown area, and is the most pleasing for visitors with its mix of heritage and modern buildings, restaurants, unique shops, galleries, nightlife and major festivals. The main artery—where you'll find the bulk of the attractions and restaurants—is **Queen Street,** which parallels the river. This part of the city is compact and easily walkable. The **Green,** a pathway that follows the river, protects the river's edge from development and provides a great place for walkers and bicyclists. If your passions include history—especially the history of British settlements in North America—you'll find Fredericton absorbing.

Up the hill from downtown, away from the river, a charming area ruled over by the Georgian-style university, parks, and residential areas serves as a buffer zone between the downtown and the hustle and bustle at the top of the hills, near the main highways, where shopping malls, motels, small industry, and services are found.

Essentials

GETTING THERE   Located beside the Trans-Canada Highway, Route 2, linking the Maritimes to the rest of Canada, Fredericton is 265km (165 miles) from Edmundston, to the northwest, near the Québec border. From Moncton, take the Trans-Canada Highway north 177km (110 miles). From Saint John to the south, it's about 112km (70 miles) via Route 7. From the U.S.-Canadian border at Houlton, Maine, it's about the same distance: Take Route 95 to Woodstock, New Brunswick, then turn onto the Trans-Canada Highway and follow it east for an hour. Look for signs directing you downtown. (From the west, follow Woodstock Road, which tracks along the river. From Saint John, look for Route 7 to Regent Street, and then turn right down the hill.)

Fredericton International Airport   (www.frederictonairport.ca; ⓒ **506/460-0920**), coded YFC, is located 10 minutes southeast of downtown on Route 102 and is served by cab and rental-car companies. Several airlines

Fredericton

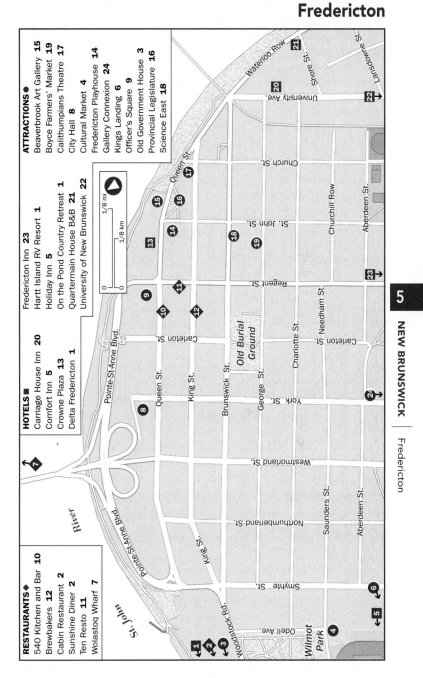

RESTAURANTS◆

540 Kitchen and Bar **10**
Brewbakers **12**
Cabin Restaurant **2**
Sunshine Diner **2**
Ten Resto **11**
Wolastoq Wharf **7**

HOTELS■

Carriage House Inn **20**
Comfort Inn **5**
Crowne Plaza **13**
Delta Fredericton **1**

Fredericton Inn **23**
Hartt Island RV Resort **1**
Holiday Inn **5**
On the Pond Country Retreat **1**
Quartermain House B&B **21**
University of New Brunswick **22**

ATTRACTIONS●

Beaverbrook Art Gallery **15**
Boyce Farmers' Market **19**
Calithumpians Theatre **17**
City Hall **8**
Cultural Market **4**
Fredericton Playhouse **14**
Gallery Connexion **24**
Kings Landing **6**
Officer's Square **9**
Old Government House **3**
Provincial Legislature **16**
Science East **18**

connect Fredericton to Canadian and American hubs. See the "By Air" section at the beginning of this chapter for details and contact information.

VISITOR INFORMATION   Fredericton maintains two visitor information centers. There's one in **City Hall** at 397 Queen St. (© **506/460-2129**), open May through October; and the second is at **King's Landing** (© **506/460-2191**), at 5804 Rte. 102 (opened on weekends). When at the City Hall Visitor Centre, ask for a visitor parking pass, which allows visitors from outside the province to park free at city lots and meters in town for 3 days without penalty. Fredericton's tourism office is open year-round at 11 Carleton St. You can also request travel information in advance by visiting the city's website, including a detailed map of the downtown, at www.tourismfredericton.ca or by calling © **888/888-4768** or 506/460-2129.

Exploring Fredericton

The free *Fredericton Visitor Guide,* available at the information centers, includes a **walking tour** of the downtown area and several driving tours.

City Hall ★, at 397 Queen St., is an elaborate Victorian building with a prominent brick tower and a 2.5m (8-ft.) clock dial. Declared a National Historic Site in 1984, the second-floor City Council Chamber occupies what used to be Fredericton's opera house until the 1940s. The basement served as a market until 1951. Tapestries adorning the **visitor's gallery** tell the town's history. Learn about these tapestries—and the rest of the building—during free tours, offered twice daily from mid-May through mid-October (both in English and French). Sentry duty changes on the hour at City Hall all summer. Contact the tourism office (© **506/460-2129**) to arrange a tour.

The **Historic Garrison District ★**, a National Historic Site sits behind a wrought iron-and-stone fence and covers a 2-block area between Queen Street and the river. The many activities here are free. Check out a visitor center or www.historicgarrisondistrict.ca to see what's happening, or just drop by.

Officers' Square ★ on Queen Street between Carleton and Regent streets is a handsome city park now, but in 1785 it was the center of the city's military activity; it was chiefly used for drills, first as part of the British garrison and then, until 1914, by the Canadian Army. Today, ceremonies take place in July and August daily at 11am and 4pm. Festivals and events—live music, theatre, croquet matches, and free guided walks also take place on these grounds. Visit www.tourismfredericton.ca for a full schedule. That handsome colonnaded stone building facing the parade grounds is the former officers' quarters.

In the center of the square, there's a prominent statue of a robed Lord Beaverbrook. It's a name you hear a lot in Fredericton—a street, a museum, and a hotel also bear his name—though it wasn't actually his name; he was born Max Aitken in Newcastle, New Brunswick. Aitken amassed a fortune, primarily in publishing, during his life and was made a lord in Britain in 1917, using the name of a stream near Newcastle where he had fished as a boy. Aitken later donated an art collection and a modern building to house it in, the **Beaverbrook Art Gallery ★★** (see p. 143).

Two blocks upriver from Officers' Square are the Soldiers' Barracks, housed in a similarly grand stone building. There's a shop with the work of local artists and crafters. Check your watch against a sundial high on the end of the barracks, a replica of the original timepiece. A small exhibit explains the life of enlisted men during the 18th century.

Fredericton is well noted for its distinctive architecture, especially its neighborhoods of fine Victorian and Queen Anne residences. Particularly attractive is **Waterloo Row ★**, a group of privately owned historic homes just south of the downtown area. Follow the riverbank south (near the University of New Brunswick).

One entertaining and enlightening way to learn about the city's history is to sign up for a walking tour with the **Calithumpians Theatre Company ★**, the troupe also responsible for theatre performances in Officers' Square. Costumed guides offer free tours in July and August, pointing out highlights with anecdotes and dramatic tales. Recommended is the nighttime "Haunted Hike" tour, done by lantern light, which runs 6 nights each week (no Sun tours). The tour takes about 2 hours and costs C$14 for adults, C$9 for children under 12; meet at the Coach House at the corner of Church and Queen streets (behind Gallery 78). Visit the website www.calithumpians.com or call the theater company at ✆ **506/457-1975** for more information.

If you're in town on a Saturday, head over to the **Boyce Farmers' Market ★★** (www.frederictonfarmersmarket.ca; ✆ **506/451-1815**) at 665 George St. (corner of Regent St.)—it's adjacent to **Science East** (see p. 144). This award-winning market, open 6am to 1pm, has existed here in one form or another since the late 18th century (although the current building was constructed in the 1950s and later expanded). About 250 indoor and outdoor vendors—butchers, bakers, even some candlestick makers—still hawk everything from fresh produce to crafts, pastries, international cuisine, and artisanal meats and cheeses, just as they always have done. *Harrowsmith* magazine once selected this market as one of the top farmers' markets in Canada. It's well worth a visit on a Saturday morning. If you can tear yourself away, also check out the **Cultural Market ★** (www.theculturalmarket.ca; ✆ **506/457-1177**) at 28 Saunders St. open Saturdays 8am to 5pm where you'll find about 40 vendors and a building full of the irresistible aromas of international home cooking like Filipino, Pakistani, and Latin, along with goods, services, crafts, and delicacies.

Also of note are the events hosted by the local artists' co-op **Gallery Connexion ★** (www.galleryconnexion.ca; ✆ **506/454-1433**) at 732 Charlotte St. The contemporary art collective presents talks, video artworks, exhibitions, musical performances, and other events. Check the website.

For a week every September, the **Harvest Jazz and Blues Festival ★★★** (www.harvestjazzandblues.com; ✆ **800/622-5837** or 506/454-2583) fills every possible venue with music and spills into the streets. The likes of Dr. John, Levon Helm, Taj Mahal, and Gregg Allman have played here.

Outdoor Pursuits

Fredericton's trail system for walkers and bikers includes 88km (55 miles) of trails. The centerpiece is undeniably the **South Riverfront ★**, a 5km (3-mile) path that follows the river past the Delta hotel (see "Where to Stay," p. 146) to near the Princess Margaret Bridge. It's a lovely walk, and passes by most of the city's key sightseeing points: the **Old Government House ★** (see below), the downtown area, and open parklands near Waterloo Row.

Connecting with this trail, a well-used pedestrian bridge crosses the St. John River using an abandoned railroad trestle just east of downtown. From this vantage point, you get superb views of downtown and the surrounding river valley. If you continue, the **Nashwaak** follows an abandoned rail bed along the attractive Nashwaak River; after about 4km (2½ miles), you can cross the river at Bridge Street and loop back to the pedestrian rail bridge via the 5km (3-mile) **Gibson Trail.**

A number of other trails link up to this network, as well. A free trail guide is available at the information centers.

Bikes may be rented at **Savage's Bicycle Center** (www.sbcoutlet.com; ✆ **506/457-7452**), 441 King St. for (C$15 half day or C$25 full day), and at **Radical Edge,** 386 Queen St. (www.radicaledge.ca; ✆ **506/459-3478**). Figure C$75 per week, C$25 per day or C$7.50 per hour for a rental.

Many visitors get out on the water in a canoe, kayak, stand-up paddleboards, or even a rowing scull with a rental from the **Small Craft Aquatic Centre** at the **Fredericton Rowing Club** next to the river at the corner of Brunswick and Smythe Streets; www.fredericton.ca/en/recleisure/smallcraftaquaticcentre.asp; ✆ **506/460-2260**). A float down the Nashwaak in a tube is doable with a rental from **Nashwaak Tubing ★** (629 Rte. 8, Durham Bridge; www.nashwaaktubing.com; ✆ **506/457-2300**) for C$10/adults, C$5 children, or luxury tubes for C$12 (reservations recommended); or **Taymouth Tubing ★** (959 Rte. 628, Taymouth; www.taymouthventures.com; ✆ **506/450-6020**). Rates start at C$9 per person (reservations recommended.)

Other less active opportunities for getting on the river include taking a river cruise with **Wolastoq Tour Boat & Charter ★** (✆ **506/471-8680**) for C$19 adults, C$17 students and seniors. Children under 5 get on free; or renting a houseboat that sleeps from 6 to 14 people farther upriver at Mactaquac with **Lakeway Houseboat Rentals ★★** (www.lakewayhouseboats.com; ✆ **888/452-5392**) for a weekend, half week, or full week.

Golfers will want to play a round or two at the **Kingswood ★★** golf course (www.kingswoodpark.com/golf.php; ✆ **800/423-5969** or 506/443-3333) named one of the top 100 courses outside the US by Golf Digest. It consists of 27 holes, a par-3 course, a driving range, and a large putting green. Greens fees for 18 holes run from C$39 to C$89.

Finally, if any city in the Maritimes is worth visiting the winter, it's Fredericton. **Frostival ★★** (www.tourismfredericton.ca; ✆ **888/888-4768**) is a giant month-long collection of over 100 activities and events, some of them of significant size themselves. You can try dog sledding, snowshoe in the moonlight, discover snowga (yoga in the snow), join an old-fashioned outdoor skating party, learn an art form, hear lots of live music, or dine around town for a single price.

Attractions Downtown

Beaverbrook Art Gallery ★★ MUSEUM   This surprisingly impressive gallery, just steps from the Historic Garrison District, is home to an extensive collection of British paintings, including works by Reynolds, Gainsborough, Constable, and Turner. Antiques buffs gravitate to the rooms with period furnishings and early decorative arts, while others find themselves drawn to Dalí's massive painting entitled *Santiago El Grande.* The secret to fully appreciating the power of this work is to lie on the floor before it and look up; gallery staff encourages it. This gallery is especially strong when showing the art of First Nations (native Canadian) artists. Stop by, or check the website, to find out what's currently on display. Renovations, expected to be completed by late 2017, promise to greatly expand the gallery, and to make the Dalí visible to passersby through a window.

703 Queen St. www.beaverbrookartgallery.org. ℂ **506/458-2028.** Admission C$10 adults, C$8 seniors, C$5 students, C$20 families; Thurs after 5pm pay what you wish. Tues, Wed, Fri, Sat 10am–5pm; Thurs 10am–9pm; Sun noon–5pm. Closed Mon Oct–Apr.

Fredericton Playhouse ★ PERFORMING ARTS   A gift from Lord and Lady Beaverbrook to the people of New Brunswick in 1964, the space was renovated in 1972 into a 709-seat modern facility for the presentation of the performing arts by local, national, and international artists and companies. To that end, it hosts musicals and contemporary dramas, music of all genres, comedians, and dance—the mix of productions is eclectic. The Playhouse is adjacent to the Provincial Legislature and across the street from the Beaverbrook Art Gallery (above). If you are travelling with children, look into their Kidstage Series.

686 Queen St. www.theplayhouse.ca. ℂ **866/884-5800** or 506/458-8344. Check the website or call ahead for schedules and ticket prices.

Old Government House ★ HISTORIC SITE   Constructed in 1828, this was the official residence of the Lieutenant-Governor and Governor, the Queen's representatives in the province. Built solidly of locally quarried sandstone in a classical style, the building's rather plain exterior gives way to a regal interior with intricate plasterwork. Over time it has housed a school, a military hospital, and a detachment of Mounties. Spared from the wrecking ball, the home was restored and reopened in 1999, and is once again the official residence of the Lieutenant-Governor, who has an apartment and an office here. Bilingual tours begin in the interpretive center and last about 45 minutes. You hike sweeping staircases and view extraordinarily high-ceilinged reception rooms; there's an art gallery on the second floor, and the rooms are full of intriguing period pieces and fixtures. Ask the helpful guides anything.

51 Woodstock Rd. www.gnb.ca/lg/ogh. ℂ **506/453-2505.** Free admission. Mid-May to Aug tours Mon–Sat 10am–4pm and Sun noon–4pm.

Provincial Legislative Assembly Building ★★ HISTORIC SITE   New Brunswick's official Assembly Building, built in 1880, boasts an exterior in bulbous, extravagant Second Empire style, but the dressed-up interior is the star. Behind heavy doors that look like the gates of Oz, you find a creaky, wooden place that's surprisingly welcoming. In the small rotunda, look first for the prints from John James Audubon's elephant folio, which are kept on display in a special case. The assembly chamber itself nearly takes your breath away, especially when viewed from the visitor gallery on the upper floors. (To get there, you climb a graceful wood spiral stairway housed in its own rotunda.) The chamber is over-the-top ornate in that fussy Victorian way all out of proportion to the legislative humdrum. Half-hour-long tours are available; plan to spend at least an hour here if you really love old buildings.

706 Queen St. (across from the Beaverbrook Art Gallery). www.gnb.ca/legis. ℱ **506/453-2506.** Free admission. Mid-June to late-Aug daily 9am–5pm; late-Aug to mid-June Mon–Fri 8:30am–4pm.

Science East ★★ MUSEUM   Children usually enjoy a visit to this science center for two reasons: First, it's located in an old jail, a sturdy stone structure built in the 1840s (and still used as a jail as late as 1996). And then there are the great exhibits: more than 150 interactive displays in all, both indoors and out. Kids can fool around with a huge kaleidoscope, use a periscope to people-watch, check out a solar-powered water fountain, make patterns with a laser beam, even create a miniature tornado—though, truth be told, the dungeon museum probably will impress them more than all that. It's an ideal place to visit with the kids on a chilly or rainy day, and there's a lot to do outside here on nice days, too. This is one of Canada's preeminent science museums, and easily worth up to 2 hours of your time.

668 Brunswick St. www.scienceeast.nb.ca. ℱ **506/457-2340.** Admission C$10 adults, C$8 seniors, C$6.50 children 3 to 17, free for children under 3. June–Aug Mon–Sat 10am–5pm, Sun noon–4pm; rest of the year, Mon–Fri noon–5pm, Sat 10am–5pm, Sun and holidays noon–4pm.

Attractions Outside of Town

Kings Landing Historical Settlement ★★★ HISTORIC REENACTMENT   Kings Landing, on the bank of the Saint John River, is about 32km (20 miles)—and 150 years—away from Fredericton. The huge (121-hectare/300-acre) authentic re-creation brings to life New Brunswick from the years 1790 to 1910: It consists of about 20 historic homes and buildings. The aroma of baking bread mixes with the smells of horses and livestock (make what you will of that), and the blacksmith's hammer clashes with church bells while costumed "settlers" chat about their lives. The best buildings—nearly all built by Loyalists relocated from New England—include Hagerman House (furniture by cabinetmaker John Warren Moore), Ingraham House (regional furniture and a formal English garden), and Morehouse House (an interesting kitchen and a clock Benedict Arnold left behind). The C. B. Boss Sash and Door Factory is a simulated turn-of-the-20th-century manufacturing plant.

There's also an ox barn, a farmhouse, several churches, and a scenic little cove to enjoy.

Afterward, hitch a ride on the *sloven wagon*—a low-slung work wagon distinctive to the Maritimes (it was invented in Saint John)—or lunch at the King's Head Inn, which served travelers along the Saint John River more than a century ago and offers grub and grog such as ale, chicken pie, and corn chowder.

Note: For those who want to become part of the action there's **edVentures:** half-day, hands-on experiences like wool processing, quilting, open-hearth baking, and rug hooking and braiding. Kids very much enjoy these programs.

5804 Rte. 102, Prince William (exit 253 off the Trans-Canada Hwy., on Rte. 2 west). www.kingslanding.nb.ca. ✆ **506/363-4999.** Admission C$17 adults, C$15 seniors and students 16 and over, C$12 children 6–15, C$39 families. Mid-June to mid-Oct daily 10am–5pm. Closed mid-Oct to May.

Shopping

Fredericton is home to a growing number of artists and artisans, as well as entrepreneurs who have filled the compact downtown with contemporary and offbeat shops.

Aitkens Pewter ★★ CRAFTS   Since 1972, this well-known shop has been crafting classically designed pewter dishes and mugs based on historical patterns, as well as modern adaptations and jewelry. Aitkens has shops in Saint John and Halifax. 408 Queen St. www.aitkenspewter.com. ✆ **800/567-4416** or 506/453-9474.

The Barracks Fine Craft Shops ★ CRAFTS   Artisans sell their ware in the historic district at the lower level of the Soldier's Barracks. They create, demonstrate, and sell their handmade, one-of-a-kind Fredericton items—wooden toys, brightly dyed silk scarves, and whimsical knitted hats with giant eyes—from June to September. Corner of Carleton and Queen sts. ✆ **506/460-2837.**

Botinicals Gift Shop ★★ GIFTS   At this little gift shop and studio, you can find excellent work by a dozen or so New Brunswick artisans, including clever and delicate metal floral arrangements by owner John Welling. 610 Queen St. www.botinicalsgiftshop.com. ✆ **506/454-6101.**

Cultures Boutique ★★ CRAFTS   If you're keen to support fair-trade, sustainable goods made ethically in community-based cooperatives, this little shop is for you. As part of a chain of YMCA-run shops that promote alternative trade to benefit craftspeople around the world, its values may reflect your own. 383 Mazzucca Lane (off York St. btw. King & Queen). www.culturesboutique.ca. ✆ **506/462-3088.**

Gallery 78 ★★★ ART   Across from the Beaverbrook Art Gallery, you'll find this private shop that sells art by the best regional artists. Paintings, prints, photos, and sculptures fill the bright rooms of this lovely historic former home with its signature turret. 796 Queen St. (near the Beaverbrook Art Gallery). www.gallery78.com. ✆ **506/454-5192.**

Owl's Nest Bookstore ★★ BOOKSTORE   As a small city with a university, Fredericton has more than its fair share of bookstores. Among them, the Owl's Nest stands out. With 300,000 books, bibliophiles will have no trouble spending an afternoon here accompanied by the feline mascot named Gretchen. 390 Queen St. ⓒ **506/458-5509.**

Where to Stay

In addition to the properties listed below, a clutch of motels and chain hotels are bunched up in a bustling mall zone on the hillside above town (along Regent and Prospect sts.), a 5- or 10-minute drive from downtown. Both the **Comfort Inn ★** at 797 Prospect St. (www.frederictoncomfortinn.com; ⓒ **506/453-0800**) and the **Holiday Inn Express and Suites ★** at 665 Prospect St. (ⓒ **506/459-0035**) are newly renovated and perfectly comfortable contemporary travel lodges. The dependable local entrant in this pack is the **Fredericton Inn ★**, 1315 Regent St. (ⓒ **800/561-8777** or 506/455-1430), situated in between two malls. It's a typical soothing-music-and-floral-carpeting sort of place that does a brisk business in the convention trade. But with its indoor pool, nice little whirlpool, and surprising fitness center, it's more than adequate for vacation travelers, as well—and the price is right. Off-season rates start at C$95 for a double and run to a peak season maximum of C$249 for an apartment or suite.

The Carriage House Inn ★★   This topnotch B&B is a short stroll from the riverfront pathway in a quiet residential neighborhood. It's bigger than the Quartermain (see p. 148) with nine rooms set on the three floors expanded little from its construction in 1875 as the grand Queen Anne–style mansion of a former mayor and lumber merchant. Rooms are furnished with period art and antiques; some public areas have so many artifacts, you feel you're inside a museum instead of a hotel. Big hot breakfasts are included and served in the sunny ballroom by bilingual hosts who get raves far and wide for their hospitality. Just shy of a luxury inn, the Carriage House is comfortable and welcoming. Adults only.

230 University Ave., Fredericton. www.carriagehouse-inn.net. ⓒ **800/267-6068** or 506/452-9924. 10 units. C$105–C$129 double. Rates include full breakfast. Free parking. **Amenities:** Restaurant, A/C, TV, Wi-Fi (free).

Crowne Plaza Fredericton Lord Beaverbrook Hotel ★★   The Crowne boasts the best location in town, right beside the Beaverbrook Art Gallery and across the street from the Fredericton Playhouse. It looks boxy from the street, but inside, the mood lightens, thanks to composite stone floors, and an ornate central staircase and chandeliers. There's an indoor pool and recreation area downstairs. Some guest rooms can be somewhat dim, and most windows don't open (ask for a room with windows that do open if that's important to you). However, the suites here are spacious and outfitted with Jacuzzis; many have excellent river views. And the hotel maintains "quiet zones"—areas where guests promise to be extra quiet—so you can ask for one of those if you're someone who struggles with sleep. There are several choices for on-site dining: The Terrace Room is the main dining area, with a deck overlooking the river. At the James Joyce, tuck into traditional Irish pub fare washed down with a craft beer while enjoying live entertainment. Finally, the Maverick lets you select your cut of beef, then grills it to your specs while a Caesar salad is made at your table.

659 Queen St., Fredericton. www.cpfredericton.com. ℭ **866/444-1946** or 506/455-3371. 168 units (12 deluxe suites). C$129–C$199 double; executive rooms and suites up to C$599. Packages available. **Amenities:** 3 restaurants, pet friendly, indoor saltwater pool, hot tub, steam room, fitness center, A/C, Wi-Fi (free).

Delta Fredericton ★★ Built in 1992, the Delta welcomes visitors in a lobby of marble and hardwood with funky artwork and crisp lighting. A pleasant riverside walk separates the Delta from downtown, making it feel more like a resort than an urban hotel. The hotel takes full advantage of that riverside proximity with an outdoor pool (with its own poolside bar) and a deck overlooking the river. On Sundays, the lobby is taken over by an over-the-top brunch buffet. The rest of the week, guests take their meals at three solid on-site eateries **The Urban Grill** ★ (seasonal and regional specialties like fiddleheads and excellent seafood), **DJ Purdy's Lounge** ★ (fish and chips and other pub grub) and **The DIP Pool Bar & Grill** ★ (gourmet burgers and lobster rolls). Rooms are recently renovated and very comfortable with excellent beds; some of the suites have Jacuzzi tubs.

225 Woodstock Rd. www.marriott.com. ℭ **888/890-3222** or 506/457-7000. 222 units. C$119 double, up to C$800 for a suite. Pets accepted. Free parking. **Amenities:** Restaurant, bar, pub, all with food service; babysitting; barber and beauty shop; foreign exchange; valet dry cleaning; fitness room; heated indoor pool; spa; fridge (some units), toll free phone, Jacuzzi (some units), Wi-Fi (free).

Hartt Island River Valley RV Resort ★ Sites are clean and spacious, set on the banks of the St. John River, and conveniently located just minutes from downtown. Those in tents will be less satisfied here than RVers, who dominate this campground. There is access to the river for boating, as well as evening guided boat tours, and canoes and kayaks for those who want to explore this unique chain of islands. There are also riverside biking and hiking trails that go into the city. Washrooms are basic, but the water park's pool and slides are great for kids.

2475 Woodstock Rd, Rte. 105. www.harttisland.ca. ℭ **506/462-9400.** C$30–C$55 Mid-May to end Oct. **Amenities:** Pools, some watersports equipment rentals, minigolf, dairy bar or canteen, playground, Wi-Fi (free at full service sites only).

On the Pond Country Retreat & Spa ★★ Located just 15 minutes out of Fredericton, this country inn and spa is nestled in a lovely woodland setting overlooking the St. John River and adjacent to the Mactaquac Provincial Park, which extends the wilderness feel. The park has beaches, nature trails, and a marina. The lodge itself is homey and inviting with common rooms—one with a fireplace, one lined with bookshelves—that lure guests. Rooms are larger than your average hotel. The spa is in the basement and offers massage, hot tub, sauna, an aesthetics room, and fitness center. The lodge sits on "The Arm"—an impoundment of the St. John River behind the nearby Mactaquac dam—in a marshy setting better for bird-watching than swimming. (Beach swimming is available across the road at the provincial park.) The Kings Landing Historical Settlement (see "Attractions Outside of Town," p. 144) is nearby.

20 Scotch Settlement Rd. (Rte. 615), Mactaquac. www.onthepond.com. ✆ **800/984-2555** or 506/363-3420. 8 units. C$125–C$145 double. Ski, golf, and other packages available. Drive west of Fredericton on Woodstock Rd.; cross Mactaquac Dam and continue to Esso station; turn right and look for sign on right. No children. **Amenities:** Jacuzzi, sauna, spa, fitness room, A/C, Wi-Fi (free).

Quartermain House B&B ★★★ The term B&B doesn't adequately describe Fredericton's best overnight experience at this luxurious five-star 1840s Gothic Revival heritage property. The period furnishings, the contemporary comforts like walk-in showers and heated ceramic floors, the views of the river, the back garden terrace, the location next to a pleasant riverside walk from the galleries, shops and historic sites of downtown would be enough to recommend it. But owner Debra Quartermain is attuned to her guests' every need in a way that's both unusual and quite lovely to experience. And then there's breakfast! Fresh pastries, soufflés, frittatas, and treats like braised pears with maple syrup and cinnamon-dusted strawberries are *de rigeur* (special dietary needs can also be accommodated).

92 Waterloo Row. www.quartermainhouse.com. ✆ **855/758-5255** or 506/206-5255. 3 units, 1 with en suite bath, 2 with private baths outside the room. C$110–C$135. Free parking. **Amenities:** Full hot breakfast, A/C, TV, Wi-Fi (free).

University of New Brunswick ★ University residences are not always the cramped, institutional cells they used to be. UNB offers 2 and 3 bedroom suites along with the more typical single rooms. All are sparsely furnished, but comfortable and they come with a great perk: full kitchens where you can prepare your own meals. The university is on the edge of town, but within walking distance of the attractions.

20 Bailey Dr. http://stay.unb.ca. ✆ **506/447-3227.** C$95 2-bedroom suite; C$130 3-bedroom suite. **Amenities:** Full kitchen, linen, towel, soap, coin-operated laundry, Wi-Fi (free).

Where to Eat

You don't have to spend big bucks for good food in Fredericton, although you'll find a proliferation of tony eateries. Locals will tell you that the **Sunshine Diner ★★** at 7 Brookmount, across from the Delta (www.sunshine diner.ca; ✆ **506/458-8470**), or tiny the **Cabin Restaurant ★** at 723 Woodstock Rd. (✆ **506/459-0094**), serve hearty bacon-and-egg style breakfast and lunch. You can't beat them for local homestyle diner food in a casual setting.

540 Kitchen and Bar ★★ GASTRO PUB 540 has an urban feel and presents an affordable menu that swings from burgers and mac 'n' cheese to such inventive items as duck confit in an orange-anise glaze or risotto with braised beef, Gorgonzola, and cremini mushrooms. As a gastro pub, there are lots of craft beer choices to pair with the eclectic foods.

540 Queen St. www.540kitchenandbar.com. © **506/449-5400.** Main courses C$12–C$29. Mon–Fri 11:30am–11pm; Sat 5–11pm.

Brewbakers ★★ MEDITERRANEAN   Although Brewbakers is no longer the most contemporary of restaurants in the downtown, it's still very much in the game. Stretched across three levels in a cleverly adapted former bakery, it's a bustling and informal meeting spot creatively cluttered with art and artifacts. Lunch hours and early evenings get very busy. The cafe section is quieter, as is a mezzanine dining room, while the third floor bustles with an open kitchen. Lunch features excellent sandwiches: smoked fishcakes, flavorful flatbreads, and blackened chicken club, for example. For dinner, the tapas selection is impressive. Pastas are the main attraction for entrees. The cocktail menu and the selection of local beers are on tap are notable.

546 King St. www.brewbakers.ca. © **506/459-0067.** Reservations recommended. Main courses C$11–C$15 at lunch, C$22–C$30 at dinner. Tues–Thurs 11:30am–10pm; Fri 11:30am–11pm; Sat 5–11pm; Sun 5–9pm; Mon 11:30am–9pm.

Ten Resto ★★★ CONTEMPORARY CANADIAN   Ten tables, ten menu items, ten all-new menus a year; A gimmick, sure, but the quality of the food is the reason locals make reservations for their next visit as they're paying the check. Husband-and-wife team Chef Keith Phillipe and server Shirley run the whole operation. Keith uses local ingredients in the many dishes he invents each year, but he also scours the world for unusual items. You might find kangaroo beside alligator beside fiddlehead ferns. Make a reservation, because it doesn't take long to fill ten tables with loyal fans.

87 Regent St. © **506/206-3951.** Main courses C$17–C$29. Tues–Sat 5am–9pm.

Wolastoq Wharf ★ SEAFOOD   It's somewhat of a surprise to find that the most popular restaurant in Fredericton is on the other side of the river from downtown. There's nothing particularly unusual about the pan-fried haddock and halibut or the seafood fettuccini, but the food is well prepared and served in a pleasant, white-tablecloth dining room.

527 Union St., Fredericton. © **506/449-0100.** Main courses C$21–C$30. Daily 11am–9pm.

Fredericton After Dark

Unlike most other places in New Brunswick, Fredericton boasts a year-round nightlife scene. Being a university town insures a goodly number of dance clubs, nightclubs, bars, and pubs that are busy most nights. But the City of Fredericton itself is particularly good at entertaining visitors and residents alike with major festivals.

Corked Wine Bar ★★   If you prefer wine, this is a popular night spot that serves flights, glasses, and bottles. It's open Wednesdays and Thursdays 4:30 to 11pm, Friday until midnight. Saturdays, it's open 6pm to midnight. 83 Regent St. www.corkedwinebar.ca. © **506/206-6010.**

Dolan's Pub and Restaurant ★   Dolan's is the place to go for live Maritime music, which is on tap most Thursdays through Saturdays. There's no cover charge Thursdays 11pm to 2am. Wednesday night is jam night. Also on tap is a large selection of microbrews. Brunch and dinner menus offer many and varied pub grub options. It's open from lunchtime all the way until 2am. 375 King St. www.dolanspub.ca. ℂ **506/454-7474.**

Lunar Rogue Pub ★★   If you're not into dance clubs, your best bet is the Lunar Rogue, which features more than 100 single-malt whiskies, a dozen draft beers, and the requisite grub (mostly fried food and burgers) in a comfortable, pubby atmosphere. It was anointed "Greatest Whisky Bar in the World" by *Whisky* magazine. Its patio is popular in warm weather. The pub is open 11am to 1am weekdays, from 10am Saturdays and from 11am to 10pm Sundays. 625 King St. www.lunarrogue.com. ℂ **506/450-2065.**

Road Trip to Gagetown ★★

About 56km (35 miles) southeast of Fredericton is the village of **Gagetown** (**www.villageofgagetown.ca**), a scenic driving detour. (Don't confuse this with Canadian Forces Base Gagetown; it's up the road in Oromocto). Gagetown's been named one of the 10 prettiest villages in Canada, and has somehow remained largely unchanged through the years—still backed by farm fields on one side, and cozied up to by Gagetown Creek, a deep water anchorage off the St. John River, on another. The peaceful surroundings and simple country architecture have attracted craftspeople and artists, who have settled here and slowly made it over into a quiet arts colony—quaint and creative, but never annoyingly so. Look for low-key enterprises like art galleries, a carver of exquisite animals and birds, a jeweler, bookstore, cider press, crafts cooperative, and several potters. Visit the farmers' market on Sunday morning and stop by one of the local vegetable stands and u-picks. **Creek View Restaurant ★** (www.thecreekviewrestaurant.com; ℂ 506/488-9806) at 38 Tilley Rd. makes new use of a former 1900s automobile dealership. Memorabilia on the walls complements the country-style cuisine; smoked haddock chowder, fiddleheads find their way into soup in season, and pumpkin gingerbread with maple sauce.

You can also **birdwatch** and explore; the region is noted for the avian life enjoying the local marshes, forests, and fields. (Nearly 150 species have been reliably identified in and around Gagetown.) Where to do it? **Gagetown Island** is just offshore and easily accessible by kayak or canoe, which some local inns provide. The island features a glacial deposit that rises some 23m (75 ft.) high, plus the ruins of a stone house dating from the early 19th century. That's all nice, but birders go for the osprey-viewing platform. There are also two Ducks Unlimited marsh preserves with trails.

While in town, drop by the **Queens County Museum ★** (www.queens countyheritage.com; ℂ **506/488-2483**), birthplace of Sir Samuel Leonard Tilley, one of the fathers of Canadian Confederation. The 1786 home, located at 69 Front St., is open daily from mid-June to mid-September; admission costs

C$3 per person, free for children 11 and under. You can also buy a pass (C$5–C$7, free for children) allowing access to several more historic homes, including the Flower House and a simple courthouse.

If you want to stay the night, check with the simple bed-and-breakfast in town, the **Step Aside B&B** ★ (*©* **506/488-1808**) at 58 Front St. Owners Elaine and Maurice Harquail maintain four rooms costing from C$70 to C$100 per night, and their inn is open year-round. Or for a slice of history, there's **16 Doctor's Hill B&B** (*©* **877/310-2723** or 506/488-2723) with two rooms from C$60 to C$75. Each room has a stocked pantry and appliances to prepare a simple breakfast.

If military history interests you, head up Route 102 to Oromocto, where the **New Brunswick Military History Museum** ★ (www.nbmilitaryhistory museum.ca; *©* **506/422-1304**) collects, preserves, and promotes Canada's military history with static and electronic displays, activities (you can try on military uniforms), and an array of retired military vehicles outside. Admission is free, and it's open year-round Monday to Friday 8am to 4pm and weekends by appointment. Also of interest to military or World War II buffs, just 50km (31 miles) east of Fredericton on Route 10 in Minto, is the **New Brunswick Internment Camp Museum** (www.nbinternmentcampmuseum. ca; *©* **506/327-3573**) located on the site where prisoners of war (POWs) were detained. In its early days, the camp housed German and Austrian Jewish refugees, then later on German and Italian Merchant Marines, and even some Canadians who spoke out against the war effort.

THE ACADIAN COAST

The diversity of New Brunswick's landscape, culture, and history becomes immediately obvious in a short drive from the Bay of Fundy or Fredericton to the Acadian Coast. From the world's highest tides to the warmest waters and longest silver-sand beaches, from Anglo European to French Acadian culture, the contrasts are many. On a drive that hugs the province's eastern coast from Port Elgin in the south to Campbellton in the north, you may conclude that you have entered not only a different province, but at times a different country where you can immerse yourself in the quirky good humor, hospitality, cuisine, and culture of the Acadian people.

Although there is a First Nations presence here and English is widely spoken, it's the red, white, and blue of the Acadian flag that seems to mark everything from mailboxes to lighthouses. Acadian cultural pride reaches a fever pitch on August 15, the Feast of the Assumption, now adopted as the national feast day during which Acadian culture is celebrated with noisy, colorful parades. At the same time, the day is a solemn acknowledgement of their troubled history at the hands of the British who, in the 18th century insisted they swear an oath of allegiance to the British crown. When the Acadians refused, the Great Expulsion *(le Grand Dérangement)*, began in 1755. Some 11,500 Acadians were expelled from their lands in Nova Scotia, their houses and farms burned. Many died at sea or of starvation. Others made it to Louisiana where they became known as the Cajuns. Some returned to France. When hostilities between England and France ceased, many Acadians returned to the Maritimes, settling along what is now New Brunswick's eastern coast.

Start Where Three Provinces Meet

From Aulac, pretty Route 16 takes you about 25km (16 miles) along the Nova Scotia border toward the Confederation Bridge to Prince Edward Island to a traffic circle near Port Elgin. From here, you can either continue on Route 16 to **Cape Jourimain,** where there is a natural wildlife area, the **Cape Jourimain Nature Centre ★** (www.capejourimain.ca/en; ℭ **506/538-2220**) and a spectacular view of Confederation Bridge; or, take Route 15 to **Shediac.** Alternatively, you can carry on along the coast on Route 955. The 46km (29-mile) stretch between Port Elgin and Shediac is home to four great beaches: Murray, Cap-Pele, l'Aboiteau, and Parlee. Parlee Beach and the town of Shediac bustle with holidayers in season, so they have all the services you could want.

You'll know **Shediac** by the giant lobster at the entrance to town on Route 133. At over 50 tons, the town claims the huge novelty sculpture is the world's largest. Kids—okay, and adults too—will love climbing into the beast's crusher claw for a photo op. You'll have no difficulty finding a restaurant to tuck into lobster and other seafood like fish and chips or clams. But don't overlook Shediac as a place to have an excellent culinary experience. **Le Petit Paris ★** (562 Main St.; ℭ **506/533-8805**) tops the list with elegant surroundings and a hybrid French-Maritime menu. Stay the night in one of four rooms for a very reasonable C$79 to C$99. For dessert or breakfast with a good pastry and coffee or lunch with a lobster croissant and French-style breads to take away, duck into **Boulangerie Francais ★** (402 Main St.; ℭ **506/351-6565**).

From Shediac, take **Route 134** to **Bouctouche** for a stop at a kind of Acadian theme park called **Le Pays de la Sagouine ★★** (51 Acadie Rd., Bouctouche; www.sagouine.com; ℭ **800/561-9188**), where music, kitchen parties, comedy, food, storytelling, and dinner theater are all part of a day's activities. La Sagouine is the best-known literary creation in a play of the same name by renowned Acadian author Antonine Maillet. The play is a set of monologues by an Acadian cleaning lady from rural New Brunswick who embodies Acadian roots, hard work, and pride. You'll meet La Sagouine—or at least an interpreter playing her—when you take the boardwalk out to a tiny island with a storybook recreation of a traditional Acadian village.

The Savonnerie Olivier Soapery ★ (821 Rte. 505 in Sainte-Anne-de-Kent; www.oliviersoaps.com; ℭ **888/775-5550**), 16km (10 miles) farther along the coast, is an econo-museum that serves up a learning experience about soap making which is full of color and fragrance (who knew skin care could be so much fun).

Bouctouche Dune ★★, on the coast road at 1932 Rte. 475, is a striking white-sand dune stretch an impressive 13km (8 miles) across **Bouctouche Bay.** At **The Irving Eco-Centre ★** (ℭ **506/743-2600**), check out the interpretation center with a staff to deliver programs and presentations. The beach is home to the endangered piping plover, a unique butterfly species, and some rare plants. The sensitive dune area itself can be viewed from a wheelchair-accessible, 2km (1-mile-plus) boardwalk that snakes along its length. On a sunny day, the sandy beach is a lovely spot to while away a couple hours, or even take a dip in the (relatively) warm seawater. Admission is free; the boardwalk is open year-round (in good weather) and the visitor center is open daily July and August, 10am to 6pm (June and Sept until 5pm).

If you're interested in spending the night in the area or grabbing a bite to eat, check out the **Dune View Inn** ★ at 589 Rte. 475 (www.aubergevuedela dune.com; © **877/743-9893** or 506/743-9893). It's open year-round, where the owners (one a trained chef who previously cooked in Montréal) serve up French-inflected local seafood. The six units here feature TVs, telephones, and private bathrooms (five with whirlpool tubs). They're pretty and light, if somewhat cramped. A double with breakfast costs from C$64 to C$150. The inn can also arrange local golf and kayaking packages—or even a romance package—with advance notice.

KOUCHIBOUGUAC NATIONAL PARK ★★

Much is made of the fact that big **Kouchibouguac National Park** (local slang: "the Kooch") has all sorts of ecosystems worth studying, from sandy barrier islands to ancient peat bogs. But that's like saying Disney has nice lakes: It misses the point. In fact, this artfully designed park is a wonderful destination for active vacationers who enjoy camping, cycling, hiking, swimming, and beachgoing (the park is blessed with very, very long stretches of lonely dunes). If you're an outdoorsy type, plan to spend a few days here doing nothing but exercising. The varied natural wonders (which *are* spectacular) will just be an added bonus—a big one.

The tongue-tangling name is a Mi'kmaq Indian word meaning "river of the long tides." It's pronounced "Koosh-uh-*boog*-oo-whack." The place is great for **cyclists,** because the park is laced with well-groomed bike trails made of finely crushed cinders that traverse forest and field or meander alongside rivers and lagoons. In those areas where bikes aren't permitted (such as on boardwalks and beaches), there are usually bike racks handy for locking up while you keep going on foot. In fact, if you camp here and bring a bike, there's no need to even use a car.

The only group this park might disappoint is gung-ho **hikers.** There isn't any hard-core hiking or climbing, just gentle walking and strolling. The pathways are wide and flat. Most trails are short—on the order of a half-mile to a mile—and seem more like detours than destinations. The exception are the beaches; miles and miles of narrow barrier island sand dunes front the entire park and are home to plentiful wildlife. They make for walks that can consume entire days.

Although the park is ideal for **campers,** day-trippers also find it a worthwhile destination. Plan to stay until sunset. The trails tend to empty out in the afternoon, and the dunes, bogs, and boreal forest take on a rich, almost iridescent hue as the sun sinks over the spruce.

Tip: Be aware that this is a fair-weather destination only—if it's blustery or rainy, there's little to do save a damp stroll on the beach or a stop at the visitor center where you'll learn the disturbing history of how this park displaced small, mostly Acadian communities totaling 1,200 people in 1969. Houses, churches, and even cemeteries were picked up and moved out of the footprint of the park. It is striking that Parks Canada not only acknowledges the displacement, but interprets the event in an attempt at reconciliation.

Essentials

GETTING THERE Kouchibouguac National Park is located about 112km (70 miles) north of Moncton; figure less than 90 minutes' driving time. The exit for the park, off Route 11, is well marked. From Fredericton, the drive is closer to 3 hours on one of three Routes (8, 10, or the Trans-Canada through Moncton) ranging from 210km (130 miles) to 285km (177 miles).

VISITOR INFORMATION The park is open daily year-round, while a **Visitor Reception Centre** (✆ **506/876-2443**) opens daily from mid-May until mid-October. The visitor center is just off Route 134, a short drive past the park entrance. (It's open 8am–8pm from mid-June through Aug, 9am–5pm in the shoulder seasons.) There's a slide show here to introduce you to the park's attractions, plus some field guides, in addition to the fascinating interpretation of the park's history.

FEES A daily pass costs C$7.80 adults, C$6.80 seniors, C$3.90 children 6 to 16, and C$20 families. (Rates are about half in Apr–June and Oct–Nov.) Seasonal passes are also available if you're planning to visit for more than 3 days. Though there are no formal checkpoints, occasional roadblocks during the summer check for pass-holding compliance. Note that, for a small extra charge, you can also get a helpful map of the park at the information center.

Outdoor Pursuits

CAMPING Kouchibouguac is at heart a camper's park, best enjoyed by those who plan to spend at least a night.

South Kouchibouguac ★, the main campground, is centrally located and very nicely laid out with 300-plus sites, most rather large and private. About 125 sites are unserviced, while 100 or so are equipped with electricity and some offer water and sewage hookups. These are stretched along several loop roads that skirt the water and dive into the forest. You can find a map of the campgrounds on the Parks Canada website or at the visitor center when you arrive. Sites here range from C$27 to C$55 per night, depending on time of year and the level of comfort you require. Reservations are accepted for about half of the sites; call ✆ **506/876-2443** starting in late April. The remaining sites are doled out first-come, first-served.

Other camping options within the park include the more remote, semi-primitive **Côte-à-Fabien** ★ across the river on Kouchibouguac Lagoon. It lacks showers and some sites require a short walk, so it's more appealing for those who are travelling light, say with a tent and just a few supplies. The cost is C$16 per night. The park also maintains three backcountry sites. **Sipu** is on the Kouchibouguac River and is accessible by canoe or foot only, **Petit Large** by foot or bike, and **Pointe-à-Maxime** by canoe or kayak only (no fresh water available at this campground). These sites cost a flat C$9.80 per night, or C$69 annually.

New to most Parks Canada campgrounds, Kouchibouguac offers 15 oTEN-Tiks, a cross between a yurt and a cabin. One night costs C$80 to C$90, depending on the season. These are popular, so book well ahead of arrival. If you arrive unprepared to stay the night, ask about Equipped Camping, which provides tent, sleeping bag, and other essentials.

BEACHES   The park features about 16km (10 miles) of sandy beaches, mostly along barrier islands of sandy dunes, delicate grasses and flowers, and nesting plovers and sandpipers. **Kellys** ★ is the principal beach, one of the best-designed and best-executed recreation areas in Eastern Canada. At a forest's edge, a short walk from the main parking area, you can find showers, changing rooms, a snack bar, and some interpretive exhibits. From here, you walk about 480m (⅓-mile) across a winding boardwalk that's plenty fascinating as it crosses a salt marsh, lagoons, and some of the best-preserved dunes in the province.

The long, sandy beach here features water that's comfortably warm, with waves that are usually mellow—they lap rather than roar, unless a storm's passing offshore. Lifeguards oversee a roped-off section about 91m (300 ft.) long; elsewhere, though, you're on your own. For kids, there's supervised swimming on a sandy stretch of the quiet lagoon.

BOATING & BIKING   Ryans ★★ (✆ 506/876-8918)—a cluster of buildings between the campgrounds and Kellys Beach—is the recreational center where you can rent bikes, kayaks, paddleboats, and canoes. All rent relatively cheaply, even the double kayaks. Canoes can be rented for longer excursions. And since Ryans is located on a lagoon, you can explore around the dunes or upstream on the winding river.

With over 60km (37 miles) of bikeway, the park is a prime biking destination. The Major Kollock Creek Mountain Bike Trail, which starts near Petit-Large, is ideal for those who want to try mountain biking. This one-way bicycle trail is 6.3km (4 miles) and takes 45 to 90 minutes to ride.

The park sometimes offers a **Voyageur Canoe Experience** ★★ during summer—Mondays and Thursdays in English; Wednesdays and Saturdays in French—with a crew paddling a sizable canoe modeled on traditional First Nations craft from the mainland out to offshore sandbars, and a naturalist/guide helps identify the wildlife and interpret the natural and human history of the area. You could see literally thousands of terns and seals on one excursion. Inquire at the park's information center when you enter. You need to reserve by calling ☏ **506/876-2443**. The fee is C$29 per-person upon reservation.

Other interpretation programs include a fun science-based exploration of the lagoons behind the barrier island, campfire storytelling by park interpreters, and Mi'kmaq cultural discovery activities. Ask for details at the visitor center.

HIKING　The hiking and biking trails are as short and undemanding as they are appealing. The one hiking trail that requires slightly more fortitude is the **Kouchibouguac River Trail,** which runs for some 13km (8 miles) along the banks of the river.

The **Bog Trail** runs just 2km (1.2 miles) in each direction, but it opens the door to a wonderfully alien world: The 4,500-year-old bog here is a classic domed bog, made of peat created by decaying shrubs and other plants. At the bog's edge, you'll find a wooden tower ascended by a spiral staircase that affords a panoramic view of the eerie habitat.

The boardwalk crosses to the thickest, middle part of the bog. Where the boardwalk stops, you can feel the bouncy surface of the bog—you're actually standing on a mat of thick vegetation that's floating on top of water. Look for the pitcher plant, a carnivorous little devil that lures flies into its bell-shaped leaves and then digests them with acid, allowing the plant to thrive in an otherwise hostile environment.

Callanders Beach and **Cedar Trail** are both located at the end of a short dirt road. There's an open field with picnic tables here, a small protected beach on the lagoon (with fine views of dunes across the way), and an 800m (about .5 mile or so) hiking trail along a boardwalk that passes through a cedar forest, past a salt marsh, and through a mixed forest. This is a good alternative for those who prefer to avoid the crowds (relatively speaking) at Kellys Beach.

THE ACADIAN PENINSULA ★★

The **Acadian Peninsula** is the heart of New Brunswick's Acadian Coast, a bulge on the northeast corner of the province, forming one of the arms of the **Baie des Chaleurs** (Québec's Gaspé Peninsula forms the other). It's a land of tidy houses, miles of shoreline (much of it beaches), harbors filled with commercial fishing boats, and residents proud of their Acadian heritage. You'll see the Stella Maris flag—the French tricolor with a single gold star in the field of blue—everywhere up here. You are in Acadian country, a warm, welcoming culture where time seems to slow down and relaxation is the norm.

After leaving Kouchibouguac, it's just a short drive to **Miramichi,** the gateway to the Acadian Peninsula. Miramichi and the river of the same name have long been known for sport fishing and hunting, a favorite of presidents and celebrities. Numerous outfitters in the region still help anglers in their quest for wild salmon. A hired guide escorts you to private pools, where chances of landing the big one are best; truth be told, however, Atlantic salmon stocks have been declining for decades, so the chances of landing one are getting slim. The town provides a delightful stopping point with river tours and music ranging from country to kitchen parties featuring local talent. There are several good chain hotels in town. From Miramichi, follow Route 11 around the coast of the peninsula or, if you want to get to Bathurst in a hurry, take Route 9.

VISITOR INFORMATION   The **Miramichi Visitor Information Centre** at 21 Cove Rd. (© **506/778-8444**) is open daily May to September. The **Caraquet Tourism Information** at 39 St-Pierre Blvd. W. (© **506/726-2676**), is a seasonal (mid-May to mid-Sept) office in the heart of downtown. The village of **Shippagan** dispenses its information from a wooden lighthouse near the Marine Centre at 200 Hotel de Ville Ave. (© **506/336-3900**); it's open year-round.

GETTING THERE   Route 11 is the main highway serving the Acadian Peninsula. Caraquet is about 260km (160 miles, or a 3½-hr. drive) north from Moncton, about 160km (100 miles, or 2+ hr.) north from the entrance to Kouchibouguac National Park, or 70km (43 miles) from Bathurst.

A Side Trip to Shippagan ★ & Miscou Island ★★

Both Shippagan and Miscou Island require a day-long detour off Route 11, but they're worth it if you're interested in glimpsing Acadian New Brunswick in the slow lane. As an added bonus, Miscou Island boasts some fine beaches and a historic lighthouse. There are places to stay and eat; they are often smaller, more intimate, and obviously local, so keep your eyes peeled.

Shippagan lies off routes 11 and 345. It's a quiet, leafy village that's also home to sizable crab and herring fleets. Feel free to saunter down to the harbor for photos and conversation among the boats on their slips.

Shippagan is home to the surprisingly modern **New Brunswick Aquarium and Marine Centre ★★**, 100 Aquarium St. (© **506/336-3013**), near the harbor; it's a good destination if you're the least bit curious about local marine life. Here you'll learn about the 125 species of native fish hereabouts, many of which are on display. Kids are especially drawn to the **harbor seal tank** outside, where trainers prompt the sleek creatures to show off their acrobatic skills. Little ones will also love watching the twice-daily feedings, when the seals down pounds of herring. Admission is C$9 adults, C$6.75 seniors, C$7 students, C$6 children age 6 to 16, and C$24 families. Open late May to late September 10am to 6pm daily; seal feedings are at 11am and 4pm.

Keep driving north on Route 113 across a low drawbridge onto **Lamèque Island.** If you're traveling through in mid-July, don't be surprised to hear fine classical music wafting from the **Sainte-Cecile Church.** Since 1975, the island has hosted the **Lamèque International Baroque Music Festival ★★** (www.festivalbaroque.com; © **506/344-3261**). For about 10 days each summer, talented musicians perform an ambitious series of concerts, held in an architecturally striking, acoustically wonderful church in a small village on the island's north coast. Tickets sometimes sell out in advance, so check before you go. Some events are free. Others range from as low as C$10 to a high of about C$50. Festival passes are also available.

If you miss the festival, do drop into the **Sainte-Cecile Church ★★** and take a look at the paint job inside—it has to be seen to be believed. In 1968, Father Gerard Estou hand-painted every inch of his church with crosses, circles, stars, cakes, and balloons in dazzling turquoise, green, yellow, and orange.

Also in the village of Lamèque, take an hour or so to explore the **Ecological Park of the Acadian Peninsula ★** at 65 Rue Du Ruisseau (www.parce cologique.ca; © **506/344-3223**). Inside, screens interpret the natural world outside where you can climb the observation tower, hike the boardwalk that snakes across an estuary into a forest, and do a little birdwatching through a scope. Interpretive guides are available. The center is open late June until the end of September. Admission ranges from C$6 to C$11.

The **Saint-Marie church ★★**, a gorgeous twin-towered white wooden structure, is also worth finding; it's located in the hamlet of **Saint-Raphael-sur-Mer,** about 16km (10 miles) from Shippagan—bear right onto Route 305 a few miles after crossing the drawbridge onto Lamèque Island. From the church, continue north on 305 another couple of kilometers (a mile or two) to see **Cap-Bateau Arch ★★**, a remarkable natural stone formation that looks like it should be somewhere in the canyons of Utah.

Backtrack to Route 113 and keep traveling north. You'll soon cross onto **Miscou Island,** which for decades was connected by a simple ferry. In the mid-1990s, an arched bridge was finally erected across the strait. Happily, this wee island still retains a sense of remoteness, especially north of the village of Miscou Centre when you start getting into boggy territory.

If you continue northward across the island until you run out of road (it won't take long), you'll come to New Brunswick's oldest lighthouse. The **Miscou Island Lighthouse ★** (© **506/344-7203**), built in 1856, marks the confluence of the Gulf of St. Lawrence and the Baie des Chaleurs. Inside, axe-hewn pine beams give the structure its strength. It's open to the public mid-June to mid-September, 9am to 6pm. Entrance costs C$3 to C$6.

The bog landscape of Miscou is as distinctive as that of the Canadian Rockies; it's flat and green, and stretches for miles in places. You'll see much of this bog habitat on northern Miscou Island, where some have been harvested for their peat. There's a well-constructed **nature trail** on Route 113, just north of Miscou Centre; a boardwalk loops through the bog and around an open pond. Here you'll see orchids and lilies that thrive in the vast and spongy mat of shrubs and roots; watch for the pitcher plants, carnivorous vessels that hold water and trap insects on sticky hairs. The loop takes about 20 minutes, and it's free. If you come in fall (late Sept to mid-Oct), you'll find these bogs suddenly aflame in coats of gorgeous crimson.

Caraquet ★★

The historic beach town of Caraquet—widely regarded as the spiritual capital of Acadian New Brunswick—is spread thinly along a single commercial boulevard that parallels the beach; this town once claimed the honorific "longest village in the world" when it ran to some 20km (13 miles).

A good place to start a tour is the **Carrefour de la Mer,** 51 Blvd. St-Pierre Est, a modern recreation complex overlooking the man-made harbor. While it hosts festivals, concerts, exhibitions, and other events, you'll also find an art gallery, shops, seafood restaurant, a snack bar, a homemade gelato stand, a children's playground, mini golf, and two short strolls that lead to picnic tables on jetties with fine harbor views. Caraquet is known as the premier place to be for the **Tintamarre,** a festival celebrating the national Acadian holiday on August 15. Accommodations can be hard to come by during this time, so if you plan to visit the first 2 weeks of August, reserve ahead.

Village Historique Acadien ★★ HISTORIC SITE   This historic village is to the Acadian coast what Kings Landing (see the Fredericton section) is to central New Brunswick. But there are many differences. For one thing, the historic time period it interprets is much longer. Some 45 buildings—most transported from villages elsewhere on the peninsula—depict life as it was lived in Acadian settlements between 1770 and 1950. The buildings are set among hundreds of acres of woodlands, marshes, and fields. You'll learn all about the settlement, deportation, and resettlement of the Acadians from interpreters in period clothing playing characters who also demonstrate skills ranging from letterpress printing to blacksmithing. Visitors can get involved by baking over a fire in a pioneer cottage. More recent buildings and exhibits include a service station with old gas pumps and antique autos. Plan on spending 4 to 8 hours on-site.

Or alternatively, stay overnight. The attractive replica of the **Chateau Albert Hotel ★★** (www.villagehistoriqueacadien.com/en/hotel-chateau-albert; ✆ **877/721-2200**) is good for those who wish to experience a night in a fine hotel from the last century (C$150 includes a full breakfast; ask about packages that include dinner theater and site admission). This hotel is open late June to mid-August daily, then Thursday to Saturday until mid-September. Rooms are snug and wonderfully peaceful due to the lack of phones and televisions (to fit the period); there's a dining room, convivial bar area, and lost-in-time vibe.

There are also several restaurants within the village. The simple, hearty 18th- and 19th-century traditional Acadian cooking in **La Table des Ancêtres ★★** at the reception center is a must for those who love food history, a chance to sample Fricot, Poutine, Fayots, and more. The hotel dining room is home to musical dinner theater, or, on other evenings, a select menu. Simpler, modern fare is available in other eateries like the **Café-Bistro du Village ★** in the reception area and the hotel bar.

Rte. 11 (6 miles west of Caraquet). www.villagehistoriqueacadien.com. ✆ **877/721-2200** or 506/726-2600. Summer admission C$18 adults, C$16 seniors and students over 18, C$11–C$13 children 6 to 18, free for children under 6, C$42 families; late Sept rates discounted 50%. Early June to mid-Sept daily 10am–6pm. Closed late Sept to early June.

WHERE TO STAY

In addition to the **Chateau Hotel Albert** in the Village Historique Acadien (see above), a few small motels offer reasonable rates including a **Super 8 ★** at 9 Avenue du Carrefour (www.super8.com; ✆ **800/536-1211**) that has a pool, free Internet, and breakfast. But the real standout is the **Hotel Paulin.**

Hôtel Paulin ★★ Ask owner Gerard Paulin to stand beside the old photograph of his grandfather in the reception area of this three-story Victorian-era hotel, and you'll see the family tree come alive. Built in 1891, the Paulin was Caraquet's first hotel. It's still the best in town. Overlooking the bay, the beautifully restored country inn has an old-world France feel, both for the decor and the hospitality. Rooms and suites are comfortably furnished with antiques. (Four luxury suites on the top floor are more stylish and contemporary.) The hotel's first floor houses a handsome, well-regarded **restaurant** ★★ where Chef Karen Mersereau prepares original seafood, local, foraged, and fusion dishes with French influences. This hotel is especially known for packages such as food-and-wine getaways.

143 Blvd. St-Pierre Ouest. www.hotelpaulin.com. © **866/727-9981** or 506/727-9981. 16 units. Mid-June to mid-Sept C$179–C$270 doubles and suites with full breakfast and 4-course dinner. Rooms without dinner available. Packages available. **Amenities:** Restaurant, Wi-Fi (free).

WHERE TO EAT

The **Hôtel Paulin's restaurant** ★★ has some serious competition from a couple of others for Caraquet's best. You'll find a surprisingly good Japanese menu at the unlikely **Mitchan Suishi** ★★ 114 Blvd. Saint-Pierre West (www.mitchansushi.ca; © **506/726-1103**), an older home converted to a restaurant with small, cozy, nearly private rooms, and generous quantities of excellent Japanese preparations at reasonable prices.

Boulangerie Grains Folie ★★ BAKERY/BISTRO Owners Claude and Lorraine are welcoming, talented bakers—and hosts—who prepare fresh sandwiches, soups, salads, quiches, and other bistro- and deli-style items. The menu changes often, but the quality is always high and the goods made on site. The bakery is in a lovely old storefront with a turn-of-the-20th-century facade and a front veranda for outdoor dining. Local performers play music here from time to time.

171 Blvd Saint-Pierre West. www.grainsdefolie.ca/en. © **506/727-4001.** Main courses C$5–C$15. Open Mon–Fri 7am–5pm, Sat–Sun 8:30am–5pm.

Deja Bu ★★ WINE BAR & RESTAURANT Originally from nearby Lemeche Island, Robert Noel learned about wine and food in the resort towns of the Rocky Mountains before returning home to open this trendy wine bar and restaurant. With an open kitchen, and a bar where there's a hip buzz, Noel says he's out to provide dining experiences by creating pairings that show off both the wines he selects (from around the world and local makers) with contemporary curveballs like his signature lobster mac and cheese made with twisty orecchiette noodles bathed in a creamy Mornay sauce. Other traditional comfort foods that appear in upscale versions include Bar Clam Poutine made with local artisan cheese and clams harvested on the sand flats over which the sun sets, the scene that is the view from the restaurant's windows.

49 Blvd Saint-Pierre West. www.dejabu.ca/english. © **506/727-7749.** Reservations recommended. Main courses C$13–C$23. Tues–Sat 4–11pm.

Grande-Anse

Grande-Anse is a wide-spot-in-the-road village of low, modern homes near bluffs overlooking the bay, lorded over by the stone Saint Jude church. The best view of the village—and a pretty good spot for a picnic—is along the bluffs just below the church. (Look for the sign indicating QUAI 45m/147 ft. west of the church.) Here you'll find a small man-made harbor with a fleet of fishing boats, a small sandy beach, and some grassy bluffs where you can park overlooking the bay.

If you'd prefer picnic tables, head a few miles westward to **Pokeshaw Park,** open from mid-June through August. Just offshore is a large kettle-shaped island ringed with cliffs that rise from the waves, long ago separated from the cliffs on which you're now standing. An active cormorant rookery thrives among the trees. There's a small picnic shelter for use in inclement weather.

For an ocean swimming experience, head to **Plage Grande-Anse,** located 2km (a mile) east of the town. This handsome beach has changing rooms, a picnic area, volleyball court, and a snack bar near the parking area.

Bathurst on to Campbellton

The beautiful Chaleur Bay draws eyes northward—that's Québec and the road to Gaspe across the water. You might want to pick up Route 134 into Bathurst. They have put some effort into developing their waterfront into a charming stop for refreshments or exploring. The boardwalks and observation tower, which rewards a climb with a great view, make for a nice break in driving. You'll also find a beach, golf, shopping, museums, and walking trails—if you overnight, you might want to take in the live local entertainment on the boardwalk every night. Bathurst is a VIA Rail stop, as is Campbellton up the line.

Chaleur Bay has been voted one of the most beautiful bays in the world, and at its top end, Campbellton acts as a welcome point for travelers from Québec's Gaspe Peninsula. That puts it at the top of New Brunswick, a region famous worldwide for the superb salmon fishing in the Restigouche River. Today it's a center for canoeing, kayaking, fishing, backpacking, hunting, nature trails, and birdwatching. **Sugarloaf Provincial Park ★** (www.nbparks. ca; © **506/789-2366**) has a great ski hill for winter enthusiasts. In the summer, they have the only lift-service mountain-bike trail in Atlantic Canada for C$25 a day for adults, C$20 for ages 6 to 18. If you're into geocaching, there are 68 caches within the 11.5 sq. km (4½-sq.-mile) park. Camp here for rates ranging from unserviced at C$25 to yurt rentals at C$39.

Campbellton is at the beginning (or end, depending on your direction of travel) of the Appalachian Range driving route, which cuts across the province to Perth-Andover. This region speaks to those who are enamored of wilderness, forests, and mountain ranges, huge skies and rock formations—409-million-year old fossils have been found near the Campbellton coast. Learning about forests and lumberjacks, cowboys and horses, native peoples and their ceremonies and crafts, even ghosts and history, are part of the journey to San Quentin and Mount Carleton.

MOUNT CARLETON
PROVINCIAL PARK ★★

In 1969, the province of New Brunswick carved out some of its choicest wood-lands and set them aside as a wilderness park—a wise decision. Today, Mount Carleton Provincial Park consists of 2,800 hectares (7,000 acres) of lakes, streams, thick boreal forest, and gently rounded mountains, the tallest of which afford excellent views of the surrounding countryside. It is the highest point in the Maritimes, and you can hike to the top. The park is home to moose, black bear, coyotes, bobcat, and more than 100 species of birds. It's so pristine that fishing isn't allowed. If you're anywhere in the area and crave a truly wild experience, it's well worth a visit—though you have to *want* to get there.

The International Appalachian Trail cuts through the park, allowing a long-distance backpacker to head northwest into Québec or southwest into Maine and on to Georgia.

Essentials

GETTING THERE   Mount Carleton Provincial Park sits in the middle of a scenic drive that the province's tourism authority has dubbed "The Appalachian Range Route" in northern New Brunswick that runs from Perth-Andover at the Trans-Canada Highway to Dalhousie at the coast. The park's access road and entrance is on Route 180, about 40km (25 miles) east of Saint-Quentin, the nearest community for supplies; there are no convenient general stores anywhere near the park's gates, so stock up.

VISITOR INFORMATION   It costs C$8 per car (cash only) to enter, and the park's gates are open daily from mid-May through mid-October, 8am to 8pm. A small **interpretive center** (© **506/235-0793**), located at the entrance gate, offers background on the park's natural and cultural history. The park remains open, though unstaffed, the rest of the year.

Camping

Armstrong Brook ★★ is the principal destination for visiting campers coming to Mount Carleton. It has 88 sites split between a forest near Lake Nictau's shore and an open, grassy field; campers can also avail themselves of hot showers and a bathhouse for washing up. A path leads to lake's edge, where there's a spit of small, flat pebbles good for swimming and sunbathing. Camping fees are C$25 for an unserviced site or C$28 to C$33 for various levels of service. Rent a cabin for reasonable rates from C$60 to C$90 a night. Note that all water supplies and toilets are shut off after September 15 due to concerns about pipes freezing.

Hiking & Biking

The park has 11 hiking trails totaling nearly 62km (38.5 miles). The helpful park staff at the gatehouse will be happy to direct you to a hike that suits your experience and mood. (There's even one wheelchair-accessible trail.)

The park's premier hike, of course, is to the summit of **Mount Carleton,** the province's highest point at 820m (2,690 ft.). Although that doesn't *sound* impressive, it's all relative: Views from the peak to the tablelands below seem endless. A craggy comb of rocks with a 360-degree view of the lower mountains and the sprawling lakes marks the summit. The trailhead is about a 25-minute drive from the gatehouse; allow about 4 hours for a round-trip hike of about 10km (6 miles).

Overlooking Nictau Lake is **Mount Sagamook Trail,** at an altitude of about 762m (2,500 ft.). This circular trail is a steep and demanding hike of about 8km (5 miles). At the summit, you're rewarded with spectacular views of Nictau Lake. For the truly gung-ho, there's the ridge walk that connects Sagamook and Carleton via **Mount Head.** The views from high above are unforgettable; but you'll need to set up a shuttle system (with a friend and two cars) to do the entire ridge in 1 day.

If you have a **mountain bike,** bring it. The cross-country ski trails, consisting of three interconnected loops (almost 14km/8 miles), are open to mountain biking in the summer. As well, the park's gravel roads here are perfect for exploring, and non-park vehicles are banned from several of these roads, which take you deep into the woods past clear lakes and rushing streams.

Finally, in winter, the park becomes part of a regional **snowmobile** trail system and also offers an 8km (5-mile) **cross-country ski trail** through the woods.

Where to Stay & Eat

Auberge Evasion de Rêves ★   The name "Dream Escape Inn," as it translates, might be a little over the top for this unremarkable property, but it does get you out of bad weather if you need to abandon the campground. Accommodations are scarce in these parts, so if you want to enjoy this wild part of the province, the Auberge is a reasonable stay. It's unpretentious, simply furnished, with a clean country motel feel. It has everything you need to give the family a break from hiking or touring—an indoor pool, dining room, lounge, and larger room that has the feel of a lodge. Some rooms are accessible for travelers with disabilities.

11 Canada St., Saint-Quentin. http://auberge-vasion-de-r-ves.jackrabbitreservations. com. ℂ **506/235-3551.** 14 units. C$109–C$146 double. Rates include continental breakfast. **Amenities:** Restaurant; bar; indoor pool; fridge (some units); no Wi-Fi, but direct cable connections in rooms (free).

6

NOVA SCOTIA

With 7,400km (4,598 miles) of coastline, it's no wonder Nova Scotia is dubbed Canada's ocean playground. It boasts a wide variety of landscapes in a relatively small province—rugged coastlines, deep wilderness, a verdant valley, ancient Appalachian highlands, feverish tidal zones, gentle northern shores, and one hip capital city.

Sightseeing   This province is best appreciated by driving it. **Cape Breton's Highlands** are ranked among the country's top scenic drives; the **Bay of Fundy**—which divides Nova Scotia from New Brunswick—is one of the natural wonders in the world.

Eating & Drinking   Freshly harvested seafood is the province's showcase, but drink is just as important: The province boasts award-winning wineries, microbreweries, distilleries, and was the producer of North America's first single malt whiskey. If you like wine, the northeast end of the Annapolis Valley around Wolfville is the home of Nova Scotia's burgeoning wine industry. Now several decades in, vintners here are making their mark on the international wine scene, particularly with crisp whites, sparkling wines, and dessert vino. Check out www.winesofnovascotia.ca to learn more about Nova Scotia specialties, Nova Scotia's appellation called **Tidal Bay ★★**, and to see a map of the province's wineries, concentrated as they are in the Annapolis Valley. Among the best are **L'Acadie Vineyards, Gaspereau Vineyards,** and **Benjamin Bridge,** but new wineries are coming on line all the time.

History   With habitation dating back to 1605, there is much to see and savor in Nova Scotia. But, on the whole, its attractions are not of the "dusty artifacts behind glass" variety. Instead, visitors find interactive museums, compelling historic sites, and whole heritage villages. Some of the best: the **Annapolis Royal, Fortress Louisbourg, Halifax Citadel, Ross Family Farm, Acadian** and **Highland Villages,** and the historic fishing vessels in **Lunenburg.**

Nature   Whether visiting with whales, riding the ocean surf, or watching sea birds fishing for dinner, the ocean that surrounds Nova Scotia is both a natural habitat and playground. Visitors can kayak hundreds of isolated, uninhabited islands and canoe vast wilderness preserves. Adventures on land include biking through the highlands, camping in a dark sky preserve, and photographing soaring eagles. Lace up your hiking boots to hunt fossils or ride the waves of the highest tides in the world. The options to explore here are endless.

EXPLORING NOVA SCOTIA

Visitors to Nova Scotia should spend a little time poring over a map—and this book—before leaving home. It's a good idea to narrow down your options, because numerous loops, circuits, and side trips are possible, and the permutations only multiply once you factor in various ferry links to and from the U.S., New Brunswick, Prince Edward Island, and Newfoundland. You don't want to spread yourself *too* thin. The only travelers who complain about Nova Scotia are those who try to see it all in a week.

Here's a bit of guidance: Looking for picture-perfect scenes of coastal villages? Focus mostly on the South Shore. Drawn to hiking amid dramatic, rocky coastal vistas? Allow plenty of time for Cape Breton Island. In the mood for more pastoral ocean scenery? Head for the Fundy Coast. Want to spend quiet time wilderness canoeing? Build your trip around Kejimkujik National Park.

Above all, schedule time for simply doing not much of anything. Strolling or biking along quiet lanes; picnicking on a beach; and watching the tides from docks, boat decks, and hotel porches—these are the best ways to let Nova Scotia's charms sink in at their own unhurried pace.

Essentials

VISITOR INFORMATION   The provincial government administers about a dozen official **Visitor Information Centres** (known as "VICs"; www. novascotia.com; ✆ **800/565-0000**) throughout Nova Scotia. These mostly seasonal centers are amply stocked with brochures and tended by knowledgeable staffers. In addition, virtually every town of any note has a local tourist information center. Request the province's excellent free road map, even if you operate by GPS.

GETTING THERE
BY CAR & FERRY   Most travelers reach Nova Scotia over land by car from New Brunswick. It's about a 3-hour drive from the U.S. border at Calais, Maine, to Amherst (at the New Brunswick–Nova Scotia border). To shorten the long drive around the Bay of Fundy, look into taking the ferry across the bay (operated by Bay Ferries) that links **Saint John, New Brunswick,** with **Digby, Nova Scotia.** Remarkably, this ferry sails daily year-round, with two sailings per day during peak travel periods.

The peak season one-way fare (June–Oct) is C$45 for adults, C$30 for children ages 6 to 13, C$5 per child under age 6, and C$35 for students and seniors. A car costs an additional C$90 (more for motor homes, trucks, vans, and buses), plus a C$20 fuel surcharge. Fares are a bit cheaper outside the peak travel months. Complete up-to-the-minute schedules for this route can be found at www.nfl-bay.com or by calling ✆ **877/762-7245.**

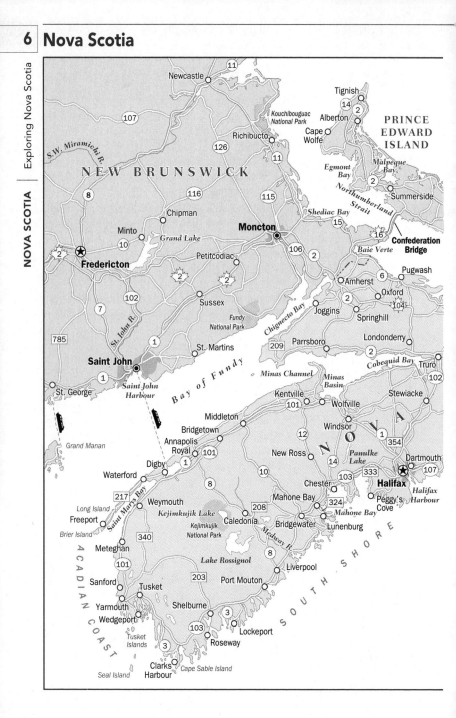

GULF OF
ST. LAWRENCE

To Îles-de-la-
Madeleine

Cape
North

To Newfoundland

Aspy Bay

Pleasant Bay
Chéticamp

Cape Breton
Highlands
National Park

Ingonish
Ingonish
Beach

Belle Côte

Prince Edward Island
National Park

Elmira
St. Peters

2

2

Stanhope
Charlottetown

Souris

3

Georgetown

Montague

4

Margaree Harbour
Margaree Forks
Inverness

CAPE BRETON
ISLAND

Sydney
Mines

105

Glace Bay

Baddeck

223

Sydney

Mira Bay

Ainslie
Lake

216

Louisbourg

Hillsborough
Bay

1

Woods
Island

High Bank

Whycocomagh

Iona

327

Scatarie
Island

Cape
George

19

105

Bras d'
Or Lake

4

Gabarus
Bay

Fortress of
Louisbourg

Pictou
Island

St. Georges
Bay

Port
Hawkesbury

St Peters

6

Pictou

245

337

Fourchu

256

New Glasgow

Antigonish

Bay
of Rocks

104

Stellarton

104

104

S   C   O   T   I   A

347

7

Guysborough

16

Chedabucto
Bay

289

348

16

316

Canso

W. St. Marys River

Melrose

316

Upper
Musquodoboit

211

Country Island

224

224

Sheet
Harbour

Liscomb

Ship
Harbour

Port
Dufferin

EASTERN   SHORE

7

Tangier

Musquodoboit
Harbour

ATLANTIC
OCEAN

Sable Island

Trans-Canada Highway
Ferry

0   50 mi

0   50 km

Another ferry service from **Maine** to **Yarmouth, Nova Scotia** has been an on-again, off-again option for many years now. Because the situation changes so often with this route, check with Tourism Nova Scotia (www.novascotia. com; *☎* **800/565-0000**) to see if there is a ship on the route; if so, ask for fee and schedule information.

For those traveling farther afield, ferries also connect **Prince Edward Island** to **Caribou, Nova Scotia** (see p. 45), and **Newfoundland** to **North Sydney, Nova Scotia**.

Also note that you can view the latest **updated highway conditions** around the province of Nova Scotia by logging onto the province's transportation website at http://511.gov.ns.ca/en. This map shows both road construction projects and unusual weather conditions affecting traffic. Or call *☎* **888/780-4440**.

BY PLANE   Halifax is the air hub of the Atlantic Provinces at **Stanfield International Airport** (www.hiaa.ca; *☎* **902/873-4422**). Seven airlines have regularly scheduled flights in and out. **Air Canada** (www.aircanada.ca; *☎* **888/247-2262**) provides daily direct service from Toronto and Boston and also flies directly to Sydney, Charlottetown, Saint John, and St. John's, as well as several more remote destinations in Eastern Canada. Other daily flights from the U.S. include American (www.aa.com; *☎* **800/433-7300**) directly from Philadelphia; Delta (www.delta.com; *☎* **800/221-1212**) from New York City; and United (www.united.com; *☎* **800/784-4444**) from Newark, New Jersey. Several airlines fly into Halifax from points within Canada, including Air Canada and **WestJet** (www.westjet.com; *☎* **888/937-8538**), connecting to several points in Ontario, as well as all other provinces. Porter Airlines (www. flyporter.com; *☎* **888/619-8622**) connects with Ontario, Québec, Newfoundland, and several U.S. cities.

BY TRAIN   **VIA Rail** (www.viarail.ca; *☎* **888/842-7245**) offers train service 3 days a week on the *Ocean* run between Halifax and Montréal; the entire trip takes between 18 and 23 hours depending on direction, with a basic summertime fare of about C$200 each way, not counting sleeping accommodations. VIA Rail connects with AMTRAK in Montréal and trains to Vancouver and Toronto. Seasonal discounts, special fares, and such make it worthwhile to shop early, and to be flexible about travel dates.

Sleeping berths and private cabins are available at extra cost—the cheapest bed, in a double-bunked cabin, is about twice the cost of the no-bed fare—and VIA has created an even higher class of service (summer-only) known as the Sleeper Touring class aboard the *Ocean*. This class includes meals, sleeping accommodations, exclusive access to lounges and a panoramic car, and continuing presentations from an onboard educator about Maritime Province culture and history. The *Ocean* departs Wednesday, Friday, and Saturday from Montréal and Halifax year-round.

THE GREAT OUTDOORS

BIKING   The low hills and gentle, low-traffic roads of mainland Nova Scotia make for wonderful cycling. The highlands of Cape Breton Island present the most challenging roads; the south coast, north coast, and Bay of Fundy regions yield wonderful ocean views while making fewer cardiovascular demands on the cyclist. A number of bike outfitters can aid in your trip planning. **Freewheeling Adventures** (www.freewheeling.ca; ✆ **800/672-0775** or 902/857-3600) is highly recommended for its guided bike tours throughout Nova Scotia (as well as Prince Edward Island). Want to go it alone? **Bicycle Nova Scotia** (www.cyclenovascotia.ca) keeps a useful and very simple website with downloadable maps, guides, and other information.

BIRD-WATCHING   More than 400 species of birds have been spotted in Nova Scotia, ranging from odd and exotic birds blown off course in storms to northern birds in their extreme southern range in summer to year-round residents like majestic **bald eagles.** Nova Scotia gained the distinction of having the highest concentration of breeding bald eagles in northeastern North America in 1975; by the mid-'80s, numbers were robust enough to supply eaglets to the northeastern United States to rebuild their population. The highest concentration is seen around Bras d'Or Lakes in the summer, but they appear throughout the province. Nova Scotia's official bird is the **osprey,** a smaller bird of prey nicknamed here "the fishhawk" because it dives dramatically for fish. You might spot poles erected for their use, topped with wide twig nests with chicks peering over the edge. Many whale-watching tours also offer specialized seabird-spotting tours, including trips to **puffin colonies.**

CAMPING   With backcountry options rather limited, Nova Scotia's forte is drive-in camping. The 20 or so provincial parks offer some 1,500 campsites. Campgrounds are uniformly clean, friendly, well-managed, and reasonably priced. For a complete list, visit www.novascotiaparks.ca. Make advance reservations at provincial or national parks during the summer. For a list of private campgrounds, check out the website run by the **Campground Owners Association of Nova Scotia** (www.campingnovascotia.com).

CANOEING & KAYAKING   Nova Scotia offers an abundance of accessible canoeing on inland lakes and ponds. The premier destination is **Kejimkujik National Park** in the southern interior, which has plenty of backcountry sites accessible by canoe. You can even trace traditional trading routes of the Mi'kmaq—check in with park staff for details. A number of other fine canoe trips allow paddlers and portagers to venture off for hours or days. **Canoe Kayak Nova Scotia** (www.ckns.ca) has a wealth of downloadable information, including route maps, on their website.

FISHING   Saltwater-fishing tours are easily arranged on charter boats berthed at many of the province's harbors or through websites such as **GetMyBoat.com**. Inquire locally at visitor information centers. No fishing license is required for *most* saltwater species for those on charters, but there are important restrictions. For questions, current fishing regulations, or lists of licensed fishing guides, check out the Nova Scotia **Department of Fisheries and Aquaculture** website at www.gov.ns.ca/fish.

Committed freshwater anglers come to Nova Scotia in pursuit of trout, bass, and the tragically dwindling Atlantic salmon, which requires a license separate from that for other freshwater fish. **Salmon licenses** must be obtained from a provincial office, campground, or licensed outfitter.

GOLF   With the opening of **Cabot Links** in 2012 and **Cabot Cliffs** in 2016, Nova Scotia golf hit the big time. These sister courses run along the coast in Inverness on Cape Breton Island. Both *Golf Digest* and *Golf Magazine* placed Links in the world's top 100 courses upon opening. *Canada Golf Magazine* named Cabot Links the country's top course. These and more than 70 other courses make a golfing holiday to Nova Scotia particularly attractive, especially when you consider that the tempering influence of the Atlantic Ocean on the weather means some courses on the South Shore are playable up to 10 months a year.

New courses are always being constructed. For one-stop shoppers, **Golf Nova Scotia** (www.golfnovascotia.com) represents about 20 well-regarded properties around the province and sells golfing packages at its member courses.

HIKING & WALKING   Serious hikers make tracks for **Cape Breton Highlands National Park,** which is home to the most dramatic terrain in the province. But trails are found throughout Nova Scotia. An energetic "rails to trails" movement has seen former railway beds converted to hiking trails, and communities have developed these and other trails as a way to give visitors and residents more to do. Ask at the visitor information centers, check the "Trails" sections in the province's official *Doers' & Dreamers' Guide* (available at www.novascotia.com or by calling ✆ **800/565-0000**), or buy any of the excellent books by Nova Scotia hiking guru **Michael Haynes.**

SAILING   Any area with so much indented coastline, and so many islands, is kismet for sailors. Tours and charters are available almost everywhere there's a decent-size harbor. The province's premier sailing experience for the non-sailor is an excursion aboard the *Bluenose II,* which is virtually an icon for Atlantic Canada, and calls at Halifax, Lunenburg, and other ports. (See the "Lunenburg" section, later in this chapter.) Bras d'Or Lakes are very popular with sailing fans. An extensive listing of boat tour operators can be found in the "Outdoors" sections in the *Doers' & Dreamers' Guide.* Skilled sailors will want to check in with the Nova Scotia Yachting Association. They have a race schedule, events, and sailing school information at www.sailnovascotia.ca.

SEA KAYAKING   Nova Scotia's 7,600km (4,722 miles) of coastline is increasingly attracting the attention of kayakers worldwide. Sea kayak excursions are especially rewarding when seals, puffins, or porpoises come alongside. Kayakers traveling on their own should be especially cautious on the Bay of Fundy side; the massive tides create strong currents that overmatch even the fittest of paddlers. More than a dozen kayak outfitters do business in Nova Scotia, offering everything from 1-hour introductory paddles to intensive weeklong trips. The town of Shelburne on the South Shore holds an annual **Kayak Festival** (www.shelburnekayakfestival.ca) in August that includes lessons, entertainment, and paddles.

Among the most respected outfitters is **Coastal Adventures,** 84 Mason's Point Rd., Tangier (www.coastaladventures.com; $\mathcal{C}$ **877/404-2774** or 902/772-2774). The company is run by veteran kayaker and doctorate-in-biology Dr. Scott Cunningham, who leads trips throughout the Maritimes and Newfoundland. For kayaking on the eastern side of Cape Breton, check with **North River Kayak** (www.northriverkayak.com; $\mathcal{C}$ **888/865-2925** or 902/929-2628). Owner Angelo Spinazzola is a native Cape Bretoner and a professional musician.

WHALE-WATCHING When on the Nova Scotia coast, you're never far from a whale-watching operation. Around two-dozen such tour outfits offer trips in search of finback, humpback, pilot, and minke whales, among others. The richest waters for whale-watching are on the Fundy Coast and Cape Breton. Fundy Bay is where the endangered right whale is often seen feeding in summer; thus, Digby Neck (the thin strand of land extending southwest from the town of Digby) has the highest concentration of whale-watching excursions in the province, but you'll find them in many other coves and harbors, as well. Pods of pilot whales on the Atlantic coast are a sight to behold. See our recommendations for Digby and Cape Breton later in this chapter.

THE PARRSBORO SHORE ★★

The shoreline route, from Amherst at the New Brunswick border south to Advocate Harbour, then on to Masstown to rejoin the Trans-Canada Highway, is far too often overlooked, and yet it is rich in history and dramatic landscapes; a great place to begin travels in Nova Scotia. This is where the ancient geological history of the Earth's crust and early life forms are exposed, and where First Nations legends and the history of early European settlers live in the landscape and in the tiny communities scattered along an otherwise wild coast.

From Amherst, take Route 6 to the 1,000-hectare (2,471-acre) **Amherst Point Bird Sanctuary ★★**, where 228 species of birds have been spotted. Some 8km (5 miles) of walking trails lead across a marsh and through woods with 300-year-old trees to a point overlooking the wetlands, where many ducks, waders, and dabblers (like the American Bittern) hang out. There is no entry fee; interpretive signs guide visitors.

From the sanctuary, find Route 302 to Route 242 to **Joggins,** the location of a UNESCO World Heritage Site. Built on top of a former 250-year-old coal mine, **The Joggins Fossil Centre ★★★** at 100 Main St. (www.jogginsfossil cliffs.net; $\mathcal{C}$ **902/251-2727;** June–Aug, 9:30am–5:30pm; Apr, May, Sept, and Oct, 10am–4pm) is a compelling introduction to the world's most complete fossil record of "the coal age." Some 15km (9⅓ miles) of 30m (100-ft.) high cliffs have eroded to reveal some 200 fossilized species from a time 300 million years ago when these latitudes were home to steamy swamps and forests where amphibians reigned and early reptiles evolved. Charles Darwin described Joggins in his revolutionary book, *On the Origin of Species.* This place truly is a world treasure. Admission ranges from C$11 to C$75, depending on the level of engagement, including options for guided tours of the cliffs and a brown-bag lunch.

From Joggins, head out on Route 209 to **Advocate Harbour** on the southernmost tip of this peninsula that juts into the Bay of Fundy. This is where you can hike and camp in one of Nova Scotia's most remote, challenging, and rewarding wilderness areas, **Cape Chignecto Provincial Park ★★★** (www.parks.gov.ns.ca/parks/cape-chignecto.asp; ℂ **902/392-2085;** open mid-May to mid-Oct). Forget the car; there are no roads, just 40km (25 miles) of trails. You'll be carrying on your back everything you need for overnights at one of 28 walk-in front-country campsites, which are a short walk from the parking lot. If you choose to hike into one of the 47 campsites in seven backcountry locations, or in one of four cabins, you'll be hiking considerable distances. The wooded landscape is characterized by flat headlands that dip suddenly into ravines, which then lead to isolated coves flanked by towering 180m (600-ft.) cliffs, past which the raging tides of Fundy roar.

The southern stretch of this scenic route from **Advocate** through **Parrsboro** to **Five Islands** is nicknamed "The Little Cabot Trail" for the undulating rural road that hugs the coast, providing grand views of the Bay of Fundy tides and the dramatic cliffs and headlands they cut into these low hills. At **Parrsboro,** you'll find a clutch of attractions that might keep you overnight and perhaps longer. The **Fundy Geological Museum ★★** at 162 Two Islands Rd. (http://fundygeological.novascotia.ca; ℂ **902/254-3814;** weekdays 9am–5pm, Sat noon–5pm, Sun noon–4pm; C$8.25/adult, C$6.75 senior, C4.75 kids 6–17) interprets the ancient geological history of the area with lifelike models and fossils of Earth's first reptiles, early dinosaurs, giant dragonflies, and bugs the size of baseball bats. At the **Ships Company Theatre ★★**, 18 Main St. (www.shipscompanytheatre.com; ℂ **800/565-7469** or 902/254-3000), a schedule of professional live theater, usually of original local material, is interspersed with concerts in every musical genre. Interestingly, the theatre is built around the steal-hulled former ferry, the MV Kipawo.

Stop at the village of **Five Islands** for a seaside lunch and views of these islands of First Nations legend (see Five Islands Provincial Park listing below). The landscape becomes gentler and increasingly pastoral as you approach **Economy,** where you can stop at Nova Scotia's first, and still one of its best, artisanal cheese makers, **That Dutchman's Cheese Farm ★★** (www.thatdutchmansfarm.com; ℂ **902/647-2751**) at 4595 Rte. 2 in Upper Economy. Pick up a wedge or a wheel of excellent Dutch-style cheeses like spicy, melt-in-your-mouth Dragon's Breath Blue or the intense Old Growler, an aged Gouda. If kids are in the car, treat them to a visit to That Dutchman's delightful homemade zoo with pigs, peacocks, and assorted pets.

Where to Stay

Five Islands Provincial Park ★★ According to Mi'kmaq legend, the first human was a giant named Glooscap who was also the creator. In one story, a giant beaver dammed his medicine garden, so Glooscap threw mud, stones, and sticks at the animal, trapping him inside one of five islands. This provincial park looks out over these islands from a headland that rises abruptly from the surging tides of the Bay of Fundy on 90m (300-ft.) sea cliffs. The park includes two of these islands—Moose and Diamond. The setting is spectacular, but the campground has few amenities. A long walk or a short drive away, the tiny village of Five Islands has a couple of restaurants and stores for supplies.

Bentley Branch Rd., Five Islands. http://parks.gov.ns.ca/parks/fiveislands.asp. ℰ **902/662-3030.** 87 sites C$26. **Amenities:** Wood, ice, trails.

Lightkeepers Kitchen & Guest House ★★ The two houses at the foot of this lighthouse—formerly a lightkeeper's residence, today a four-room inn and restaurant—are blessed with one of the most dramatic settings in all of Canada. Perched on the edge of a cliff, with waves battling below (part of the "Dory Rip," the pounding surf produced by the heaving of the world's highest tides), it would be impossible to stay the night in a more deliciously isolated spot . . . without camping out. But there are creature comforts here: In the restaurant guests are treated to a three-course feast of a dinner; and while guestrooms either share a bathroom or use one down the hall, they are otherwise very comfortable, with colorful bedding on top of good mattresses and shiny hardwood floors. *One warning:* Guests park above the inn and then walk down a rocky path, carrying their belongings: not ideal for those with mobility impairments. To get there, follow the big blue Cape d'Or Scenic Area signs from Advocate Harbour up a 6km (3¾ miles) dirt road and over a headland to the parking lot.

Cap d'Or. www.capedor.ca. ℰ **902/670-0534.** 4 units. C$80–C$110 double or C$340 whole house. **Amenities:** Restaurant, trails, no Wi-Fi.

The Maple Inn ★★ This 1893 Victorian mansion, built for a shipbuilder, is within walking distance of everything you'll want to see and do in Parrsboro. From the affordable C$99 "Buttercup Room" with twin beds, floral wallpaper, and Victorian-era chairs to the grand "Empire Suite" with its regally ornamented Viennese bed, Jacuzzi-style tub, chandelier, dramatic wallpaper (red-and-white striped with a border of scenes from Botticelli paintings), and a bay window cushioned for sitting, each room is elegant in its own way. The Buttercup is the only room of the seven without an en suite bathroom. Deeply cushioned rugs keep sounds from traveling from room to room. An excellent breakfast is included in the nightly rate.

2358 Western Ave., Parrsboro. www.mapleinn.ca. ℰ **877/267-5346** or 902/254-3735. 6 units. C$95–C$200. Rates include full breakfast and afternoon tea. **Amenities:** Air-bubble tub (some units), Wi-Fi (free).

Where to Eat

Black Rock Bistro ★★ BISTRO "Fried" is not a food group, but you'd be forgiven for thinking so in these parts. The antidote to all that unhealthy

If you're headed from the Truro area southwestward along the Fundy Coast toward the Annapolis Valley, **Route 215** offers a wonderful **coastal detour ★** from Maitland to Windsor. This winding, fast, and rather narrow road (not recommended for bicyclists) passes through a number of quiet hamlets, some with handsome early buildings. But the chief appeal comes in the sudden vistas of lush green farmland and broad views of Minas Basin beyond. At the town of Walton, there's a solid lighthouse on a rocky bluff with a nearby picnic area just off the main route (it's well marked). This detour runs about 90km (56 miles) from South Maitland to Brooklyn. Few services for tourists are offered, other than a handful of restaurants, B&Bs, and campgrounds. Look for general stores and farm stands if you need a snack.

eating is Black Rock, where a chef is his early 20s has made partnerships with local farmers to put food that doesn't need to be battered to be tasty on the plate. Many dishes are a marriage of local and exotic, imported ingredients, like the blackened haddock served with quinoa and a lemon hollandaise sauce. Other dishes are all Nova Scotian, like the primo fish chowder, vegan-friendly farmer's plate, and salads accented with Dutchman cheeses from up the shore.

151 Main St., Parrsboro. www.blackrockbistro.ca. © **902/728-3006.** Mains C$15–C$23. May–Oct, daily for lunch and dinner with special openings in Nov, Christmas, New Years.

Wild Caraway ★★★ CANADIAN   Far from the madding crowd is a humble restaurant in an old Nova Scotia home where a chef named Aitken scours the fields, forest, and sea for delicacies to supply his kitchen. This place really is the most remarkable in the Maritimes for making the best use of wild, foraged ingredients. A few items from the spring foraging menu will demonstrate the breadth of his knowledge and imagination: seaweed popcorn; mackerel tartare with corn lilies; local flounder with sea lettuce, oyster leaf, and clam goodness; rose crème brûlée, elderflower cake, sweet cicely flower ice cream; mountain ash caramel profiterole. At other times, the menu is less exotic (in a local way), but every bit as fine—seafood chowder, pulled pork sandwich, fishcakes—and always employing local ingredients whenever possible.

3727 Hwy. 209, Advocate Harbour. www.wildcaraway.com. © **902/392-2889.** Mains C$22–C$30. Open May to mid-Oct, Thurs–Sun 11am–9pm summer, 11:30am–7pm spring & fall.

ANNAPOLIS VALLEY ★★

Wolfville ★★

The trim Victorian village of **Wolfville** (pop. 4,300) has a distinctively New England feel to it, both in its handsome architecture and its compact layout—a small commercial downtown just 6 blocks long is surrounded by shaded neighborhoods of elegant homes. And it's not hard to trace that sensibility back to its source: The area was largely populated in the wake of the American Revolution by transplanted New Englanders, following the expulsion of the original Acadian settlers by the British.

More recently, the farmlands around Wolfville are being transformed into productive vineyards, making for a new **wine industry** that has matured over the past 3 decades to become a producer of increasingly quaffable—now award-winning—wines, particularly whites, sparkling, and dessert wines. Check out www.winesofnovascotia.ca to learn more about Nova Scotia specialties, Nova Scotia's appellation called **Tidal Bay,** and to see a map of the province's wineries, concentrated as they are in the Annapolis Valley.

The town's mainstay is the pastoral **Acadia University,** which has nearly as many full-time students as there are residents of Wolfville. The university's presence gives the small town an edgier, more youthful air. Don't miss the university's **Art Gallery** at 10 Highland Ave. (at the corner of Main St.) ★ (http://gallery. acadiau.ca; ✆ **902/585-1373;** Tues–Sun noon–4pm, Thurs noon–7pm; free admission), which showcases both contemporary and historical Nova Scotian art.

EXPLORING WOLFVILLE

Strolling through the village is a good way to spend a half-day; the leafy hardwood trees that shade the extravagant Victorian architecture make for an ideal walk. Check out the excellent **Wolfville Farmers Market** ★★ at 24 Elm Ave. (www.wolfvillefarmersmarket.ca; ✆ **902/697-3344**) every Saturday morning from 8:30am to 1pm and Wednesdays from May to December 4 to 7pm. The main drag is lined with shops and restaurants to explore, and there's a refurbished old cinema that now houses **The Al Whittle Theatre** ★ at 450 Main St. (www.alwhittletheatre.ca; ✆ **902/542-3344**) where you can catch live entertainment, films, and in November, parts of a Nova Scotia signature festival of international stature called **Devour! The Food Film Fest** ★★ (www.devourfest.com; ✆ **902/440-1551**). Yes, a festival about food films with great culinary events from fine dining to food trucks and farmers markets.

Info on current events can be found at the **Wolfville Tourist Bureau** (www. wolfville.ca; ✆ **877/999-7117** or 902/542-7000) at 11 Willow Ave. (in Willow Park) on the northern edge of the downtown area; it's open daily from mid-April through October. The nearby train station at 21 Elm Ave. is now a National Historic Site, and home to the **Wolfville Memorial Library** (www. valleylibrary.ca; ✆ **902/542-5760**).

At **Blomidon Provincial Park** ★★ (www.novascotiaparks.ca; ✆ **902/662-3030**), 24km (15 miles) north of Route 101 (exit 11), some 14km (8.7 miles) of trail take walkers through forest and along the coast. Among the most dramatic trails is the 6km (3.7-mile) **Jodrey Trail** ★, which follows towering cliffs that offer broad views over the Minas Basin. It's open from April through early October. Stay at the 70-site campground by checking availability and booking online at the site above.

The drive from Wolfville to Scots Bay on Route 358 is a scenic one through small towns and farmland. Stop at **Fox Hill Cheese House** ★ at 1678 Church St. (www.foxhillcheesehouse.com; ✆ **902/542-3599**) 2km (1¼ miles) the other side of Port Williams to load up on delicious local cheeses (a hiking snack?). Then it's up and over what's known as the North Mountain. This ancient, worn remnant of the Appalachians is now little more than a long, high ridge that separates the verdant Annapolis Valley from the cooling effects and fog of the Bay of Fundy. From the top of this ridge, the view across the valley to the South Mountain and the Minas Basin is one of Nova Scotia's finest vistas.

For a truly rewarding adventure, drive 25 minutes on Route 358 to the end of the road in Scots Bay, and park near the beginning of the **Cape Split Trail ★★★**, perhaps mainland Nova Scotia's most rewarding; you can't miss the trailhead. This 16km (10-mile) trail offers breathtaking vistas, especially on cresting oceanside cliffs that approach 122m (400 ft.) in height over tides that sometimes roar past the rocks below. Allow a couple of hours to walk (it's about an hour of challenging mountain biking) to the end, and most of a day to truly enjoy an in-and-back excursion through shady mixed forest to cliff-edge fields at the end of this hook of land that extends far into the Bay of Fundy.

EXPLORING GRAND-PRÉ

A side trip to neighboring Grand-Pré will happily fill a day and enhance your appreciation of the area and its Acadian heritage. Horticulturalists in particular should allow time to savor the area. Begin with a fresh roasted coffee at Nova Scotia's very successful fair-trade coffee merchants (the first in Canada to go fair trade) **Just Us! Grand-Pré Coffee House ★★** at 11865 Hwy. 1, Grand-Pré (www.justuscoffee.com; ✆ **902/542-7474**). Browse the small fair-trade coffee museum and the many Just Us! products, including excellent chocolate and teas. Just down the road, at 11827 Hwy. 1, Grand-Pré, the **Tangled Garden ★** (www.tangledgardenherbs.ca; ✆ **902/542-9811**) transforms herbs and fruit into jewel-like chutneys, liqueurs, vinegars, and jellies like garlic rosemary or raspberry lavender. It's a delightful place to stop and wander about, drinking in the aromas of the herbs and enjoying the whimsy of the artwork in the small gallery and gardens.

Grand-Pré National Historic Site ★★ HISTORIC SITE   To appreciate the troubled history of these lands, a stop at this UNESCO World Heritage Site is required. Hardworking Acadians vastly altered the local landscape, in large part by constructing a series of dikes outfitted with ingenious log valves, which allowed farmers to convert the saltwater marshes to productive farmland. At the modern, unobtrusive **visitor center,** visitors learn about these dikes and the history of the Acadians who populated the Minas Basin from 1680 until their expulsion *(le Grand Dérangement)* at the hands of the British in 1755. Some 11,500 were forcefully deported from these and other Acadian communities, their homes and farms burned when they refused to sign oaths of allegiance to the British crown. Many died on their way to Louisiana, where they became the Cajuns. Today, Grand-Pré ("great meadow") features superbly tended grounds with green lawns studded by weeping willows, excellent for picnics. A graceful stone church—built in 1922 on the presumed site of the original Acadian church as an interpretive center—features commemorative works of art and fascinating artifacts, like a ledger that lists all

For proof that the Bay of Fundy really does have some of the world's highest tides, take **Hwy. 1** to **Route 341,** which turns into **Route 359** and follow it to **Halls Harbour ★**. There you'll find fishing boats moored as at the wharf as you'd expect . . . if it's high tide when you arrive. If it's low tide—or if you want to wait around for about six hours—you'll see those same boats stranded far below the deck of the wharf on the mud flats. This tiny fishing village dates from 1779; its history relayed by interpretive panels. There's a boardwalk and shoreline to explore. The buildings of the **Hall's Harbour Lobster Pound and Restaurant ★** ((📞 **902/679-5299**) date from the 1820s, and today house a restaurant with tables on the wharf and all the seafood you can eat.

those deported. Evangeline Bellefontaine, the revered (albeit fictional) heroine of Longfellow's epic poem *Evangeline,* was said to have been born here; look for the tragic heroine's iconic statue (created in 1920 by Canadian sculptor Philippe Hérbert) in the garden gazing longingly over her shoulder at the church. From here, you can bike the 9km (5.6 miles) of hardpacked-dirt trail along the tops of the dike.

2205 Grand-Pré Rd., Grand-Pré. www.grand-pre.com. 📞 **902/542-3167.** Admission C$7.80 adults, C$6.55 seniors, C$3.90 children age 6–16, C$19.60 families. Mid-May to mid-Oct daily 9am–5pm.

WHERE TO STAY

Wolfville boasts more than its fair share of grand, Victorian era inns . . . and little else. Among them, the ornate **Gingerbread House Inn ★** at 8 Robie Tufts Dr. (www.gingerbreadhouse.ca; 📞 **888/542-1458** or 902/542-1458), which looks like a giant dollhouse in pink, frilly trim (surprisingly, most rooms feature contemporary decor—cool blue walls and white-wicker furniture in one) with three double rooms and four suites, is a good choice. A full, hearty breakfast is included in the rates. Here are two others that really stand out.

Blomidon Inn ★★★ This rambling 1800s sea captain's mansion, now a 33-unit inn, is perhaps Wolfville's finest lodging. The rooms come with eye-candy period furnishings like four-poster beds or beds with elaborately carved headboards, wardrobes, and ornate fireplaces, Victorian loveseats, antique carpets, and artwork. The ambience of an English manor house is enhanced by the extensive Victorian style gardens. Dining is superb here, the kitchen drawing on foraged delicacies and an array of fine and fresh ingredients including local vegetables and Nova Scotia seafood. Afternoon tea from 3 to 4:30pm and continental breakfast are included in the room rate. *One warning:* It's a steep climb to third-floor bedrooms, so ask to be switched if you have mobility issues.

195 Main St. www.blomidon.ns.ca. 📞 **800/565-2291** or 902/542-2291. 29 rooms C$119–C$159; 2 suites C$159–C$209; cottage C$249–C$269. **Amenities:** Restaurant, Internet (free). Restaurant open for lunch and dinner. Mains C$17–C$36.

The 110km (68-mile) drive along **Route 1** from Wolfville to Annapolis Royal is the best way to see the intervening small towns, farms, and scenic country-side of the Annapolis Valley. Once you get past the busy commercial district of New Minas and the much nicer town of **Kentville ★**, you'll stumble upon farm-ers markets stuffed with local produce, pleasant small picnic parks, u-picks, and historic attractions in and between towns and villages like Kingston and Middleton. Alternatively, even more rural **Routes 201 and 221** offer their own charms through long stretches of the valley.

The first stop on a tour of this agri-culturally rich valley has to be **Noggins Corner Farm Market ★★** beside the road on Rte. 1 at 10009 (www.noggins farm.ca; *𝄞* **902/542-5515**) for buys on old variety apples like Cox's Orange Pippin and Russet, and many other fruit and vegetable choices. Check the freezer for wild boar sausage. Out back, the Noggins giant **Corn Maze ★★** will delight kids and adults. It's open week-days 11am to 6pm from late August to November when the corn is high.

If your accommodations allow you to cook for yourself, stop at **Meadow-brook Farm Meat Market ★** 314 Pleas-ant Valley Rd.—from Hwy. 1, take Route 360 3km (1.9 miles) through Berwick before turning right onto Pleasant Valley Road and driving 1.7km (1 mile) until you see the sign (www.meadowbrook meatmarket.com; *𝄞* **902/538-1106**). Open Monday to Saturday 8:30am-5:30pm. You'll find locally raised, top-quality pork, poultry, and beef cuts, sausages, and deli meats as well as local apple ciders, preserves, and other Valley specialties.

To complete the Annapolis Valley meal you're building, stop for fruit, berries, vegetables, and creative condiments like Fire Engine Jelly and Lebanese Pickles at **Dempsey Corner Orchards ★★** at 2717 Route 221 off Exit 16 near Ayles-ford (www.dempseycorner.com; *𝄞* **902/847-1855**), a fifth generation family-run farm with a fantastic u-pick—57 varieties of apples and lots more of cherry, plum, peach, pear, blue-berry, raspberry, and so on. There's a petting zoo where witty co-owner Allison Maher might introduce you to a rooster named Russell Crowe or Hamlet the pig-let (get it?). Or there's the apple-driving range for golfers with a sense of humor.

Back across Hwy. 1 through Ayles-ford, treat the kids (or yourself, if you enjoy zoos) to an afternoon at **Oaklawn Farm Zoo ★** at 997 Ward Rd (www.oak lawnfarmzoo.ca; *𝄞* **902/847-9790**) where lions and lemurs, pythons and pigs vie for the hearts of visitors. Open daily 10am to dusk, C$8 adults, C$5 seniors and students, C$2.50 children 3 to 12, free for children 2 and under.

For a family-oriented place to stay in central Annapolis Valley, you know you gotta pick **Yogi Bear Jellystone Park ★★** which is at, get this, 43 Boo Boo Blvd, 4km (2½ miles) from Kingston (www.jellystonens.com; *𝄞* **888/225-7773**). The overnight options are many, from cabins to serviced RV sites to tent-ing. Fun activities like free archery with an inflatable bear, bumper cars, jumping pillows, swimming pool, playground, and mini golf . . . and of course, Yogi Bear cartoons are all part of the deal. From Kingston, head north on Maple Street onto Bishop Mountain Road. Turn left onto Brooklyn Street, then right onto Boo Boo.

Tattingstone Inn ★★   Built in 1874 as a farmhouse, this registered heritage property was once home to Leslie R. Fairn, an outstanding Canadian architect who designed many of Nova Scotia's public buildings. He raised a family in the main house and worked out of the Carriage House. Decorated with a deft touch and furnished with antiques, the carriage house rooms are a little smaller than in the main house, but still pleasant—and they showcase fine examples of modern Canadian art. The blue-and-cream "Toad Hall" room in the carriage house has the most privacy, because it's in a separate building on the back of the property. There's a living room downstairs, while the upstairs offers a queen-size bed and two-person Jacuzzi. The heated outdoor pool is a bonus, as is the enclosed sun porch, which nicely captures the early evening light.

620 Main St. www.tattingstone.ns.ca. ℂ **800/565-7696** or 902/542-7696. 9 units. July–Oct C$128–C$178 double; Nov–Apr C$98–C$160 double, Apr–June C$118–C$165. Rates include full hot breakfast. **Amenities:** Outdoor pool, Jacuzzi (some), fireplace (some), no phone, Wi-Fi (free).

Victoria's Historic Inn ★★   This stellar inn, a 10-minute walk from downtown, was constructed by apple mogul William Chase in 1893, and remains a head-turner for its ornate ornamentation. The sturdy Queen Anne–style building features bold pediments and pavilions adorned with balusters and elaborate Stick-style trim. Inside, it feels like you've wandered into a Victorian parlor. There's dense mahogany and cherry woodwork throughout, along with exceptionally intricate ceilings. Several of the inn's suites have fireplaces and Jacuzzis. The deluxe two-room Chase Suite (the most expensive unit), for instance, features a large sitting room with a gas fireplace, double Jacuzzi, queen-size bed, and an oak mantle. Less expensive third-floor rooms are smaller and somewhat less historical in flavor.

600 Main St. www.victoriashistoricinn.com. ℂ **800/556-5744** or 902/542-5744. 16 units. C$119–C$229 double and suite. Rates include full breakfast. **Amenities:** Jacuzzi (some), Wi-Fi (free).

WHERE TO EAT

For a small town, Wolfville's dining options are eclectic and, for the most part, topnotch. From gastro pubs to fine dining, coffee shops to ethnic fare, the possibilities are many. In addition to Blomidon Inn and Just Us! (see above), **Il Dolce Far Niente Espresso Bar** ★ at 15 Elm St. (ℂ **902/542-5307**) beside Troy Restaurant (see below), is a top spot for coffee, pastries, or light lunch. Below is a selection of the best eateries in their categories.

LeCaveau Restaurant ★★★   GOURMET CANADIAN   Chef and cookbook author Jason Lynch landed a recent "Restaurant of the Year" award for chef-inspired fine dining from The Taste of Nova Scotia, as well as the Prestige Award from the same organization. And we'll add to the accolades: This is one of the finest restaurants in all of Nova Scotia. Chef Lynch prepares regional specialties like wild scallops, sustainably farmed salmon, locally farmed rabbit, and even wild partridge with a cosmopolitan flair. Call ahead to ask about martini nights on the patio and for reservations.

11611 Hwy. 1, Grand-Pré. www.grandprewines.ns.ca. ⓒ **866/479-4637** or 902/542-7177. Lunch entrees C$11–C$15, dinner entrees C$29–C$36. Daily May–Oct 11:30am–2pm & 5–8:30pm. Nov–Dec open for dinner only and Sun brunch. Closed Jan–Apr.

Naked Crêpe Bistro ★ CRÊPERIE   Surprisingly, the best thing on this crêperie's menu is its superb thin-crust pizza. Not to say the crêpes aren't also good, they are: well-made, generously portioned, and either savory or sweet (the Nicolette is both: melted brie, spinach, strawberries, sliced almonds, all drizzled with maple syrup). We find the crêpes seasoned with Mexican or Thai are tempting, but we usually head here for the excellent 'za.

402 Main St. ⓒ **902/542-0653.** Breakfast crêpes under C$10; mains C$7.50–C$17. Sun–Thurs 9am–11pm; Fri–Sat 8am–midnight.

The Port Pub ★★ CANADIAN   The on-site Sea Level Brewery and great pub food put this gastro pub on the map as soon as it opened. Situated in a new building beside the tidal Cornwallis River in nearby Port Williams (under a 10-minute drive from Wolfville on Rte. 358), the prices here are very reasonable and the atmosphere friendly, mostly because this is a community-owned venture created to showcase local beers ("Blooberry Pail Ale" is made with wild blueberries), foods ("Moo, Cluck, Oink" is a trio of sliders—beef, chicken, pork—with home fries), and wines, as well as to rejuvenate the community and take advantage of pastoral views across the dike lands. Everything from the salad ingredients to the cheese is locally sourced and delicious. Check the website for the live entertainment schedule.

980 Terry's Creek Rd, Port Williams. www.theportpub.com. ⓒ **902/542-5555.** Entrees $13–$22. Sun–Wed 11am–9pm, Thurs–Sat 11am–10pm.

Troy Restaurant ★ MEDITERANNEAN   At Troy, you'll find a busy dining room with a decorous warehouse feel, and an outdoor garden patio where Med fare like flame-seared kabobs are prepared in an open kitchen, along with traditional lamb, seafood, and vegetarian dishes. If you're here on a Wednesday, enjoy live music and specials on drinks and mezze platters. There's parking on the street, free Wi-Fi, and takeout available.

12 Elm Ave. www.troyrestaurant.ca. ⓒ **902/542-4425.** Mains C$16–C$25. Mon–Sat 11am–9pm; Sun noon–8pm.

ANNAPOLIS ROYAL ★★

Annapolis Royal is arguably Nova Scotia's most historic town—it bills itself, with some justification, as "Canada's birthplace"—and it is a treat to visit. Because the region was largely overlooked by later economic growth (the bulk of the trade and fishing moved to the Atlantic side of the peninsula), it requires very little in the way of imagination to see Annapolis Royal as it once was. (The current year-round population is less than 500.) The original settlement was rebuilt on the presumed site of explorer Samuel de Champlain's famous

1604 visit; old Fort Anne still overlooks the upper reaches of the basin, much as it did when abandoned in 1854. The village maintains much of its original historic charm, with narrow streets and historic buildings fronting a now-placid waterfront.

Annapolis Royal is also considered by many historians to be the birthplace of the continent's historic preservation movement. Town residents have been unusually activist about preserving the character of their town, and as a testament to their dedication, some 150 buildings and homes in town are now officially designated heritage sites (and presumably can't be altered much by future owners). The affordable Victorian-era accommodations continue the historical theme of a visit. For anyone curious about Canada's early history, Annapolis Royal is one of Nova Scotia's absolute don't-miss destinations.

Essentials

GETTING THERE Annapolis is located at exit 22 off Route 101. It is 200km (124 miles) from Halifax, and 129km (80 miles) from Yarmouth.

VISITOR INFORMATION The **Annapolis Royal and Area Visitor Information Centre** (www.annapolisroyal.com; ⓒ **902/532-5454**) is 1km (⅔ mile) north of the town center at 236 Prince Albert Rd. (follow Prince Albert Rd. and look for the Annapolis Royal Tidal Generating Station). It's open daily 10am to 8pm, May 15 to October 15, and 10am to 6pm otherwise.

Exploring the Town

Start at the Visitor Information Centre, which is located at the **Annapolis Royal Tidal Power Generation Station ★** (ⓒ **902/532-5454**), where the extreme fall in the tides has been harnessed since 1984 to produce electricity. It's the *only* such tidal generator in North America. If you're so inclined, you can learn about the generator at the free exhibit center upstairs, open roughly from mid-May until mid-October. Pick up a copy of the free walking-tour brochure with an annotated map providing architectural and historic information. It's pretty amazing to stop and think, as you stroll down lower St. George Street, that you're walking down the oldest street in Canada.

In the evening, there's often entertainment in downtown Annapolis Royal at **King's Theatre ★**, 209 St. George St. (www.kingstheatre.ca; ⓒ **902/532-5466** or 532-7704). Shows range from movies to musical performances to variety shows to touring plays—and there are plenty of offerings for kids, too. Stop by or call to find out what's happening during your stay.

Children and adults alike adore the **Upper Clements Parks ★** (www.upperclements.com; ⓒ **888/248-4567** or 902/532-7557) on Route 1, about 5 minutes south of Annapolis Royal. It's an old-fashioned amusement park (you arrive after driving through an old orchard), full of low-key attractions that will delight younger kids. Highlights include the flume ride (originally built for Expo '86 in Vancouver), a wooden roller coaster that twists and winds through trees left standing during the coaster's construction, and a mini train. It's open daily in season from 11am to 7pm; admission to the grounds is C$11 plus tax, C$5 for children 3 and under. The rate includes admission to the wild animal park next door. At the adjacent **Tree Top Adventure Park,** try free falling and zip lining. Bracelets permitting unlimited access to rides run from about C$30 per day or C$20 for half a day. Ask for special offers if you are military or emergency services personnel.

Fort Anne National Historic Site ★ HISTORIC SITE   Not much is left of the many buildings and fortifications that have occupied these grounds since 1643, but there's enough to make it interesting. The 1708 gunpowder magazine is the oldest building in the entire Canadian National Historic Sites collection. There's a museum in the 1797 British field officers' quarters, including a model of what the place looked like in 1710 to contemplate its former glory. Many come here for a picnic or hike on the **Perimeter Trail** ★, an easy 530m-long (⅓ mile) path that follows the top of the star-shaped fort.

Entrance on St. George St. www.pc.gc.ca/eng/lhn-nhs/ns/fortanne/index.aspx. 🅲 **902/532-2397,** 532-2321 off-season. Admission C$3.90 adults, C$3.40 seniors, C$1.90 children, C$9.80 families. June–Sept 9am–5:30pm; off season by appointment only (grounds open year-round).

Historic Gardens ★★★ GARDEN   An hour or two at these exceptional gardens and you'll see why they were named the 2015 Canadian Garden of the Year at the Canadian Garden Tourism Awards. Open to the public since 1981, the 4-hectare (10-acre) grounds are uncommonly beautiful, with a mix of formal and informal gardens dating from various epochs. Set on a gentle hill, the plantings are placed among lawns and shady trails, all overlooking a beautiful salt marsh. You'll see a geometric Victorian garden, a knot garden, a vegetable garden, and a perennial border garden. About 2,000 rosebushes (of 230 cultivars) track the history of the flower's cultivation from earliest days through the Victorian era to the present day. Also on site: a replica Acadian pioneer cabin and garden, a cafe, and a gift shop.

441 St. George St. www.historicgardens.com. 🅲 **902/532-7018.** Admission C$12 adults, C$9.75 seniors and students, C$5 children 12–18, C$2 children 6–11, C$25 families, free for children under 6. July–Aug daily 8am–8pm; May–June and Sept–Oct daily 9am–5pm. Closed Nov–Apr.

Port-Royal National Historic Site ★★ HISTORIC SITE   Across the river from Annapolis, this site was selected by explorer Samuel de Champlain and survivors in his company after spending the disastrous winter of 1604 on St. Croix Island between New Brunswick and Main. For 8 years, the group lived here. To keep spirits up, they formed the Order of Good Cheer, a periodic feast designed to distract them during the long, cold winters. The buildings here are rustic shelters built with techniques the pioneers brought with them from France. This 1939 reproduction is convincing; costumed interpreters work away at traditional handicrafts like carpentry. Have the interpreters show you some of the techniques and tools (such as "rat-tailing" and "mortise and tenon") used in construction; they'll also talk about life in the colony during those difficult early years when the French first forged an uneasy alliance with local First Nations (demonstrations include ancient Mi'kmaq healing remedies).

10km (6¼ miles) south of Rte. 1, Granville Ferry (turn left shortly after passing the tidal generating station). www.pc.gc.ca. ✆ **902/532-2898.** Admission C$3.90 adults, C$3.40 seniors, C$1.90 children, C$9.80 families. May 15–Oct 15 Tues–Sat 9am–5:30pm, daily mid-June to Aug 9am–5:30pm. Closed mid-Oct to mid-May.

Outdoor Pursuits

A short drive from Annapolis Royal and Port Royal are the **Delaps Cove Wilderness Trails,** which provide access to the rugged Fundy coastline. Directions and a brochure are usually available from the visitor information center. Otherwise, head to Delaps Cove from Granville Ferry; veer left on the dirt road that cuts steeply downhill at a rightward bend shortly before the cove. Follow this dirt road to the end, where you'll find parking and trail maps.

Two trails lead from an overgrown farm road to the rocky coastline. Take the **Bohaker Trail** ★ (2km/1.2 miles) first, then decide whether you want to continue on to **Charlies Trail** ★ (1.9km/1.2 miles). Both are linked by the Shore Road Trail (2.7km/1.7 miles one-way). The return walk will take 3 to 4 hours. The Bohaker is a lovely loop through woodlands to a short coastline trail. The highlight is a cobblestone cove piled with driftwood, into which a small waterfall tumbles. The trails are well marked—once you find them, that is.

Where to Stay

With its rich fishing and merchant trade history, this region has a slew of mansions and heritage homes that have found new life as inns and bed-and-breakfast accommodations. This is your chance to experience the historic homes of movers and shakers, the sea captains and entrepreneurs of yesteryear, at inns like the 1849 **Hillsdale House Inn** ★ at 519 St. George St. (www.hillsdalehouseinn.ca; ✆ **877/839-2821** or 902/532-2345) with rates from C$89 to C$169 that is pet friendly and has lawn games; or the handsome 1868 **King George Inn** ★ at 548 Upper St. George St. (www. kinggeorgeinn.20m.com; ✆ **888/799-5464**) furnished with period pieces with rates from C$79 to C$150. Both include full hot breakfasts and free Wi-Fi in their rates. In addition, the following three are standouts:

Dunromin Campsite ★★ Private Dunromin was picked by *Today's Parent* as one of Canada's top 25 campgrounds. The attractive 9-hectare (22-acre) waterfront property on Route 1, just across the bay from the famed tidal generating station, has full hookups for trailers and RVs, and scenic tenting sites along the water's edge, plus high-speed Internet access, kayak and canoe rentals, water bikes, an on-site cafe, and a few cabins, RV rentals, a gypsy wagon, and "tipi." It's a short drive from Annapolis Royal.

4618 Hwy. 1, Granville Ferry. www.dunromincampground.ca. ✆ **844-292-1929** or 902/532-2808. 192 sites, 8 cabins. May to mid-Oct camping & RV sites C$28–C$43, cabins C$68 to C$113. **Amenities:** Fishing, rental boats, kayak lessons, playground, laundromat, Wi-Fi (free).

Garrison House Inn ★★ This 1854 registered heritage property faces Fort Anne in the heart of the town center and has a well-regarded **restaurant ★★**. Rooms give the feel of the Victorian era without the usual frou frou; instead you'll find pretty floral wallpapers, comfy beds, and pine floors overlaid with hook rugs. While the inn is close to the main road into town, traffic is very light. Still, if you're sensitive to noise, ask for a room overlooking the back yard rather than the street. Breakfast (included) is simple, but tasty and hearty.

350 St. George St. www.garrisonhouse.ca. ℂ **866/532-5750** or 902/532-5750. 7 units. C$99–C$149 July–Sept, C$89–C$135 mid-Apr to May and Oct, C$95–C$145 June, double. Street parking. **Amenities:** Restaurant, bar, Jacuzzi (1 unit), no phone, Wi-Fi (free).

Queen Anne Inn ★★★ You get the full Victorian at this 1865 mansion—and that's a great thing. Guestrooms are spacious, high-ceilinged, and decorated with tasteful antiques: four-poster lace canopy beds, ornate sleigh beds, Persian carpets, carved fireplaces, claw-foot tubs. It's a bit too elegant for toddlers, but the two-story attached carriage house, split into two bi-level suite units, is perfect for families. And children will love running about on the parklike grounds that enclose the inn. In the beverage room, a selection of local wines and beers are laid out for guests, and the included breakfast is a gourmet feast. Best of all is the high level of service from the cheerful young couple who own and run the Queen Anne. A truly special place.

494 Upper St. George St. www.queenanneinn.ns.ca. ℂ **902/532-7850.** 12 units. Early Apr to late Oct C$99–C$189. Rates include full 3-course breakfast. Closed late Oct to early Apr. Free parking. **Amenities:** Beverage room, Jacuzzi (some), no phone, Wi-Fi (free).

Where to Eat

Annapolis is just the kind of quiet, historic waterfront town where cafes abound, most concentrated in the short 4-block walk along stately St. George Street in front of Fort Anne and around the corner past King's Theatre to the wharf. None will disappoint, but the following are my favorites:

The Bistro East ★★ BISTRO Everything is handmade at this sunny little bistro, from the pizza and sandwich dough to the pasta. And that guarantees food that always tastes fresh, even when it's just a simple salad or plate of noodles. Not that all the food is basic: one of our favorites is the "Seafood Extreme," a rich and satisfying plate of pasta loaded with local lobster and scallops in "extreme lemon cream." Friday evenings feature live entertainment with no cover charge.

274 St. George St. www.bistroeast.com. ℂ **902/308-7992.** Reservations recommended. Main courses C$17–C$27. Open daily 11am–10pm.

Café Restaurant Compose ★★ CANADIAN/EUROPEAN Of course, you can't eat the view, but this restaurant's location, next to the boardwalk along the Annapolis River, means that diners are guaranteed tasty vistas. Complementing the "eye candy" is an Austrian-accented menu with several schnitzel dishes, and lots of excellent local seafood dishes like fish chowder or Scallops Charan in a European-style tomato-based sauce. Lobster and salmon also star on a number of plates.

235 St. George St. www.restaurantcompose.com. © **902/532-1251.** Reservations recommended. Main courses C$17–C$27. Open daily for lunch and dinner.

Ye Olde Town Pub ★ PUB FARE   Set in a cozy, 1884 brick building that was once a bank (hence the bars on the windows), Annapolis's only pub has an excellent selection of craft beers and a way with comfort food—mother of owner Brian Keevil invented "potachos," an addictive hybrid of fries and nachos (deep fried lattice potatoes are smothered in melted cheese, tomatoes, and green peppers and served with sour cream and salsa). Free Wi-Fi, a solid kids menu, and the chance to eat in the "smallest pub in Nova Scotia" are other reasons to take a meal—or a pint—here.

9-11 Church St. http://yeoldetownepub.wordpress.com. © **902/532-2244.** Main courses C$8–C$14. Mon–Fri 11am–11pm, Sat 10am–11pm, Sun noon–8pm.

KEJIMKUJIK NATIONAL PARK ★★

About 45km (28 miles) southeast of Annapolis Royal is a popular national park that's a world apart from coastal Nova Scotia. **Kejimkujik National Park,** founded in 1968, is commonly known as Keji and located in the heart of south-central Nova Scotia, and it is to lakes and bogs what the South Coast is to fishing villages and fog. Bear and deer, porcupine and raccoon are the full-time residents here; park visitors are the transients. Most stay in the **Jeremy's Bay campground** where over 300 sites, along with a few yurts and cabins, make for a busy front-country experience. The park, which was largely scooped and shaped during the last glacial epoch, is about 20% water, which makes it especially popular with canoeists and kayakers who reach backcountry campsites along waterways. Other remote sites take long hikes to reach. Shorter hikes take anywhere from 10 minutes to 2 hours, but are rewarding.

Bird-watchers are also drawn to the park in search of the 205 species that have been seen both here and at the **Kejimkujik Seaside Adjunct ★★** a 22-sq.-km (8½-sq.-mile) coastal holding west of Liverpool. Among the more commonly seen species are pileated woodpeckers and loons, and at night you can listen for the raspy call of the barred owl. The Adjunct is an hour drive from the inland park, and are alike in name only because white-sand beaches with seabirds and seals are the reward at the end of a half-hour hike. Kejimkujik was designated as Nova Scotia's first Dark Sky Preserve in 2010 by the Royal Astronomical Society of Canada, resulting in new programs relating to the ecological and cultural importance of night skies. Cultural heritage is celebrated through presentations such as a guided walk to view petroglyphs which portray the observations of Mi'kmaq people in the 18th and 19th centuries.

Essentials

GETTING THERE   Kejimkujik National Park is approximately midway on Kejimkujik Scenic Drive (Rte. 8), which extends 115km (71 miles) between

Annapolis Royal and Liverpool. Plan on about a 2½-hour drive from Halifax. Kejimkujik Seaside Adjunct is located off Route 103 at Port Joli southwest of Liverpool.

VISITOR INFORMATION   The park's **visitor center** (*©* **902/682-2772**) is open daily and features slide programs and exhibits about the park's natural history.

FEES   The park opens daily at 8:30am year-round, closing at 8pm in peak season (late-June through Labour Day), earlier on weekends in spring and fall. Entrance fees are C$5.80 for adults, C$4.90 for seniors, C$2.90 for children ages 6 to 16, and C$15 for families. Seasonal passes can cut the cost of a longer stay; they cost C$40 for adults, C$25 for seniors, C$15 for children ages 6 to 16, and C$74 for families. The campground kiosk stays open an hour later in peak season, until 9pm, to receive campers. Entry to the Seaside Adjunct is slightly less, with the family seasonal pass costing C$49. The park is closed November to mid-May.

Exploring the Park

Part of what makes the park so appealing (and serene) is its lack of access by car: One short park road off of Route 8 gets you partway into the park—but from there, you're forced to continue either on foot or by canoe. Over 80% of the park is only accessible by hiking or paddling.

A stop at the **visitor center** is worthwhile, both for its exhibits on the region's natural history, and a stroll on one of three short trails, including the Beech Grove loop (2km/1¼ miles), which takes in a glacial hill called a drumlin. The park has an audio-taped walking tour available for borrowing.

Canoeing is the best means of traversing the park, if you're into that. Bring your own craft or rent one at **Jakes Landing** from **Keji Outfitters** (www.whynotadventure.ca; *©* **902/682-2282**), 3km (2 miles) along the park access road. (You can also rent paddleboats, kayaks, rowboats, and cycles at the facility. If you arrive with nothing, they can outfit you with a complete camping package.) Route maps are provided at the visitor center, and rangers also lead short, guided canoe trips for novices. Multiday trips from backcountry campsite to campsite are a good way to get to know the park intimately, or cobble together an excursion from one lake to another (which might involve portaging your canoe over dry land between bodies of water. But the portage routes are on trails kept even and open, so the carries are relatively easy).

The park also has 15 **walking trails,** ranging from short and easy strolls to, well, longer easy strolls, and very long treks to backcountry campsites, including the 60km (37 miles) **Liberty Lake** trail. In other words, there's no elevation gain here to speak of. The 5km (3½-mile) **Hemlocks and Hardwoods Trail** loops through stately groves of 300-year-old hemlocks; the 3km (2-mile) one-way **Merrymakedge Beach Trail** skirts a lakeshore to end at a beach. **Snake Lake** and **Peter Point** begin on the same trail and are both 3km (2 miles) return. Each leads through shaded forest to scenic lakeside ends. A free map that describes the trails is available at the visitor center. Several of the trails are multi-use so bikers and hikers should be aware of each other.

Mountain bikers can explore the old **Fire Tower Road,** a round-trip of about 19km (12 miles); the road becomes increasingly rugged until it ends at a fire tower near an old-growth forest of birch and maple. There are four other trails in the park where bikes are allowed, as well, including the 16km (10-mile) **New Grafton Distance loop.** The other three trails are somewhat shorter, and are shared with hikers.

Camping

Backcountry camping ★★★ is this park's chief draw for locals. The more than 40 backcountry sites here are in such demand that they actually cost as much as the drive-in campsites. Overnighting on a distant lakeshore is the best way to get to know the park, so even if you're planning to car-camp, it's worth the extra time and expense of renting a canoe and paddling off for a night to one of these campsites just for the experience.

The canoe-in and hike-in sites are assigned individually, which means you needn't worry about noisy neighbors. Backcountry rangers keep the sites in top shape, and each is stocked with firewood for the night (the wood is included in the campsite fee). Most sites can handle a maximum of six campers. Naturally, the best sites are snapped up on weekends by urbanites from Halifax; midweek, you've got a much better shot, but either way, make a reservation as far ahead as possible. You can reserve backcountry sites up to 60 days in advance by calling the **visitor center** (ⓒ **902/682-2772**). *Note:* Your deposit is nonrefundable even if you have to cancel.

The park's drive-in campground at **Jeremy's Bay ★** offers about 360 sites, as well as yurts, cabins, and the hybrid oTENTiks, and this campground is open mid-May to mid-October. Campground rates are C$22 to C$29 per night. Make reservations by calling ⓒ **877/737-3783** or online at www.reservation.pc.gc.ca.

DIGBY TO YARMOUTH ★★

The 113km (70-mile) shoreline from Digby to Yarmouth has been described as down-home Canada at its best. Choose the meandering coastal Route 1, rather than Route 101 (faster but without scenery or community). Here you'll find Acadian enclaves; lively summer festivals; historic buildings; fishing villages; miles of sandy, lonely beaches; and spruce-topped basalt cliffs.

The unassuming port town of **Digby** is located on the water at Digby Gap—where the Annapolis River forces an egress through the North Mountain coastal range. Set at the south end of the broad watery expanse of the Annapolis Basin, Digby is home to the world's largest inshore scallop fleet. These boats drag the ocean bottom nearby and bring back the succulent Digby scallops famous throughout Canada. The town itself is an active community where life centers around the fishing boats, convivial neighborhoods of wood-frame houses, and no-frills seafood eating places. It also serves as Nova Scotia's gateway for those arriving from Saint John, New Brunswick, via ferry. Aside from the Digby Pines Golf Resort and Spa, which warrants its own trip (see p. 191), the town is worth checking out.

Digby Neck ★★

Look at a map of Nova Scotia and you'll see the thin strand of **Digby Neck** extending southwest from Annapolis Basin. This scenic peninsula is a nature lovers' paradise lying between the Bay of Fundy and St. Mary's Bay. You can catch any number of boats to watch whales, or kick back and relax secure in the knowledge that rush hour will never hit this long, bony finger of high ridges, spongy bogs, dense forest, and ocean views. Maybe you're like me and just get a kick out of following a road to its end. The last two knuckles of this narrow peninsula are islands, both of which are connected via quick, 10-minute ferries across straits swept by currents as strong as 9 knots.

Neither the neck nor the islands have a lot of services for tourists beyond a mix of basic accommodations (a lodge, B&Bs, and so on) and a few general stores. But it's well worth the drive if you're a connoisseur of end-of-the-world remoteness. The village of **Sandy Cove** on the mainland is picture-perfect, with its three prominent church steeples rising from the forest and a footprint so narrow it has wharfs on both sides of the peninsula. There really is a sandy beach in this cove. Both Tiverton on Long Island and Westport on Brier Island are unadorned fishing villages.

ESSENTIALS

GETTING THERE   Digby is Nova Scotia's gateway for those arriving from **Saint John,** New Brunswick, via ferry. The ferry terminal is on Route 303, west of Digby. The ferry terminal is on Rte. 303, just west of Digby. Trips can and from Nova Scotia can be booked through **Bay Ferries** (www.ferries.ca; ✆ **877/762-7245**) for C$45 per adult in peak season, C$90 per car.

If you're indeed arriving by ferry and want to visit the town before pushing on, look sharp for signs directing you downtown from the bypass, lest you end up on Route 101 and headed out of town by mistake. Coming from the rest of Nova Scotia, take exit 26 off Route 101 to reach Digby.

From Digby, Route 217 runs about 72km (45 miles) south to **Brier Island.** Two **ferries** bridge the islands, and they run 24 hours a day, year-round. The first boat leaves **East Ferry** (about a 45-min. drive from Digby) on the mainland for **Tiverton,** Long Island, every half-hour; the second ferry departs Long Island for **Brier Island** on the hour. (The ferries are timed so that you can drive directly from one ferry to the next, if you don't dally too much on the road between.) The fare is C$5 for each ferry (C$10 total), and you pay each full fare on the outbound leg. Make sure you have the correct fare because it's cash only.

VISITOR INFORMATION   The province maintains a visitor information center (✆ **888/463-4429**) in downtown Digby open mid-May to September.

On Long Island, you can pick up local information inside the **Islands Museum ★** at 3083 Hwy. 217 (www.islandshistoricalsociety.com; ⓒ **902/839-2034**) in Tiverton. It's a tiny place, but the museum gives considerable room to Joshua Slocum, the first person to sail solo around the world and the most famous person in the history of the island. The museum is open June to mid-October and is free to enter.

If you're in the area in early August, don't miss **Digby Scallop Days ★** (www.digbyscallopdays.ca), a salty local celebration of the shellfish that gives the town its fame. Expect scallop-shucking contests, raffles, food, busking, and general merriment. A fancy event? No. A slice of real Nova Scotia life? Yes. Another slam-dunk event for motorcycle enthusiasts: the **Wharf Rat Rally ★★★** (www.wharfratrally.com; ⓒ **902/245-5924**), held on Labour Day weekend, is one of the largest rallies in Atlantic Canada, bringing thousands to town and filling the streets with bikes, competitions, stunts, and parades. This is a huge event, filling rooms with a radius of at least an hour's drive. If you like bikes and biker culture, this is nirvana. If you don't, stay away.

EXPLORING DIGBY NECK

BICYCLING   Brier Island is a stellar destination for mountain bikers. Just 6×2km wide (4×1½ miles), it's the right scale for spending a slow afternoon poking around dirt roads that lead to two of the island's red-and-white lighthouses. Brier Island maps are available for free at island stores and lodges. If you park your car on the Long Island side and take your bike over on the ferry, you'll save money; there's no charge for bikes or pedestrians.

You can rent a bike cheaply at the local youth hostel, the **Digby Backpackers Inn ★** (ⓒ **902/245-4573**) at 168 Queen St. (see "Where to Stay & Eat," below).

HIKING   On **Long Island,** two short but rewarding woodland hikes bring you to the open vistas of St. Mary's Bay and the Bay of Fundy. The trail head for the first, the 800m (½-mile) hike to **Balancing Rock ★★**, is about 4km (2½ miles) south of the **Tiverton** ferry on Route 217; look for a well-marked parking area on the left. The steep, dramatic trail ends at the ocean's edge where boardwalks lead over the surging ocean to get a dead-on view of the iconic column of basalt balancing improbably atop another column.

For the second short hike, return to the parking lot and drive 5km (3 miles) south to the **picnic area** on the right. From the parking lot atop the hill, a hike of about 1km (½-mile) descends gradually through a forest of moss, ferns, and roots to the Fundy shore. The coastline here looks almost lunar, its dark rock marbled with thin streaks of quartz.

Farther along, **Brier Island** is also laced with **hiking trails** offering fantastic opportunities for seaside exploration. Pick up one of the maps offered free around the island. One good place to take a walk is at the **Grand Passage Lighthouse ★** (turn right after disembarking the ferry and continue until you can't go any farther). Park near the light and walk through the stunted pines to the open meadows on the western shore, where you can pick up a **coastal trail.**

Birdwatchers make pilgrimages here to witness the fall migration when the air fills with flocks of particular species of hawks, songbirds, and shorebirds.

WHALE-WATCHING ★★ Here in the Bay of Fundy, ocean currents mingle and the vigorous tides cause upwelling, which brings a rich assortment of plankton up to the surface from the briny depths. That means a free, all-you-can-eat buffet for some species of whales, which feed on these minuscule creatures, making it the prime whale-watching location on mainland Nova Scotia. As the fishing industry has declined and the interest in whales increased, the number of fishermen offering whale-watching tours has boomed. Most of these are down-home operations on converted lobster boats or newer versions on fast zodiacs—don't expect gleaming ships like you might find elsewhere.

Your chances of seeing fin, minke, or humpback whales is excellent, and many guides offer guarantees. (Right, sperm, blue, and pilot whales have also occasionally been spotted over the years.) Plan on spending around C$50 to C$60 per adult for a 3- to 4-hour cruise; less per child.

Among the many choices of operators, we recommend the following three. Local resident Penny Graham operates **Mariner Cruises ★** (www.novascotia whalewatching.ca; ✆ **800/239-2189** or 902/839-2346) in **Westport** on Brier Island, using the *Chad and Sisters Two,* which is equipped with a heated cabin. Both whale- and bird-watching tours are offered.

Petite Passage Whale Watch ★ (www.ppww.ca; ✆ **902/834-2226**) sails the *Passage Provider 04,* which has a partially covered deck, out of **East Ferry.** It runs two to three cruises daily from June through October for C$58 per adult, less for children, seniors, students, and group members.

For a saltier adventure, join biologist Tom Goodwin with **Ocean Explorations ★** (www.oceanexplorations.ca; ✆ **877/654-2341** or 902/839-2417), which offers tours out of **Tiverton** on rigid-hulled inflatable Zodiacs—they call it ocean rafting. The largest boat holds up to a dozen passengers and moves with tremendous speed and dampness through the fast currents and frequent chop around the islands and the open bay; guests are provided with survival suits for warmth and safety. The 2- to 3-hour trips cost C$65 per adult, less for children, seniors, students, and group members.

WHERE TO STAY & EAT

Brier Island Lodge ★ The property resembles a summer camp (dated furnishings, no A/C, and few creature comforts), but most don't mind because they're here for the spectacular nature all around, and the Lodge's well-run whale- and/or bird-watching tours. If you approach this as a nature-oriented stay, you won't be disappointed; along with the set tours, hiking trails connect the lodge with the Fundy Shoreline. Saving grace: The food at the restaurant is solid and you eat it looking through soaring glass windows overlooking the Grand Passage 40m (131 ft.) below.

Brier Island, Westport. www.brierisland.com. ✆ **800/662-8355** or 902/839-2300. 40 units. Open May–Oct. C$99–C$159 double. **Amenities:** Dining room, lounge, courtesy phone in lounge, Wi-Fi (some rooms, free).

Digby Backpackers Inn ★★ Toody the cat welcomes guests to this comfortable hostel, with a fully equipped kitchen and a barbecue out back for cooking your own meals. There's a spacious garden with a firepit and a size-able living room where guests gather around the fireplace to play guitar, dip into the book exchange, or watch TV. Take your choice of dorm rooms or doubles—either will be clean and pleasant. All bathrooms are shared, but breakfast and Wi-Fi are included in the reasonable rates.

168 Queen St., Digby. www.digbyhostel.com. © **902/245-4573.** 40 units. Open May–Oct. Dorm room C$30, double C$65. **Amenities:** Kitchen & barbecue, breakfast, linens, towels, Wi-Fi (free).

Digby Pines Golf Resort & Spa ★★ An iconic Nova Scotia resort, the red-roofed Digby Pines, situated on 121 hectares (299 acres), has sweeping views of the Annapolis Basin close to the Digby–Saint John ferry terminal. As the name suggests, the resort is surrounded by pines, and is a throwback to an era when moneyed families headed to fashionable resorts for the summer. For many years, the province of Nova Scotia owned and operated this 1929 classic in Norman château style, but it's now privately owned and recently renovated. Rooms have white-paneled walls and carpeted floors with modern furnishings; they come in a variety of sizes from small rooms with twin beds to luxury suites. Alas, the walls could be thicker (if you have loud neighbors, you'll hear them). Thirty or so cottages of one- to three-bedrooms each are ideal for families, most of them outfitted with fireplaces, air-conditioning, and mini refrigerators. Amenities are a reason for coming: An Aveda spa offers a full menu of treatments and services, plus an 18-hole Stanley Thompson–designed golf course threads its way through pines and over a brook—kids 15 and under can play for free. The resort's Annapolis Room is open for three meals daily, serving Nova Scotian cuisine with a French flair.

103 Shore Rd., Digby. www.digbypines.ca. © **800/667-4637** or 902/245-2511. 79 rooms, 6 suites, 31 cottages. C$159–C$442 double. Packages available. Closed mid-Oct to mid-May. **Amenities:** Restaurant, bar, bike rentals, concierge, golf course, health club, heated outdoor pool, sauna, spa, 2 tennis courts, A/C (cottages only), fireplaces (cottages only), fridge (cottages only), Wi-Fi (free).

Summer's Country Inn ★ Unlike many Maritime B&Bs, Summer's is not overflowing with character. Still, it's just a 5-minute walk into the heart of town and well-maintained, with spotless guestrooms (some with four-poster canopy beds and wingback chairs, others looking more like modern motels) and service that can't be faulted—the owners and staff here are genuinely friendly and helpful. Along with B&B rooms, the owners also rent out a couple of housekeeping units closer to the action in "downtown" Digby, although the action might be little more than a few fishermen gossiping on the wharf. The housekeeping units are popular with families who make use of the fully equipped kitchens—basically, you're renting an apartment.

16 Warwick St., Digby. www.summerscountryinn.ca. © **902/245-2250.** 11 units (9 B&B, 2 off-site housekeeping units). Open May–Oct. C$89–C$129 double. **Amenities:** Breakfast included with B&B rooms only, fully equipped kitchens in housekeeping units only, Wi-Fi (free).

The Acadian Coast

The Acadian Coast (called the "French Shore" by English-speaking locals) runs roughly from St. Bernard to Salmon River. This hardscrabble coast, where the fields were once littered with glacial rocks and boulders, was one of the few areas, along with the eastern coast of New Brunswick and parts of Cape Breton, where Acadians were allowed to resettle after their 1755 expulsion from English Canada.

Today, you'll find abundant evidence of the robust Acadian culture. The colors of the ubiquitous Stella Maris (the Acadian red, white, and blue flag, with its prominent star) are everywhere. Summer festivals celebrate this culture with traditional live music and dancing, often performed in historic Acadian costume. Towering Catholic churches mark the center of each of the small towns that stretch along this coast from one to the other. There's a French language university here, too, where Acadian culture is studied and celebrated. Fishing is still the economic fuel, so wharves and boats and businesses catering to fishermen's needs are abundant.

ESSENTIALS

GETTING THERE   The Acadian Coast is traversed by Route 1. Speedy Route 101 runs parallel, but some distance inland; take any exit from 28 to 32 and follow Route 1 that hugs the coast and cuts through towns and villages.

VISITOR INFORMATION   It's best to collect information in the major towns bracketing either end of this stretch; that means heading to either the **Yarmouth Visitor Centre** (p. 195) at 228 Main St. or Digby's **information center** (p. 188) on Route 303.

EXPLORING THE ACADIAN COAST

A drive along this seaside route offers a pleasant detour, in both pace and culture. You can drive its whole length, or pick up segments by exiting from Route 101 and heading shoreward. The distance is only just over 100km (62 miles), so take your time and savor the sights.

Start with the magnificent **St. Mary's Church ★★★** at Church Point (adjacent to the campus of Université Sainte-Anne, the sole French-speaking university in Nova Scotia). Many towns here are proud of their impressive churches, but none is quite so awe-inspiring as St. Mary's. You can't miss it: The imposing, gray-shingled French Breton–style church has the feel of a European cathedral—yet St. Mary's, built between 1903 and 1905, is made entirely of wood. It's said to be the tallest and biggest wooden church on the entire continent. Outside, the church is impressive enough—a steeple rises some 56m (184 ft.) above the grounds, with some 40 tons of rock helping to provide stability in the wind. Inside, though, it's even more extraordinary— entire tree trunks serve as columns (they're covered in plaster to lend a more traditional appearance), and there are plenty of windows and arches to give architectural weight to the place. A small museum in the rear offers glimpses of church history. Open mid-May to October, 9am to 5pm. Admission by donation; please leave one.

Also here you'll find the flavors of the coast at **Rapure Acadienne Ltd.** ★ (✆ **902/769-2172**), a small specialty shop. Rappie pie is an Acadian wholemeal pie, typically made with beef or chicken. The main ingredient is grated potatoes, from which the moisture has been extracted and replaced with chicken broth. The full and formal name is "pâté a la rapure," but look for signs for "rapure" or "rappie pie" along Route 1 on the Acadian Coast. This unassuming shop on Route 1, just south of Church Point, prepares one of the best examples. You can pick up a freshly baked beef or chicken rappie pie here for about C$5. The shop is open daily year-round, usually from around 8am.

Find Acadian culture in Church Point at **Rendez-vous de la Baie Cultural and Interpretive Centre** ★ (✆ **902/769-2345**). Located on the Université Sainte-Anne campus, this center houses an artist-run gallery, souvenir boutique, theater, and an Internet cafe. The Interpretive Centre is a top place to learn about Acadian culture. Admission is free, but donations are appreciated.

In Meteghan, one of the oldest Acadian houses on the French Shore is now a small historical museum called **La Vieille Maison** ★ (✆ **902/645-2389**). It displays artifacts of Acadian life in the 19th century (like a scrap of original French wallpaper uncovered during restoration of the summer bedroom) and is furnished with Acadian antiques. Open daily in summer. Admission is free; guided tours are available.

A few minutes south of Metaghan, the small provincial park called **Smuggler's Cove** ★ has a picnic area and steps running steeply down to a cobblestone cove. From here, you'll have a view of a tidal cave across the way. Rum runners were said to have used this cave—about 5m (16 ft.) high and 18m (59 ft.) deep—as a hide-out during the Prohibition era. Admission is free.

Farther along the coast, the **Mavillette Beach** ★★ is now a provincial park and has nearly all the ingredients for a pleasant summer afternoon—lots of sand, grassy dunes, changing stalls, a nearby snack bar with ice cream, interpretive panels, and views across the water to scenic Cape Mary. Some hardy souls take dips in the usually frigid waters on weekends when swimming is supervised. The beach is 1km (⅔ mile) off Route 1, and the turnoff is well marked. It's open mid-May through mid-October. Admission is free.

Another lovely provincial park, **Port Maitland Beach** ★★, is near the breakwater and town wharf. It isn't quite as scenic or pristine as Mavillette Beach, and it is closer to Yarmouth, attracting larger crowds, principally families. Still, this sand and cobblestone beach is backed by a grassy picnic area and dunes. Change houses are available, and there's supervised swimming in summer. Open mid-May to mid-October.

WHERE TO STAY

Accommodations are pretty thin in this area; most are small, unpretentious B&Bs offering varying degrees of comfort. They are quite affordable, however; you could pay as little as C$50 for a night in a double room. It all depends on what you want. Push to the Annapolis Valley if you want a fancy inn, or to Yarmouth for a family motel or chain hotel if you'll be heading for the South Shore next. Head inland at Annapolis Royal to **Kejimkujik National Park** ★★ (p. 185) if you're after a wilderness experience.

If you'd like to stay on the Acadian Coast, here are three selections. **A la Maison D'Amitie** ★ (www.houseoffriendship.ca; ☎ 888/645-2601) sits on a clifftop down a dirt road in Mavillette, with two oceanfront suites starting at C$145 in peak season and a much more expansive, ground-floor suite with vanity sinks and a Jacuzzi. The home boasts an impressive 152m (500 ft.) of ocean frontage in addition to its views, and lives up to its name, translated as "House of Friendship." You might also try **L'Auberge au Havre du Capitaine** (www.havreducapitaine.itgo.com; ☎ 902/769-2001) on Route 1 in Meteghan River, a standard motel with eight rooms at rates ranging from about C$60 to C$99 per night; a few even have Jacuzzi tubs. As a bonus, there's a local Acadian-cuisine restaurant on the premises. **Château Sainte-Marie** at 959 Hwy. 1 (☎ 902/769-3113) has seven rooms in a 1920 oceanfront home with a sitting room and deck for enjoying the view. It's open April 1 to December 31 with rates from C$95 to C$129.

Yarmouth & the Acadian Shore

It's a mixed bag of people who've inhabited Yarmouth. Mi'kmaq called the area "Keespongwitk," meaning "lands' end." France's Samuel de Champlain named a fishing village here Cape Forchu in 1604 and Acadians exiled from Grand-Pré returned to settle here. United Empire Loyalists, settlers loyal to Britain who fled the United States, arrived in the late 1700s. Ideally located at the southwestern tip of Nova Scotia closest to the United States, Yarmouth quickly became a thriving shipbuilding center and seaport, at one point boasting more tonnage per capita than any other port in the world. One of the first screw propellers was built here. Seafaring history was made in 1932 when Molly Kool was issued master's papers, making her the first female ship captain in the world.

Visitors will see the legacy of this seafaring heritage when they visit Yarmouth today. There are some 400 sea captains' homes in the region, built between 1850 and 1900 with riches gained at sea. The architectural styles of the homes reflect the ports of call and grandeur experienced by these world travelers. Take time to explore these neighborhoods and this rocky sea coast, part of the world's largest lobster fishing grounds.

Yarmouth today is a great base for exploring the Acadian Shore, which extends on both sides of the town along the coast. The state of the ferry to Maine has been in flux for several years, carriers coming and going. Check with the Visitor Information Centre (below) or Tourism Nova Scotia (www.novascotia.com; ☎ 800/565-0000) for the latest on contact information, American departure ports, and fees.

ESSENTIALS
GETTING THERE   Yarmouth is at the convergence of two of the province's principal highways, routes 101 and 103. It's approximately 300km (186 miles) from Halifax.

WORLD CLASS WILDERNESS LODGE—trout point

With the looks of one of the classic National Park lodges (think: the majesty of the Old Faithful Inn in Yellowstone) and the soul of a Ritz Carlton, the **Trout Point Lodge ★★★** has won accolades from every major reviewer form *The New York Times* to *National Geographic Traveler.* We're adding our voice to the chorus of approval. Set in an isolated and pristine area on 40 hectares (100 acres) of forest next to the enormous Tobeatic Wilderness Preserve, the three-story lodge is created from massive spruce logs and hand-cut granite. Rooms and public areas are decorated with Tiffany lamps, oriental carpets, and furniture cunningly created from what look like bent twigs (in some cases, and including some bed frames). The luxuries continue with a riverside, wood-fired hot tub, a real library, and a staff that bend over backwards to make sure all is right in this little world. Guests spend the day hiking on nature trails, and paddling, kayaking, or fly fishing on the rivers that surround the lodge. After a day of activity (and before one), guests are coddled by truly fine dining—Trout Point's cooking team of Vaughan Perret and Charles Leary bring a distinctly Cajun approach to local and foraged Nova Scotia delicacies. Their careers saw stops in Louisiana, Costa Rica, and Spain, so they bring to the wilderness an extremely sophisticated sensibility. (Cooking classes are among the sought-after activities here). A memorable vacation experience.

189 Trout Pt. Rd., East Kemptville. www.trout point.com. ℂ **902/761-2142.** Inn 11 units plus 1 cottage. Open mid-May to Oct. C$169–C$350. Children must be 14 and older. No cell-phone coverage. **Amenities:** Restaurant, 2 bars, sauna, hot tub, canoes and kayaks, massage, bicycles, hiking trails, guided fishing, phones in room, Wi-Fi (some units, free).

VISITOR INFORMATION   The **Yarmouth Visitor Centre** (ℂ **902/742-5033**) is at 228 Main St., in a modern, shingled building you simply can't miss. Both provincial and municipal tourist offices are located here, open June to mid-October, daily from 8am to 4:30pm.

EXPLORING THE AREA

The tourist bureau and the local historical society publish a very informative walking-tour brochure covering downtown Yarmouth. It's well worth requesting at the Yarmouth Visitor Centre (see above). The guide offers general tips on what to look for in local architectural styles (how do you tell the difference between Georgian and Classic Revival?), as well as brief histories of significant buildings. The entire tour is 4km (2½ miles) long.

The most scenic side trip—an ideal excursion by bike or car—is to **Cape Forchu** and the **Yarmouth Light ★★** (www.capeforchulight.com; ℂ **902/742-4522**). Head west on Main Street (Rte. 1) for 2km (1¼ miles) from the visitor center, then turn left at the horse statue. The road winds out to the cape, past seawalls and working lobster wharves, meadows, and old homes.

When the road finally ends, you'll have arrived at the red-and-white-striped concrete lighthouse that marks this harbor's entrance. (The lighthouse dates from the early 1960s, when it replaced a much older octagonal lighthouse that succumbed to wind and time.) There's a museum, gift shop, and tea room where you can refresh with a light lunch locally known as a "mug up." The museum is open daily 9am to 7pm, the tearoom 11am to 7pm.

Leave enough time to ramble around the dramatic rock-and-grass bluffs—part of Leif Ericson Picnic Park—that surround the lighthouse. Don't miss the short trail out to the point below the light. It's a great place for a picnic.

Art Gallery of Nova Scotia (Western Branch) ★★ GALLERY

This gallery in Yarmouth is a satellite of the famed AGNS in Halifax (see p. 275), a specialist in folk art and the very best of Canadian contemporary art. Works usually in the Halifax gallery travel here for display; it's the only other place in the province to see them, and they're often quite compelling viewing.

341 Main St. www.artgalleryofnovascotia.ca. ℭ **902/749-2248.** Admission by donation. Wed–Fri 8:30am-4:30pm, Sat–Sun 11:30am–4:30pm.

Firefighters' Museum of Nova Scotia ★★ MUSEUM

Here's a real surprise, a museum to Nova Scotia firefighting that is truly engrossing to more than just emergency response workers. Kids will love the antique equipment, including hand-drawn pumpers and other historic fire trucks. They can climb up on some of the trucks and pretend to drive or check out the antique toy engine collection. Canada's oldest horse-drawn steam engine from 1863 is here. For adults, the history of the firefighting craft and the shocking story of devastating fires in Nova Scotia's history will engage.

451 Main St. http://firefightersmuseum.novascotia.ca. ℭ **902/742-5525.** Admission C$4 adults, C$3 seniors, C$2 children 6–17, C$8 families, free for children under 6. Open Mon–Fri 9am–4pm, Sat 1–4pm.

WHERE TO STAY

Yarmouth is home to a number of mom-and-pop and chain motels. Some of the better choices in town follow are the **Best Western Mermaid Motel ★** 545 Main St. (www.bwmermaid.com; ℭ **800/772-2774** or 902/742-7821), with rates of around C$106 to C$160 double and an outdoor pool; the **Lakelawn B&B Motel ★** 641 Main St. (www.lakelawnmotel.com; ℭ **877/664-0664** or 902/742-3588) is a combination of motel and B&B with very reasonable rates at around C$59 to C$99 double; and the business-hotel-like **Rodd Grand Hotel ★** 417 Main St. (www.roddvacations.com; ℭ **800/565-7633** or 902/742-2446), with rates ranging from C$101 to C$161 double per night and an indoor pool. All offer free Wi-Fi.

A number of quality B&Bs in historic homes stand out in Yarmouth as well, including **Harbour's Edge ★**, 12 Vancouver St. (www.harboursedge. ns.ca; ℭ **902/742-2387**), with four rooms that go for C$145 to C$175 in a Victorian home set on sizable grounds; and the **MacKinnon-Cann Inn ★★** at 27 Willow St. (www.mackinnoncanninn.com; ℭ **866/698-3142** or 902/742-9900). Though pricey at C$125 to C$239, it has a restaurant and seven very nice rooms themed by decade from 1900 to 1960. Both provide free Wi-Fi.

Ellenwood Provincial Park ★★ About the same distance from town as Lake Breeze, but along Route 340, this charming Provincial Park and campground is set between two lakes on a 114-hectare (280-acre) wooded site. Walking trails lead through mature hardwood, there's a playground, and the beach is supervised. If you're towing a boat, you can launch it in the sizeable lake and try some fishing. The campground is closed in winter, but visitors are welcome to hike and ski here any time.

1888 Mood Rd, Deerfield. www.novascotiaparks.ca. ✆ **888/544-3434** or 906/761-2400. 87 sites, C$26. Open mid-May to early Sept. Reservations required. **Amenities:** Hiking trails, playground, showers.

Guest-Lovitt House ★★ The four rooms here will please those who appreciate ornate, lacey, floral furnishings and decorations that suit the historic character of the downtown property (down to the backyard gazebo). Think white upholstered love seats, four-poster beds, antique wooden furniture, and, in some rooms, a fireplace. If that sounds too frou-frou for you, look elsewhere.

12 Parade St. www.guestlovitt.ca. ✆ **866/742-0372** or 902/742-0372. 4 units C$149– C$239. Breakfast included. Free parking. **Amenities:** Laundry service, Wi-Fi (free).

Lake Breeze Campground and Cottages ★ Fifteen kilometers (9⅓ miles) west of town on Route 1 is this little, privately run spot with an appealingly low-key character. It sits right on the shores of tiny Lake Darling for easy access to the water. Boat rentals are available for $5 an hour. Five cottages on site are relatively small, but fully equipped. Though a little close to the main house, the cottages do share a large backyard and front lawn. Everything is well tended by the owners.

2560 Hwy. 1. www.lakebreezecampground.com. ✆ **902/649-2332.** 50 sites, C$21– C$29; 5 cottages C$65–C$104. Open mid-May until mid-October. **Amenities:** Washrooms with showers, canteen, horseshoe pit, fishing, Wi-Fi (free).

WHERE TO EAT

Yarmouth is one of those few larger centers in Nova Scotia and, indeed, across the Maritimes, that has yet to undergo the same widespread culinary revolution as the rest of the region and produce a stand-out restaurant. While there are a couple of reasonable standbys, the options are overwhelmingly fast food, and only a few independents are worth trying. (The one exception—if at a stretch you consider it a Yarmouth-based restaurant—is **Trout Point Lodge,** above.)

Having said that, Chef Michael at the **MacKinnon-Cann Inn** (see above) does give a solid three-course performance featuring fresh, local ingredients creatively prepared for a set price of C$50 per person. It's open Wednesday to Saturday, and reservations are required (✆ **866/698-3142** or 902/742-9900). If you wish, you can bring your own wine. In addition, here's where to find something other than a chain burger.

Old World Bakery and Deli ★★ BAKERY Fresh bread, baked daily, is the foundation for very good deli sandwiches at a place some Yarmouthians say is a local saving grace. Besides the hearty deli sandwiches, calzones,

When you leave Yarmouth, travel east on scenic Route 3. Pubnico, about 40km (25 miles) down Route 3, is the oldest Acadian Village in the world. Visit the restored Acadian Village to get a taste of pioneer life. Facing the wharf (where one of the biggest fishing fleets in Atlantic Canada ties up), **Dennis Point Café** ★ (www.dennispoint cafe.com; © **902/762-2112**) is a solid diner usually loaded with fishermen. The heaping servings of seafood are so large, they're presented on serving platters. Another 40km (25 miles) along scenic Route 3, you'll come to a small commercial area at the entry to the causeway to Cape Sable Island. If you haven't already dined, pop into **The**

Lobster Shack ★★ (www.lobstershack. ca; © **902/637-1788**) where a former fisherman offers up simple but well-prepared lobster, fish, and other dishes created for the restaurant by a professional chef, a menu that won this little eatery the "Restaurant of the Year, Essence of Nova Scotia Award." Head across the causeway on the short, circular drive around Cape Sable Island for a look at a thriving fishing community. Stop at the wharves and chat up the fishermen, most of whom will be glad to stop for a yarn. Ask directions to The Hawk, Nova Scotia's most southern point and a beach known for bird-watching and views of the province's tallest lighthouse, the Cape Sable Light.

soups, and salads, there's a bit of an international flair here with sauces and dips like tzatziki, hummus, and tabouli, as well as the house specialty, loaves of bread (with such unusual ingredients as olive sage, sweet potato walnut, and rye) and tons of pastries to takeaway.

232 Main St. www.facebook.com/pages/Old-World-Bakery-and-Deli/124191087621923. © **902/742-2181.** Price range C$4 to C$7. Open Tues–Sat 7am–6pm, closed an hour early on Sat in winter.

Rudder's Seafood Restaurant & Brewpub ★ BREWPUB

When Rudder's opened its doors as an early Nova Scotia brewpub, the promise was good that there was finally a great place to eat in Yarmouth. However, over time, the quality of the food declined to be just okay. The craft beer is good. Eat here, but don't expect exceptional. The location, on the other hand, couldn't be better. Set right on the waterfront in a former warehouse, the feel is refurbished industrial with a long wooden bar and views inside of either fermentation tanks or through the windows of wharves and fishing boats. The sizeable deck overlooks the busy harbor very close to the ferry terminal. Call ahead for the schedule of live entertainment.

96 Water St. www.ruddersbrewpub.com. © **902/742-7311.** Mains C$11–C$29. Open daily from 11am.

Shanty Café ★★ FUSION

Cuban croquetas and plantain sliders appear beside Indian samosas, burgers, and club sandwiches on the menu, all at unbelievably affordable prices—the only thing on the menu over C$10 is a bottle of wine. That's partly because the Shanty is a social enterprise supporting people with disabilities. The food is creative, fresh, and tasty, served in a quirky little stone building with a small patio between Main Street and the harbor. It's a great place for breakfast, too.

68 Central St. www.shantycafe.ca. ✆ **902/742-5918.** Mains C$5–C$9. Open Mon–Fri 7am–5pm, Sat until 3pm.

SOUTH SHORE ★★★

Named one of the world's ten best coastal destinations by *National Geographic Traveler,* the Atlantic coast between Yarmouth and Halifax is quintessential Nova Scotia. Dozens of secluded silver beaches, lighthouses, working fishing wharves, colorful small towns, quiet villages, and real folks are the norm. Get off highway 103—it's the shortest distance from A to B, but there's little of interest to see. Instead, take Route 3, aka the Lighthouse Route, 300-plus kilometers (186-plus miles) of winding seaside road. The closer you get to Halifax, the busier and more crowded with tourists the towns become until you arrive at the postcard village of **Peggy's Cove,** the province's mecca for bus tours. **Mahone Bay** is dressed up in bright colors for shoppers and sightseers, **Chester** is a historic summer haven for wealthy American families, **Shelburne** brimming with Loyalist and Black Loyalist history, **Lunenburg** is a UNESCO World Heritage Site—one of three in the Maritimes, all in Nova Scotia—for its authentic fishing history and architecture. But to meet working fishermen, hear their tales, and see their boats docked shoulder to shoulder, head for the wharves of Cape Sable Island, Barrington, and Lockeport and many of the small villages along this coast. Don't be shy around wharves; visitors are as welcome there as they are everywhere along these friendly shores.

Barrington ★

Once a thriving age-of-sail community, Barrington is now a quiet little turn in the road on Route 3, but it's worth a stop because of its concentration of museums and a one-of-a-kind interactive experience (see below).

ESSENTIALS

GETTING THERE   Barrington is about 240km (150 miles) southwest of Halifax on Route 3. It's just a kilometer (⅔ mile) from Route 103 at exit 29.

VISITOR INFORMATION   The local **visitor information center** (✆ **902/637-2625**) is a white wooden building in the middle of the museum area. It's open daily mid-May to October.

EXPLORING HISTORIC BARRINGTON

Barrington Museum Complex ★★ MUSEUM   This eclectic cluster of four museums, all within a stroll of each other, gives a concentrated taste of life in another age. The best two are the **Seal Island Light Museum ★** that offers a rare chance to enter a lighthouse and see one of the large lenses once used to guide sailors to safety. The second is the **Barrington Woolen Mill Museum ★**, a creaky old riverside mill that takes visitors back to the days of water-powered wool processing (used for sturdy clothing for fishermen).

Recently, Darren Hudson, world-champion log roller (many times over), started the **Lumberjack AXEperience ★★** here at 5 Petticoat Lane (www.wildaxe. com; ⓒ **902/637-7609**), an uproariously fun set of activities including log rolling, axe throwing, and competitive sawing. The activity fee is C$90 for adults, C$25 or C$50 for youth, depending on adult accompaniment. It's open mid-May to mid-October, Thursday to Saturday starting 1pm; call ahead to arrange for an alternative time. The grounds for these activities are laid out beside the Barrington River just behind the Woolen Mill. Darren created a lumberjack coloring book for sale on site and even has a beer named after him—Wild Axe Pilsner from **Boxing Rock Brewery** (www.boxingrock.ca; ⓒ **902/494-9233**) in nearby Shelburne, which makes unique, extra hoppy beers.

Route 3. www.capesablehistoricalsociety.com. ⓒ **902/637-2185.** June 1–Sept 30 Mon–Sat 9:30am–5:30pm, Sun 1–5pm. Seal Island Light Museum and Woolen Mill Museum admission C$5, C$15 families. Old Meeting House and Military Museum admission by donation.

Shelburne ★★

Shelburne's 10-block heritage district along the historic waterfront is one of the most undervalued, under-promoted, and under-visited neighborhoods in the Maritimes. The town's history is a microcosm of world events since its founding in 1783 by United Empire Loyalists and Black Loyalists both seeking refuge after the American Revolution in what was then a British colony. At one point, the population swelled to 10,000, making it the fourth-largest settlement in North America at the time. Freed slaves and others of African descent stopped here in hopes of a better life, but promises of land and work were not fulfilled. Instead, the little settlement of Birchtown became the departure point for those headed back to Africa, where they created the state of Sierra Leone. Made famous in Lawrence Hill's novel *The Book of Negroes* (the movie of the same name shot here), Birchtown is the missing link in the great saga of African slavery. The multi-million-dollar **Black Loyalist Heritage Centre,** with its glass floors, and the names of Black Loyalists etched on its windows, is the newest edition to the province's museums, and it will move you.

Proof that Shelburne thrived in the great age of sail can be found in the many buildings and dozens of brightly colored, carefully kept 19th century captain and merchant homes lining the streets. The several **museums** on the waterfront (see below) interpret this epic history. The sailing heritage lives on here in the local and private **Shelburne Harbour Yacht Club** and **Sailing Academy** that fills the large harbor with sails, jibs, and races all summer long. The fishing industry is a shadow of its former glory. Lobster is the only remaining catch of any value. Shelburne County fishers land more of the sweet crustacean than anywhere in the world, but that doesn't mean you can't find fresh local fish.

Starting in the 1990s, Hollywood location scouts realized they could take advantage of the historic district and the wooded shore across the harbor to stand in for pre-industrial America. Films like *Moby Dick, The Scarlet Letter, Mary Silliman's War,* and most recently *The Book of Negroes* were filmed here. The movie industry left behind a few permanent buildings and a streetscape now untainted by electrical wires.

ESSENTIALS

GETTING THERE Shelburne is about 223km (139 miles) southwest of Halifax on Route 3. It's a short hop from Route 103 via either exit 25 (southbound) or exit 26 (northbound).

VISITOR INFORMATION The local **visitor information center** (*©* 902/875-4547) is in a tidy waterfront building at the corner of King and Dock streets. It's open daily mid-May to October.

EXPLORING HISTORIC SHELBURNE

The 10-block heritage district runs along the waterfront where you can see early-19th-century streetscapes that are well kept and colorful. Visitors tend to linger at the museum complex, the Saturday morning farmers market, gift shops, a working cooperage where wooden barrels are still made (technically, it's not open to the public, but ask nicely for a look), the **Osprey Arts Centre ★,** open year-round (www.ospreyartscentre.ca; *©* **902/875-2359**) where live performance and films provide entertainment, the harbor-edge **Sea Dog Saloon ★** (*©* 902/875-1131) which offers up a good, traditional fishcake and entertainment most weekends. A block inland from the water is Shelburne's commercial stretch for services like banks, shops, gas, and snacks.

The town has developed a 3.5km (2.2-mile) section of an abandoned rail line as a trail, which links with a section that runs from the Roseway River to **Islands Provincial Park.** A bicycle routes brochure contains four scenic routes. Pick one up at the visitor information center.

Beer lovers have to stop at **Boxing Rock Brewing ★★** (www.boxingrock. ca; *©* **902/494-9233**) for a tasting of their handcrafted brews. My favorite is Temptation Red, a hoppy, richly malted, satisfying ale. It's at 78 Ohio Rd., just off the highway across from the Tim Hortons coffee shop at exit 26.

If you're here in September, don't miss the whimsical and colorful **Whirligig and Weathervane Festival ★★** (www.whirligigfestival.com) where you'll find dozens of homemade, wind-propelled lawn ornaments. Rug-hooking displays, a ukulele camp, and more fun often happens simultaneously.

Black Loyalist Heritage Centre ★★ MUSEUM As above, this museum is a tribute to the history of the Black Loyalists who fled slavery and oppression in the United States and sought refuge, first in this former British colony in the late eighteenth century, and then in Sierra Leone in Africa. In this case, that tribute is taking the shape of a multi-million dollar building, just outside of town with a swell view of the harbor. Inside, multimedia exhibits tell the story, as does the cleverly designed building itself, the glass floors a window on the artifacts beneath—including a replica of the covered hole dug in the ground that served as shelter for some Black Loyalists through their first winter. The windows are also etched with the names of those in what is called "The Book of Negroes," who were seeking freedom so long ago.

119 Old Birchtown Rd. http://blackloyalist.novascotia.ca. © **902/875-1310.** Admission C$8 adult, C$5 senior and child 6–17, C$20 family, free for children 5 and under. Open daily mid-May to Sept.

Shelburne Historic Complex ★★ MUSEUM   The historic complex is an association of three local museums located within steps of each other, animated by costumed interpreters who give tours and lead small activities like dressing in period clothing, hand-dipping candles, and churning butter. The most engaging is the **Dory Shop Museum ★★** right on the waterfront. On the first floor, you can admire examples of the simple, elegant Shelburne dory and view videos about the late Sidney Mahaney, the master builder who built 10,000 dories from the time he was 17 until he was 95. Then head upstairs, where all the banging is going on and see dories under construction. You'll learn about the rivalry between the Shelburne and the Lunenburg shops, which drove innovations in the construction of the boats such as the streamlining of the framing process. The **Shelburne County Museum** features a potpourri of locally significant artifacts from the town's Loyalist past. Most intriguing is the 1740 fire pumper equipped with wooden wheels and leather buckets; it was made in London and imported here in 1783. Behind the museum is the austerely handsome **Ross-Thomson House** built in 1784 through 1785. The first floor contains a general store as it might have looked in 1784, with bolts of cloth and cast-iron teakettles. Upstairs is a militia room with displays of antique and reproduction weaponry. You could easily spend a half-day here, particularly if you're travelling with kids, who will be captivated by the craftspeople and the hands-on activities offered—such as dressing like a Loyalist or churning butter.

Dock St. www.shelburnemuseums.com. © **902/875-3219.** Admission to 3 museums C$10 adults, C$20 family; free for children 16 and under; individual museums C$4 adults, free for children 16 and under. June to mid-Oct daily 9:30am–5:30pm. The Shelburne County Museum is also open mid-May to June daily 9am–noon & 1–5pm.

WHERE TO STAY

The Cooper's Inn ★★   Facing the harbor in the Dock Street heritage district, the impeccably historic Cooper's Inn was built by Loyalist merchant George Gracie in 1785. Subsequent additions and updates have complemented the original building. The downstairs sitting rooms set the mood nicely, with worn wood floors, muted wall colors, and classical music in the background. A tranquil courtyard has a pond and bell fountain. Rooms are furnished in a comfortably historic-country style, one with claw foot tub and wingback chairs, another with four-poster canopy king-sized bed, another with antique reproduction twin beds, and so on. A third-floor suite features wonderful detailing, two sleeping alcoves, and harbor views—worth the extra cost.

36 Dock St. www.thecoopersinn.com. © **800/688-2011** or 902/875-4656. 8 units. C$110–C$185 double and suite. Rates include full breakfast. **Amenities:** Kitchenette (1 unit), Wi-Fi (free).

Islands Provincial Park ★★   Facing Shelburne at the very end of the harbor beside the Roseway River sits a lovely little provincial campground with sites beneath tall pines next to the water. There's a small wharf for a view of Shelburne's historic district and for watching ducks and sailboats in the harbor. There are no RV hookups here, so it favors those in tents seeking a quiet refuge. Make a reservation on line and check in via automated kiosk at the entrance.

183 Barracks Rd., Hwy. 3. www.novascotiaparks.ca/parks/theislands.asp. ℭ **888/544-3434.** 70 sites. C$39. Open June–Oct. **Amenities:** Water, picnic areas, unsupervised beach, Wi-Fi (free at the registration desk).

MacKenzie's Motel ★   The rates at this tidy little motel are as small as the pool, but the hospitality is supersized, and there are roomy cottages for those who need to stretch out. Former fisherman Captain Jim Goodick and his wife Sandra are warm and welcoming. Their establishment is easily identifiable by the surprisingly detailed chainsaw carvings of sea captains made from tree stumps still rooted to the ground. It's an easy 10-minute walk to Shelburne's heritage district.

260 Upper Water St. www.mackenzies.ca. ℭ **866/875-0740** or 902/875-2842. 15 units. C$70–C$150. Rates include continental breakfast. **Amenities:** Heated pool, full kitchens in cottages, barbecues, Wi-Fi (free).

Sandy Lane Vacations ★★   From humble to grand, from funky cottages to historic old houses, the selection of 40 or more homes available through this all-local, family-owned and operated rental service is worth considering. The properties have to meet the company's standards, and are regularly inspected. The rentals are scattered along the coast from Barrington to Liverpool—most with an ocean view—and include all the amenities of a fully furnished home. Some are best suited to a couple, but others are large enough for sizeable groups, like the "Heart of the Ocean Cottage"—not a cottage at all, but a lovely renovated fisherman's house with a bright new kitchen and a deck that overlooks West Green Harbour and a small, private beach. Most have a 3-night minimum.

135 Water St. www.sandylanevacations.com. ℭ **800/646-1577** or 902/875-2729. 40 houses. C$900–C$1,500 weekly. Many have a minimum 3-night stay.

WHERE TO EAT

Charlotte Lane Café ★★★ CONTEMPORARY CANADIAN   Scrumptious food and warm service make this small dining room on a quiet lane in the heart of Shelburne's heritage district an award winner—it was named Nova Scotia's "Restaurant of the Year" in 2011 and "Best Small Restaurant" in 2013. Long-time staffer Cora Beck won "Server of the Year" in 2014. Chef Roland Glauser serves up Swiss-inspired food with Nova Scotia flair, some of it entirely local, like his award-winning chowder made with maple smoked salmon and Shelburne's Boxing Rock beer. The food here can be light and zesty, like the Bluenose Spinach Salad with dried blueberries, candied pecans, and blue cheese; or substantial, like spaghettini Gorgonzola with chicken,

Lockeport is a laidback little fishing town on an island linked to the mainland by the famous **Crescent Beach,** so picturesque it was once featured on the back of the Canadian $50 bill. Take exit 24 from Jordan Falls or 23 from Sable River off Highway 103 and drive about 20km (12½ miles). This road known as "The Lockeport Loop" on Route 3 is part of the Lighthouse Route and leads into town via a short causeway across the beach. There's an attractive contemporary building right at the beach with tourist information, changing rooms, and nifty views from a second story loft. Head into town for a bite to eat at one of several restaurants, including classic fish and chips at the **White Gull ★** (*(C)* **902/656-2822**). I always drop in on the **Lockeport Town Market ★★** (*(C)* **902/656-2514**), a tiny grocery store that employs a butcher for homemade sausage and other preparations that

harken back to a bygone era of small-town service.

If you decide to extend your stay beyond an afternoon—many do—I recommend the **Ocean Mist Cottages ★★**. Set right on the beach at the edge of town (everything is in easy walking distance), these cozy little houses include fully equipped kitchens, comfortable furnishings, and a gas stove for those cold, foggy days. Ask owner Bill Crosby, an avid photographer and bird watcher, about the best birding spots in the area. Book well ahead, because this is a popular vacation destination for repeat visitors.

1 Gull Rock Rd. across the street from the red brick high school as you enter town. www. oceanmistcottages.ca. *(C)* **902/656-3200.** 6 two-bedroom cottages. C$119–C$195 per night or C$725–C$1,250 weekly. Open year-round. **Amenities:** Full kitchen, gas fireplace, Wi-Fi (free).

broccoli, and green peppercorns or their famous lobster and scallops brandy gratin. Regardless of your choice, it will be gorgeously presented and packed with flavor.

13 Charlotte Lane. www.charlottelane.ca. *(C)* **902/875-3314.** Lunch items C$12; dinner items and larger entrees C$18–C$33. Open mid-May to Christmas. Tues–Sat 11:30am–2:30pm and 5–8pm. Closed Jan to mid-May. Reservations recommended.

Ship's Galley Pub and Eatery ★ PUB FARE   Despite the rather bland setting, this place has the best pub-style seafood and burgers in town. The fries are house-made and the burger selection runs from Portobello burger to the substantial bacon and bleu burger. Most weekend evenings, there's live entertainment on a small corner stage and there's always local craft beer on tap from Boxing Rock and Hell Bay, among others.

156 Water St. *(C)* **902/875-3260.** Main course C$8–C$18. Tues–Thurs & Sun 11am–8pm; Fri–Sat 11–12am.

Liverpool ★

Liverpool has some lovely residential neighborhoods and several fun museums. As with Lockeport and so many other South Shore towns, European settlement replaced Mi'kmaq First Nations here in the mid-1750s, when New England planters began fishing and named it after the Liverpool in England with its own

Mersey River. The American Revolution led to some interesting twists and turns in the town's history that pivoted around the violent doings of privateers (what amounted to legalized pirates). Visit the **Perkins House Museum** to find out more—Colonel Perkins led the defense of the town against them. Fishing, logging, and shipbuilding later sustained the town, with rum running during Prohibition adding a colorful chapter. The town's major employer—a paper mill—closed in 2012, leaving it less prosperous but a lot cleaner.

ESSENTIALS

GETTING THERE Liverpool is about 148km (92 miles) southwest of Halifax on Highway 103. Exits 18, 19 and 20A lead to town with the middle exit being the most direct.

VISITOR INFORMATION The local **visitor information center** (© 902/354-5421) is on Henry Hensey Dr. next to the river at the bridge leading to the small downtown. It's open daily mid-May to mid-October, 10am to 6pm.

EXPLORING LIVERPOOL

For live entertainment, it's always worth checking the **Astor Theatre** ★ at 59 Gorham St. (www.astortheatre.ns.ca; © 902/354-5250) to see what's on in the handsome former movie theatre. It might be a high-profile comedian, a rock concert, or a movie.

Lovers of British-style beers will appreciate a stop at the **Hell Bay Brewing Co.** ★ (www.hellbaybrewing.com; © 902/356-3556) at 38 Legion St. in a red building next to the water. Their English Ale is a mild, thirst-quenching tribute to the classics.

Stop by the **Perkins House Museum** ★ (http://perkinshouse.novascotia.ca; © 902/354-4058) at 105 Main St. to learn more about the privateers that today are celebrated during the annual Privateer Days festival at the end of June. For a taste of the quirky, check out the **Museum of the Outhouse** ★, one of six museums and five galleries in the **Rossignol Cultural Centre** ★ (www.rossignolculturalcentre.com; © 902/354-3067) at 205 Church St., a block up the hill from Main Street. Find out everything you wanted to know—and some things you didn't—about the little house over yonder.

Fort Point Lighthouse Park ★★ MUSEUM Interpretive panels, a video, an on-site guide, and artifacts provide information about this lighthouse—astonishing to imagine that a family of 13 once lived here—and the town's history. But the fun comes in the increasingly cramped climb to the top. There's a good view from here of the mouth of the harbor, though the scenery is somewhat marred by the idle pulp mill on the other side.

21 Fort Lane (at the end of Main St. going east). www.regionofqueens.com/attractions/lighthouses/fort-point. © **800/655-5741** or 902/354-5741. Admission free. Open mid-May to Oct.

Hank Snow Home Town Museum ★★ MUSEUM Even if you're not a country music fan, the story of this hometown legend is fascinating. The Grand Ole Opry star and composer of classics like "I'm Moving On" and "I've Been Everywhere," Snow made 140 records (copies of most are on the museum wall) and placed 85 singles on the Billboard country charts from 1950 to 1980. At the museum (set in the old train station) are the two Cadillacs he owned or some of his many stage costumes.

148 Bristol Ave. www.hanksnow.com. ✆ **888/450-5525** or 902/354-4675. Admission C$5 adult, C$4 senior. Open daily mid-May to mid-Oct Mon to Sat 9am–5pm, Sun noon–5pm; mid-Oct to mid-May Mon–Fri 9am–5pm.

WHERE TO STAY & EAT

Lane's Privateer Inn ★★ If you're looking for a place within walking distance of everything in Liverpool, Lane's is it. Situated beside the bridge on the riverbank, Lane's is often the center of the action itself, with a very good restaurant and a darkened pub with a classic British feel, both of which host live entertainment and other events (a book launch, perhaps, or a workshop on creating art with concrete). Take part in quiz night or sign up for a wine tasting. On the premises, you can browse the small bookstore, shop for gourmet and handcrafted items, sip a coffee, or sample Nova Scotia craft beers. Upstairs, the rooms are spacious and homey, the best with gleaming hardwood floors and ships' portraits on the walls.

27 Bristol Ave. www.lanesprivateerinn.wordpress.com. ✆ **800/794-3332** or 902/354-3456. 27 rooms. C$110–C$165 double. **Amenities:** Restaurant, Wi-Fi (free).

Quarterdeck Beachside Villas and Grill ★★ There isn't a bad view from the villas at the Quarterdeck. Built right on spectacular Summerville Beach, front doors and upstairs balconies open onto private decks overlooking a wide stretch of sand and the mesmerizingly beautiful bay. Inside of the units—most are two-story, two-bedroom villas, though some are smaller units (too small, frankly)—all is spotless, the walls are a natural wood and the furnishings in pretty, muted colors. On-site is a good **restaurant** and, as of the summer of 2016, a large, indoor recreation facility. Although this isn't an all-inclusive resort like White Point just up the road, it is a most spectacular location for a Nova Scotian holiday, mostly because the beach is one of the most idyllic and accessible in the province.

7499 Hwy. 3. www.quarterdeck.ns.ca. ✆ **800/565-1119** or 902/683-2998. 13 2-bedroom villas; two 1-bedroom suites; one 3-bedroom cottage. C$159–C$399. **Amenities:** Restaurant, units equipped with Jacuzzi, fireplace, full kitchen, barbecue, Wi-Fi (free).

White Point Beach Resort ★ Whether it's a convention of 200 ukulele players or travelers enjoying lazy summer days at the seashore, White Point is busy year-round. It's a complete, self-contained resort. The main lodge was rebuilt after a fire in 2011, so the feel here is no longer that of a historic hunting and fishing lodge, which is how it started out in 1928, but it's still grand. And activity packed—there's enough here to keep a family busy for a week. The resort is sandwiched between the ocean (with a nice beach for strolling and waves for surfing) and a small lake (paddling of all sorts). The onsite golf course offers ocean vistas, the indoor pool is a boon on chilly days. There's also a spa, tennis, horseshoes, croquet, and bocce ball; and the indoor games

Between Liverpool and Bridgewater (the South Shore's largest town and a good place to stock up on all sorts of supplies and access any number of services), there's a 37km (23-mile) stretch of coastal road that is as quintessentially Nova Scotian as you can find. From Highway 103, take Exit 17 just past Mill Village onto Route 331 and enjoy the scenery along this coastal drive as you pass through idyllic little villages like Cherry Hill, Broad Cove, Petite Rivière, Rissers Beach, Crescent Beach, and finally LaHave, where the ocean meets the LaHave River. From the LaHave Ferry ($7; open 7am–11pm; ✆ **902/527-7632**) you can continue on into Bridgewater to shop or jump back onto Highway 103 or cross by the cable ferry to the other side of the river to either drive into Bridgewater or continue your coastal explorations on into **Lunenburg** on Route 332. Stop to explore beaches, islands, and antique shops or to take photos of, say, a single fishing boat

moored in a wooded cove, the whole scene reflecting off the glassy surface of the water. Stop just before the ferry at the delightful **LaHave Bakery ★★** (www.lahavebakery.com; ✆ **902/688-2908**) for lunch in a fabulous old building (tin ceilings, old wooden shelves groaning with memorabilia) next to the water. It's open 8:30am to 6:30pm in summer, 9am to 5pm otherwise.

If you fall in love with this little stretch of heaven and want to stay in the area, you can camp in the middle of it all next to a beach within sight of the LaHave Islands, some of which are linked by road. Route 331 runs right through the seaside **Rissers Beach Provincial Park ★★** (www.novascotia parks.ca). The beach is the main attraction, but there's also a boardwalk along an inland marsh and an interpretation center. The campground offers 93 sites, 15 of which are equipped with electrical and water hookups. Site 31 is best; it is beside the ocean and relatively private.

including billiards, table tennis, and shuffleboard. Kids adore White Point for the beach, the pool, for marshmallow roasts around the bonfire, but mostly for the famous bunnies that nibble at grass all over the grounds. Some of the cabins feel their age, and some should not be rented—ask to see yours before staying. Unfortunately, the quality of the accommodations can vary greatly from unit to unit, with major problems—loose tiles, faulty plumbing—in some bathrooms.

Rte. 3, White Point. www.whitepoint.com. ✆ **800/565-5068** or 902/354-2711. 131 units C$135–C$460; housekeeping cottages C$2,100–C$3,500 weekly. Specials and packages are worth exploring. Free parking. **Amenities:** Restaurant, golf, pools and hot tub, spa, fitness center, playground, tennis courts, Wi-Fi (free).

Lunenburg ★★★

Lunenburg is just plain lovable, compressing everything you came to see in Nova Scotia into one tidy package: ocean tides, fishing boats, terrain, architecture, museums, and fish. It's one of Nova Scotia's most historic and most appealing villages, a fact recognized in 1995 when UNESCO declared the old downtown a World Heritage Site.

The town was first settled in 1753, primarily by German, Swiss, and French colonists. It was laid out on the "model town" plan then in vogue. (Savannah, Georgia and Philadelphia, Pennsylvania are also laid out using similar plans.) The plan consists of seven north-south streets, intersected by nine east-west streets. Lunenburg is located on a harbor and flanked by steep hills—yet the town's planners decided not to bend the rules for geography. As a result, some of the town's streets go straight uphill and can be exhausting to walk.

Still, it's worth trying. About three-quarters of the buildings in the compact downtown date from the 18th and 19th centuries, many of them are possessed of a distinctive style and are painted in bright pastel colors. Looming over all is the architecturally unique, red-and-white painted **Lunenburg Academy** with its exaggerated mansard roof, pointy towers, and extravagant use of ornamental brackets. The school sets a tone for the town the same way the Citadel fort does for Halifax. (The Academy is now a music school and sometimes offers public performances, allowing outsiders to see its inside.)

What makes Lunenburg so appealing is its vibrancy. Yes, it's historic, but this is no static outdoor museum. This place bustles with funky shops and galleries, some of the best fine and casual dining in the Maritimes, museums, and just a little Nova Scotia tartan and Sou'Wester kitsch.

ESSENTIALS

GETTING THERE Lunenburg is about 100km (62 miles) southwest of Halifax on Route 3.

VISITOR INFORMATION The **Lunenburg Visitor Information Centre** (www.lunenburgns.com; ⓒ **902/5360-4677**) is located at 125 Cornwall Rd. in Blockhouse. It is open daily from May through October, usually from 9am to 8pm.

EXPLORING LUNENBURG

Leave plenty of time to explore Lunenburg by foot. An excellent walking-tour brochure is available at the Visitor Information Centre. Alternatively, sign up with **Lunenburg Walking Tours ★** (www.lunenburgwalkingtours.com; ⓒ **902/518-6867**) for any of several tours at a reasonable C$20 adult, C$10 youth.

While exploring the steep streets of the town, note the architectural influence of its European settlers—especially the Germans. Some local folks made their fortunes from the sea, but serious money was also made by carpenters who specialized in the ornamental brackets that elaborately adorn dozens of homes here. Many homes feature a distinctive architectural element known as the "Lunenburg bump," a five-sided dormer-and-bay-window combo installed directly over an extended front door. (Other homes feature the simpler, more common Scottish dormer.) Also look for double or triple roofs on some projecting dormers, which serve absolutely no function other than to give them the vague appearance of a wedding cake.

St. John's Anglican Church ★★★ (www.stjohnslunenburg.org; ⓒ **902/634-4994**) at the corner of Duke and Cumberland streets is one of the most impressive architectural sights in all of Eastern Canada—even though it's a reconstruction. The original structure was built in 1754 of oak timbers shipped from Boston in simple New England meetinghouse style. Between 1840 and 1880, the church went through a number of additions and was overlaid with ornamentation and shingles to create an amazing example of the "carpenter Gothic" style. All this changed on Halloween night of 2001: A fire nearly razed the place, gutting its precious interior and much of the ornate exterior. In 2005, the church reopened after a painstaking 4-year restoration project using new materials but the old design. It's a must-see, and free to enter.

A contrasting stop is the **Ironworks Distillery** ★★ at 2 Kempt St. (www.ironworksdistillery.com; ⓒ **902/640-2424**), a craft distillery and shop in a former blacksmith shop built in 1893 that supplied ironworks for the once-booming shipbuilding trade. Their liqueurs—blueberry and cranberry—are so intense (without being sweet) that they give the sensation of devouring a handful of berries fresh from the field.

Several boat tours operate from the waterfront, most tied up near the Fisheries Museum. **Lunenburg Whale Watching Tours** ★ (www.novascotiawhalewatching.com; ⓒ **902/527-7175**) sails in pursuit of several species of whales, along with dolphins, seals, sea turtles, and seabirds on 3-hour excursions. There are four departures daily from May through October, with reservations recommended (and all bookings must be confirmed 24 hr. in advance with a phone call). Cost is C$52 per adult, C$35 for children age 5 to 14, and C$21 for children 5 and under (though infants are free). Alternately, if you have less time, **Star Charters** ★★ (www.novascotiasailing.com; ⓒ **877/386-3535** or 902/634-3535) takes visitors aboard a 48-foot wooden ketch on shorter, mellow 90-minute tours of Lunenburg's inner harbor five times daily from June through October. These tours cost C$35 for adults, C$23 for students, C$16 for children, and C$90 for a full family. Sunset cruises are the same price and depart at 6:30pm.

Fisheries Museum of the Atlantic ★★ MUSEUM   Right on the waterfront, this museum has a one-two punch, offering exhibits and activities both inside a historic building; and in a set of former fishing vessels, tied up at the wharf ready to board and explore. The intriguing spaces include a working boat shed and a scallop-shucking house. Sometimes, the famous *Bluenose* (see "The Dauntless *Bluenose*" box, below) is even tied up here, Lunenburg being her home port. Inside, kids will enjoy the aquarium and touch tank, as well as the sea monster exhibit. Twice daily, kids can help with the launch of a model schooner. Adults will want to tuck into meatier material like the history of fishing and shipbuilding, and a section on the rum runners of prohibition days.

On the waterfront. 68 Bluenose Dr. http://fisheriesmuseum.novascotia.ca. ⓒ **866/579-4909** or 902/634-4794. Admission C$10 adult, C$3 children, C$7 seniors (C$4 per person off season) children free. Mid-May to June and Sept to mid-Oct daily 9:30am–5pm; July–Aug to 5:30pm; mid–Oct to mid-May Mon–Fri 10am–4pm.

SHOPPING

Lunenburg is known for its galleries and unique shops. Here are just a few.

Laurie Swim Gallery ★★★ HOME GOODS   Laurie Swim has taken quilt-making to a fine art form. Her pieces could be mistaken at a distance for photographs or paintings, they are so exquisitely and painstakingly rendered. While some of her work captures the innocence of childhood or a moment in a quiet cove, other work is commemorative of great tragedies like storms that claimed many fishermen at once or the Halifax Explosion. Her work is known across the country and fetches big prices. 138 Lincoln St. www.laurieswim.com. ✆ **877/272-2220.**

Lexicon Books ★★ BOOKSTORE   Crammed with books of every kind— including lots of local work—Lexicon is a warren of stacks with quiet corners where reading is encouraged. From the stone foundation, a ledge or two sticks out, doubling as a shelf or a seat. Author readings and book club meetings are held regularly. 125 Montague St. www.lexiconbooks.ca. ✆ **902/634-4015.**

The Lunenburg Makery ★★ CRAFTS   This unique shop began through consultations with local residents who expressed a wish to have a place to sew and to learn fabric arts. The Makery offers on-site sewing machine rentals, supplies like craft kits and fabrics, as well as lots of fabric workshops for adults and kids. 228 Lincoln St. www.lunenburgmakery.ca. ✆ **902/640-4100.**

SHORT ROAD TRIPS FROM LUNENBURG

Blue Rocks ★★ is a tiny, picturesque harbor a short drive from Lunenburg. It's every bit as scenic as Peggy's Cove, but without any of the tour buses. Head out of town on Pelham Street (which turns into Blue Rocks Rd.) and just keep driving east, watching for signs indicating either THE POINT or THE LANE, and steer in that direction. The winding roadway gets narrower as the homes get more and more humble. Eventually, you'll reach the tip of the point, where it's just fishing shacks, bright boats, rocks, and views of spruce- and heath-covered islands offshore. The rocks are said to glow in a blue hue in certain light, hence the name; bring a camera and see if you can capture some of it.

If you continue onward instead of turning toward "the point," you'll soon come to the enclave of **Stonehurst,** another cluster of homes gathered around a rocky harbor. The road forks along the way; the narrow, winding route to South Stonehurst is somewhat more scenic. This whole area is ideal for exploring by bicycle, with twisting lanes, great vistas, and limited traffic.

Heading eastward along the other side of Lunenburg Harbor, you'll end up eventually at the **Ovens Natural Park ★★** (www.ovenspark.com; ✆ **902/766-4621**) in Riverport, a privately owned campground and day-use park that sits on 1.6km (1 mile) of dramatic coastline. You can follow the seaside trail to view and descend into the "ovens" (sea caves, actually) for which the park was named. Cannon Cave gets its name from the sound of the surf echoing from the rocks inside. The park also features **Ol' Gold Miner Diner,** which serves up traditional homemade meals and a great view. Entrance fees are

THE DAUNTLESS bluenose

Take a Canadian dime out of your pocket and have a close look. That graceful schooner on one side? That's the *Bluenose*, Canada's most recognized and most storied ship. You'll also see it gracing license plates from Nova Scotia.

The *Bluenose* was built in Lunenburg in 1921 as a fishing schooner. But it wasn't just any schooner. It was an exceptionally fast schooner.

U.S. and Canadian fishing fleets had raced informally for years. Starting in 1920, the *Halifax Herald* sponsored the International Fisherman's Trophy, which was captured that first year by Americans sailing out of Massachusetts. Peeved, the Nova Scotians set about taking it back. And did they ever! The *Bluenose* retained the trophy for 18 years running, despite the best efforts of Americans to recapture it. The race was shelved as World War II loomed. In the years after the war, fishing schooners were displaced by long-haul, steel-hulled fishing ships, and the schooners sailed into the footnotes of history. The *Bluenose* was sold in 1942 to labor as a freighter in the West Indies. Four years later, it foundered and sank off Haiti.

What made the *Bluenose* so unbeatable? Several theories exist. Some said it was because of last-minute hull design changes. Some said it was frost "setting" the timbers as the ship was being built. Still others claim it was blessed with an unusually talented captain and crew.

The replica *Bluenose II* was built in 1963 from the same plans as the original, in the same shipyard, and even by some of the same workers. It sails throughout Canada and beyond as Nova Scotia's seafaring ambassador. The *Bluenose*'s location varies from year to year, and it schedules visits to ports in Canada and the United States. In midsummer, it typically alternates between Lunenburg and Halifax, during which time visitors can sign up for 2-hour harbor sailings (C$40 adults, C$25 children age 3–12). Find each summer's sailing schedule online at www.bluenose.novascotia.ca. To hear about the ship's schedule, call the ***Bluenose II* Preservation Trust** (© **855/640-3177** or 902/640-3177).

C$10 adults, C$5 seniors and children age 5 to 15, free for children under 5. Campsites cost C$28 to C$60 per night—the most expensive sites are on the water, with the best views—and there are discounts for weekly stays. Ten camping cabins of various sizes are C$55 to C$190 nightly, C$380 to C$1,300 weekly. The park is open from mid-May to late September.

WHERE TO STAY

Lunenburg is chockful of good inns and B&Bs, the top 10 or so nearly indistinguishable for quality, comfort, affordability, and service, so the selection can be overwhelming.

Alicion Bed & Breakfast ★★★   Accommodations from a more gracious and elegant era, this 1911 home will spoil you for other B&Bs. Everything is done to a T here, from the period furnishings, which perfectly complement the richly hued walls, to the feasts that start the day, to such lovely extras as hydrotherapy tubs in some rooms and a wraparound porch filled with colorful chaises. And you can feel righteous about staying here because at this eco-friendly B&B, everything's organic, from the breakfast ingredients to the linens and bedding, and recycling bins are in every room. The house is set on a hill in a quiet residential neighborhood, about a 10-minute walk from downtown.

66 McDonald St. www.alicionbb.com. ✆ **877/634-9358** or 902/634-9358. 4 units. C$119–C$169. Open year-round, low season rates available. Rates include full breakfast. **Amenities:** Bikes, Jacuzzi (2 units), Wi-Fi (free).

Boscawen Inn ★★ The 1888 Queen Anne–style Boscawen mansion stands on guard up the hill from the harbor, so the views are grand from many rooms and from the deck (where you can get a cocktail come evening). Our favorite rooms here are the evocative turret suites with their sloped ceilings, bay windows, Victorian decor, and a corner Jacuzzi, perfect for a romantic holiday. But all rooms are tastefully furnished, with crisply painted neutral walls, and a mix of "extras," from working fireplaces to spa bathtubs. *Note:* Some bathrooms are cramped, so ask to move if you're not pleased with the room you get (there are 15 rooms in all).

150 Cumberland St. www.boscawen.ca. ✆ **800/354-5009.** 16 units. C$95–C$225 double. Rates include hot breakfast. No pets. Free parking. **Amenities:** Pub, sun deck, hot breakfast buffet, 2 accessible rooms, Jacuzzi (1 unit), indoor pool and spa next door upon request, fireplace (some units), Wi-Fi (free).

Lunenburg Arms Hotel & Spa ★★ In the heart of Lunenburg, this boutique hotel in what was once a boarding house offers a wide variety of rooms from standard through roomier deluxe options. At the high end, lofts here are two-level suites with living room on the lower floor and bedroom upstairs. One overlooks the harbor, the other has a town view. In a town and province where most inns are furnished with antiques fitting the period of the building, the decor is contemporary and rather plain, but certainly comfortable. Rooms are accessible, and there is an elevator. The onsite spa includes a soaker tub, hot tub, aromatherapy-and-steam showers.

94 Pelham St. www.eden.travel/lunenburg. ✆ **800/679-4950** or 902/640-4040. 24 units. Rates C$129–C$299. Free parking. **Amenities:** Restaurant, lounge, garden deck, spa, pet-friendly, Wi-Fi (free).

Lunenburg Board of Trade Campground ★ Within walking distance of town, this little campground has views of both front and back harbor. It's a tight fit, so ask about a site on the less-crowded far side of the Visitors Centre.

11 Blockhouse Hill Rd next to the Visitors Centre. ✆ **888/615-8305** or 902/634-8100. 55 sites. C$28–C$42. May–Oct. **Amenities:** Showers, Wi-Fi (free).

WHERE TO EAT

Fleur de Sel ★★★ FINE DINING Here it is, the best restaurant in Lunenburg and vying for the best in the province. Chef Martin Ruiz Salvador and his eatery have won many awards and competitions, and made multiple top Canadian restaurant lists (in fact, too many to list here!). In farm-to-table fashion, mains include scallop and lobster from local harvesters; pork from a small, nearby farm; and PEI beef. Locally caught tuna is seared rare and served with confit of local eggplant and a rarity, black garlic. Prices are on the high side for small town Nova Scotia, but dining here is a memorable experience.

Interestingly, the same team has gone casual with two excellent, affordable eateries. **The Fish Shack ★★** at 108 Montague St. (www.southshorefish shack.com; ☎ **902/634-3232**) serves nothing but fish—deep fried haddock with home fries, lobster poutine, lobster rolls, deep fried clams, and a Maritime delicacy, deep fried cod tongues. Two Propeller Brewery beers are on tap—bitter and pale ale. **The Salt Shaker Deli ★★** at 124 Montague St. (www.saltshakerdeli.com; ☎ **902/640-3434**) offers up dishes packed with flavor for reasonable prices—smoked seafood chowder, pad Thai, thin-crust pizzas. The selection of craft beers here is better than at the other two establishments, most from Nova Scotia, along with over a dozen solid wines.

53 Montague St. www.fleurdesel.net. ☎ **902/640-2121.** Reservations recommended. Mains C$30–C$40. Wed–Sun from 5pm.

The Knot Pub ★ PUB FARE   For a casual night out at a classic British-style pub, the Knot is the place. Try the cream of mussel soup, a house specialty and an uncommon preparation for this shellfish. Otherwise, the menu's hearty and classic pub fare, like stacked burgers, a good chicken Caesar, and fish and chips. As for tipples, you'll do best with the Knot Pub Ale, made by an excellent microbrewery in Halifax. Frankly, we wish they had a larger selection of craft beers—but that's why the Knot gets just one star from us.

4 Dufferin St. www.theknotpub.ca. ☎ **902/634-3334.** Meals C$5–C$17. Daily 10am–midnight; kitchen closes 9pm in summer, 8:30pm in winter.

Lincoln Street Food ★★ CONTEMPORARY CANADIAN   There's a joy about the inventiveness of the ever-changing menu created by Chef Paolo Colbertaldo, who forages at the local farmers market for the freshest ingredients and is on speed dial to local suppliers of seafood. Look for artistically presented dishes like mushroom and cashew pâté or tequila-cured organic salmon gravlax. Sounds rather precious, but, in fact, the place is casual—the kitchen is open, as is the ceiling to reveal steel beams for a warehouse feel. Plus the prices are quite low for touristy Lunenburg (and the quality of the grub).

200 Lincoln St. www.lincolnstreetfood.ca. ☎ **902/640-3002.** Reservations recommended. Mains C$8–C$18. Open Thurs–Sat from 5pm.

Mahone Bay ★★

Ask anyone in Nova Scotia where to find the town with the three churches and they'll direct you to Mahone Bay. The churches stand shoulder to shoulder at the foot of the bay a few steps from the town center. Dressed up in bright pastel colors, Mahone Bay is probably the closest to what Nova Scotians would consider a tourist trap, but compared to such places in other parts of the world, that's not very close. It's more that Mahone Bay is a great little town for shopping when it comes to independent, funky little shops stuffed with handmade jewelry, pottery, and knitted items.

Settled in 1754 by European Protestants, Mahone Bay is bright, tidy, and trim, with an eclectic Main Street that snakes along the lovely bay of the same name and is lined with inviting shops, markets, and eateries. Locals are friendly and knowledgeable. The winds attract plenty of sailboats to this bay of 365 islands. This is a town that's remarkably well-cared-for by its 900-or-so full-time residents. Architecture buffs will find a range of styles to keep them ogling, too.

One of the best **visitor information centers** (www.mahonebay.com; ✆ **888/624-6151** or 902/624-6151) in Nova Scotia is located at 165 Edgewater St., near the three church steeples. It's open daily in summer from around 9am until 7:30pm, only until 5:30pm in the shoulder seasons.

Mahone Bay has become a specialist in putting on a good festival. In October, the town fills with scarecrows of every description, many costumed like celebrities. In November, they bring on Father Christmas. It's all an excuse to dress up the town with various fun themes and activities.

EXPLORING THE TOWN

The free **Mahone Bay Settlers Museum** ★, 578 Main St. (www.mahonebay museum.com; ✆ **902/624-6263**), provides a historic context for your explorations. From June through September, it's open daily 10am to 5pm. The little museum includes a selection of antique ceramics, an exhibit on local architecture, and another on boatbuilding. All are quite informative. Before leaving, be sure to request a copy of "Three Walking Tours of Mahone Bay," a handy brochure that outlines easy walks around the compact downtown.

Thanks to the looping waterside routes nearby, this is a popular destination for walkers and bikers. Rent a bike from **Sweet Ride Cycling** ★ at 523 Main St. (www.sweetridecycling.com; ✆ **902/531-3026**) where a half-day costs you just C$20, or C$30 for a full day. And the deep, protected harbor offers superb sea kayaking. Contact **East Coast Outfitters** ★★ (www.eastcoastoutfitters. com; ✆ **877/852-2567** or 902/852-2567), based in the Peggy's Cove area near Halifax, for rentals and tours. They offer half-day introductory classes and a 5-day coastal tour of the area. Among the more popular adventures is the daylong introductory tour, in which paddlers explore the complex shoreline and learn about kayaking in the process. The price is C$135 per person, C$115 if you bring your own picnic. Rentals are also available, starting at about C$50 per half-day for a single kayak.

Ross Farm Museum ★★ (http://rossfarm.novascotia.ca; ✆ **877/689-2210** or 902/689-2210) at 4568 Rte. 12, off Route 103, is an unusually entertaining "living experience museum" that draws visitors in to life of the 1800s. Guests can ride horse-drawn sleighs, make horseshoes, pet lambs, "go to school" in the one-room schoolhouse, and will smell cookies or stew cooking over a wood fire. The oxen that graze here are a highlight: big, lumbering, and beautiful. Costumed interpreters discuss heritage animal breeds and many things related to running a farm or a family home. This is one of my favorite stops, winter or summer. I love the slowdown to quieter times, walking the interpretative trails, getting my hands dirty in the kitchen or the barn, and visiting the people and the animals. Allow half a day to truly enjoy country life.

SHOPPING

Mahone Bay serves as a magnet for all manner of creative types, and Main Street has become a mini-shopping mecca for handmade goods. Shops here are typically open from late spring until Christmas, when Halifax residents often travel down here for some holiday shopping away from the malls. Here's a small selection in a town known for its many independent shopping locations.

Amos Pewter ★ ARTS & CRAFTS   Watch pewter come fresh out of the molds at this spacious workshop and gallery located in an 1888 building. You can get anything from tie tacks and earrings to candle holders and vases here; the Christmas-tree ornament is a popular souvenir. 589 Main St. www.amospew ter.com. 🕿 **800/565-3369** or 902/624-9547.

Jo-Ann's Deli Market & Bake Shop ★★ MARKET   Gourmet and farm-fresh basic fare are sold at this wonderful food shop, where a bag of carrots serves as a counterweight on the screen door. It's the best place for miles around to stock up on local and organic produce, deli delicacies, and knockout sweets. If you're in the mood for a picnic, this is your destination. The coffee drinks from the bar are exceptionally good. 9 Edgewater St. www. joannsdelimarket.ca. 🕿 **902/624-6305.**

Suttles & Seawinds ★★ CLOTHING   Vibrant and distinctive clothing designed and made in Nova Scotia is sold at this stylish boutique. (There are other branches stretching from Halifax to Toronto, but this is the original.) The adjacent shop is crammed with quilts and resplendent bolts of fabric. 466 Main St. www.suttles.ca. 🕿 **902/624-8375.**

WHERE TO STAY

You'll find a clutch of bed-and-breakfast choices along Mahone Bay's Main Street, and also on the roads leading to surrounding coves. Right in the center of town, the lovely **Mahone Bay Bed & Breakfast** ★ at 558 Main St. (www. mahonebaybedandbreakfast.com; 🕿 **866/239-6252** or 902/624-6388) is a winner. It's the yellow Victorian home with the elaborately decorative veranda. Built in the 1860s by one of the town's many former shipbuilders, the home says "Mahone Bay" more than any other. Rooms are simple and comfortable with shiny wooden floors. Rates are from C$110 to C$145 per night.

There's also **Fisherman's Daughter Bed & Breakfast,** 97 Edgewater St. (www.fishermans-daughter.com; 🕿 **902/624-0660**), with its maritime theme and four rooms with names like Gull's Nest and Captain's Quarters at C$135 to C$145. The rooms have excellent views, though Emma's Hideaway at the top is truly special: It has a chimney running through the middle of it, views of the garden, and a skylight—kids will enjoy the hideaway feel of it.

Amber Rose Inn ★★   This restored 1875 heritage home is both B&B and an art gallery. The roomy suites in the inn are furnished with comfortable modern loveseats and armchairs, the wall and bedding floral-printed, but not overly so. The roomy apartment called The Treehouse has a full kitchen, stone fireplace, and a lovely deck beneath a shady tree. Outside, there's a deck with a gorgeous stone patio beyond surrounded by plantings, benches, and a fountain.

319 W. Main St. www.amberroseinn.com. ⓒ **902/624-1060.** 3 units, all suites, and 1 apartment. C$125–C$175. Rates include full breakfast. **Amenities:** Art gallery, patio, gardens, Wi-Fi (free).

WHERE TO EAT

Mahone Bay's little main street has more than its share of places where you can grab a bite or sit down to dinner.

Affable and affordable, the **Gazebo Cafe ★** at 567 Main St. (ⓒ **902/624-6484**) dishes up filling, healthy sandwiches and bowls of thick seafood chowder. They also do juices, smoothies, and topnotch coffee. Fresh desserts are delivered several times weekly. The de facto arts headquarters in town, the Gazebo is as much an info center about local culture as it is a sometime venue.

The delightful little **Biscuit Eater Café ★★** at 16 Orchard St. (www.biscuiteater.ca; ⓒ **902/624-2665**), in Mahone Bay's oldest building from 1775, is a bookstore, a garden patio, and a place to refresh with a hybrid English-Maritime tea with big biscuits, preserves, and a pot of tea. There are other menu items for a light lunch as well, and a wine menu to go with it. Check their schedule for readings, performances, and films.

At the **Mug and Anchor Pub ★** at 643 Main St. (ⓒ **902/624-6378**), you'll find dependable pub grub, about 20 beers on tap and (occasionally) live entertainment in the evening. The outdoor patio overlooks the bay, so beer or lunch here can be quite enjoyable.

Kedy's Inlet Café ★★ SEAFOOD   This restaurant has a long tradition as Mahone Bay residents' upscale night out on the town. Everything here is good, if not all that creative, instead relying on the appeal of freshly picked vegetables and fish and seafood freshly plucked from the waters. The best seats in the house are on the stone patio, with its fine view of the harbor and the famous three steeples. If you end up sitting inside, though, that's okay: The airiness of the interior make it just as inviting. The atmosphere here is informal and relaxed, never stuffy.

249 Edgewater St. www.kedysinlet.com. ⓒ **902/624-6363.** Most main course items C$16–C$28. Wed–Mon 11:30am–9pm

Mateus Bistro ★★ BISTRO   The roots of this adventurous bistro, in a renovated heritage building at the middle of Mahone Bay—you'll catch a whiff of grilled meat as you walk down Main Street—can be traced back to Czechoslovakia where Matthew Krizan learned to cook in his mother's kitchen. Mateus brings farm and sea to table, preparing local ingredients with a European flair and putting the grills to good use. Think fresh, local microgreen salads, lobster risotto, and rack of lamb, among other treats.

533 Main St. www.mateusbistro.com. ⓒ **902/531-3711.** Reservations recommended. Mains C$16–C$35. Mon, Thurs, Fri 5–9pm; Sat, Sun 10am–9pm.

Chester ★★

Chester is a short drive off Route 103 and has the feel of a moneyed summer colony somewhere on the New England coast back in the roaring '20s. That's because wealthy families have been retreating here since the late nineteenth century. The town was first settled in 1759 by immigrants from New England and Great Britain; today it has a population of about 1,600. Chester is noted for its regal homes and quiet streets, along with the numerous islands offshore. The atmosphere here is uncrowded, untrammeled, lazy, and slow—the way life used to be in summer resorts throughout the world. There's not really a public beach, but the views and boat rides are more than enough to compensate.

The **Chester Visitor Information Centre** (www.chesterareans.com; ✆ **902/275-4616**) is inside the old train station on 20 Smith Rd., Route 3, on the south side of town. It's open daily from 10am to 5pm.

EXPLORING THE AREA

Like so many other small towns in Nova Scotia, Chester is best seen on foot. But unlike other towns, where the center of gravity seems to be in the commercial district, here the focus is on the graceful, shady residential areas that radiate out from the tiny main street.

In your rambles, plan to head down Queen Street to the waterfront, then veer around on South Street, admiring the views out toward the mouth of the harbor. Continue on South Street past the yacht club, past the statue of the veteran (in a kilt), past the sundial in the small square. Then you'll come to a beautiful view of Back Harbour. At the foot of the small park is a curious municipal saltwater pool, filled at high tide. On warmer days, you'll find what appears to be half the town, out splashing and shrieking in the bracing water.

Some artsy shops are finding a receptive audience in and around Chester, and there's good browsing for new goods and antiques, both downtown and in the outlying areas. A good stop is the **Village Emporium ★** at 11 Pleasant St. (www.villageemporiumns.com; ✆ **902/275-4773**), an eclectic clustering of folk-arty lavender soaps, simple pottery, knit purses, and the like; it's in the same building as the Kiwi Café (see "Where to Eat," below). At **Chez Glass Lass ★★**, 63 Duke St. (www.kilnart.ca; ✆ **902/275-4300**), the fused glass kiln art is bright and beautiful. Even pieces that look painted—an intricate fish on a clear glass plate—are all-glass with no glazes or paints, so everything is dishwasher safe and non-toxic. **Jim Smith's Pottery ★★** (www.jimsmithstu dio.ca; ✆ **902/275-3272**), at the corner of Duke and Water Streets, is a Chester landmark. Smith's work is brightly colored with distinctive floral designs, influenced by his travels to Mexico and Europe, in particular a 6-month stay on the island of Crete (where he decided to take up pottery).

For an even slower pace than the quiet streets of Chester, plan an excursion out to the **Tancook Islands ★** (www.tancookislandtourism.ca), a pair of lost-in-time islands with 200 year-round residents. Cabbage put the islands on the map. German farmers were so good at growing them and making sauerkraut that the product became quite famous. You will still find Tancook Sauerkraut in stores throughout the region. The islands, accessible via a short ferry ride, are good for biking (or walking, if you're willing to spend more time getting around). Rent wheels for kids and adults at **Tancook Bikes ★** (© **902/300-9839**) at the head of the wharf hill, open 8am to 5pm May through October. On the rocky shores, look for fossils. There's a small cafe or two, but little else to cater to travelers. The **Tancook Island Ferry** (© **902/275-7885**) makes several trips daily between 6am and 6pm. Ferry tickets are C$7 round-trip, free for children under 12. You might also want to check out **Oak Island.** One of many small islands in Mahone Bay, it is home to the "Oak Island Money Pit," one of the world's longest-running hunts for lost treasure (it was the subject of a popular reality TV show). Privately owned, the island is connected to the mainland by a causeway; advanced permission is required for visitation. **The Friends of Oak Island Society** (on Facebook) provides information and tours.

In the evening, the intimate **Chester Playhouse ★★**, 22 Pleasant St. (www.chesterplayhouse.ca; © **800/363-7529** or 902/275-3933), hosts plays, concerts, a summer theater festival, and other high-quality events from March through December; it's a town institution, and a terrific option if you're a theater or folk-music buff.

WHERE TO STAY

Graves Island Provincial Park ★★   This lovely campground sits on a hill overlooking the 365-island bay. Cross a small bridge onto a grassy field and it's like driving onto an old estate. The 50-hectare (124-acre) park has 95 sites—a third of those have electricity and water—a boat launch, swimming area, and playground for the kids. There's a walk-in woodland camping area for more privacy. Wi-Fi is available at administration.

Rte. 3 (3km/1¾ miles north of the village on East River). © **902/275-4425.** 95 sites. C$26–C$35.

Mecklenburgh Inn ★★   You'll know this popular and highly regarded B&B by its double-covered balconies with handsome Adirondack chairs. It was built on a hill at the turn of the twentieth century in a quiet residential area. Rooms are bright, with a light Victorian touch and pine floors. But beyond the Inn's good looks, we recommend it because it's warm and welcoming with a great breakfast—Suzi, the innkeeper, attended London's Cordon Bleu and cooks on chartered yachts in the Caribbean in winter. You're likely to leave feeling as much one of the family as a guest.

78 Queen St. www.mecklenburghinn.ca. © **902/275-4638.** 4 units. C$95–C$155 double. Rates include full breakfast. Closed Jan–Apr. **Amenities:** Truffles, no phone, Wi-Fi (free).

WHERE TO EAT

If it's baked goods you want, **Julien's Pastry Shop** (© **902/275-2324**) at 43 Queen St. does them extremely well, as does the Kiwi Café (see below).

The Fo'c'sle ★★ PUB FARE   This is one of the town's chief gathering spots; locals have appropriately dubbed it "Chester's Living Room" (it sits on the main corner in town). Not only is it Nova Scotia's oldest rural pub, the building dates to 1764 and was previously a grocery store, stable, and inn. These worn wooden floors have been trod by man and beast for centuries, although the pool table brings it more into the 1950s. The pub grub is good— the grilled pizza, especially, is well made—and the on-tap beer plentiful. Check the website for the live music schedule.

42 Queen St. www.focslechester.com. ✆ **902/275-1408.** Main courses C$12–C$20. Daily from 11am.

Kiwi Café ★★ CAFE   Breakfast, all-day breakfast, and lunch are the thing at this funky little eatery. You'll find the usual assortment of wraps, panini, and conventional sandwiches. But there's originality here, too, from owner and New Zealand transplant Lunda Flynn, like eggs benny with smoked salmon and lobster or fishcakes with mango salsa. On Sundays, jazz accompanies the dining.

19 Pleasant St. www.kiwicafechester.com. ✆ **902/275-1492.** Main courses C$6–C$18. Daily 8am–5pm.

Hubbards

Nova Scotia's last great dance hall has been luring folks to Hubbards for more than 65 years. From late April to Halloween, the **Shore Club** ★★★ at 250 Shore Club Rd. (www.shoreclub.ca; ✆ **800/567-1790** or 902/857-9555) tunes up the music every Saturday for one great party. They serve up the best in classic and contemporary rock, blues, R&B, reggae, zydeco, swing, and big band, so check the line-up on their website. But dancing is only part of the fun. The Shore Club's unique lobster suppers have been going even longer, approaching a century now. Tuck into boiled lobster with all-you-can-eat salad and mussels. Alternatives include steak, chicken, and a kids' menu. Open weekends in May, then Wednesday to Sunday, 4 to 8pm for the rest of the summer until the end of September, when they close until the next season. Every Saturday, save by combining the supper and dance.

For a local stay, book into the **Dauphinee Inn** ★★ nestled on the shores of Hubbards Cove at 167 Shore Club Rd. (www.dauphineeinn.com; ✆ **800/567-1790** or 902/857-1790). Magnificent views of St. Margaret's Bay from decks, rooms, and pool are standard. There's a restaurant here, too, that offers a mixed menu, the seasonal **Tuna Blue Bar and Grill** ★. Every Friday night, there's music. Room rates range from C$95 to C$195.

HALIFAX ★★★

Geographically, Halifax should come next in a chapter on Nova Scotia. But the city is of such importance, we decided to give it its own chapter. See p. 267 to read about Nova Scotia's vibrant capital.

THE EASTERN SHORE ★★

Heading from Halifax to Cape Breton Island (or vice versa), you need to choose between two routes. If you're burning to get to your destination, take **Route 102** to Route 104 (the Trans-Canada Highway, the one with the maple leaf). If you have loads of time, and are more content venturing down scenic narrow lanes, allow a couple of days to wind along the Eastern Shore, mostly along **Route 7**. (*Note:* Some tourism materials refer to this stretch as the Marine Drive instead of the Eastern Shore.) Along the way, you'll be rewarded with glimpses of a rugged coastline that's among the most wild and remote in the province. Long inlets are punctuated by sweeping white-sand beaches and rocky headlands, the bays dotted with hundreds of secluded islands. The farther you go from Halifax, the fewer and farther apart are the communities, which tend to be stocked with fewer services—and tourists. With its rugged terrain and remote locales, this region is for those drawn to the outdoors and seeking coastal solitude.

Essentials

GETTING THERE   Routes 107 and 7 run along or near the coast from Dartmouth to Stillwater (near Sherbrooke). Other local routes—including numbers 211, 316, 16, and 344—continue onward along the coast to Canso at the extreme northeastern tip of the mainland and on to the causeway to Cape Breton. An excursion along the entire coastal route—from Dartmouth to Cape Breton Island with a detour to Canso—is about 400km (250 miles) in length. Driving time will vary wildly, depending on your willingness to make detours.

VISITOR INFORMATION   Several tourist information centers are staffed along the route. You'll find the best-stocked and most helpful centers in **Musquodoboit Harbour** where the Visitor Information Centre occupies the waiting room of the **Musquodoboit Harbour Railway Museum** at 7895 Hwy. 7 (www.mhrailwaymuseum.com; ℭ **902/889-2689**); **Sheet Harbour** inside the **MacPhee House Museum** (next to the waterfall; ℭ **902/885-2092**); and in **Canso** at 1297 Union St. in the **Canso Museum** (ℭ **902/366-2170**). All are open daily in summer.

A Driving Tour of the Eastern Shore

This section assumes you'll drive northeastward from Halifax toward Cape Breton. Between Halifax and Sheet Harbour, the route plays hide-and-seek with the coast, touching coastal views periodically and then veering inland again. The first stop is Lawrencetown Beach, surfing capital of the Maritimes.

Continuing on past Lawrencetown Beach, the most scenic areas are around wild, open-vista **Ship Harbour** and **Spry Harbour,** noted for its attractive older homes and the islands looming offshore. But before you get there, a side trip to Lawrencetown Beach is in order (facing page).

At the **Fisherman's Life Museum** ★ (http://fishermanslife.novascotia.ca; ℭ **902/889-2053**) on Route 7 in Jeddore Oyster Pond, you'll get a glimpse of life on the Eastern Shore a century ago. The humble white-shingle-and-green-trim

surf's up AT LAWRENCETOWN BEACH

Word that the surf is up spreads like a fever among those who get their kicks from riding the waves. Very close to Halifax, Lawrencetown Beach Provincial Park (www.lawrencetownbeach.com; ✆ 800/565-2224), supervised by the Nova Scotia Lifeguard Service, is renowned as a prime destination for local and international surfers. A south-facing stretch of sand unfurls for nearly 1.5km (almost 1 mile) along the Atlantic Ocean. It's positioned perfectly to experience exceptionally high surf conditions resulting from tropical storms and hurricanes. Beach conditions are recorded daily by lifeguard staff and can be accessed July and August by calling the Beach Line at ✆ 902/429-0635 or viewing the website (see above). You don't have to be a pro to enjoy the beach, which is also popular with body boarders. Swimmers need to be cautious of undertows, and so are advised to stay in the areas with life guards. Hikers and mountain bikers love the trail system near the beach. Nature enthusiasts will find the area home to lots of watchable wildlife, especially seabirds, and enjoy outings such as guided flora and fauna walks.

Happy Dudes Surf Emporium

(www.happydudes.wordpress.com; ✆ 902/827-4962) located at 4891 Hwy. 207 in Three Fathom Harbour, just 3km (almost 2 miles) east of Lawrencetown Beach, is open 9am to dusk daily. They sell or rent everything you need for surfing, but you don't have to go there. When the surf is up, look for their rental van on the head bank overlooking the beach.

One Life Surf School

(www.onelifesurf.com; ✆ 902/449-9488) offers surf lessons for all ages and abilities; it is women-run and women-owned, but they also teach guys. Private, semi-private, and group lessons, as well as surf yoga classes, are offered.

Kannon Beach Wind and Surf

(www.kannonbeach.com; ✆ 902/434-3040) has just about everything you'll need for surfing and windsurfing in their shop at 4144 Lawrencetown Rd. in East Lawrencetown. It overlooks popular surf spots and one of the more popular windsurf and kite spots (Stoney Beach). Open Monday to Friday 9am to 6pm; Saturday 9am to 5pm.

cottage was built by James Myers in the 1850s; early in the 20th century, it became the property of his youngest son, Ervin, who raised a dozen daughters here—a popular stop for local boys, evidently—and the home and grounds have been restored to look as they might have around 1900 or 1920. It's replete with hooked rugs and a reproduction pump organ, among other period touches. A walk through the house and barn and down to the fishing dock won't take much more than 20 minutes or so. Open June to mid-October, daily 8am to 4pm. Admission is C$3.90 adults, C$2.80 seniors and children age 6 to 17, C$8.65 families.

Nova Scotia's longest sandy beach is nearby—**Martinique Beach Provincial Park** ★★ (www.novascotiaparks.ca) in East Petpeswick is a 5km (3 miles) crescent of white sand with dunes and woodland where you can walk for hours. Swimming is supervised in the summer months, and there are changing houses, boardwalks, and trails. The park is open mid-May to mid-October, but you can take a beach walk any time.

At the town of Lake Charlotte, you can opt for a side road that weaves along the coast (look for signs for Clam Harbour). The road alternately follows wooded coves and passes through inland forests; about midway, you'll see signs for a turn to **Clam Harbour Beach Park ★★**, one of the best beaches on this coast. A long, broad-crescent beach attracts sunbathers and swimmers from Halifax and beyond; it also helps that there's a boardwalk, clean sand, and toilets and changing rooms, plus lifeguards supervising the action on summer weekends. Look for the picnicking area set amid a spruce grove on a bluff overlooking the beach. There's a funky **sandcastle competition ★** (www.halifax.ca/sandcastle) here in mid-August (which draws big crowds), so you know the sand is plentiful and good. There's no admission charge; gates close around 8pm. Continue on up the coast from the park and you'll reemerge on Route 7 in Ship Harbour.

On the rugged, windswept 6.5km (4-mile) long peninsula that is **Taylor Head Provincial Park ★★** (www.novascotiaparks.ca), it seems like ocean is battling stone. Huge boulders called "erratic" punctuate the landscape, evidence of glaciers that retreated eons ago leaving these monoliths behind. The park is 16km (10 miles) of coastline, eroding headlands, salt marshes, and woodland. Maps are downloadable from the website and available at a visitor information center.

Between Ship and Spry Harbours is the town of Tangier, home to a top tour outfit **Coastal Adventures** (www.coastaladventures.com; ✆ **877/404-2774** or 902/772-2774) at 84 Mason's Point Rd., which specializes in kayak tours. It's run by Scott Cunningham, who literally wrote the book on Nova Scotia kayaking (he's the author of the definitive guide to paddling this coast). This well-run operation is situated on a beautiful island-dotted part of the coast, but it specializes in multiday trips throughout Atlantic Canada.

Continuing northeast, **Sheet Harbour** is a pleasant little town of 800 or so souls, with a campground open May through September, a couple small grocery stores, and two motels, behind which is a short nature trail and boardwalk that descends along low, rocky cascades. Inland from Sheet Harbour on Route 374 you can find the **Liscomb Game Sanctuary ★★**, a huge wilderness area for those properly equipped with canoe and backcountry gear. (There are no services to speak of here for casual travelers.) Then, east of Sheet Harbour, you pass through the wee village of **Ecum Secum,** which has nothing to attract the tourist—but is unusually gratifying to say out loud to friends after the journey.

Adjacent to the well-marked Liscombe Lodge (see p. 224) and just over the main bridge is the **Liscomb River Trail** system. Trails follow the river both north and south of Route 7. The main hiking trail follows the river upstream for 5km (3 miles), crosses it on a suspension bridge, and then returns on the other side. The shorter **Mayflower Point Trail** follows the river southward toward the coast, then loops back inland for a total of 2.9km (1.8 miles). Both trails are rated "difficult." For a "moderate" walk, the 400m (¼-mile) **Wood-pecker** and **Prospector Trails** are both short strolls along wooded trails.

Continuing on Route 211 beyond historic Sherbrooke Village (see below), you'll drive through a wonderful landscape of lakes, ocean inlets, and upland bogs, and soon come to the scenic **Country Harbour Ferry** (✆ **902/387-2200**). The 12-car cable ferry crosses the broad river every half-hour in summer and hourly from October to June, weather and river conditions permitting. The fare is C$7 per car, which includes driver and passengers. If the ferry isn't running, you'll have to turn right around and head back, so it's wise to check at the Canso or Sherbrooke visitor centers before detouring this way.

Farther along (you'll be on Rte. 316 after the ferry), you'll come to **Tor Bay Provincial Park.** It's 4km (2½ miles) off the main road but well worth the detour on a sunny day. The park features three sandy crescent beaches backed by grassy dunes and small ponds that are slowly being taken over by bog and spruce forest. The short boardwalk loop is especially worth a walk.

Way out on the eastern tip of Nova Scotia's mainland is the end-of-the-world town of **Canso** (pop. 800), a rough-edged fishing town, wind-swept and foggy. The main attraction here is the ruined fort at the **Grassy Island National Historic Site** (www.pc.gc.ca/eng/lhn-nhs/ns/canso/index.aspx; ✆ **902/295-2069;** also known as the Canso Islands National Historic Site). A park-run boat takes you out to the island, which once housed a bustling community of fishermen and traders from New England, where a small interpretive center on the waterfront (open daily 10am–6pm June to mid-Sept) features artifacts recovered from the island and boat schedules. A trail also links several historic sites within the island. Admission is by voluntary donation. If you're coming to Canso in summer, watch for the annual music festival held the first week of July to honor what many consider Canada's most-loved folk musician Stan Rogers, who perished in an airline fire in Cincinnati in 1983 at the age of just 33. The **Stan Rogers Folk Festival ★★** (www.stanfest.com; ✆ **888/554-7826**), also known in these parts as StanFest, focuses on the craft of songwriting. But big names do sometimes play here. Weekend passes are C$130 per adult, day passes between C$55 and C$60.

Route 16 between the intersection of Route 316 and Guysborough is an especially **scenic drive.** This road runs high and low along brawny hills, giving soaring views of Chedabucto Bay and grassy hills across the way. Also pleasant, although not quite as distinguished, is Route 344 from Guysborough to the Canso causeway. That road twists, turns, and drops through woodlands with some nice views of the strait. It might make you wish you were the owner of a large and powerful motorcycle.

Memory Lane ★★ HISTORIC VILLAGE   For a change in the Victorian-era obsessed Maritimes, the *recent* past is celebrated at this 1940s heritage village museum. (The interpretation period includes World War II.) The village encompasses a school, a church, barns, houses, and a fascinating gold miners' shack and work shed where visitors can operate rock-crushing machinery. A recording is triggered in each building as people enter, immersing them in the sounds of the time. Barnyard animals peck and graze about the yard. Cookhouse meals are great fun; a very basic menu, yes, but that's in keeping with the historical character of the place. And the baked beans, brown bread, gingerbread, and fresh lemonade served in glass milk bottles are all delicious (and just C$12/adult). The cookhouse itself is a re-created mining camp building with plank tables. Elsewhere, there's a general store with loads of goods that will make some nostalgic.

5435 Clam Harbour Rd., Lake Charlotte. http://heritagevillage.ca. © **877/287-0697** or 902/845-1937. Admission C$6 adults, C$4 children, C$16 families. Mid-June to mid-Sept daily 11am–4pm, off season by appointment.

Sherbrooke Village ★★ HISTORIC VILLAGE *Another* historic village, but this one is like a Victorian greeting card, a window to a time in the past when horses moved people, and when small communities were self-sufficient. Sherbrooke is the largest restored village in all of Nova Scotia, and is unique in several respects. For one, almost all the buildings here are on their original sites (only two have been moved, unlike Memory Lane, above). That's very rare in museums like this. Second, many of the homes are still occupied by local residents—and other private homes are interspersed with the ones open to visitors. So it's not just a historic exhibit. About two-dozen buildings have been restored and opened to the public, from a convincing general store to an operating blacksmith shop and post office. Look also for the former temperance hall, courthouse, printery, boatbuilding shop, drugstore, and schoolhouse. All are capably staffed by genial interpreters in costume, who can tell you what life was like around here from the 1860s forward. Be sure to ask about the source of the town's early prosperity; you might be surprised.

Rte. 7, Sherbrooke. http://sherbrookevillage.novascotia.ca. © **888/743-7845** or 902/522-2400. Admission C$13 adults, C$9.75 seniors, C$4.75 children age 6–17, C$32 families, free for children under 6. June–Sept daily 9:30am–5pm.

Where to Stay & Eat

Liscombe Lodge Resort ★★ This modern complex consists of a central lodge plus a series of smaller cottages and outbuildings. It's situated on a remote part of the coast, adjacent to hiking trails and a popular boating area at the mouth of the Liscomb River. The lodge bills itself as a nature lover's resort, and certainly it offers access to both forest and sea. But it's not exactly wilderness here; the well-tended lawns, modern architecture, shuffleboard, marina, and free Wi-Fi testify to the middle-to-upper income summer-campness of the place. What makes it swell for vacationing families are the tons of kid-friendly offerings (table tennis, horseshoe pitches, and so forth). Outdoor types will enjoy the guided kayak trips, hikes, and bird watches. Rooms here are modern and motel-like; the cottages and chalets have multiple bedrooms: again, good for families. The **Riverside Dining Room** ★ is open to the public and competently prepares seafood, beef, chicken, and other mains, but with no particular originality. For simple pub fare, a boxed lunch, and cocktails, head for **Lone Cloud's Lounge** ★.

Rte. 7, Liscomb Mills. www.liscombelodge.ca. © **800/665-6343** or 902/779-2307. 68 inn & cottage units. C$129–C$350. Packages and meal plans available. Closed mid-Oct to mid-May. Pets allowed in chalets. **Amenities:** Marina, restaurant, lounge, free bikes, kayaks, canoes, paddle boats, fitness center, indoor pool, sauna, whirlpool, tennis courts, fireplace & woodstove (cottages only), fridge (some units), no phone, Wi-Fi (free).

Murphy's Camping on the Ocean ★★   Many sites line the shore in this little campground between Ship Harbour and Tangier, though there is also a field where RVs set up. The two sites at the very end of the road are private and roomy with fantastic views of the islands. The Murphy's are seventh-generation owners of this property. Their home is at the entrance, and their tiny wharf, complete with fishing boat, sits in the middle of the campground for fishing and swimming. Talk to the Murphy's at the little reception building about ordering in some local oysters to cook over the fire. Drop into jolly Brian Murphy's hangout across from the wharf for free coffee, conversation, and cribbage lessons. He'll take you out in his little fishing boat to the shores of nearby islands—100 of them have just become a protected area—for the scenery and to gather wild mussels for the communal feast that evening around the campfire.

308 Murphy's Rd., Murphy Cove. www.murphyscamping.ca. © **902/772-2700.** 48 sites. C$27–C$39. Open mid-May to mid-Oct. **Amenities:** Marina, boat tours, fishing, communal fire pit, free mussel boil nightly, Wi-Fi (free).

SeaWind Landing Country Inn ★★★   This lovely, 8-hectare (20-acre) oceanfront compound is exactly the type of place one hopes to find in an isolated area such as this—the hospitality is genuine and the owners have smartly made the most of the superb natural surroundings. The property has three private sand beaches, and coastal boat tours and picnic lunches can be arranged for an extra charge. Some of the guest rooms are located in the handsome, 130-year-old home, which has been tastefully modernized and updated. The rest are in a more recent outbuilding, whose rooms feature a whitewashed brightness, terrific peninsula and ocean views, and double Jacuzzis. For an extra fee, the inn also serves excellent breakfasts and dinners, featuring local products and wines.

159 Wharf Rd., Charlos Cove. www.seawindlanding.ca. © **800/563-4667** or 902/525-2108. 13 units. C$99–C$169 double. Packages available. **Amenities:** Dining room, trails, motorcycle shelter, Wi-Fi (free).

AMHERST TO ANTIGONISH ★★

This, the northernmost shore of mainland Nova Scotia—dubbed the **Northumberland Shore** or **Sunrise Trail** by tourism promoters—is a coastline of rolling hills, water views, and pastoral landscapes interspersed with small towns. Driving from the New Brunswick border along Route 6, you pass through farmlands along the western reaches from **Amherst** to **Pugwash** and beyond; around **Tatamagouche** the landscape sometimes mirrors the one found on the other side of the straits on Prince Edward Island: softly rolling fields of grain, punctuated by well-tended farmhouses and barns, and rust-red soil appearing where fields are freshly plowed. Cows might dominate one field; massive bull's-eyes of rolled hay the next. This Amherst-to-Pictou drive is especially scenic very early or late on a clear day, when the low sun highlights the green of the local fields and forests.

Beyond **Pictou,** get on the Trans-Canada Highway to continue on to **Antigonish** either quickly via the Trans-Canada or via the scenic Sunrise Trail, which swings around Cape George into town. From there, it's a short hop to Cape Breton.

VISITOR INFORMATION Nova Scotia's principal **Visitor Information Centre** (www.novascotia.com; ⓒ 902/667-8429) is at the New Brunswick–Nova Scotia border just off exit 1 of the Trans-Canada Highway. In addition to the usual vast library of brochures, there are videos, helpful staff, extraordinary views across the windy **Tantramar Marsh,** and, often, a bagpiper. It's open year-round, and staffed daily starting 9am, closing mid-October to April at 4:30pm; May and June, September to mid-October at 6pm; July and August at 8pm.

Amherst

Amherst is a lovely small town of 9,500, perched on a low hill at the edge of the sweeping Tantramar Marsh, which demarcates the border between Nova Scotia and New Brunswick. It's the beginning of Route 6 (the Sunrise Trail along Nova Scotia's northern shore) and Route 2 (known as the **Glooscap Trail,** which skirts the Minas Basin, part of the Bay of Fundy). Just east of the provincial visitor center is the **Amherst Tourist Bureau** (www.amherst.ca; ⓒ **902/667-0696**) for local information.

If you're not in a hurry to get farther along the Trans-Canada Highway (*Note:* There is a C$4 **toll** on this road about 70km [43 miles] east of Amherst) or onto either of the scenic routes that originate here—Sunrise and Glooscap—it's worth stopping in Amherst just for the historic streetscapes and murals painted on the sides of buildings in the small downtown—one particularly colorful piece depicts the sports history of the town. Because of its key geographic location and the building of the railway in the 19th century, Amherst became an important commercial hub, sparking a manufacturing boom—pianos, shoes, luggage, and woolen products were all made here. This history is evident in the large brick and sandstone buildings about town—notice the elaborately pedimented 1888 **courthouse** at the corner of Victoria and Church. A short stroll north is the sandstone **Amherst First Baptist Church,** with its pair of prominent turrets. Farther north are the stoutly proportioned Doric columns announcing the 1935 **Dominion Public Building.** While the era of prosperity fueled by the railway has largely passed, there is still some manufacturing on the edges of town near the Trans-Canada.

If you need a pick-me-up, a good place for organic coffees and/or a meal is **Bella's Café and Bistro ★** in the heart of downtown at 117 Victoria St. (ⓒ **902/660-3090**), which is also Route 6. Here you'll find elaborate sandwiches, pastas, and homemade soups—a special might consist of an open-face chicken and avocado on light rye with a bowl of roasted carrot soup.

Heading east on Route 6 from the center toward **Pugwash** on the coast, you'll glimpse homes from the past 150 years or so, displaying an eclectic range of architectural styles and materials. Info on Amherst's history is available at **Cumberland County Museum ★** (www.cumberlandcountymuseum. com; ✆ **902/667-2561**), 150 Church St. Set in the 1836 home of R. B. Dickey, one of the Fathers of Canadian Confederation, the museum is especially strong in documenting details of local industry and labor—it's big on rugs, fabrics, knitting, census records and oral histories. The museum is open Tuesday to Friday, 9am to 5pm and Saturdays noon to 5pm (closed Sat in winter and fall). Admission is C$3 adult, C$5 per family.

Pugwash to Pictou

It takes roughly 1½ hours to drive from **Amherst** to **New Glasgow** on the Trans-Canada Highway (which dips southward through Truro) or about 2 hours along Route 6 along the northern shore. Both are about 160km (100 miles) long. If speed is your chief objective, take the Trans-Canada, most of which is divided highway. But you'll also notice your eyes glazing over, and you'll pay that **C$4 toll** I mentioned above.

Route 6 ★ from **Pugwash** to **Pictou** has far more visual interest, and you'll still move speedily among sprawling farms, fields of wheat and corn, blue ocean inlets, and green coastal marshes along the wide **Northumberland Strait** that divides Nova Scotia and Prince Edward Island. If you're not in any rush, you'll want to stop and walk on beaches, visit a museum, or shop at one of the crafts stores in the middle of nowhere. If you take Route 6, you'll also pass through **Pugwash, Tatamagouche,** and **Pictou** described below.

From PEI, you can arrive via the **Prince Edward Island ferry** (www.ferries.ca; ✆ **877/762-7245**) with a terminal several kilometers north of Pictou at the coast near Caribou. (See chapter 4 for details on this ferry.)

The **Tatamagouche Visitor Information Centre** is in a lovely yellow house which doubles as the **Fraser Cultural Centre ★** at 362 Main St. (www.fraserculturalcentre.org; ✆ **902/657-3285**). In addition to the Fraser Gallery, where you'll find art exhibits rotating year-round and an exhibit on a 19th-century 7' 9" giantess—Anna Swan—who became famous as a touring oddity. While she was with P. T. Barnum, she had to be rescued from a fire. It took 18 men with a block and tackle to lower the 413-pound Anna from a hole knocked in the wall on the third floor. Access free; Wi-Fi inside.

In **Pictou,** the **Visitor Information Centre** (www.townofpictou.ca; ✆ **902/301-3466**) is located just off the big rotary west of downtown (at the junction of Rte. 6 and Rte. 106).

EXPLORING THE REGION

This region is home to a number of picnic parks, as well as local and provincial beaches. Signs along Route 6 point the way; most require a detour of a few miles. Pack a picnic and make an afternoon of it.

Pugwash, which comes from the Mi'kmaq word *pagweak,* meaning deep waters, has a slightly industrial feel. That white stuff you see piled across the water, or being loaded onto ships at the small cargo port is salt—yes, Pugwash has a salt mine. Pugwash sits on top of a salt deposit some 450m (1,476 ft.) thick. **Seagull Pewter ★** (www.seagullpewter.com; *☏* **888/955-5551** or 902/243-3850) is well known throughout the province and is made in a factory on the east side of town; look for the retail store (which also stocks antiques) on the other side of town, just west of the Pugwash River bridge on Route 6. A second pewter manufacturer called **Basic Spirit ★** is at 73 Water St. (www.basicspirit.com; *☏* **902/243-3390** or 877/245-3821) with a retail shop also on Route 6 at 9828 Durham St. Both factories produce giftware like Christmas ornaments, picture frames, and jewelry; both are open daily in summer.

Tatamagouche is a pleasant fishing village with a cameo on TV (the CBC miniseries *The Week the Women Went* was based here) and a surprisingly large annual **Oktoberfest ★★**, held at the local recreation center. For details on the festival, visit the event's website at www.nsoktoberfest.ca.

There's a very good Saturday morning **farmers market** at **Creamery Square ★★** (www.creamerysquare.ca; *☏* **902/657-**3500) a historic waterfront development, a collection of red-shingled buildings, beside the Waugh River. Inside one of these, guides demonstrate their skill at building wooden boats. Another houses a small performing-arts venue.

You can even go craft shopping here with several shops in town. **Sara Bonnyman Pottery ★** (www.sarabonnymanpottery.com; *☏* **902/657-3215**) has a studio and shop just outside town on Route 246, where you'll find rustic country-style plates, mugs, and more in a speckled pattern embellished with blueberries, sunflowers, and other pleasing country motifs. For regional tipples, the **Tatamagouche Brewing Company ★★** (www.tatabrew.com; *☏* **902/657-4000**) at 235 Main St. offers brews like Hippie Dippie Pale Ale (they claim no hippies were harmed in its making) and Butcher Block Red, a boldly hopped, richly malty beer named for the building they occupy, a former butcher shop. **Jost Vineyards ★★** (www.devoniancoast.ca; *☏* **800/565-4567**), on the Malagash Road 17km (10½ miles) west of Tatamagouche off Route 6, is Nova Scotia's largest winery and one of its oldest; the first vines were planted here in 1978. Their whites are best, the Muscat a good choice to pair with Nova Scotia seafood. It's open daily for tours and tastings, March to mid-June and mid-September to Christmas 10am to 5pm; mid-June to mid-September until 6pm.

A couple of provincial museums preserve and interpret the history and workings of two mills. Tucked in a wooded gorge, the lovely **Balmoral Grist Mill ★★** (http://balmoralgristmill.novascotia.ca; *☏* **902/657-3016**), with a brook tumbling over a dam next to a giant waterwheel, is restored to 1874 condition and still creaks and grinds inside. Try the oat cakes made with oats ground here. Find it at 544 Peter MacDonald Rd. off Route 311, 14km (9 miles) from Tatamagouche off Route 6 as it crosses the Waugh River. Equally intriguing, the 1890s **Sutherland Steam Mill ★★** (http://sutherlandsteammill.novascotia.ca; *☏* **902/657-3365**) is at 3169 Route 326 in Denmark (off Route 6 at Brule Corner), 15km (9 miles) east of Tatamagouche. The recently

Pugwash gives the impression of being a sleepy little town, but remarkably, this is the site where some of the world's great thinkers came together and had a huge impact on world politics and world peace. When World War II ended, Bertrand Russell, Albert Einstein, and several scientists published the Russell-Einstein Manifesto, calling for nuclear disarmament. They wanted to debate these issues in a location free from scrutiny from any government. Finding funding with "no strings attached" was a problem until Cyrus Eaton, an American industrialist, stepped forward and agreed to fund the entire project with one condition: They must hold the conference in Pugwash. In his honor, attendees named it the Pugwash Conferences on Science and World Affairs. The first Peace Conference was held in 1957 at what is now known as the "Thinkers Lodge" at 249 Water St. (www.thinkerslodge.org). The Pugwash Movement grew and is now held in cities throughout the world. Important conferences are still held periodically at the Lodge. Mr. Eaton received the Lenin Peace Prize in 1960. In 1995, the Pugwash Conferences on Science and World Affairs won the Nobel Peace Prize. Thinkers Lodge is now a National Historic Site. The lodge is open Tuesday to Sunday, 10am to 5pm.

restored boilers and machinery are fired up regularly in summer to demonstrate the operations of this sawmill where trees went in one end and out the other came everything from lumber to wooden bathtubs. Both are open June through September, Tuesday to Saturday from 10am to 5pm, Sundays opening 1pm. Fees are very reasonable: C$3.90 adult, C$2.80 students and seniors, C$8.65 family.

Pictou is where Route 6 ends. The First Nations Mi'kmaq presence here goes back eons. Long before first contact, Pictou was their summering grounds. The first Europeans arrived here in 1773 as part of a development scheme. Under the terms of a land grant, speculators from Philadelphia needed to place settlers at the harbor. The company sent a ship called the *Hector* to Scotland to drum up a few hundred desperately impoverished souls who might be amenable to starting their lives over again in North America. The ship returned with some 200 passengers, mostly Gaelic-speaking Highlanders. The stormy voyage was brutal, and the passengers nearly starved, but they made it—disembarking in high style, wearing tartans and victoriously playing bagpipes.

Today, Pictou is a historic harborside town with tons of interesting buildings. There are so many sandstone edifices adorned with five-sided dormers here that you might feel at times like you've wandered into an Edinburgh side street by mistake. Water Street is especially pleasing, with its boutiques, casual restaurants, and pubs filling the storefronts.

The harbor is marred by the large pulp mill across the water that often fills the air with unpleasant sulfurous odors. Still, the waterfront can be animated. Check out the three-story post-and-beam interpretation center, the **Hector**

Heritage Quay Visitor's Marina (www.shiphector.com; © **902/485-4371**) at 37 Caladh Ave. Docked beside it is a replica of the tall ship *Hector* that brought the first Scottish immigrants here. It looks like it's right out of a swashbuckling Errol Flynn movie. Aboard the ship, visitors learn about the difficult conditions that hearty souls had to endure for an 11-week crossing of the Atlantic. It's open from June through October, 10am to 5pm.

The Performing Arts are alive and well in Pictou at the 420-seat **deCoste Entertainment Centre** ★★ at 99 Water St. (http://decostecentre.ca; © **902/485-8848**), which presents live music of all kinds, theatre, and dance year-round.

WHERE TO STAY

This coast is Nova Scotia cottage country. Small neighborhoods of cottages are stretched along the shore to take advantage of the warm waters. **Cottage Coast** ★★ (www.cottagecoast.ca; © **902/701-0976**) rents seven housekeeping units by the week. The best are modern beach houses with floor-to-ceiling windows, cathedral ceilings, and decks overlooking beaches. Others are simple but comfortable cabins. Most come with fully equipped kitchens; washer/dryer; and new, comfortable sofas, chairs, and beds. Decks are equipped with barbecues and patio furniture. Rates range from C$600 to C$2000, depending on the unit and the season.

Auberge Walker Inn ★   This 1865 heritage property is so loaded with character, a murder mystery could be set here, and indeed, the innkeepers will warn you about the (friendly) ghost. Inside the large brick townhouse, furnishings are looking a bit tired, all walls are plain white, and some of the renovations missed the mark—rooms upstairs can be small. The best rooms in front—some with a handsome fireplace, one with a kitchenette—overlook the streets of Pictou; everything is within easy walking distance, and it's affordable.

78 Coleraine St., Pictou. www.walkerinn.com. © **800/370-5553** or 902/485-1433. 10 units. May–Oct C$79–C$169 double and suite. Rates include continental breakfast. Free parking. **Amenities:** Conference room, kitchenette (1 unit), no phone, Wi-Fi (free).

Pictou Lodge Beachfront Resort ★★   For a century, this little resort, a 10-minute drive from Pictou, has been a landmark on this coast. Here, it's all about the water; the resort is sandwiched between the sea and a large pond. As a result, water views from the inn and the chalets and cottages are *de rigeur* (and windows in these accommodations are large to take in the views). Guests stroll the beach, paddle around the pond, walk the trails, and play lawn games. Some rooms are equipped with kitchenettes. The floors and cathedral ceilings in the chalets are of varnished wood and harken back to a statelier era. Alas, rooms in The Birches are more like motel units. Dining is in the rustic lodge (see "Where to Eat," below).

172 Lodge Rd., Pictou. www.pictoulodge.com. © **800/495-6343** or 902/485-4322. 58 units. C$109–C$425 double, chalets and cottages. Mid-May to Oct. **Amenities:** Restaurant, playground, beach, outdoor pool, fitness room, room service, laundry, kitchenette (some units), fireplace (some units), Jacuzzi (some units), Wi-Fi (free).

Seafoam Campground ★ Among the many campgrounds along this coast, there's none better equipped than Seafoam. Grassy fields lead down to the beach and the warm, very calm waters of the Northumberland Strait. Kids will be entertained for days at the beach, where fishing boats putter along the shore. On the down side, there's little privacy in the big field where rigs are parked shoulder to shoulder in front of picnic tables lined up in rows. Those who prefer a less social setting should go elsewhere.

3493 Rte. 6, River John. www.seafoamcampground.com. ℂ **902/351-3122.** 157 sites. Early May to late Sept C$32–C$39. **Amenities:** Beach, convenience store, arcade, horseshoes, volleyball, laundromat, showers, chip & putt golf, playground, billiards, table tennis, Wi-Fi (free).

Train Station Inn ★★★ This is one of the most unique lodgings in Nova Scotia—and in Canada, for that matter. Located down a side street in Tatamagouche's former railyard, the Train Station itself (a handsome, century-old brick building) contains just one unit: the Station Master's Suite, consisting of the entire second floor of the station. It comes with a small Victorian parlor, three bedrooms, a kitchenette, and balcony. It's nice, but not nearly as fun as the rest of the units that sit in the railyard, in seven Canadian National cabooses and one boxcar. Honest. The rail cars have been refurbished as very simple rooms and vary in comfort and character. Some are decorated in Edwardian parlor motifs with bead-board paneling and striped wallpaper; others come outfitted with hardwood floors, gas woodstoves, kitchenettes, king beds, and little sitting areas with plastic patio chairs. Needless to say, book into one of these. All bookings include a continental breakfast served in a men's waiting room lined with lanterns and railway memorabilia. (It doubles as a cafe.) The reception area and gift shop is located in the ladies' waiting room. Amazingly, there is even a dining car here, serving lunches and dinners.

21 Station Rd., Tatamagouche. www.trainstation.ca. ℂ **888/724-5233.** 9 units. Caboose and boxcar rooms C$120–C$180 double; station suite C$320. Rates include continental breakfast. Closed Nov–Mar. Pets allowed with advance notice. **Amenities:** Restaurant, kitchenette (2 units), Wi-Fi (free).

WHERE TO EAT

The **Pictou Lodge Resort ★★** (see above) features several distinct dining areas, one with ocean views and one with fireplaces, and from time to time, entertainment. It's definitely the preferred pick in town. Main courses like pulled chicken pappardelle pasta with cremini mushrooms or local lamb rack with polenta cake range from C$18 to C$36; it's open daily 7am to 9pm.

If you want something more casual, Pictou has a wide choice of cafes, pubs, chip shops, and tearooms lining **Water Street** and its continuation to the east (Front St.). Several more choices can be found by walking a block to the water and Caladh Avenue. A standout, the **Stone Soup Café ★★** at 41 Water St. (www.facebook.com/Stonesoupcafeandcatering; ℂ **902/485-4949**), serves tasty breakfasts and lunches, as well as takeout. You might find heart-shaped ravioli or curried sweet potato soup for lunch for C$11 to C$16. Ingredients are locally sourced whenever possible, as is the on-tap beer. It's open daily 7am to 3pm.

In Tatamagouche, the restaurant on the dining car at the **Train Station Inn** ★★ (see above) from mid-May to mid-October offers lots of variety on their menu from fishcakes and lobster quesadillas to a steak dinner and daily pasta specials; prices for main courses range from C$16 to C$30.

Antigonish

Of the several towns between Pictou and Cape Breton, **Antigonish** is the best center for exploring the eastern part of this coast. This university town can trace its European roots back to the 1650s (the French came first; the Irish, Black Loyalists, and Scottish Highlanders later), and today the town of 4,000-plus residents is still the local market town, with a bustling main street and **St. Francis Xavier University,** which was founded in 1853. Part of the university, **The Coady Institute** attracts students from around the world to study community development; it's named for Father Moses Coady, who rallied people in the 1920s around these parts to stick up for themselves against big companies that were taking advantage of their workers. As a result, credit unions and cooperatives sprung up as part of what became known as the Antigonish Movement, which spread worldwide by the 1950s. There's still a credit union in town as part of a busy commercial center; be prepared for some traffic midsummer. There are several cafes on Main Street and a shop or two worth browsing.

For a mild outdoor adventure, drive about 8 to 9km (5 or 6 miles) northeast of town on Route 337 (past the hospital) and look for the **Fairmont Ridge Trail** ★. Here you'll find a half-dozen gentle hiking loops, ranging from 3 to 11km (2–7 miles) in length, that take you through hayfields and past beaver ponds and babbling brooks into ravines and forests of old-growth trees. There are many junctions and intersections on the trail, but trail maps are posted. Check with the tourist office (see "Visitor Information" below) about current conditions.

While you're on Route 337, continue on for fantastic scenery of rolling hills over the ocean. You can see Cape Breton and PEI from here. If you're interested in fossils, stop at **Arisaig** ★, a coastal village where the eroding cliffs are full of fossilized shells. A small provincial picnic park overlooks a wharf full of fishing boats and the Northumberland Strait. Viewing platforms and interpretive panels along a 1.5km (1-mile) loop trail offer a window into life on the planet half a billion years ago.

The Name Game

The origins of the name Antigonish—correctly pronounced, it sounds more like "ahn-*tee-gun*-ish" than "anti-goan-ish"—has created contention among linguists. In the original Mi'kmaq tongue, it meant either "five-forked rivers of fish" or "the place where branches get torn off by bears gathering beech nuts to eat." Those Mi'kmaq sure were practical, when it came to place names.

To return to Antigonish, double back to **Malignant Cove** to find Route 245. The whole drive is only 84km (52 miles) round trip.

ESSENTIALS

GETTING THERE   Antigonish is on Route 104 (Trans-Canada Hwy.) 53km (33 miles) west of the Canso Causeway (the connection to Cape Breton Island).

VISITOR INFORMATION   The **tourist office** (www.visitantigonish.ca/visitor-information-centre; *©* **902/863-4921**) is located at the **Antigonish Mall Complex** (exit 33 north off the Trans-Canada Hwy., Rte. 104 to Church St.). It's open daily 10am to 8pm, May to October.

SPECIAL EVENTS   The **Highland Games** ★ have been staged in mid-July annually since 1863. What started as a community diversion has become an international event—these are now the oldest continuously played Highland games in North America, a place to experience everything Scottish from piping to dancing to the feat of dexterity known as "tossing the caber" (the *caber* being a heavy log or pole that's tossed end to end for accuracy, not distance). Contact the local **Antigonish Highland Society** (www.antigonish highlandgames.ca; *©* **902/863-4275**) for each summer's dates and details. Rooms are scarce during the 3-day games (Fri–Sun), so if you plan to attend, book well ahead. You can buy daily and event tickets (C$35–C$95 per adult for passes, less for individual events, discounts for children).

The **Festival Antigonish** ★ (www.festivalantigonish.com; *©* **800/563-7529** or 902/867-3333) is a summer-long program of theater and live performances held on the campus of St. Francis Xavier University. Shows might range from productions written by local playwrights to Agatha Christie tales. Tickets for children's and "Stage 2" productions are C$10 or less; tickets for the main-stage, adult performances range from about C$12 to C$35. Or you can pre-order one of several all-inclusive passes for about C$100.

WHERE TO STAY

Antigonish is located just off the Trans-Canada Highway, the last town before you reach Cape Breton Island. As such, it's home to a number of chain motels, both downtown and on the "strip" leading into town. But there are alternatives.

In summer, budget travelers can book no-frills dorm rooms, or more comfortable apartments (some with full kitchens), at **St. Francis Xavier University** ★★ (www.sites.stfx.ca/conference_services/planning/accommodations; *©* **902/782-9289**) from mid-May through mid-August. The dorm rooms are simple and share hallway washrooms, but they include all the basics: linens, pillows, towels, and soap. Guest rooms have private bathrooms and kitchens—but no utensils; bring your own. Guests have access to a fitness center, the pool, and laundry facilities. Single and double rooms C$45 and C$60; single and double guest rooms cost C$92 and C$150. Meals are available in the Morrison Dining Hall for a small charge. There's free Wi-Fi throughout.

Antigonish Victorian Inn ★★   Despite the name, some rooms at this downtown inn (across the street from the Maritime Inn, below) are a combination of period and contemporary—carved four-poster beds, say, and new armchairs. The best, like The Library, are grand rooms with hardwood floors showing off the tiled fireplace and decorative mantel. Less roomy and less expensive are those at the top of the building, with sloped ceilings and less ornate furnishings. The new Garden Suite has a luxurious king-size bed and a kitchenette; it opens onto a back yard that's like a private park, it's so large—totally unexpected in the middle of town. You can't miss this big, red 1904 Victorian building with the round turret in the heart of Antigonish.

149 Main St. www.antigonishvictorianinn.ca. ✆ **800/706-5558** or 902/863-4001. 13 units. C$110–C$175 double. **Amenities:** Breakfast, garden, Wi-Fi (free).

Maritime Inn Antigonish ★ Location, location, location is what recommends this comfortable, clean motel/inn. Step out the front door and you are in the middle of a Main Street bustling with shops, restaurants, and services. The rooms are clean and comfortable; the least expensive are drive-ups on the main floor. But there are suites here, too, of varying sizes, equipped for longer stays with living rooms (with sofa, chairs and entertainment center) and mini-fridges. The restaurant is open daily 7am to 9pm (opens 1 hour later on weekends).

158 Main St. www.maritimeinns.com/en/home/maritime-inn-antigonish/default.aspx. ✆ **888/662-7484** or 902/863-4001. 32 units. C$123–C$200 double. **Amenities:** Restaurant, Wi-Fi (free).

WHERE TO EAT

Brownstone Café ★ MEDITERRANEAN   The selections on the sizeable, Mediterranean-inspired menu vary widely from basic to surprising. Besides the usual Paninis, pizzas, burgers, and pasta is a selection of Greek dishes like moussaka and souvlaki. One particularly intriguing offering is *saganaki:* sautéed fennel, tomatoes, and peppers with shrimp or chicken flambéed with the licorice-flavored drink *ouzo* topped with melted feta cheese. This place is often packed, so make a reservation (try to get space on the roomy sidewalk patio where you can watch small-town life go by).

244 Main St. www.brownstonecafe.ca. ✆ **902/735-3225.** Main courses C$13–C$22. Mon-Sat 11am–9pm. Closed Sunday.

Dream Catchers Deli and Treats ★★ BISTRO   Though this is a counter-service joint, the food here is a cut above, as is the service. You'll feel welcomed as soon as you walk in the door—friendly smiles, prompt attention, and general good cheer. As for the grub, there's a lot of variety, from salads to hearty mains (like baked chicken, meatballs, or ribs in a house-made sauce) to potent potables (a selection of Nova Scotia craft beers is on tap, the best of which is Rare Bird Pumpkin Ale), and desserts from two glass cases. If you just want something quick, the deli sandwiches are good, and there's also a deep fryer for fish and chips. The room is a bit odd in that it's an open, triangular space with the tables too close for much privacy.

219 Main St. www.dreamcatchersdeli.ca. ✆ **902/863-1300.** Main courses C$7–C$20. Mon–Sat 9am–9pm; Sun 11am–7pm.

Gabrieu's Bistro ★★ BISTRO   Halifax-quality food—and that's a major compliment in these parts—and an extremely comfortable and pleasant dining room have won this bistro a slew of fans and awards over the years. The flavors here are quite sophisticated, whether you're sipping a cocktail like the Haskaparita (made with blueberry-like haskap berries, a new Nova Scotia sensation); picking your way through the extensive tapas menu (we're fans of the delicate tempura artichoke hearts with chipotle aioli); or feasting on such main courses as braised lamb shank (marinated in red wine, garlic, and herbs) or risotto of seafood (lobster, seared sea scallops, and asparagus with coconut milk and green curry). If you're in a hurry, alert the waitstaff, because service can be leisurely.

350 Main St. www.gabrieaus.com. ✆ **902/863-1925.** Main courses C$16–C$30. Mon–Thurs 10am–9pm; Fri 10am–9:30pm; Sat 4–9:30pm. Closed Sun.

CAPE BRETON ISLAND ★★★

Isolated and craggy Cape Breton Island—Nova Scotia's northernmost land-mass—should be tops on a list of bucket list destinations for travelers to Nova Scotia, especially those who like outdoor adventures and great views. The island's chief draw is the knockout **Cape Breton Highlands National Park,** up at the top of the island's western lobe. Celtic music and the lure of Scottish heritage, world class golf, whale and bird watching, the historic fort at **Louisbourg,** and scenic the **Bras d'Or Lakes** (an inland saltwater lake that nearly cleaves the island in two) are just a few of the reasons for visiting.

Above all, there are the drives: It's hard to find a road on this island that's *not* a scenic route. Some of the vistas are wild and dramatic, some green and pastoral, but all of them will have you clicking your camera furiously.

When traveling on this island, be aware of the cultural context. Just as southern Nova Scotia was largely settled by Loyalists fleeing the United States after England lost the War of Independence, Cape Breton was principally settled by Highlander Scots whose families came out on the wrong side of rebellions against the crown overseas. You can still hear their heritage here, both in the accents of people in the villages (listen carefully, you might even hear the Gaelic language) and in the popularity of Scottish-style folk music.

You'll often hear references to the **Cabot Trail ★★★** while on the island. This is the official designation for the 300km (186-mile) roadway circling around the northwest corner of the island and the national park. It's named for John Cabot, whom some believe first set foot on North American soil near Cape North. Most scholars disagree, asserting that Cabot made landfall on Newfoundland or elsewhere.

The entry area at Port Hastings and Port Hawksbury across the Canso Causeway to the island is not an attractive place to stay—although there are motels on both sides of the water, if you need them. Instead, base yourself in **Baddeck,** which is centrally located and has a small concentration of lodgings and restaurants. You can reach both the national park and the historic settlement of

Louisbourg from Baddeck, though both are long daytrips. Alternatively, you'll get more of an immersion in the culture and the scenery if you stay in accommodations along the way, or if you camp in the national park.

For your convenience, this section is divided into two parts: one on the bulk of Cape Breton Island, and then one on Cape Breton Highlands National Park itself. (For specific information on just the park, jump ahead to p. 263.) Geographically, though, the park is likely second on your itinerary: Most travelers enter the island, scoop up info, then make a beeline for lovely uplands areas in Mabou or the Margaree Valley for the night or to Baddeck. Then, from either location, they head straight for the **Cabot Trail,** the winding, spectacular coastal road which passes in and out of the national park.

Essentials

GETTING THERE   Cape Breton is connected to the mainland via the Canso Causeway, a man-made stone causeway built in 1955 with 10 million tons of rock. (You can see the mountain which was sacrificed for the cause as you approach the island on the Trans-Canada Hwy.) The causeway, which is 61m (200-ft.) high and 1km (¾-mile) long, is 262km (163 miles) from the New Brunswick border at Amherst and 272km (169 miles) from Halifax—a little less than 3 hours' drive from either point by the most direct routes. Once on the island, everything is within a 3-hour drive, and most within 2.

VISITOR INFORMATION   A number of tiny local tourist information centers dot Cape Breton Island (Baddeck, Inverness, St. Peters, North Sydney, Sydney, Margaree, Louisbourg, and Chéticamp), but you're best off grabbing a pile of info at the bustling **Port Hastings Information Centre** (www.cbis land.com; © **902/625-4201**), which is on your right just after you cross the causeway onto the island. It's open daily 9am to 7pm in summer (closes 5pm in spring and fall). (It's closed Nov to mid-May.)

SPECIAL EVENTS   Celtic Colours ★★★ (www.celtic-colours.com; © **888/355-7744** or 902/567-3000) is an island-wide, annual music shindig timed to approximate the peak of the lovely highland foliage in early October. The concentration of Celtic musicians—local and international—getting together for good times and music at 250 community events and upwards of 50 concerts across the island for over a week makes it a signature Nova Scotia festival. It usually begins in the second week of October for a foot-stompin', pennywhistlin', fiddle-playin' 10 days. International stars from around the Celtic world like the Chieftains have performed here, but much of the attraction is the chance to attend a local dance called a *ceilidh* at a small community hall. Ticket prices range from about C$10 to C$60 for a single event. The most popular performers sell out months in advance; check the website or call well ahead if you've got your heart set on a particular act.

Mabou & Vicinity ★★

Turning left after crossing the Canso Causeway and driving along the western coast of the island on **Route 19,** you'll pass through small villages until you

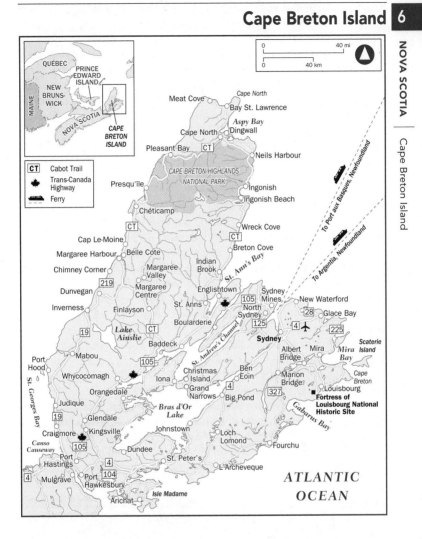

reach **Margaree Harbour.** Provincial tourism promoters dubbed this section of the island the **"Ceilidh Trail"** ★★ because it is the heart of Celtic culture on the island. Along the route, the views of the Northumberland Strait to PEI and mainland Nova Scotia are the highlight of the drive. From the road, you'll see rental cottages and walking trails, beaches and rivers. By the end of the Ceilidh Trail, hills become larger, valleys greener and more pronounced. If you're here at dusk, stop and admire the sun sinking beyond the lands to the west.

Within 58km (36 miles) of the causeway, you'll come to the little village of **Mabou** ★★, a central base from which to explore the area. It sits on a deep, protected inlet along the island's western shore and boasts lovely scenery and

237

intriguing nightlife (see below). This former coal-mining town has made itself over as a lobster-fishing town, though you don't come here for crustaceans; the seafood is shipped out to Halifax and beyond. Attractive drives and bike rides are easy to find in the area; almost any road you choose is an opportunity to break out the camera. The town itself consists of a short main street, a clump of homes, a gas station, a few eateries and services, plus a scenic little beach.

But there's a hidden bonus to the area, giving it an importance disproportionate to its size: Local residents are strongly oriented toward **music,** even more so than is usual on already-musical Cape Breton Isle. The local kids, nearly all of Scottish descent, grow up playing instruments, singing, and dancing; amazingly, this tiny town has produced several international hit Celtic music acts.

Evening entertainment in Mabou revolves around fiddle playing, square dancing, and the traditional gathering of musicians and dancers known as a *ceilidh* (*kay*-lee) ★★★. These planned and impromptu musical events take place in pubs, civic buildings, outdoors, people's homes . . . anywhere. To find out what's going on, stop by the village **grocery store,** the **Mull** cafe right across the street, or the **Red Shoe** pub (see p. 242) and scope out their bulletin boards and calendars. You might also check with the **Strathspey Place Theatre** (www.strathspeyplace.com; ✆ **902/945-5300**) at 11156 Rte. 19. It offers a variety of performing arts events, including occasional Celtic music events too, usually for C$15 to C$40 per person.

If you want to see Nova Scotia's largest freshwater lake, turn right at **Strathlorne** toward **Lake Ainslie** ★. A campground and a few cottages offer accommodations around the lake, so if you'd prefer it to the coast, you can spend time here. Otherwise, there are few services or attractions.

The most exciting thing to happen on this coast in decades is the development of two adjoined world-class golf courses in Inverness—**Cabot Links** ★★★ and **Cabot Cliffs** ★★★ (www.cabotlinks.com; ✆ **902/258-4653**) at 15933 Central Ave. If you play, you'll be in golfer's heaven; if you don't, you'll still be pleased with the way these courses have transformed Inverness from one of the most run-down towns in the region to a trendy little place with new amenities for travelers, including unrivaled restaurants and accommodations at the golf courses (see below). It's impossible to miss the courses when driving through town on Route 19—they sweep down from the road over what was once a coal mine slag heap and plateau at the shore. Cabot Links is edged by the small harbor where fishing boats are docked and ends at a gorgeous sand beach backed by grassy dunes where townsfolk gather to hang out at the beach or stroll the boardwalk. Cabot Cliffs stops short of the sea where, you guessed it, the beach gives way to shoreline cliffs. Every hole has an ocean view. Both are built to echo the world's first courses where the game began in Scotland. Cabot Links is said to be the only one in Canada. Both *Golf Digest* and *Golf Magazine* placed it in the world's top 100 courses upon opening in 2012. *Canada Golf Magazine* named it the country's top course. Cabot Links opened in 2016; it will surely gather similar accolades.

In a handsome valley between Mabou and Inverness is another world-class site, the distinctive post-and-beam **Glenora Distillery ★★★** (www.glenora distillery.com; © **800/839-0491** or 902/258-2662). This modern distillery—North America's first and Canada's only single-malt whiskey (it's "Scotch," but for legal reasons, they can't call it that) producer—began making **Glen Breton ★★★** whiskey in 1990, using water from the pure local stream that flows right through the property. Kentucky bourbon casks are used to age the whiskey, because the distillers here believe those impart a mellower taste than the traditional sherry casks. Tours are offered May through October and cost C$7 for a half-hour (offered daily 9am–5pm), culminating in free samples. The distillery also runs an adjoining **restaurant** (open seasonally) and a nine-room **hotel** (see below); traditional music is often scheduled for weekends or evenings in the contemporary pub.

Continuing up the western coast brings us to the end of Route 19 at **Margaree Forks.** This is where you pick up the Cabot Trail. The trail can be driven either clockwise or counterclockwise from here. If you would prefer a little bit of road between you and the cliff edges in the highest sections, turn left toward Chéticamp. If you prefer the complete view from the outside lane, turn right and head inland toward Baddeck. For our purposes, we'll stick to the coast and continue on toward Chéticamp.

The **Margaree Valley** consists of the area from the village called Margaree Valley (near the headwaters of the Margaree River) to Margaree Harbor, downriver on Cape Breton's west coast. Some seven small communities are clustered along this valley floor, a world apart from the rugged drama of the surf-battered coast—it's more reminiscent of Vermont than Maine. The **Cabot Trail** gently rises and falls here on the shoulders of rounded hills flanking the valley, offering views of farmed floodplains and glimpses of a shining river. The whole area is best explored by slow and aimless driving, or by bike or canoe if you've brought one along with you. In autumn, the foliage here is often among Eastern Canada's very best.

The **Margaree River** is a bona fide celebrity in fishing circles—widely regarded as one of the best Atlantic salmon rivers in North America, and the salmon have continued to return to spawn here in recent years, which is unfortunately *not* always the case on many waterways of Atlantic Canada. The river has been closed to all types of fishing except fly-fishing since the 1880s, and in 1991 it was designated a Canadian Heritage River.

Beyond fishing, we recommend a stop at **Cape Breton Clay ★★** (www.capebretonclay.com; © **902/235-2467**), though getting there takes careful navigation; basically, if you're in Margaree Valley off the Cabot Trail, just follow the signs. Bell Fraser's work is truly unique. Jellyfish, crab, sheep, and other motifs are worked into her platters and bowls in ways that will surprise and delight. The shiny black mussels ringing the outside of a brick-red bowl look like they've just been plucked from the ocean. The shop is open daily from June through late-October, 10am to 5pm; individual pieces might run from C$40 to C$400. Don't miss "the Koop" next door, a place where real—and Bell's ceramic—chickens comingle. There's now a second location in Chimney Corner on Route 19 about 8km (5 miles) south of Margaree Harbour.

WHERE TO STAY

Cabot Links Resort ★★★ Cabot's pride-and-joy is its "links course" which is, to many, the purest form of golf. In brief, links courses are seaside playing greens that keep the natural bumps and gullies of the terrain rather than smoothing them out. It's what the great courses of Scotland do, and in creating a course with these features, the owners of Cabot Links have conjured up a resort that's a dead ringer for Scotland (appropriate: "Nova Scotia" means "New Scotland"). That translates inside the lodge, as well, with a bar that serves 36 different types of Scotch and hospitality that will make you feel you've jumped the pond. Don't expect tartan everywhere, though. Rooms are sleek and contemporary, done up in neutral colors, with such unexpected treats as super-cushy beds, heated bathroom floors and extra-powerful showers. Luxury rooms boast floor-to-ceiling, wall-to-wall windows flanking several holes, including the 18th. Luxury villas have similar decor but are fully equipped with high-end kitchen appliances. While the resort is within easy walking distance to the few eateries and shops in town, the on-site **Cabot Bar ★★** and **Panorama Restaurant ★★★** (see below) are hands down the cream of the crop; be prepared to pay handsomely for this kind of luxury.

15933 Central Ave., Inverness. www.cabotlinks.com/lodging. ✆ **855/652-2268.** 48 units. C$235–C$315 double. **Amenities:** Dining room, bar, golf course, terrace (some units), Wi-Fi (free).

Glenora Inn & Distillery ★★ When was the last time you spent the night sleeping next to a huge stash of moonshine? Okay, I exaggerate. A little. This distiller of single-malt whiskey offers nine modern hotel rooms over a courtyard next to a pub, beside the distillery. They're contemporary yet rustic, with easy access to the aforementioned pub and a restaurant (which often feature live performers from the area). There are also a half-dozen attractive log chalets, one to three bedrooms each, with woody interiors on the hills overlooking the distillery. These are ideal for either lovebirds or families. Each has a Jacuzzi, satellite TV, and a fab view of the mist-covered valley below. It all has the feel of being tucked in a remote vale in the Scottish Highlands.

Rte. 19, Glenville. www.glenoradistillery.com. ✆ **800/839-0491.** 15 units. C$140–C$195 double; C$190–C$299 chalet. Closed Oct 31 to mid-May. **Amenities:** Restaurant, bar, Jacuzzi (some units), Wi-Fi (free).

Hillcrest Hall ★★ Harborside in Port Hood, this large 1910 Queen Anne Revival inn, offers a friendly Cape Breton welcome to its guests. Each room is unique and set off the rambling hallways. Although their decor isn't as precious as other Nova Scotia B&Bs, it's cheery and kept immaculately clean. Room number 6 is the best; the maid's quarters at one time, it's now a large suite with four-poster bed on hardwood floors and commanding views of nearby islands and a beach with a boardwalk behind it. If you're a senior, you are in luck—discounts are offered. One unit is wheelchair accessible. The owners run a small, unremarkable motel across the street next to an inviting pub.

24 Main St. Port Hood. www.hillcresthall.com. © **888/434-4255** or 902/787-2211. 11 units. C$90–C$180 double. **Amenities:** Breakfast, Wi-Fi (free).

Mabou River Inn ★★   Located not far from the river and adjacent to the Mother of Sorrows Pioneer Shrine (dedicated to the settlers of the Mabou area), this former boarding school was converted twice, first into a winning youth hostel and then into this homey little inn just off the main road. Hosts Donna and David Cameron keep things running smoothly and dispense great advice; nature lovers will appreciate the opportunity to hike, kayak, fish, and mountain-bike on the scenic Ceilidh Trail using the inn's rental equipment, while night owls can stroll a few minutes across the bridge and into town to check out the local traditional music offerings that fill Mabou in summer. A variety of room types are offered from those with queen- and king-size beds (that take up most of the room!) to what the Camerons call apartments, which amount to spacious two- and three-bedroom suites suitable for up to eight people, with full kitchens, the largest with washer/dryer and a separate entrance. Continental breakfast is included in the nightly rate and features tasty homemade baked goods.

19 Southwest Ridge Rd., Mabou. www.mabouriverinn.com. © **888/627-9744** or 902/945-2356. 10 units. C$105–C$175 double; C$145–C$265 suite. Closed Nov-Apr. **Amenities:** Complimentary continental breakfast, restaurant, bike and sea kayak rentals, kitchenette (some units), no phone (some units), Wi-Fi (free).

MacLeod Campground ★★★   Nestled between two green hillsides that dip into the ocean is an inviting quarter-mile stretch of sand that feels like a discovery every time you descend along the narrow path through the trees. This is your beach, if you camp at MacLeod's Beach Campsite. Just north of Inverness lies a green field where you can pitch a tent or drive a rig onto the grass. The open field offers little privacy, but there are more secluded sites in the trees. The same family runs the **Inverness Beach Village ★**, a compound between the two golf courses of 41 simple, dated housekeeping cottages (C$110–C$160)—small, brown shed-like buildings with small windows and decks set in a large field with spectacular views—and the romantic 6-room **MacLeod Inn ★★** (with wraparound veranda and five modern, comfortable rooms with quiet artwork and sheer curtains to enjoy the leafy, green surroundings) tucked away on a wooded hill before the campground (C$140–C$150). If you aren't equipped to camp, look into these two alternatives on their website.

1485 Broad Cove Marsh Rd., Dunvegan. www.macleods.com. © **902/258-2433.** 150 sites. C$34–C$38 double. **Amenities:** Full hook-ups, showers, recreation room, playground, store, trails.

WHERE TO EAT

Downstreet Coffee Company ★★ CAFE   Right on Route 19 in the middle of town, the aroma of fresh baking and brewed coffee will pull you into this funky place (with lots of local artwork on the walls and live music from time to time). Stop by for breakfast (the lemon-cranberry scones and eggs benny are primo) or for one of the lunch specials, like club sandwiches or homemade tomato basil soup with a couple of egg-salad brioche sliders. Downstreet also stocks a small selection of baked goods and alternative groceries like granola, rare chocolate bars, sauces, maple syrup, and the like.

15844 Central Ave., Inverness. www.facebook.com/downstreetcoffeecompany. ✆ **902/258-3477.** Sandwiches C$7–C$14. Daily 7am–6pm (3pm in winter).

Panorama Restaurant ★★★ GOURMET CANADIAN   On the second floor of the Cabot Links Resort, the Panorama lives up to its name; a wall of windows takes in the stunning view over the greens of the golf course to the beach and ocean beyond, the whole scene facing west to pull sunsets right into the room. The menu for this dinner-only dining room shows off the best of Nova Scotia with a deft touch (lobster ravioli served in a rich, buttery, roasted garlic cream sauce, for example; or snow crab salad with pink grapefruit, avocado and wasabi vinaigrette). And some 30 of the world's best Scotches and whiskeys are available for brown liquor lovers. In the **Cabot Bar** ★★ (open daily 6:30am–10pm), on the lower level, the views are the same and the menu is just as sure, but more affordable. I gotta say, the slow-roasted brisket sandwich with onion rings and slaw takes pub food to the next level. The only disappointment? The on-tap and in-bottle beer selection, which includes none of the excellent Nova Scotia craft beers.

15933 Central Ave., Inverness. www.cabotlinks.com/dining. ✆ **902/258-4653.** Reservations recommended. Mains C$25–C$45. Daily 5–10pm.

The Red Shoe Pub ★★ PUB FARE   The famous musical family the Rankins reopened this neighborhood pub in 2005 to continue its long tradition as the daily gathering place for the best local folk musicians. The Red Shoe menu is healthier than other pubs. Yes, you can find a burger or fish and chips, but fried foods don't dominate. For an appetizer, we're partial to the "Drinkin Mussels" steamed in Red Shoe Ale, bacon, and garlic. The house special Red Shoe Meatloaf, a flavorful rendition made healthier with the addition of—what could be more Celtic?—oatmeal, is also superb. More stars of the menu include the vegetable lasagna and the pan seared scallops and bacon. The Red Shoe is cozy and sometimes crowded, but the hospitality and music are first class.

11573 Rte. 19, Mabou. www.redshoepub.com. ✆ **902/945-2996.** Entrees C$16–C$28. June to Oct Mon–Wed 11:30am–11pm; Thurs–Sat 11:30am–2am; Sun noon–11pm. Closed mid-Oct to May.

Chéticamp ★★

The Acadian town of **Chéticamp** is the western gateway to Cape Breton Highlands National Park, and the center of French-speaking culture on Cape Breton. The change is rather obvious as you drive northward from Margaree Harbour—the family names suddenly go from MacDonald to Doucet, the landscape from wooded to windswept fields, and the cuisine turns on its head.

So does the obvious sense of humor: look for "tourist traps" (stacks of lobster traps for sale to visitors), scarecrows with celebrity faces, and brightly painted folk art, including one entire house. In this vein, do stop at **Gallery La Bella Mona Lisa ★★★** (12225 Cabot Trail; www.labellamonalisa.com; ⓒ **902/224-2560**) in Le Moine, before you hit Chéticamp, where you'll find whimsical, original artwork that will have you laughing out loud and marveling at the range of the human imagination. Much of the brightly painted work is by Michel Williatte-Battet; his paintings and sculptures have a folk art feel with a surrealist edge—a man in a red hat stands in a field under moonlight while a dog dashes past in the distance: Title—"Looking for my dog."

The town is an assortment of restaurants, boutiques, and tourist establishments spread along a Main Street closely hugging the harbor. A winding **boardwalk ★** follows harbor's edge through much of town, a good spot to stretch your legs from the drive and have a look at the local geography. Chéticamp Island sits just across the water; the mighty coastal hills of the national park are visible just up the coast.

Chéticamp is famous worldwide for its hooked rugs, a craft perfected here by the early Acadian settlers. Those curious about the craft should stop at **Les Trois Pignons,** which houses the **Elizabeth LeFort Gallery** and the **Hooked Rug Museum ★** (on Main St.; www.lestroispignons.com; ⓒ **902/224-2642;** mid-May to mid-October, daily 9am–5pm and until 7pm in July and Aug; C$5/adult, C$4/seniors, C$3.50/students, C$12/families, free for children 5 and under.) The museum displays some 300 fine tapestries, many created by Elizabeth LeFort, who was Canada's premier rug-hooking artist for many decades until she passed away in 2005—check out her tableau of U.S. presidents from 1959, which required 1.7 *million* loops to be hooked. You can also view tools used for the craft. Several boat tour operators are based in Chéticamp Harbor. **Love Boat Seaside Whale and Nature Cruises** (www.loveboatwhalecruises.ca; ⓒ **877/880-2899** or 902/224-2899) sets out on *Love Boat 1* and *Love Boat 2* in search of whales, seals, and scenery, and has hydrophones on board for listening to any whales you may encounter. The tours take 2½ to 3 hours. The **Visitor Information Center** is also in this building.

The most pleasing drive or bike ride in the area is out to Chéticamp Island, connected to the main highway by a road and bridge. Look for the turnoff just south of town.

Several restaurants and pubs in town offer live entertainment, including **The Doryman Pub and Grill** at 15528 Cabot Trail (www.doryman.ca; ⓒ **902/224-9909**) for local music like Saturday afternoon fiddle sessions.

WHERE TO STAY

A handful of motels service the thousands of travelers who pass through each summer. **Laurie's Motor Inn ★** on Main Street (ⓒ **800/959-4253** or 902/224-2400; May–Oct only) is the largest in Chéticamp with 48 rooms and 5 suites in a string of buildings situated right in town; rates run from C$124 to C$259 per night (mostly toward the lower end of that range). The inn also manages nice rental homes around town for longer stays.

Maison Fiset House ★★ For a bit of luxury right in town, this B&B, with a view across the road of the harbor (from private patios and a glassed-in terrace), is the answer. Any of the eight carpeted units in the house is comfortable and spotlessly clean; all have mini-fridges and private patios, though some views are only of a driveway. One is wheelchair accessible from the parking lot out back. The furniture is new and selected to match the color scheme of each room—eggplant, robin's egg blue, burnt orange. An oddity in a couple of rooms is the corner Jacuzzi's position beside the bed. Breakfast is a serious matter, with quality and quantity surpassing most B&Bs. The owners offer a three-bedroom house nearby with a private patio, a barbecue, and a view of the harbor. Fiset is pricey, but if it's within your budget, it's the place to stay in Chéticamp; just be sure to ask for a room with a view of the water.

15050 Cabot Trail. www.maisonfisethouse.com/en. ✆ **855/292-1794** or 902/224-1794. 8 units and a 3-bedroom house. C$139–C$250. **Amenities:** Hot breakfast, Wi-Fi (free).

Pilot Whale Chalets ★ Lodgings don't get more kid-friendly than the Pilot Whale. The reception room holds a corner full of toys for the beach and for rainy days, as well as games and movies. The beach lies just out of site beyond a grassy bank. The grounds are rather odd, in that the cottages are scattered here and there around a big field that allows little in the way of privacy. But the cottages, although plain from the outside, are fully outfitted for a fun family vacation; full kitchens (plus gas barbecues outside), woodstoves, and decks and cheery, sturdy furnishings that you don't have to worry about damaging. Nine of ten are two-bedroom, one is a three-bedroom. Some are outfitted with Jacuzzi and fireplace. Oddly, some of the cottages include two suites, so only take one if you don't mind sharing the building with other guests.

15775 Cabot Trail. www.pilotwhalechalets.com. ✆ **902/224-1040.** C$95–C$125 double; C$159–C$249 cabin. **Amenities:** Private beach, laundry, Jacuzzi (some units), kitchenette (some units), Wi-Fi (free).

WHERE TO EAT

Many eateries are spread along the main drag beside the Cabot Trail that runs through town. Most serve reasonably priced and reasonably edible local seafood and traditional Acadian dishes like *rappie pie* or *rapure pie*, a meat-and-potato pie in which grated potatoes are reduced to a thick gelatin; it tastes better than it sounds. Some of the larger ones are set up to feed bus tours.

A staple in Chéticamp since the 1950s, **La Boulangerie Aucoin** ★ (✆ **902/224-3220**) is located just off the Cabot Trail between the town and the national park at 14 Lapointe Rd. (look for signs). The place is known for fresh-from-the-oven goods that have the look and flavor of grandmother's baking. Among the options: rolls, scones, bread, cookies, squares, and berry pies.

But for more sophisticated baked goods—a taste of France in Acadian Nova Scotia—stop at the **Frog Pond Café** ★★★ at 15856 Cabot Trail (www.sunsetartgallery.ca; ✆ **902/224-1831**). You can't miss it; it's the place with the bright folk art signs and pieces around the small parking lot on the right as you leave town. This is the **Sunset Folk Art Gallery** ★★★, a small, private room with the most wonderful (usually) wooden sculptures roughly thrown together and painted brilliant colors. You might see a larger-than-life Elvis or fish to hang on your clothesline or a giant bird with a rainbow of tail feathers. The cafe is basically a shed with a takeout window full of pastries, savory treats, buttery croissants, sourdough bread, and coffee so deliciously authentic, they will transport you to a Paris sidewalk cafe; enjoy them under the awning of the outdoor patio. It's open mid-June to mid-September daily 9:30am to 5:30pm in summer, closed Mondays in spring June and September.

Harbour Restaurant and Bar ★★ ACADIAN   Management refers to its fare as "fine dining," but it's closer to traditional Nova Scotia fare, done well, and in huge portions. To be frank: If you welcome the "Apple Garden Cake," included with the meal after making your way through the "Seafood Sensation Dinner," you've accomplished quite a feat. The former comes with pan-fried haddock, half a dozen scallops, and two skewers of shrimp topping a heap of vegetables and another side—whew! The Fishermen's "Best of Both" Dinner, which includes both crab and lobster, is another lollapalooza of a dish. But the menu is varied and full of options (including some smaller ones). The bar is well-stocked with spirits and big brewery beers, although you won't find any craft beers or Nova Scotia wines. As the name implies, this harborside restaurant is set right beside the wharves and boats.

15299 Cabot Trail. www.baywindsuites.com. © **902/224-1144.** Reservations recommended. Mains C$3.50–C$5. Daily 7am–9pm.

Pleasant Bay ★

Just outside Chéticamp, the Cabot Trail enters the national park. At the north end of the Trail's exhilarating run along the island's western cliffs, the road turns inland through the park, winds up over a coastal tabletop mountain on a route that will test your nerve and your brakes on hairpin turns and steep descents. Take your time; expect slow progress and traffic that ranges from squadrons of motorcycles and bicycles to trucks, as well as other tourists. Eventually, the road heads back down to the northern edge of the park on this coast to the village of **Pleasant Bay.** You need to sneak off the Trail (down Harbour Rd., naturally) to find a surprise: a simple, attractive little harbor protected by a man-made jetty, complete with bobbing brightly painted fishing boats. It's just a short walk off the main road and sits at the base of rounded, forested mountains.

The **Whale Interpretive Centre ★** (© **902/224-1411**), built on a rise overlooking the harbor, features exhibits to help explain why the waters offshore are so rich with marine life—not to mention a *life-size* model of a pilot whale and a tank filled with smaller sea creatures. It's open daily, June through mid-October 9am to 5pm; admission is C$5 for adults, C$4 for children and seniors, and C$16 for families.

Whale-watching tours are offered three to five times daily from June through mid-October from the harbor by Captain Mark Timmons of **Capt. Mark's Whale and Seal Cruise ★★** (www.whaleandsealcruise.com;

© **888/754-5112** or 902/224-1316). Timmons's 2½-hour cruises on his 13m (42-ft.) cabin cruise *Double Hookup* and a choice of two Zodiac-style boats, *TourMaster* and *North Star,* provide unrivaled glimpses of the rugged coast both north and south, and often a close-up look at whales (almost always pilot whales, frequently finbacks and minkes, occasionally humpbacks). The boat has a hydrophone on board, so you can hear the plaintive whale calls underwater. Trips are C$39 to C$49/adult, C$35 to C$44 students and seniors, C$19 to C$24 children 3 to 18.

If you bear right at the "Y" and continue northward, the road wraps around the coastal hills and turns to gravel after 5km (3 miles). Keep going another 3 to 5km (2 or 3 miles). Here you'll come to a spectacular **coastal hiking trail ★★**, which runs to **Pollett's Cove,** about 10km (6 miles) up the coast. A dozen families once lived here; all that remain now are two cemeteries and an open field where a stream empties into the ocean, which makes the most spectacular location for a tent. Be prepared for a challenging 3-hour hike into the wilderness; you're likely to see eagles, deer, and even whales. The cove and the trail are on private land, but hiking and other quiet recreation are allowed.

On this road, you'll pass a Buddhist Monastery called **Gampo Abbey ★★** (www.gampoabbey.org; © **902/224-2752**), which offers retreats and welcomes visitors for free tours (July–Aug at 1:30 and 2:30) inside the buildings and on the wooded grounds and gardens. If you arrive outside touring hours, you're free to wander the grounds and visit the "Stuppa of Enlightenment," an intriguing sculpture decorated with prayer flags and surrounded by stones etched with phrases. In town, you're likely to meet a robed monk or two picking up the mail or buying supplies.

If you want to stay here, a couple of motels and a hostel offer basic accommodations with great views. Private rooms, dorm-style rooms, and a wilderness cabin are available with **Hi-Cabot Trail Hostel** at 23349 Cabot Trail (www.cabottrailhostel.com; © **877/776-0707** or 902/224-1976). The hostel provides use of a kitchen, a barbecue, and free Wi-Fi. You can rent a bike to get around, or if you have one in need of servicing, they'll fix it for you. You'll have to bring your own shampoo, soap, and towel, but the rates are cheap, starting at C$25.

Cape North ★★

Cape North is a recommended detour for adventurous travelers who want even more of the scenery and culture they find on the Cabot Trail, but in a place that feels even more remote. If you drive to the end of the road in Meat Cove, you will feel you've reached the end of the world.

The cape is reached via a signed turnoff at the northern tip of the Cabot Trail, after you descend into the Aspy Valley. You'll soon come to **Cabot Landing Provincial Park ★★**, where local lore claims that John Cabot first made landfall in North America in 1497. (Historians are doubtful of this claim, however.) Debate the issue among yourselves near the statue of Cabot, or take a long walk on the lovely 3km (2-mile) ochre-sand beach fronting the bay. The views of the remote coastline are both noteworthy and camera worthy.

The road then winds onward to the north; at a prominent fork, you can veer right to **Bay St. Lawrence,** if you wish, and find the tiny harbor and several summertime whale-watching outfits.

Family-owned *Oshan* **Whale Watch**'s ★★ (www.oshan.ca; ℂ **877/383-2883** or 902/383-2883) thrice-daily tours on Captain Cyril Fraser's 13m (42-ft.) lobster boat cost C$30 per adult, C$20 senior and student, and C$12 per child from July through October. The former fishing boat is equipped with a hydrophone so you can hear the whales as well as see them. The birdwatching from the boat is topnotch, as is the deep-sea fishing (they'll clean your fish for cooking afterward). **Captain Cox's Whale Watch** (www.whalewatching-novascotia.com; ℂ **888/346-5556** or 902/383-2981) costs more but also offers a different experience, that is, in an inflatable 8m (24-ft.) inflatable Zodiac named *Hazel Mable.* Trips aboard the safety-certified, speedy craft are available from mid-June through September. These tours cost C$45 adults (discounts for seniors) and C$25 per child, but require a four-person minimum; don't show up expecting a tour unless you're four or more.

From Bay St. Lawrence, go left at the fork in the road and continue along the stunning cliffside road to **Meat Cove.** The last 5km (3 miles) are along a dirt road that runs high along the shoulders of coastal mountains, then drops into shady ravines to cross brooks and rivers. The road is potholed and in places carved from the cliff; it ends at a rough-hewn settlement that's been home to hardy fishermen—seemingly all named McClellan—for generations.

WHERE TO STAY

Four Mile Beach Inn ★★   Overnight in a museum—that's what a stay at this rambling, old inn, and former general store, feels like. The store in the front room is still intact, fully stocked with items that would have been for sale throughout its history, starting in 1898. Small sitting rooms are filled with period furniture and fascinating odds and ends, and from time to time, live musicians come by to play tunes. Some of the bedrooms and suites are cozy nooks with sloped ceilings tucked away in what seems like an endless warren of hallways and corners. Some are self-sufficient, with kitchenettes and separate entrances, while others require a trip across the hall to get to the bathroom. Behind the house, a trail leads to the isolated bay and the lonely beach where shorebirds feed and oysters grow in the shallow waters. Wake up to a home-made breakfast that will get you on your way . . . if you can stand to leave.

1520 Bay St. Lawrence Rd. www.fourmilebeachinn.com. ℂ **877/779-8275** or 902/383-2282. 8 units. C$89–C$129 double. Rates include full breakfast. Packages available. Closed mid–Oct to mid-June. **Amenities:** Canoe and kayak rentals, kitchenette (some units), Wi-Fi (free).

Meat Cove Camping ★★   You have arrived at the end of the Earth. Perched on a grassy clifftop at the end of the road, this private campground has some of the most dramatic ocean- and cliff-views of any campground in Nova Scotia. The more than two-dozen campsites are unserviced, but there are hot showers and bathrooms, as well as other amenities. Four very basic cabins that resemble garden sheds with 2×4 bunks share the same views, but you'll have to bring your own bedding. Descend to a pebble beach, take a sea kayak out for a look at the cliffs from the ocean, and hike trails in the nearby hills. This campground is a full immersion into dramatic Cape Breton landscape.

2479 Meat Cove Rd. meatcovecampground.ca. ℰ **902/383-2379**. 29 sites C$25; 4 cabins C$70. Open June–Oct. **Amenities:** Pebble beach, trails, sea kayaks, restaurant, showers, firewood, Wi-Fi (free).

WHERE TO EAT

For inexpensive eats, check out **Angie's Family Restaurant** (ℰ **902/383-2531**) in Cape North, serving a menu of pizzas and local seafood. The restaurant at **Markland Coastal Beach Cottages** ★ (www.themarkland.com; ℰ **855/872-6048**) in Dingwall has reopened after years of being closed. It serves well-prepared local seafood like snow crab and oysters, as well as alternatives like pasta and chicken; waitstaff recommend wine pairings by a sommelier.

White Point & Neil's Harbour ★

From South Harbour (near Dingwall) you can drive on the Cabot Trail inland to Ingonish, or stick to the coast along an alternate route that arcs past White Point, continues to **Neil's Harbour,** then links back up with the Cabot Trail. If the weather's clear, this **coastal road** ★★ is a far better choice. Bear left at **South Harbour** onto White Point Road. Initially, the road climbs upward amid jagged cliffs with sweeping views of Aspy Bay; at **White Point** ★, you can veer a mile-and-a-half out to the tip of the land for even *more* dramatic views.

The road then changes names (to New Haven Rd.) and tracks inland before emerging at **Neil's Harbour** ★, a postcard-worthy fishing village of a few hundred souls. On a rocky knob located on the far side of the bay is a square red-and-white lighthouse (now an ice-cream parlor). From Neil's Harbour, it's just a 2-minute drive back to the Cabot Trail.

Ingonish ★★

The Ingonish area includes a gaggle of similarly named villages—Ingonish Centre, Ingonish Ferry, South Ingonish Harbour—which collectively add up to a population of perhaps 1,300 or so (on a good day). Like Chéticamp on the peninsula's east side, Ingonish serves as a gateway to the national park and is home to an information center and a handful of motels and restaurants. There's really no critical mass of services in any one of the villages, though—instead, they're spread along a lengthy stretch of the trail. So you never quite feel you've arrived in town. You pass a liquor store, some shops and restaurants, a handful of cottages. And that's it—suddenly you're in the wild park.

Highlights in the area include a sandy beach (near Keltic Lodge) good for some chilly splashing around, and a number of shorter hiking trails. (See "Cape Breton Highlands National Park," later in this chapter.)

For golfers, the wind-swept **Highlands Links course** ★★★ (www.high landslinksgolf.com; ℰ **800/441-1118** or 902/285-2600)—adjacent to the

Keltic Lodge (see "Where to Stay," below) but under completely separate management—is considered one of the best in Atlantic Canada, though its position at the top of the list has been usurped by the very different Cabot Links (p. 238). It's a 6,035m (6,600-yard), links-style course with grand views and some stupendously difficult holes. Peak-season rounds cost C$103 per adult (C$27–C$45 for children); spring and fall rates are about C$20 lower, and twilight rates are also available. Ask about packages whenever booking a hotel, and be sure to reserve your tee time in advance—it's popular.

South of Ingonish, the Cabot Trail climbs and descends the hairy 305m (1,000-ft.) promontory of Cape Smokey, which explodes into panoramic views from the top. At the highest point, there's the free **Cape Smokey Provincial Park**—really little more than a picnic area and a trailhead—where you can cool your engine and admire the views. A 10km (6-mile) hiking trail studded with unforgettable viewpoints leads to the tip of the cape along the high bluffs.

WHERE TO STAY & EAT

A number of serviceable cottage courts and motels are located in the area. In addition to the choices below, **Seascape Coastal Retreat ★★** in Ingonish at 36083 Cabot Trail (www.seascapecoastalretreat.com; © **866/385-3003** or 902/285-3003) offers 10 luxury oceanfront cottages (off a private beach with handsome gardens and near a pond). The cottages are roomy and have fireplaces and private decks. The bathrooms are equipped with whirlpool tubs. Home-grown veggies and herbs appear in meals at the **restaurant ★**. For outings in the park, ask the kitchen to pack you a picnic lunch. Pets are permitted, but managements says their "facility is not suitable for children." Rates are high at C$169 to C$259 (closed Nov–Apr).

In addition to the dining room mentioned above, there are any number of small eateries in the Ingonishes. Stop in at the **Bean Barn Café ★** (© **902/285-2767**) at 36743 Cabot Trail in Ingonish for coffee and dessert or lunch items like sandwiches, pizzas, and panini. It's open daily in summer 6:30am to 8pm, otherwise 7am to 5pm.

Castle Rock Country Inn ★   The hillside perch from which Castle Rock overlooks the Ingonish area and the ocean beyond feels like an eagle's eyrie. It's the last view of the Ingonish enclave and the park before climbing over Cape Smokey. As you'd expect, the rooms facing that direction come with extraordinary views and cost more than others. The **Avalon Restaurant ★**, with deck, shares this spectacular vantage point and offer an Asian–Nova Scotian fusion menu; organic produce and local seafood star in dishes like crab dumplings in Asian dipping sauce. Unlike the views, the rooms themselves in the large, white house with pale blue shutters are rather ordinary, furnished with queen-size beds and a small table and chairs on carpeted floors. Pets are permitted in some rooms.

39339 Cabot Trail, Ingonish Ferry. www.castlerockcountryinn.com. © **888/884-7625** or 902/285-2700. 17 units. C$129–C$173 double. Packages and off-season discounts available. **Amenities:** Restaurant, bar, continental breakfast, no phone, Wi-Fi (free).

For whatever reason, this sparsely populated 68km (42-mile) section of the Cabot Trail is like a drive-through art gallery with studios and shops along the way. You'll find pewter, blown glass, fine art, woodworking, leather goods, and craft shops. Among them, **Glass Artisans** ★★ (www.glassartisans.ca; ℂ **902/929-2585**) at 45054 Cabot Trail is one of the most intriguing. The yard is full of colorful blown-glass works, and there's a studio with a white-hot fire where you can watch glass being made, colored, and blown into wonderful shapes by skilled owner Wendy Smith and others. Walk across the road to **The Clucking Hen Café and Bakery** ★★ (ℂ **902/929-2501**) for a meal: the creamy linguine alfredo with lobster, shrimp, or chicken is tops as are the chocolate haystack cookies. Chickens—ceramic, painted, printed—peer from every shelf and corner.

Coastal Waters Restaurant & Pub ★★★ PUB FARE   The menu at Coastal looks like it came in a dream to a cafeteria-weary college student; indeed, owners Jason LeBlanc and Keith Moore did meet in college and dream up Coastal Waters. Inside the unexceptional roadside building is a kitchen with a quirky sense of humor and considerable skill with pub grub. Astonishingly affordable burgers have names like "The Quagmire" and "The Big Lebowski." The Coastal Ringer Burger (featured on TV's *You Gotta Eat Here*) is a 6-ounce patty, with homemade smoky sauce topped with a giant onion ring, bacon, and mozzarella all stuffed into a Kaiser bun and served with a steak knife stuck through its heart so you can cut it up rather than try to fit it into your mouth. It was built to be washed down with an on-tap craft beer. The waitstaff wear humorous T-shirts, and there's live entertainment some nights. You're as likely to share the open room or even a table with a crew of bikers or a gaggle of plaid-garbed golfers fresh from the greens.

36404 Cabot Trail, Ingonish. www.coastal-restaurant.com. ℂ **902/285-2526.** Mains C$10–C$15. Open daily mid-May through Oct noon–8pm (Sat until 2am); summer breakfasts 8–9am and weekends until 2am.

Keltic Lodge Resort & Spa ★   Once Nova Scotia's premier resort, the Keltic Lodge has, sadly, seen better days. Service is only so-so, with the maids making a racket long before most guests want to rise, and harried waiters in the several restaurants. Meals can be hit or miss. The kitchen sources fine fresh products, but sometimes a piece of fish will spend a little too long under the grill or a dish that should be hot emerges from the kitchen chilled. Some rooms in the lodge can feel like luxury from another era, while others are outdated with bathrooms that need new fixtures, and small, view-free windows. Avoid room 201, an overpriced small space with no view situated above the casual **Highland Sitting Room,** which delivers thumping bass through its ceiling into that room, and others nearby, late into the night. Rooms in the more modern **Inn at Keltic** are better, with commanding views and contemporary furnishings and bathrooms. Cottages on the premises are set among white birch, but are less private than you'd hope as living rooms are shared with other guests in the building. All that being said, the place still has a definite grandeur to it. Just the drive out a narrow wooded peninsula to catch a view of the improbably placed Tudor-style main lodge is worth it, as is roaming the exquisite grounds. They include the **Highland Links** golf course—within easy walking distance of any room, a lovely outdoor pool and trails to the end of the peninsula.

383 Keltic Inn Rd., Ingonish Beach. www.kelticlodge.ca. © **800/565-0444** or 902/285-2880. 74 rooms & suites, 10 cottages. C$155–C$395 double and cottage. Rates include breakfast. Packages available. Closed mid-Oct to mid-May. **Amenities:** 2 restaurants, lounge, children's programs, golf course, outdoor pool, spa, tennis courts, fridge (some units), no phone, Wi-Fi (free).

St. Ann's

Traveling clockwise around the Cabot Trail, you'll face a choice when you come to the juncture of Route 312. One option is to take the side road to the **Englishtown ferry** and cross over St. Ann's Harbor in slow but dramatic fashion. The crossing of the fjordlike bay is scenic, and it only takes about 2 minutes. The ferry runs around the clock, for C$7 per car. If you take this route, the rest of the road to Baddeck is on the relatively busy Trans-Canada Highway.

Your second option is not to cross via ferry but rather to stay on the Trail, heading down along the western shore of St. Ann's Harbour.

One good launching point for exploring the waters is **North River,** where local guide/musician Angelo Spinazzola offers tours through his **North River Kayak Tours** ★★ (www.northriverkayak.com; © **888/865-2925** or 902/929-2628) company from mid-May through mid-October. The full-day tour (C$119 per person) includes a steamed-mussel lunch on the shore; 3-hour tours cost C$69. There's also a more expensive "romance tour" where couples camp overnight on a remote beach—the owner cooks dinner, sets up a tent, and then departs for the night. Most every trip, claims Spinazzola, involves sightings of bald eagles. Kayaks can also be rented (or even purchased) from the outfit.

In the village of St. Ann's, be sure to drop by the **Gaelic College of Celtic Arts and Crafts** ★★ (www.gaeliccollege.edu; © **902/295-3411**), 51779 Cabot Trail Rd., located about a kilometer (⅔ mile) off the Trans-Canada Highway at exit 11. The 142-hectare (350-acre) campus was informally founded in 1938, when a group of area citizens began offering instruction in Gaelic language in a one-room log cabin. Today, classes are offered in bagpiping, fiddle, Highland dance, weaving, spinning, and Scottish history, among other things. The **Great Hall of the Clans** ★ makes for a quick lesson in Scottish culture via interactive displays. Exhibits provide answers to burning questions like "What's the deal with the plaid?" and "What do Scotsmen really wear under a kilt?" The Hall is open weekdays mid-May to mid-October 9am to 5pm. Admission is C$8 per adult, C$6 for students, and C$20 for families.

WHERE TO STAY & EAT

Chanterelle Inn and Cottages ★★ Set on a 61-hectare (150-acre) wooded estate, the inn offers that rare combination of outdoor adventure and gustatory gratification. Within 5 to 20 minutes of the inn, there's primo hiking, kayaking, and golf; not much farther are boat tours with whale watching. And if you get peckish from all of the exercise, the restaurant here is sure to satisfy. The chef is a wizard with locally sourced eats, whether they're foraged mushrooms, line-caught trout, or greens and herbs from the on-site garden. As for the digs, they're crafted from reclaimed wood and furnished with pretty antiques, oriental carpets, and original artwork. The cottages have full kitchens and decks with views of virtually nothing but treed mountainsides. (One cottage is wheelchair accessible.)

48678 Cabot Trail, North River Bridge. www.chanterelleinn.com. *C* **866/277-0577** or 902/929-2263. 12 units, inn open May–Oct; cottages open year-round. C$145–C$225. Rates include buffet breakfast (inn only). **Amenities:** Restaurant, trails, gazebo, paddle boats, electric fireplace (some units), air-jet tub (some units), Wi-Fi (free).

Baddeck

Although **Baddeck** (pronounced *Bah*-deck) is some distance from the national park, it's often considered the de facto "capital" of the Cabot Trail. This is partly because Baddeck is centrally positioned on the island, and partly because its main drag happens to offer more hotels, B&Bs, and restaurants than any other town on the loop. (That's how thinly populated it is up here.) There are also a clutch of practical services here you can't easily find on the Trail: grocery stores, laundromats, gas stations, and the like.

Baddeck was once the summertime home of telephone inventor Alexander Graham Bell, now memorialized at a national historic site (see facing page). It's also a compact, easy town to explore by foot and is scenically located on the shores of big Bras d'Or (say bra-*door*) Lake. If you're on a tight schedule and plan to drive the Cabot Trail in a day (figure on 6–8 hr.), this might be the best place to bed down afterward; it's on the way to Sydney and/or Louisbourg. If, however, your intention is to spend a few days exploring the hiking trails, bold headlands, and remote coves of the trail and the national park (which I certainly recommend), find an inn farther north. Baddeck is just too far away from the park for day trips.

The friendly **Baddeck Welcome Center** (www.visitbaddeck.com; *C* **902/295-1911**) is located just south of the village at the intersection of routes 105 and 205. It's open daily from June through mid-October.

EXPLORING BADDECK

Baddeck, skinny and centered around a single main street (called Chebucto St. rather than Main St.), is just off the lake. Many get onto that lake with **Paddledog Kayak Tours** ★ (www.paddledog.ca; *C* **888/865-2925** or 902/295-8868) at 22 Water St. They'll get you to Kidston Island (see below) for tea and scones on the beach or a swim in the exceptionally warm waters, all for C$49. The thrice-daily tours are short at just 1½ hours, so you'll have lots of time for other fun. **Amoeba**

The seasonal **Giant MacAskill Museum** ★★ (504, Rte. 312; ✆ **902/929-2875;** open daily July–Aug 9am–5pm; admission is C$4/adults, C$2.50/seniors and youth) honors the memory of local Scottish transplant Angus MacAskill, who lived here from 1825 to 1863 and gave new meaning to the term "living large." Angus, you see, was *huge.*

Supposedly MacAskill's father was of normal height, and Angus was a regular-size baby, too. But when he hit adolescence, something went haywire: The boy shot up to 7 feet tall before the age of 20. At 7' 9" tall and 425 pounds, MacAskill is believed to have been the tallest natural giant who ever lived. According to the *Guinness Book of World Records*, he was the strongest man in recorded history. MacAskill's feats of strength—tipping over his fishing boat to drain water from it; lifting 1-ton anchors off a dock easily—are legendary, and he later made a successful go of it as owner of Englishtown's local general store. Angus was well-liked (he would have to have been), but caught a fatal infection during a trip to Halifax to purchase supplies and died a week later, just shy of 40. He is buried nearby.

Children will enjoy sitting on MacAskill's massive chair (if they can reach it) and trying on his sweater; the actual-size replica of the coffin MacAskill was buried in is simply astounding. In fact, most adults find the museum fascinating, too, in a Ripley-esque kind of way.

Englishtown, where the museum is located, is about 64km (40 miles) south of Ingonish, on the way down to the middle "lobe" of Cape Breton Island.

Sailing Tours ★ (www.amoebasailingtours.com; ✆ **902/295-7780** or 902/295-1426) has a turn-around trip of about the same length. You'll find its tall ship at the Baddeck Wharf on the waterfront; the C$25 tour passes Alexander Graham Bell's palatial former estate and other attractions.

About 180m (590 ft.) offshore is **Kidston Island** ★, owned by the town of Baddeck. It has a wonderful sand beach with lifeguards (sometimes—check with the visitor center) and an old lighthouse to explore. A shuttle service comes and goes, so check with the visitor center.

The lovely **Uisge Ban Falls** ★★ (that's Gaelic for "white water") is the reward at the end of a 3km (1.8-mile) hike. The falls cascades 16m (52 ft.) down a rock face; the hike is through hardwood forest of maple, birch, and beech. Ask for a map at the visit center.

Alexander Graham Bell National Historic Site ★★ HISTORIC SITE   Each summer for much of his life, Alexander Graham Bell—of Scottish descent, but his family emigrated to Canada when he was young—fled the heat and humidity of Washington, D.C., for this hillside retreat perched above Bras d'Or Lake. The mansion, still owned and occupied by the Bell family, is visible across the harbor from various points around town. Today it's part homage, part science center. The modern exhibit center highlights Bell's amazing mind; you'll find exhibits on his invention of the telephone at age 29, of course, but also information about other projects: ingenious kites, hydrofoils, and airplanes, for instance. Bell also invented the metal detector—who knew? Science buffs will love the place, and most visitors are surprised to learn Bell actually died in this home. (He's buried on the mountaintop.) Then there's an extensive "discovery" section, where kids are encouraged to apply their intuition and creativity to science problems. All in all, it's a very well-thought-out attraction—and attractive, too.

559 Chebucto St. www.pc.gc.ca/bell. ℂ **902/295-2069.** Admission C$7.80 adults, C$6.55 seniors, C$3.90 youth age 6–16, C$20 families. Mid-May through Oct, daily 9am–5pm.

WHERE TO STAY

Auberge Gisele's Inn ★   Gisele's isn't for everyone—it has a faux-Italian sensibility, with a bit too much pink and floral patterning for our tastes. And it's popular with bus tours, so it can feel crowded. Still the rooms are newly renovated with large windows, some with swell views. Suites are of different sizes, all roomy and equipped with wood-burning fireplaces, fridge, and microwave; you'll find gas fireplaces in some doubles. A chef originally from Germany has run the kitchen in the **restaurant** ★★ for 20 years, and gives classic mains—like pork tenderloin, duck breast, and rack of lamb—a European flair. Meals are reasonable at C$15 to C$25.

387 Shore Rd. www.giseles.com. ℂ **800/304-0466** or 902/295-2849. 78 units. C$115–C$300. Open mid-May to late Oct. **Amenities:** Restaurant, whirlpool, sauna, fireplace (33 units), Wi-Fi (free).

Inverary Resort ★★   The Inverary sweeps from Shore Road down to the lake across wide, green lawns studded with trees and gardens. Cottages, special event buildings, hotel buildings, and the main lodge built in 1850 are all painted a signature slate and spread across this sprawling 5 hectare (11-acre) property, which is within walking distance of town. Loads of activities await couples and families; you'll find tennis and shuffleboard courts, a pool, fishing and paddle-boats, kayaks and bikes. The rooms vary widely in size, but all are clean and bright, and most come with a fireplace. Each cottage has two side-by-side apartments, each equipped with a kitchen, as well as a deck with a barbecue. Good eats can be had at **The Thistledown Restaurant and Pub** ★; both are open daily in summer, the dining room 5 to 10 pm, the downstairs pub until midnight (in winter, only the pub is open and only from Thurs–Sat). As you might expect, it's elevated pub grub, like burgers, fish and chips, pasta, and pizza in the downstairs eatery. The menu at the restaurant on the upper level is closer to fine dining, with such treats as a delicious cranberry-stuffed roast chicken and for dessert, a decadent peanut-butter pie. It's Cape Breton, so both program live entertainment daily in summer. There's also a **cafe** ★ at the marina. The hotel hosts many large groups like wedding parties, bus tours, and conventions.

368 Shore Rd. www.capebretonresorts.com. ℂ **800/565-5660** or 902/295-3500. 141 units. C$109–C$189 double; C$159–C$390 suite. Packages available. Closed Dec–Apr. **Amenities:** 2 restaurants, pub, bikes, Jacuzzi, indoor pool, room service, sauna, spa, 3 tennis courts, watersports, marina, private beach, kitchenette (some units), fireplace (many units), Wi-Fi (free).

Telegraph House ★ Since 1861, Telegraph House has hosted royalty and, for many years, Alexander Graham Bell himself. You have three room choices here—the main inn or simple motel units and cottages behind the house. Most rooms are rather ornate with floral wallpaper, lacey bedspreads, and carpeted floors. Some—particularly in the cottages—have a less cluttered look with hardwood floors and painted walls. The motel and cottages are uphill, so they do get glimpses of the lake, as do small balconies in the lodge. The **dining room** ★★★ has been reinvented with the arrival of a chef affectionately known as Chef George who has turned this place into *the* place for fine dining in Baddeck with dishes like roasted quail in crabapple-honey whiskey and white tablecloth service on the outdoor patio.

479 Chebucto St. www.baddeckhotel.com. ℂ **888/263-9840** or 902/295-1100. 39 units. C$85–C$130 double; C$100–C$275 cabins. **Amenities:** Restaurant, Jacuzzi (some units), no phone, Wi-Fi (free).

WHERE TO EAT

Every hotel in town has a restaurant attached to it and most are fine (though we like the ones above best). For a quick meal, head to the Highwheeler:

Highwheeler Cafe ★★ DELI/BAKERY/CAFE Staff at the Highwheeler proudly display their homemade breads, salads, wraps, and desserts in a glass case, one that at mealtimes attracts a line of hungry visitors oohing and ahhing with anticipation. Though not everything is vegetarian or gluten free, those options are plentiful: think black bean quinoa salad, spelt flour breads, fresh vegetarian soups, and cranberry scones. Patrons can eat on the roomy, street side patio.

468 Chebucto St. www.facebook.com/Highwheeler-Cafe-Bakery-268590753326950. ℂ **902/295-3006.** Sandwiches under C$10. Open daily May to mid-Oct.

Bras d'Or Lake

With so much beauty on Cape Breton Island, Bras d'Or Lake doesn't get its fair share of attention from travelers. It's bizarre: almost anywhere else in the world, Bras d'Or—a vast inland sea that's so big it nearly cleaves the island in two—would be a major tourist attraction ringed by motels, boat tour operators, water parks, and chain restaurants. But today, along the twisting shoreline of this 112km (70-mile) saltwater lake, all you find are a few small towns and villages—including First Nations reserves—the odd motel and campground, and a whole lot of wilderness. Yes, roads circumnavigate the whole lake, but service areas are far apart. (By the way, most Nova Scotians use the plural Bras d'Or Lakes when referring to this body of water.)

Bras d'Or is a difficult lake to characterize, because it changes dramatically from one area to the next—wild and rugged in some parts, pastoral and tamed in others. Wherever you go on the lake, though, keep an eye peeled for the regal silhouettes of bald eagles soaring high above the water (or for a telltale spot of bright white in the trees, indicating a perching eagle). Dozens of eagle pairs nest along the lake's shores or nearby, making this one of the best places in Canada for observing eagles in their natural habitat.

EXPLORING BRAS D'OR LAKE

What's a good strategy for touring the lake? For starters, I would caution against trying to drive around it in 1 day—or even 2 days. There's no equivalent to the Cabot Trail tracing the lake's outline. The lake is a connected group of smaller bodies of water, so there's no one route that travels the entire shore without backtracking and detouring. The circumnavigating roads serve up breathtaking views from time to time, but parts of the route are dull, running some distance from the lake's shore and offering little more than views of scratchy woods. Pick one or two small sections of the lake and focus on those.

On the southeastern shore is the historic little town of **St. Peter's ★**, where the lake comes within 800m (½-mile) of breaking through to the Atlantic Ocean and splitting Cape Breton into two half-islands. There's evidence this neck of land was settled as early as the 16th century by the Portuguese. Later the French used it strategically for shipping out timber—it was known as Port Toulouse at that time. Still later, the British built a fort and the town grew by leaps when Loyalists began fleeing America.

Nature couldn't quite manage to split the mass up here, but humans did it when they built **St. Peter's Canal** in 1854. This canal still operates, and you might see impressive pleasure craft making their way up-canal to the lake. The pathway along the canal makes for a good walk, too.

The village of **Marble Mountain ★**, on the lake's southwestern shore, is hard to find but offers an intriguing glimpse into island history. (If you intend to come here, get a *good* local map of the island first, then take the back roads from **Dundee, West Bay,** or **Orangedale.**) Believe it or not, this town was briefly a little metropolis. In 1868, a seam of high-quality marble was discovered here, and by the early 20th century, full-scale mining operations were exporting it to builders around the world. At its peak, the quarry employed 750 miners, and the town was home to a thousand or more souls.

Now the marble has played out, though, and the village has reverted to form: a sleepy backwater. You can glimpse the scar of the former mine (which offers great views over the lake) by car or on foot from town (ask a local for directions), and there's a **beach** right in town with scenic swimming. The beach looks like it features pure white sand from a distance, but it doesn't: It's made up of marble chips washed down from the old quarry.

Also worth a quick detour is **Isle Madame ★**—which is the largest in an *archipelago,* a group of small islands—just south of the lake off Route 104 and Route 4 as you return west from St. Peter's to the island's "entrance" at Port Hawkesbury. Shortly after Columbus arrived in North America, French, English, and Basque fishermen used these islands as a base for fishing, whaling, and walrus expeditions. Over the years, people settled, fished, and survived both the wars between French and English and being exploited by business monopolies. A few turned to smuggling, giving the island a bit of a romantic history, but cod was the mainstay. Today, this region is almost entirely French-speaking (though everyone speaks English too).

three for the road: LAKESIDE DRIVES

Bras d'Or Lake is huge and scenic—in fact, that's the problem. It's simply *too* big (and too hard to see from most roads) to be worth the trouble of circum-navigating. It's best to explore the lake piece by piece. Here are my picks for the three best short sections of Bras d'Or to tour by car when you're pressed for time:

○ Drive the stretch of quiet shore-line that begins in **Iona** and hugs the St. Andrews Channel on **Route 223;** if you're headed to **Sydney,** go this way as far as **Barrachois.** It's about a 40km (25-mile), 45-minute ride—longer if you stop a while at the good **Highland Village Museum ★★** (below).

○ Another nice section is the hump of land that rises and falls between **Dundee** and **St.** Peter's, which runs attractively over hill and dale. There are two or three different ways you can go; each takes about a half-hour.

○ A third segment is the stretch of **Route 4** that heads northeast from **St. Peter's** to **East Bay,** running along the eastern arm of the lake as it narrows to a point. You'll get the very best views of the lake from this route, and the best sense of its surprisingly vast size. You'll also pass little coves, a famous tearoom (see "Where to Eat," p. 258), and a First Nations reserve (at **Chapel Island**). This is a longer haul—about 64km (40 miles)—but the road is mostly straight and quick, and it'll very likely take you less than an hour to traverse.

Highland Village Museum ★★ HISTORIC VILLAGE   Highland Village is located outside Iona, on a grassy hillside with sweeping views over the lake. When you finally turn your back on the great panorama, you'll find a good living history museum. This 16-hectare (40-acre) village features a set of buildings reflecting the region's Gaelic heritage, some of them actual historic structures relocated here from elsewhere on the island and some of them quite impressive replicas. Inside, they contain rug-hooking tools, furniture, old Celtic music scores, info on the Gaelic language, and many more artifacts. Poke through the (ca. 1790) Black House, a stone-and-sod hut of the sort an immigrant would have lived in prior to departing Scotland, or the schoolhouse and general store, which date from the 1920s. Staffers dressed in historical costumes are happy to answer your (or your kids') questions about island life in the early days. It's worth spending at least an hour, more if you've got a group of kids keenly interested in history.

4119 Hwy. 223, Iona. http://highlandvillage.novascotia.ca. ℂ **866/442-3542** or 902/725-2272. Admission C$11 adults, C$9 seniors, C$5 children 6–17, C$25 families. June to mid-Oct daily 10am–5pm; Mid-Oct to May Mon–Fri 9am–5pm gift shop only.

WHERE TO STAY
Ben Eoin Beach RV Resort & Campground ★★   On a hook of sand reaching into the gentle Bras d'Or Lake, campers crowd together in RVs, tents, and cabins to enjoy one of the few beaches on the lake, swim in the

warm waters, and take in the views of the low, green mountainsides that enclose and protect these waters. In spite of—and possibly because of—the tight quarters, regulars return year after year, to let the kids run loose, meet old friends, boat around the lake, and gather around campfires at night.

6140 East Bay Hwy. (Rte. 4). http://beneoinbeach.ca. © **902/828-3100**. 212 sites. C$30–C$47 double. Closed mid-Sept to mid-June. **Amenities:** Store, canteen, recreation hall, showers, laundromat, wood, boat rental and launch, playground, Internet (free).

Bras d'Or Lakes Inn ★   The advertised "pool" is a hot tub, the fitness room is lean on equipment, and the grounds are small. But in this area of the world, you're not going to do better and to be fair, service here is quite friendly, the housekeeping can't be faulted, and the dock out back is a lovely spot for quiet contemplation of the lake (also a launching place for a kayak or canoe). We also have a soft spot for the rooms: Yes, they too are lilliputian—there's little space between the foot of the bed and the far wall—but they're comfortable, with a subdued decor of neutral-colored bedding, quiet artwork, and one wall of rustic knotty pine. And evening meals, in the spacious cedar log **dining room ★**, are well-made and nicely presented. The menu ranges from unusual and delicious brandy-flambéed shrimp skewers in Cajun cream sauce to standard fare like burgers, chicken, steak, and fried seafood. An a la carte entree averages C$13, or you can splurge on the three-course Table d'Hôtel for C$30.

10095 Grenville St. Peter's. www.brasdorlakesinn.com. © **800/818-5885** or 902/535-2200. 19 units. C$144 double. Packages available. Closed Nov–Mar. **Amenities:** Dining room, lounge, live entertainment, exercise room, patio, dock, outdoor hot tub, gift shop, bike and water craft rentals, Wi-Fi (free).

WHERE TO EAT

Quality eateries outside Baddeck are few and far between around the lake, but in addition to the dining room at the Bras d'Or Lakes Inn (above), there are a couple of interesting smaller places for a bite or two.

Farmers Daughter ★★ MARKET & CAFE   Started as a roadside fruit and vegetable stand, Farmers Daughter has grown into a bakery, deli, cafe, and gift shop while retaining that original market component. Stop for a hot or a cold drink and the house specialty: a hot savory meat pocket called "Stuffed Crust Flora Buns." For picnics, visitors gather armloads of bread and deli items or buckets of fried chicken. The red roadside market is a regular stop for many who travel this main route.

9393 Trans Canada Hwy., Whycocomagh. www.thefarmersdaughtercountrymarket.ca. © **902/756-9042.** Sandwiches C$4–C$9. Open daily 7am–8pm.

Rita's Tea Room ★ CAFE   Well known Cape Breton singer-songwriter Rita MacNeil started this tea room in the village of Big Pond where she grew up (and often reminisced about on stage as she toured the world). She converted a 1939 schoolhouse into a home and then into a gift shop and thriving little dining room for light lunches (soups, salads, baked goods) and, of course, tea. Sadly, Rita is no longer with us, but her spirit still infuses this place. In the summer there's live music most Sundays.

8077 Hwy. 4, Big Pond. www.ritamacneil.com/pages/ritas-tea-room. (C) **902/828-2667.** Snacks, soups, and sandwiches C$7–C$15; afternoon tea sets C$10–C$15. Late June to mid-Oct daily 10am–5pm. Closed mid-Oct to late June.

Sydney

The province's third-largest city (pop. 31,000) was northern Nova Scotia's industrial hub for decades. Recent economic trends have not been kind to the area, however, and the once-thriving steel mills and coal mines are gone. So this gritty port city has been striving to reinvent itself as a tourist destination, though with limited success—partly because Cape Breton's natural wonders offer such tough competition. Although its commercial downtown is a bit bland, some of Sydney's residential areas might appeal to architecture and history buffs. Three early buildings are open to the public in summer, all within easy walking distance of one another and of the spruced-up waterfront, where you'll find a giant fiddle welcoming the odd cruise ship.

The **Cossit House Museum** ★, 75 Charlotte St. (http://cossithouse.nova scotia.ca; (C) **902/539-7973**), is Sydney's oldest standing house, built in 1787 and now carefully restored and furnished with a fine collection of 18th-century antiques. If you ask the interpreter about ghosts, the doors will be closed, and the flickering lights extinguished for the relating of hair-raising tales. It's open from June through mid-October, Tuesday through Saturday 9am to 5pm. Admission is C$2 for adults, C$1 for seniors and children ages 6 to 17.

The nearby **Jost Heritage House** ★, 54 Charlotte St. ((C) **902/539-0366**), was built in 1787 and had a number of incarnations in the intervening years, the architectural changes made intentionally visible for visitors. Highlights of the home include an early apothecary. Open June through August Monday through Saturday from 9am to 5pm, September and October 10am to 4pm. Admission costs C$2 per person.

The handsome **St. Patrick's Church** ★, 87 Esplanade ((C) **902/562-8237**), locally known as "St. Pat's," is the island's oldest Roman Catholic church and dates to 1828. It's suitably impressive, made of rugged stone. From June through Labour Day, a **museum** in the church with artifacts that tell some of the island's religious history opens Monday to Saturday, 9am to 5pm.

PUFFIN STUFF

If you are a birdwatcher with any level of interest and commitment, you have to see the **Bird Islands.** Thirty minutes west of Sydney (just off the Trans-Canada Hwy., en route to St. Ann's or Baddeck) is the home port of **Bird Island Boat Tours** ★★★ (www.birdisland.net; (C) **800/661-6680**). On a 2¾-hour narrated cruise, you'll head out to the Bird Islands, home to a colony of around 300 nesting puffins. You'll get within 18m (60 ft.) of the colorful endangered birds (which nest in grassy burrows above rocky cliffs); you may also see razorbills, seals, guillemots, cormorants, the occasional eagle, as well as seals. Two or three tours are offered daily from mid-May through late

September, though the timing varies by day; cost of the tours is C$45 for adults, C$19 for children 7 to 12. Seniors, those with reservations, and others get a C$3 discount. To find directions to the landing, check the website.

AN UNDERGROUND TOUR

Northeast of Sydney is the town of **Glace Bay,** a former coal-mining center. The mines have slipped into an economic twilight, but the province made lemonade from lemons by creating the surprisingly intriguing **Cape Breton Miners' Museum ★★** at 17 Museum St. (www.minersmuseum.com; © 902/849-4522). The museum provides background on the geology of the area, and offers insight into the region's sometimes-rough labor history. In the **Miners' Village** next to the museum is a company store and a humble miner's home from the late 19th century; there's also a restaurant. In summer, the Men of the Deeps men's choir gives concerts. The highlight of the trip is the 20-minute descent into the mine itself (for an extra charge). Retired miners lead the tours, because they can tell you what it was like to work here better than anyone else. Admission is C$12 adults, C$10 children for the museum, and an additional C$12 adults and C$10 children for the mine tour. The museum is open daily from June through October, 10am to 5pm (Tues until 7pm when Men of the Deeps is performing), by appointment the rest of the year.

Louisbourg ★★★

Louisbourg, on Cape Breton's remote and wind-swept easternmost coast, was once one of Canada's most impressive French settlements. Then, the colony basically disappeared after the British forced the French out (for the second and final time) in 1760. Through the miracle of archaeology and historic reconstruction, much of the imposing settlement has now been re-created, and today this is among Canada's most ambitious National Historic Sites and the largest historic reconstruction project on the continent.

A visit does require a little effort. Being 35km (22 miles) east of Sydney means this attraction is an end in itself, but one well worth the trip. The hours spent wandering the wondrous rebuilt town, engaging with dozens of interpreters who bring the place alive through seemingly endless tasks and activities, and then walking along the coastal trail could be one of the highlights of a trip to Eastern Canada.

The Gabarus Wilderness Area ★★★ (www.novascotia.ca/nse/protected areas/wa_gabarus.asp) south of Louisbourg is a magnificent 3,745-hectare (9,250-acre) stretch of isolated wild beach, dunes, lagoons, and rocky headlands where you might witness a bald eagle tearing apart its prey or find a whale carcass washed ashore—and there's a ghost town in one cove. There are no services here; it's just you and the natural beauty of a rugged coastline. Contact a visitor information center for maps and information.

EXPLORING THE VILLAGE

The hamlet of Louisbourg—which you pass through en route to the historic park—is low-key. A short **boardwalk** with interpretive signs runs along the town's tiny waterfront. (You'll get a glimpse of the historic site across the water.) Nearby is a cool faux-Elizabethan theater, the **Louisbourg Playhouse** ★ (www.louisbourgplayhouse.com; © **902/733-3838**), at 11 Aberdeen St. The 17th-century-style playhouse was originally built near the old town by Disney for the movie *Squanto*. After production wrapped, Disney donated it to the village, which dismantled it and moved it to a side street near the harbor. Live theater and Cape Breton music are staged here throughout the summer.

As you come into town on Route 22, you'll pass the **Sydney and Louis-bourg Railway Museum** (© **902/733-2720**), which shares the gabled railway depot with the local **visitor information center** (same phone). The museum commemorates the former railway, which shipped coal from the mines to Louisbourg harbor between 1895 and 1968. You can visit some of the old rolling stock (including an 1881 passenger car) and view the roundhouse. It's open daily from mid-May through October; in July and August, from 8am to 8pm, and in spring and fall 9am to 5pm. Admission is free.

Lighthouse Point ★ is the site of Canada's very first lighthouse. (The lighthouse you see there today is a replacement version, however.) The rocky coastline at this spot is quite dramatic and undeveloped, and open—no trees. It's a swell spot for a little hike, a picnic, and some photographs. Look for Havenside Road (the lighthouse access road), which diverges from the main paved road near the visitor information center in the center of town.

Fortress of Louisbourg National Historic Site ★★★ HISTORIC SITE   The lonely, often cold and foggy eastern edge of Cape Breton seemed like a strategic necessity to French forces in the early 18th century. From here, they thought, they would protect Atlantic fishing interests and, as importantly, the entrance to the St. Lawrence River and therefore the French-controlled cities of Québec and Montréal. Thus the stone stronghold of Fortress Louis-bourg was conceived and built. In its heyday, it was North America's third-busiest port behind Boston and Philadelphia, home port of over 60 fishing schooners and a fleet of some 400 *shallops* (two-masted open boats for daily inshore fishing ventures). After possession changed several times between France and England as wars waxed and waned, the British finally destroyed it in 1758. In the 1960s, Parks Canada began a long reconstruction of the for-tress (and the town within) to 1744 condition using an army of archeologists and unemployed coal miners. It became North America's largest reconstruc-tion project.

Today, Louisbourg is a place to experience life inside a rough New World military stronghold. You arrive by boarding a bus at the interpretation center—no cars allowed near the fortress. As you climb down off the bus and are accosted by costumed guards, the illusion of entering a time warp begins. Farm animals peck and poke about. The smell of fresh baking drifts on salty air that might suddenly be shattered by the blast of a cannon or a round of musket fire. Soldiers march about and intimidate visitors who could be British spies. Children play the games of 3 centuries ago in the streets. Fishermen, servants, officers, and cooks greet guests at the doors of their respective homes and places of work. Meals here consist of rustic, historically accurate beef stew or meat pie sided by rum specifically made for the Fortress (a full meal is about C$15 in one of four restaurants designated by class—upper or lower). If you want a more complete immersion, you can become a colonial French military student in training to fire the cannon or get your hands dirty as you help tend the medicinal and food gardens. Twice-daily guided walking tours take about an hour and cost C$3.90, accessible tours about 45 minutes and cost about double. Count on a full day here; check the website for numerous special events.

259 Park Service Rd. www.fortressoflouisbourg.ca or www.pc.gc.ca/eng/lhn-nhs/ns/louis bourg/index.aspx. © **902/733-3552.** Open year-round, late May to mid-Oct daily 9:30am-5:30pm; mid-Oct to late May Mon–Fri 9:30am–4pm. Admission C$18 adult, C$15 seniors, C$8.80 children, C$44 families; 60% discounts in reduced service periods.

WHERE TO STAY

Cranberry Cove Inn ★★   This big Victorian inn, painted, well, cranberry, with a wide veranda at the front overlooking the harbor, is a local landmark. Inside, the Victorian theme and cranberry red continue with opulent period furniture and floral wallpaper. The seven units are each decorated to fit their own theme; greens, yellows, and greys from a tartan pattern dominate Isle Royale, while a ship's wheel and nautical knick-knacks appear in The Captain's Den. Most rooms have fireplaces and Jacuzzis, others skylights in sloped ceilings. Because of an open stairwell, this property is not suitable for children.

12 Wolfe St., Louisbourg. www.cranberrycoveinn.com. © **800/929-0222** or 902/733-2171. 7 units. C$105–C$160 double. Rates include full hot breakfast. Closed Nov to mid-May. **Amenities:** Dining room, fireplace (some units), Jacuzzi (some units), Wi-Fi (free).

Point of View Suites ★★   This large, new three-story hotel faces the fortress, so views are grand indeed. Situated on a 1.6-hectare (4-acre) peninsula, this is the closest accommodation to the fortress. There's a private beach from which to enjoy that same view. Suites and apartments have hardwood floors, which brighten already well-lit rooms, some with glass doors that open onto balconies or terraces. Walls, too, are a warm and knotty wood—very attractive. Apartments are equipped with Jacuzzis, three queen beds, and full kitchens. Units with no ocean view start at C$125, oceanfront units at C$145, and apartments at C$199. The building is wheelchair accessible.

12 Wolfe St. www.louisbourgpointofview.com. © **888/374-8439** or 902/733-2080. 19 units. C$129–C$299. Rates include full breakfast. Closed mid-Oct to mid-May. **Amenities:** Dining room, balcony (some units), Jacuzzi (some units), private beach, Wi-Fi (free).

WHERE TO EAT

If you haven't had enough of historic restaurants in period costume at the fortress, **Beggars Banquet** ★★ (www.louisbourgpointofview.com/dining; © **888/374-8439**) in the village outside the fortress will surely satisfy you. While you chow down on steamed lobster or snow crab, halibut or half a roasted chicken with fixings, waitstaff in 18th-century costumes serve and entertain with tunes, lyrics, and stories about love and life back then. Ginger cake with whipped cream is dessert. Dinner for C$50 is at 6pm nightly. While choice is limited, the fun is not.

Alternatively, to re-enter the 21st century, there's family casual dining at the **Lobster Kettle ★**, popular with locals and tourists, at 41 Strathcona St. (*©* **902/733-2723**). It's just what you'd expect: an emphasis on steamed lobster, chowder, surf 'n' turf, and other seafood dishes, everything done well enough for C$10 to C$35.

CAPE BRETON HIGHLANDS NATIONAL PARK ★★★

Cape Breton Highlands National Park covers nearly 1,000 sq. km (370 sq. miles) and stretches across a rugged peninsula from the Atlantic to the Gulf of St. Lawrence. It's famous for its starkly beautiful terrain, featuring one of the most dramatic coastal drives in North America. One of the great pleasures of this park is that it holds something for everyone, from tourists who prefer to sightsee from the comfort of their cars to those who like backcountry hiking in the company of bears and moose.

The mountains of Cape Breton are probably unlike those you're familiar with elsewhere. The heart of the park is fundamentally a huge plateau; in the vast interior, you'll find a flat, melancholy landscape of wind-stunted evergreens, bogs, and barrens. This is called the "taiga," a name that refers to the zone between tundra and the northernmost forest. In this largely untracked area you might find 150-year-old trees that are still only knee-high. Up here, moose browse hardwood saplings and wade into lakes. (It's best not to drive at night on these roads because moose can suddenly appear on them.)

It's the park's edges that really capture attention. On the western side of the peninsula, the tableland has eroded right into the sea, creating a dramatic landscape of ravines and ragged, rust-colored cliffs pounded by the ocean, where eagles soar in the updrafts and whales feed close to shore in the deep waters. The **Cabot Trail ★★★**, a paved road built in 1939, winds dramatically along the flanks of these mountains, offering extraordinary vistas and camera shots at every turn. On the park's eastern flank—the Atlantic side—the terrain's a bit less spectacular and the ocean a little farther away, but those lush green hills still offer a backdrop that's exceptionally beautiful.

Note that this section of the book focuses only on the park proper, which offers *no* lodging or services other than campgrounds. You can find lodging and restaurants in the handful of villages and towns that ring the park. See the previous section, which begins on p. 235, for detailed information about lodgings in the various towns (such as Chéticamp, Ingonish, and Baddeck) near the park's boundaries.

Essentials

GETTING THERE   Access to the park is via the **Cabot Trail,** which is very well marked by provincial signage. The entire loop is about 305km (190 miles), though the section that passes through the national park—from the entrance at Chéticamp to the one at Ingonish—is only about 105km (65 miles). You'll drive slowly to navigate the hairpin turns, climb or descend the steep inclines, pull over at the many viewing stations, and take in the vistas. Although the loop can be done in either direction, we present it here in a clockwise direction.

VISITOR INFORMATION   Two **visitor information centers** are located at either end of the park, in **Chéticamp** and **Ingonish.** Both are open daily from mid-May through mid-October, 8am to 7pm in summer (July–Aug) and 9am to 5pm during the shoulder seasons. The Chéticamp center has much more extensive information about the park, including a slide presentation, natural history exhibits, a cool large-scale relief map, and a very good bookstore. The park's main phone number is ⓒ **902/224-2306** and the website is www.pc.gc.ca/eng/pn-np/ns/cbreton/index.aspx.

FEES   A park pass is required for use of all services and facilities including campgrounds and trails while the park is open and can be purchased either at information centers or at tollhouses at the two main park entrances. Daily fees are C$7.80 adults, C$6.80 seniors, C$3.90 children age 6 to 16, and C$20 families. If you'll stay in the vicinity of this park for a week or more, buy an **annual pass,** which saves you money; the yearly pass is about C$98 for families, about C$39 per adult. If you want to visit more than one national park in the Maritimes, buy an all-Canada National Pass (www.pc.gc.ca).

Exploring the Park
SCENIC DRIVES

Cape Breton Highlands National Park basically only offers one drive, but it's a doozy: With few exceptions, it's jaw-droppingly scenic along nearly the entire route. The most breathtaking stretch is probably the 40km (25-mile) section from **Chéticamp to Pleasant Bay** ★★★ along the island's northwestern coast. Budget lots of extra time for driving this part, because you'll be stopping at the pullouts to gawk at the views, reading interpretive panels, and snapping photos. Other drivers will poke along, too. If you have time, there's even a nice out-of-park detour at the northern apex of the loop to **Meat Cove;** see "Cape North," p. 246 in this chapter, for details.

If it's a foggy day, though, you might want to save yourself the entrance fee and time. Some folks say that without the views, there's little reason to drive the loop, and advise waiting for a day when the fog has lifted. On the other hand, a foggy landscape can be ethereal; cloud-shrouded peaks make for mystery and drama. When fog hangs near the water or over the bogs, slow down and savor the unique views. If the mountain tops disappear, explore villages near your hotel in the atmospheric mist instead.

HIKING

The park offers no fewer than 26 distinct hiking tracks departing from the Cabot Trail. Many excursions are quite short and have the feel of a casual stroll rather than a vigorous tramp, but those determined to get a workout and get into the wilderness will find suitable trails, too. All the trails are listed, with brief descriptions, on the reverse side of the map you get when you pay your park entry fee at the gates.

One of the most rewarding short hikes is straight across the road from the information center in Ingonish. **Freshwater Lake Lookoff ★★** is only .3km (.2-mile) return, but it's as steep as it is short, climbing the side of a hill to a small clearing atop a rocky cliff where there's a bench to sit and take in the picturesque view of Ingonish Beach with a large pond in the foreground and Cape Smokey in the background.

The **Skyline Trail ★★★** is perhaps the park's finest; it offers oodles of altitude and views, without the climbing. You ascend a tableland from Chéticamp by car, then follow a 9km (6-mile) loop out along dramatic bluffs and through wind-stunted spruces and firs where moose might be browsing. A spur trail descends to a high, exposed point overlooking the surf and another slope across the Cabot Trial; it's capped by blueberry bushes.

Farther along the Cabot Trail, **Lone Shieling ★** is an easy 800m (.5-mile) loop through lush hardwood forest in a valley that's home to 350-year-old sugar maples. The re-created hut of a Scottish crofter (shepherd) is another interesting feature of this trail.

If you're looking to leave the crowds behind, the **Glasgow Lakes Lookoff ★** is a relatively gentle 9km (6-mile) round-trip hike that takes you through barrens and scrubby forest to a rocky, bald overlook with distant views of the ocean and some highland lakes. This trail is alternately swampy and rocky, so wear rugged footwear.

On the eastern shore, try the 4km (2.5-mile) **hike to Middle Head ★★**, which starts beyond the Keltic Lodge resort. This dramatic, rocky peninsula thrusts well out into the Atlantic. The trail is wide and relatively flat, and you'll cross open meadows with wonderful views both to the north and south. The tip of the peninsula is grassy and open, a good spot from which to watch for passing whales—or see waves crashing in after a storm. Allow about 2 hours for a relaxed walk out to the point and back.

BIKING

The full 290km (180-mile) **Cabot Trail loop ★★★** is the ironman tour for bikers, both arduous and rewarding. The route twists up ravines and plummets back down toward the coast. One breathtaking vista after another unfolds, and the plunging, brake-smoking descent from Mt. MacKenzie to Pleasant Bay is one cyclists aren't likely to forget. Campgrounds and motels are well spaced out, making a 3- or 4-day excursion possible. However, the road is almost uniformly narrow and free of shoulders, so you'll be battling constantly with errant drivers for the side of the road. If you're not inclined to pedal the entire loop, especially scenic stretches for bikers in good shape include the sections from **Chéticamp to Pleasant Bay ★★** and back, and the climb and descent from **Lone Shieling eastward to the Aspy Valley ★★**.

Note that mountain bikes are allowed on just a few trails within the park—check with the visitor center when you arrive for details. The longest backcountry trail is the 12.2km (7.6-mile) route called **Salmon Pools ★**, a level trail that follows the bottom of the Chéticamp River canyon with towering cliffs. Bikes are permitted on part of this trail.

Camping

The best way to experience the park is to stay a while: to live close to nature by camping. The park has five drive-in campgrounds. The largest are at **Chéticamp** (on the west side) and **Broad Cove** (on the east), both of which have the commendable policy of never turning a camper away; even if all regular sites are full, they'll still find a place for you to pitch a tent or park your RV. All these campgrounds are well run and well maintained, though Chéticamp and Broad Cove have the most facilities, including three-way hookups for RVs. Rates run from around C$18 to C$38 per night, depending on the level of services you require, time of year, and the campground you've selected. Remember that you're also required to buy a park entry (or have a park pass in hand) and that you can only make advance reservations at Chéticamp and Broad Cove, where sites are set aside for advance bookings, made by calling © **877/737-3783** or using the website www.reservation.pc.gc.ca/Home.aspx. At all the other campgrounds, it's first-come, first-served. A hybrid of tent and cabin called the oTENTik is available at these two campgrounds for C$100 a night.

The park also has a stunning **backcountry campsite at Fishing Cove ★★**, set on a pristine, scenic cove with a grassy hillside, cobblestone beach, and river. It's an 8km (5-mile) hike into the site from your car, and there's no potable drinking water once you arrive; pack enough in. (No campfires are allowed there, either.) Once there, however, you can watch for pilot whales at sunset from the cliffs to your heart's content. The site costs C$9.80 per night; make arrangements at one of the visitor information centers.

HALIFAX

Harborside Halifax is the biggest city in the Maritime Provinces by far, yet it doesn't feel big at all. It actually feels like a collection of loosely connected neighborhoods, which, in fact, it is. The municipal boundaries of the city stretch from Hubbards in the south to Musquodoboit Harbour in the north, nearly 100km (60 miles) apart, engulfing many smaller communities and rural areas that cannot otherwise be considered urban. When Nova Scotians speak of Halifax, they generally mean the small city on the peninsula between the harbor and the inlet known as the Northwest Arm. Downtown Halifax faces the former City of Dartmouth, now a neighborhood in the Halifax Regional Municipality.

Established in 1749, the city was named for George Montagu Dunk, 2nd Earl of Halifax. The city plodded along as a colonial backwater for the better part of a century, overshadowed by nearby towns building more ships and boats (Shelburne and Lunenburg, to name two); one historian even wrote of Halifax as "a rather degenerate little seaport town."

But the city's natural advantages—that well-protected harbor, its location near major fishing grounds and shipping lanes—eventually caused Halifax to overtake its rivals and emerge as an industrial port and military base. Several universities, including a significant art college, were established early and have thrived ever since, populating the city with intellectuals, students, and artists. In recent decades, this city has grown aggressively and carved out a niche for itself as the commercial and financial hub of the Maritimes.

It's these multiple personalities of the city that make it so vibrant. The music scene here is humming and continues to produce pop, folk, and alt stars the likes of Sarah McLachlan, Sloan, and Denny Doherty, a member of the '60s group, The Mamas & the Papas. Nightlife in Halifax is lively and friendly; whole sections downtown are dedicated to dining, music, and drinking, with many festivals animating the streets year-round. A big chunk of real estate at the city center was given over long ago as a common area, which it remains today. Green spaces at the Commons, Citadel Hill, the Halifax Public Gardens, and Point Pleasant Park at the tip of the peninsula make Halifax a walkable, relaxed small city.

ESSENTIALS

GETTING THERE Coming from New Brunswick and the west, the most direct route to Halifax by car is via Highway 102 from Truro; allow 2 or 2½ hours to drive here once you cross the invisible provincial border at Amherst. Others arrive via ferry either from Saint John, New Brunswick to Digby, Nova Scotia and on to Halifax on Highway 101 or from Maine to Yarmouth, then to Halifax on Highway 103. (Note that the ferry to Yarmouth has been in flux for some years, so check with Tourism Nova Scotia to learn about the latest American departure port and fees.) There is a bus service, the **Maritime Bus** (www.maritimebus.com; ℂ **800/575-1807**), which connects to the rest of the world from the train station at 1161 Hollis Street.

Many travelers arrive in Halifax by air. Halifax's **Stanfield International Airport** (www.hiaa.com; ℂ **902/873-4422;** airport code YHZ) in Elmsdale is 34km (21 miles) north of the city center. To get to Halifax, take Route 102 south. Airlines serving Halifax currently include Air Canada, WestJet, American, Delta, Porter Airlines, United, and Air Saint Pierre, along with some seasonal and vacation carriers (see "Fast Facts: The Maritimes," p. 299). Nova Scotia's variable weather means it's always a good idea to call your airlines before heading out to the airport to make sure your flight will depart on time, especially in winter.

For transportation to and from the airport, you can either take a cab (a flat fare of C$53–C$56 by law); rent a car (plenty of big-name chain options in the terminal); or take the **Airport Shuttle** operated by **Maritime Bus** (www.maritimebus.com; ℂ **800/575-1807**), which makes frequent runs from the airport to major downtown hotels daily from 4:30am to 11:15pm. The rate is C$22 per person one-way with children under 12 riding for free. There are also a surprising number of **long-haul shuttles** ★ from the airport directly to Cape Breton, Yarmouth, Moncton, Antigonish, and Prince Edward Island. Some shuttle services require advance reservations, because they only run once per day and the vans may be full up. Check the airport's website (www.hiaa.ca), or stop at the **Visitor Information Centre** (VIC) located in the domestic arrivals area of the main airport terminal, open year-round from 9am until 9pm.

You can even arrive by train. **VIA Rail** (www.viarail.ca; ℂ **888/842-7245**) offers overnight train service 3 days a week between Halifax and Montréal. The entire trip takes between 18 and 21 hours, depending on direction. Stops include Moncton and Campbellton (with bus connections to Québec City). Halifax's train station, at 1161 Hollis St. (adjoining the Westin Hotel), is within walking distance of downtown attractions.

Cruise ships tie up adjacent to the train station, if you happen to want to arrive in that style.

VISITOR INFORMATION The government-run **Visitor Information Centre** (VIC) (www.destinationhalifax.com; ℂ **902/424-4248**) on the waterfront at 1655 Lower Water St. (Sackville Landing on the boardwalk) is open

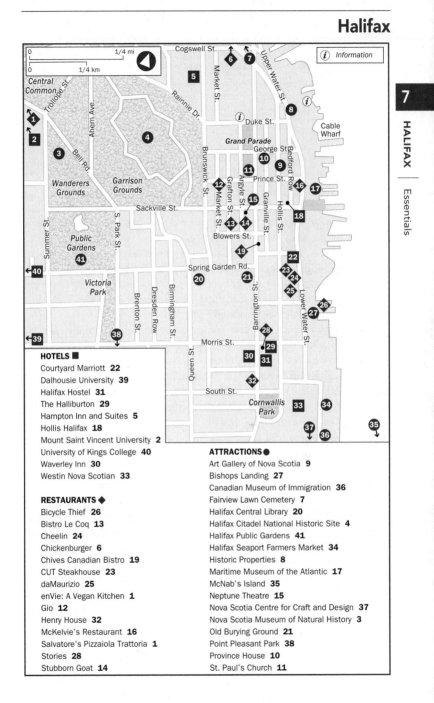

Central Common

Trollope St.

Ahern Ave.

Bell Rd.

Wanderers Grounds

Garrison Grounds

Summer St.

S. Park St.

Public Gardens

Victoria Park

Brenton St.

Dresden Row

Birmingham St.

Cogswell St.

Market St.

Rainnie Dr.

Brunswick St.

Grafton St.

Market St.

Upper Water St.

Duke St.

Grand Parade

George St

Prince St.

Argyle St.

Granville St.

Bedford Row

Hollis St.

Cable Wharf

Sackville St.

Blowers St.

Spring Garden Rd.

Barrington St.

Lower Water St.

Morris St.

Queen St.

South St.

Cornwallis Park

HOTELS ■
Courtyard Marriott **22**
Dalhousie University **39**
Halifax Hostel **31**
The Halliburton **29**
Hampton Inn and Suites **5**
Hollis Halifax **18**
Mount Saint Vincent University **2**
University of Kings College **40**
Waverley Inn **30**
Westin Nova Scotian **33**

RESTAURANTS ◆
Bicycle Thief **26**
Bistro Le Coq **13**
Cheelin **24**
Chickenburger **6**
Chives Canadian Bistro **19**
CUT Steakhouse **23**
daMaurizio **25**
enVie: A Vegan Kitchen **1**
Gio **12**
Henry House **32**
McKelvie's Restaurant **16**
Salvatore's Pizzaiola Trattoria **1**
Stories **28**
Stubborn Goat **14**

ATTRACTIONS ●
Art Gallery of Nova Scotia **9**
Bishops Landing **27**
Canadian Museum of Immigration **36**
Fairview Lawn Cemetery **7**
Halifax Central Library **20**
Halifax Citadel National Historic Site **4**
Halifax Public Gardens **41**
Halifax Seaport Farmers Market **34**
Historic Properties **8**
Maritime Museum of the Atlantic **17**
McNab's Island **35**
Neptune Theatre **15**
Nova Scotia Centre for Craft and Design **37**
Nova Scotia Museum of Natural History **3**
Old Burying Ground **21**
Point Pleasant Park **38**
Province House **10**
St. Paul's Church **11**

daily, year-round until 9pm in summer, until 6pm in winter. There's another VIC at Halifax's airport (℃ **902/873-1223**), also open year-round.

GETTING AROUND   Parking in Halifax can be problematic. Long-term metered spaces are in high demand downtown, and many of the parking lots and garages fill up fast. In recent years, parking capacity has expanded at private lots. If you're headed downtown for a brief visit, you can usually find a 2-hour meter. But if you're looking to spend the day in town, I'd suggest venturing out early and snagging a spot in an affordable parking lot or garage, or taking a taxi or public transit from your hotel. **Metro Transit** operates buses throughout the city. Route and timetable info is available at www.halifax.ca/transit or by calling ℃ **311.** Bus fare is C$2.50 for adults and students; C$1.75 for seniors and children. Transfers are free.

EVENTS   Year-round, Halifax excels at presenting unique festivals and events. A complete list can be found at www.destinationhalifax.com. Some of the most notable are:

Savour Food and Wine Festival ★★ (www.savourfoodandwine.com; ℃ **902/429-5343**) from the end of January to mid-March is a series of culinary events that pair fab food with the best of Nova Scotia wines, craft beers, and cocktails. Stars of the festival include **Decadence: Chocolate, Wine and Cheese** and the **Craft Beer Cottage Party.**

The Halifax ComedyFest ★★ (www.halifaxcomedyfest.ca) brings some of the finest Canadian and international comedians to town at the end of April each year. It's a chance to see great stand-up live in intimate venues across the city.

The annual **Royal Nova Scotia International Tattoo** ★★★ (www.nstattoo.ca; ℃ **800/563-1114** or 902/420-1114) features military acrobatics and marching bands totaling some 2,000-plus performers. The rousing event takes place over the course of a week in early July and is held indoors at the **Scotia Bank Centre** at the foot of Citadel Hill. Tickets are from about C$45 to C$100, depending on seating, less for seniors and children.

The annual **Halifax Jazz Festival** ★★ (www.halifaxjazzfestival.ca; ℃ **902/420-9943**) has performances ranging from global to avant-garde to local and traditional music each July. Venues include nightclubs and outdoor stages, and prices vary considerably; consult the website for details.

Halifax International Busker Festival ★★ (www.buskers.ca) takes place in early August, and attracts a slew of street performers—folk singers, fire-eaters, clowns, jugglers, you name it They descend on Halifax for 10 days, performing along the waterfront walkway. The talent is often quite remarkable. The festival is free, though donations are requested (you can donate *and* get complete info by buying a comprehensive festival guide for C$2 on the waterfront before and during the festival).

The **Atlantic Film Festival** ★★ (www.atlanticfilm.com; ℃ **902/422-4006**) offers screenings of more than 150 films at theaters around Halifax over a 10-day period in mid-September. The focus is largely on Canadian filmmaking, with an emphasis on independent productions and shorts, and the quality level is high. The lineup usually includes Oscar and Golden Globe nominees.

Panel discussions with industry players are also part of the festival, meaning you get a chance to see mid-level directors and stars up close and personal.

The annual mid-October **Nocturne** ★ (www.nocturnehalifax.ca) is a fun, free art museum-and-gallery walk that kicks off at 6pm and concludes around midnight, highlighting what's fresh on the local art scene. Free shuttle buses ease the load on your feet, too. Only drawback? It only lasts 1 night.

EXPLORING HALIFAX

These days, Halifax sprawls out for miles in every direction but east—that is the Atlantic Ocean. Downtown Halifax is fairly compact, thus easily navigated if you don't mind steep hills and some traffic. The major landmark is the **Citadel**—that stone fortress looming over downtown from a grassy height. (From the ramparts, you can look into the windows of the 10th floor of downtown high-rises.) The Citadel is only 9 blocks uphill from the **waterfront**—9 *steep* blocks. It's along the east and south side of the hill that the city's core is concentrated. The waterfront area crams a huge number of activities, experiences, restaurants, and shopping into about 9 city blocks. You can get a sampling in a day, but plan for longer if you want to really explore the museums, theaters, pubs, and eateries (or go on tours or try sailing or . . .).

Another lively neighborhood worth seeking out runs along **Spring Garden Road** between the Public Gardens and Barrington Street. Here you'll find intriguing boutiques, bars, and restaurants along 6 blocks, set amid a bohemian street scene. If you relish a little exercise, start on the waterfront and walk uphill and over the Citadel, descend to the lovely **Public Gardens ★★** (see p. 277), then return via Spring Garden Road.

On the other side of Citadel Hill, Quinpool Road, another commercial and retail area, extends west away from the Halifax Commons. The **Oxford Theatre** at 6408 Quinpool Rd. (www.cineplex.com; ✆ **902/422-2022**) dates from 1937, and the classic feel of the theater takes patrons back to the golden age of cinema. It's one of the only remaining single-screen movie houses in the province, playing both Hollywood and art films.

You'll need wheels to get to the **Hydrostone Market ★★** (5515–5547 Young St.), a small neighborhood called **The Hydrostone,** often referred to as a "European experience." The district rose from the ashes of the catastrophic Halifax Explosion (1917) and was designed after an English garden suburb. The neighborhood houses unique shops and some excellent eateries like **Salvatore's Pizzaiola Trattoria ★★★** (see p. 286).

The Waterfront

Halifax's rehabilitated waterfront extends from Casino Nova Scotia (near Purdy's Wharf) south to Pier 21 with boardwalks and piers extending the full length, making it a very accessible, exceedingly walkable area. To the north, naval dockyards and Canadian Forces Base Halifax are restricted but often provide a view of naval vessels from the Canadian fleet. On sunny summer afternoons, this stretch of waterfront bustles with tourists enjoying the harbor, business folks sneaking ice-cream cones, or skateboarders trying to make (or stay out of) trouble.

To fortify yourself for what lies ahead—or better, to relax at the end of the long stroll if you walk north to south—stop in at **Garrison Brewing** ★★ at 1149 Marginal Rd. (www.garrisonbrewing.com; ✆ **902/453-5343**) for a tour and sampling. It's at the south end of the waterfront boardwalk near **Pier 21** (see below for more on this immigration museum) and the cruise-ship docks.

Halifax Seaport Farmers' Market ★★★ at 1209 Marginal Rd./Pier 20 (www.halifaxfarmersmarket.com; ✆ **902/492-4043**) is a special place. Over 150 vendors peddle everything from fresh farm products to hot, delicious takeaway food to high quality arts and crafts. Although the market is open 7 days a week (weekdays 10am–5pm, Sun 9am–3pm), it's Saturdays from 7am to 3pm when it's bustling with the most vendors and large crowds.

As you walk north from the market, you have a terrific view of Georges Island, a small drumlin in the middle of Halifax harbor which has been the scene of constant military activity and harbor defense for 200 years. You can glimpse the top of fortifications from here, but most of it is hidden. In 2012, Parks Canada took over access to the island, but it is still not open visitors.

Passing a beach of trucked-in sand, you'll soon come across **Bishops Landing,** an upscale development of condos and nifty little shops. Among them, **Bishop's Cellar** ★★ (www.bishopscellar.com; ✆ **902/490-2675**) is a stellar wine shop open until midnight Friday and Saturday. **The Bicycle Thief** ★★★ (see p. 284), right on the boardwalk adjacent Georges Island, is a favorite restaurant in the area for its old world charm and Italianesque Canadian fare. **Rum Runners Rum Cake Factory** ★ (www.rumrunners.ca; ✆ **902/421-6079**) is another fun stop; it bakes rum or whiskey into delicious cakes.

Continue a short distance along the boardwalk, keeping the water on your right. **Sackville Landing** ★ is studded with intriguing shops, takeout food emporia, artisans, and monuments. Think of it as an alfresco scavenger hunt. If you're interested in nautical history, make your next stop the **Maritime Museum of the Atlantic** ★★★ (see below). You'll pass North America's oldest operating **naval clock,** which was built in 1767 and chimed at the Halifax Naval Dockyard from 1772 all the way up until 1993.

Next you'll come to the **Halifax Ferry Terminal;** a ferry service has been in operation here since 1752. It gets hectic during rush hour with commuters coming and going to Dartmouth across the harbor. But at other times of the day, boarding a ferry here is a cheap and relaxing way to get a quick, sweeping city and harbor view. The passenger-only **ferry** ★ runs every 15 minutes. The fare is the same as the city busses at C$2.50 per adult or student each way, C$1.75 for seniors and children age 5 to 15. You need to have cash. Change machines are nearby, and remember to ask for transfers for a bus or to return. It only takes 15 minutes to get to Dartmouth, and 15 minutes to get back.

The waterfront's shopping core is located in and around the 3-block **Historic Properties** ★. These buildings of wood and stone are Canada's oldest surviving warehouses, and were once the heart of the city's shipping industry.

Today, their historic architecture provides ballast for boutiques and restaurants. This area is busy during the day with walkers, shoppers, buskers, and small-time vendors. At night, a contagious energy spills out of the public houses here as workers get off work and tipple pints. You'll find a bustling camaraderie and live music. On summer evenings, live music is staged in the spaces between the historic buildings.

The top sights of the area are:

The Canadian Museum of Immigration at Pier 21 ★★ MUSEUM
Over a million immigrants flowed through this seaport terminal from 1928 to 1971 on their way to new lives in Canada. Some of Canada's immigration policies and practices were less than admirable, and the museum does not gloss over these. For example, in a campaign to attract western American farmers to Canada's prairies, African Americans were openly discouraged from immigrating. Most intriguing are the personal stories told on interpretive panels and in videos and audio displays. Don't hesitate to bring the little ones; there are meaningful activities for kids, too.

1055 Marginal Road. www.pier21.ca. ✆ **855/526-4721** or 902/425-7770. C$10 adult, C$8.35 seniors, C$7 children 6 to 16, C$25 family, free for children 5 and under. Open daily 9:30am–5pm.

Fairview Lawn Cemetery ★ CEMETERY
When the *Titanic* went down on April 15, 1912, nearly 2,000 people died. Ship captains from Halifax were recruited to help retrieve the corpses. Some 121 victims, mostly ship crewmembers, were buried at this quiet cemetery located a short drive north of downtown Halifax. Some of the simple graves have names, but many others only bear numbers. Plaques and signs highlight some poignant stories from the tragedy. It's definitely worth an hour or more for *Titanic* fans; others might just spend a few minutes here. (Without a car, though, skip it entirely—too far.) A brochure with driving directions to this and two other *Titanic* cemeteries in the city can be obtained either at the Maritime Museum (below) or the city's visitor information centers.

Chisholm Ave. www.novascotia.ca/titanic/connection.asp. ✆ **902/490-4883.** Always open. Admission free.

Maritime Museum of the Atlantic ★★★ MUSEUM
Visitors with even a passing interest in local history owe themselves a stop at this standout museum, situated on a prime piece of waterfront. The exhibits are well executed and involving—you'll be surprised how fast 2 hours can fly. Visitors are greeted by a cool 3m (10-ft.) lighthouse lens from 1906, then proceed through a series of shipbuilding and seagoing displays. These include the deckhouse of a coastal steamer (ca. 1940) where travelers learn the colorful history of Samuel Cunard, the Nova Scotia native (born in 1787) who founded the Cunard Steam Ship Co. to carry royal mail—but established a travel dynasty instead. Another highlight is the shocking exhibit on the Halifax explosion of 1917, when two warships collided in the harbor not far from this museum, detonating tons of TNT. It was the world's most powerful blast until atomic

bombs were dropped on Hiroshima and Nagasaki; more than 1,700 people died, and windows were shattered 60 miles away.

Perhaps the most poignant exhibit here is just a single deck chair from the Titanic—a somber reminder that 150 victims of that disaster are buried here in Halifax (see above), where the rescue efforts were centered.

Outside is the permanently docked **CSS** *Acadia* ★★, a steam-powered vessel used by the Canadian government to chart the ocean bottom from 1913 until its retirement in 1969. A self-guided tour is worth it just to see the fine woodwork in many of the rooms. The *Acadia* is a National Historic Site and the museum's largest artifact. Allow half an hour.

1675 Lower Water St. www.maritime.museum.novascotia.ca. © **902/424-7490.** May–Oct admission C$9.55 adults, C$8.50 seniors, C$5.15 children 6–17, C$25 family; Nov–Apr, admission discounted about 50%. May–Oct daily 9:30am–5:30pm (to 8pm Tues); Nov–Apr closed Mon and only 1–5pm Sun.

On the Water

A number of boat tours depart from the Halifax waterfront. You can browse the offerings on **Cable Wharf,** near the foot of George Street, where many tour boats are based. On-the-water adventures range from 1-hour harbor tours (about C$18) to half-day deep-sea fishing trips (about C$55). **Murphy's on the Water** ★★ (www.mtcw.ca; © **902/420-1015**) runs the most extensive tour operation, with several boats and a choice of tours ranging from tall ship, pirate, or cocktail sailing cruises to whale-watching and fishing trips. If you have little ones, *Theodore Too,* a replica of the tugboat from the Theodore cartoon series, a popular Canadian show, will be a hit. It will cost you C$65 to take the family for a harbor tour. The **Harbour Hopper** amphibious craft crosses both land and sea during a harbor tour that takes about an hour. It costs C$31 for adults, C$29 for seniors, C$17 for children ages 6 to 15, and C$10 for children 5 and under. The ticket office is located on the north side of the Maritime Museum.

Moored to one of the wharves near the Maritime Museum and the CSS *Acadia* is the **HMCS** *Sackville* ★★ (www.hmcssackville.ca; © **902/429-2132,** off season 427-2837), a World War II veteran corvette (a warship one step down from a destroyer) painted a distinctive blue and white. The ship is outfitted just as it was in 1944, maintained as a memorial to the Canadians who served in World War II. Bedford Basin, at the western end of the harbor, served as the staging point for great convoys of ships like this that brought supplies and relief to war-torn Europe during World War II. The thousands of seafarers who passed through this port are honored by nearby monuments. Admission starts at C$4 adult. It's open June to October, 10am to 5pm.

The Citadel & Downtown

Downtown Halifax cascades 9 blocks down a hill between the imposing stone Citadel and the city's waterfront. There's no fast-and-ready tour route; don't hesitate to follow your own whims, ducking down quiet side streets or striding along the main roads. A good spot to regain your bearings periodically is the

Grand Parade, where military recruits once practiced their drills. It's a lovely piece of urban landscape—a broad terrace carved into a hill. At the south end is **St. Paul's Anglican Church ★★** (www.stpaulshalifax.org; © **902/429-2240**), the first Anglican cathedral outside England, and Canada's oldest place of worship for Protestants. A piece of flying debris from the great explosion of 1917 (see Maritime Museum of the Atlantic, p. 273) is lodged in the wall over the doors to the nave. The fine stained-glass windows are one of the highlights of a guided tour. At the north end stands Halifax's **City Hall,** a sandstone structure built between 1887 and 1890 and exuberantly adorned in the usual Victorian ways: prominent clock tower, dormers, pediments, arched windows, pilasters, Corinthian columns. (Alas, there's not much to see inside.)

If the weather is nice, the Grand Parade is a prime spot to bring a picnic.

Art Gallery of Nova Scotia ★★ GALLERY   The province's art gallery, perhaps the best in the Maritimes with 17,000 works in the permanent collection, is situated two blocks south of the Grand Parade. You'll find challenging and exciting contemporary Canadian art like that of Garry Neill Kennedy (he's won many awards, including Canada's top visual arts prize, the Governor General's Award) alongside the region's best folk art. That latter display includes the entire house where the province's most famous folk artist, Maude Lewis, lived and worked . . . and painted the walls. Annie Leibovitz gifted the gallery with a major collection of works, worth an estimated C$20 million; as this book went to press the works were slated to go on display in mid-2017. To re-energize, try the on-site **Cheapside Café ★**.

1723 Hollis St. www.artgalleryofnovascotia.ca. © **902/424-5280.** Admission C$12 adults, C$10 seniors, C$7 students, C$5 children age 6–17, C$25 families. Daily 10am–5pm (Thurs to 9pm). Tours daily.

Halifax Citadel National Historic Site ★★★ HISTORIC SITE   The Citadel is the perfect introduction to Halifax: It provides a good geographic first look at the city, and anchors it in history, as well. Even if a big stone fort weren't here, it would still be worth the uphill trek to this site just for the astounding views—the panoramic sweep across downtown, the city's harbor, and the Atlantic Ocean are breathtaking. And the ascent to your goal quickly makes it obvious why this spot was chosen for Halifax's most formidable defense: There's simply no sneaking up on the place. Four forts have occupied this same hilltop since Col. Edward Cornwallis was posted to the colony in 1749, but today the Citadel has been restored to look much as it did in 1856, when the fourth and final fort was built out of concern over American expansionist ideas. Yet the fort has never been attacked, perhaps a testament to its effectiveness as a deterrent.

The architecture is basic: Sturdy granite walls topped by grassy embankments form a star. In a sprawling gravel and cobblestone courtyard, you'll find convincingly costumed interpreters in kilts and bearskin hats marching in unison, playing bagpipes, and firing a cannon at noon. The former barracks and other chambers are home to exhibits about life at the fort. If you have questions, just stop a soldier, bagpiper, or washerwoman and ask. Don't expect to be alone—this National Historic Site is the most heavily visited in all of Canada. On the plus side, you won't need more than 45 minutes or an hour to see everything here, probably, unless you want to linger afterward and snap lots of pics of the tableau below you.

Citadel Hill. www.pc.gc.ca/eng/lhn-nhs/ns/halifax/index.aspx. ℂ **902/426-5080.** Admission June to mid-Sept C$12 adults, C$10 seniors, C$5.80 children 6–16, C$29 families; off season pay about 70%. Parking C$3.15. July–Aug daily 9am–6pm; May–June and Sept–Oct daily 9am–5pm. Nov–Apr visitor center closed but grounds and washrooms open. Ghost tours and other tours available.

Nova Scotia Centre for Craft and Design ★ GALLERY

Inside the center, you'll find a gallery, studios, and shop established by the government to launch and develop the careers of Nova Scotian craftspeople. Wood, metal, textile, and ceramic studios offer courses and residences for artists; the gallery exhibits new work.

1061 Marginal Rd., Ste. 140. www.craft-design.ns.ca. ℂ **902/492-2522.** Free admission. Tues–Fri 9am–5pm; Sat–Sun 11am–4pm.

Nova Scotia Museum of Natural History ★ MUSEUM

On the north side of the Citadel, opposite the new high school, this modern, midsize museum offers a good introduction to the flora and fauna of Nova Scotia. Kids will enjoy visiting Gus, the resident tortoise, now a century old. Pop him a little lettuce or banana, his favorite foods. Otherwise exhibits tell about the birds, mammals, geology, and human history of Nova Scotia, including the life and culture of the first nations Mi'kmaq people. A highlight is the colony of honeybees that make a home in the museum, entering and exiting through a clear tube. Kids and parents will enjoy an afternoon here.

1747 Summer St. www.naturalhistory.novascotia.ca. ℂ **902/424-7353.** Admission C$6.30 adults, C$5.70 seniors, C$4.05 children 6–17, C$13–C$18 families. Daily 9am–5pm (Wed until 8pm), Nov to mid-May closed Mon.

Province House ★ HISTORIC SITE

Every year since 1819, the Nova Scotia Legislature has met in Province House, making it the country's oldest seat of government. Although it is smaller than others across Canada, this one is considered architecturally important, because it is one of the continent's best examples of the rigorously symmetrical Palladian style. The dour stone exterior hides gems of ornamental detailing and artwork inside, especially the fine plasterwork, which is rare in a Canadian building from this era.

It was here that the first responsible government in the British Empire, outside Great Britain, was established. A free, well-written booklet is available when you enter; it provides helpful background about the building's history and architecture. (Sample legend that may or may not be true: It's said the headless falcons in several rooms were decapitated by an agitated, free-swinging legislator with a cane who mistook them for eagles during a period of feverish anti-American sentiment in the 1840s.) Consider sitting in on a legislative session if you're interested in watching parliamentary democracy in action as lawmakers debate—it can get quite heated. Or you can phone ahead to book a tour, available year-round. History buffs should allow an hour for this visit.

1726 Hollis St. www.nslegislature.ca. ✆ **902/424-4661.** Free admission. July–Aug Mon–Fri 9am–5pm, Sat–Sun and holidays 10am–4pm; Sept–June Mon–Fri 9am–4pm.

Green Spaces & Parks

Halifax Central Library ★★★ ATTRACTION   Near the foot of Spring Garden Road, a block west of Barrington Street, the exciting new library building stands as the city's most innovative architectural work. From the outside, it looks like a stack of boxes . . . or books. Inside, it's an airy, open space full of light, with secret, quiet corners for reading or watching the city. Stairwells crisscross like those at Hogwarts, Harry Potter's fictional school. Danish architects designed the funky new building that opened in late 2014 to wild enthusiasm from residents. Even if you aren't looking for a book or need to check your e-mail, it's worth taking a look inside to experience the building. There are two cafes and a rooftop terrace where you can enjoy fabulous views. Remarkably, artist Cliff Eyland painted over 5,000 library card–sized paintings that adorn one wall.

5440 Spring Garden Rd. www.halifaxpubliclibraries.ca. ✆ **902/490-5700.** Free. Mon–Thurs 9am–9pm, Fri & Sat 9am–6pm, Sun noon–6pm.

Halifax Public Gardens ★★ GARDEN   The Public Gardens took seed in 1753, when they were founded as a private venture. The tract was acquired by the Nova Scotia Horticultural Society in 1836, and these gardens assumed their present look around 1875 during the peak of the Victorian era. As such, the garden is one of Canada's Victorian masterpieces, rarer and more evocative than any mansard-roofed mansion. You'll find here wonderful examples of 19th-century trends in outdoor landscaping, from the "naturally" winding walks and ornate fountains to the duck ponds and Victorian band shell. Like Point Pleasant Park, the big trees were victims of Hurricane Juan, but not to the same degree. Following the storm, a radio campaign raised a million dollars in 48 hours to restore the gardens. Today, there are plenty of leafy trees, lush lawns, cranky ducks who have lost their fear of humans, and little ponds. It is the best place in this area to find reprieve from urban overstimulation.

Spring Garden Rd. and S. Park St. www.halifaxpublicgardens.ca. Free admission. May–Nov 11 8am–dusk.

McNab's Island ★ PARK   Nobody has lived here since 1985, and today this large swath of wooded wilderness at the mouth of Halifax Harbour is a provincial park with trails and shoreline to explore. At its southern tip are fortifications from the 19th century. If you want to stay on the island, ask about camping privileges. During World War I and World War II, all ships entering the harbor were required to signal the fort or risk being fired upon. Worth the trip as an urban wilderness oasis, but only if you have time in Halifax to spare.

In Halifax Harbor. www.mcnabsisland.com. ✆ **800/326-4563** or 902/465-4563 (ferry service). Admission to island free; ferry from Eastern Passage C$20 round-trip adult, C$15 round-trip seniors and children 5–17.

Old Burying Ground ★ CEMETERY   At the corner of the two main streets downtown—Barrington and Spring Garden—is Halifax's first cemetery. You'll know it by the locally famous sculpture at the entrance of a lion with the Medusa-like mane. Some 12,000 people were buried on these small grounds between 1749 and 1844, although only 1 in 10 souls owns a headstone. With two historic churches across adjacent streets viewed through leafy old trees, this corner is steeped in the history of this city's founders.

Corner of Spring Garden and Barrington. ℂ **902/429-2240.** Free admission. Daily mid-May to mid-Oct 9am–5pm; guides until late Aug. Closed rest of year.

Point Pleasant Park ★★ PARK   Joggers mix with families and dog walkers at the southern tip of the wooded Halifax peninsula, one of the finest parks in Canada. Hurricane Juan nearly flattened the entire 75-hectare (186-acre) park in 2003, but it is recovering (the new trees planted are starting to grow). For years the area actually served as one of the linchpins in the city's military defense. Look carefully and you'll find the ruins of early forts, plus a nicely preserved Martello tower. Interestingly, Halifax still has a 999-year lease from Great Britain for this park, for which it pays 1 shilling—about U.S. 10¢—per year. The park is located about 2km (1¼ miles) from downtown.

Point Pleasant Dr. (south end of Halifax; head south on S. Park St. near Public Gardens and continue on Young). www.pointpleasantpark.ca. Free admission. Daily 6am–midnight.

Shopping

Halifax has a large, eclectic mix of shops, from mainstream retailers to offbeat boutiques. There's no central retail district to speak of; shops are scattered throughout downtown, and the best way to go about finding cool stuff is just to walk around and happen upon unique, independent shops. Of the many malls in Halifax, my favorite is the small **Sunnyside Mall** ★★ in Bedford at 1595 Bedford Hwy. (www.sunnysidemall.ca; ℂ **902/835-5099**). The anchor is the unique **Pete's Fine Foods** ★★, an independent (until 2015 when it was bought by Sobeys) grocer that stocks fresh fruit, vegetables, and other groceries from around the world, in particular from the United Kingdom where founder Pete Luckett started out. With Pete's on site, the food court in this mall is loaded with unique food stalls. Stop in at Freak Lunchbox for throwback candy. Take Exit 4A off Highway 102 or take the Bedford Highway out of peninsular Halifax.

For souvenir shopping, head to the Historic Properties buildings on the waterfront; one of the star attractions is **Nova Scotian Crystal** ★★ at 5080 George St. (www.novascotiancrystal.com; ℂ **888/977-2797** or 902/492-3044), where mouth-blown, hand-cut crystal is made in full view. For one-of-a-kind shops, try the independents on and around Spring Garden Road between Brunswick and South Park streets. Queen Street is the destination for vintage and local clothing.

Art Gallery of Nova Scotia Shop ★ CRAFTS The museum's gift shops feature limited but choice selections of local crafts, ranging from creative postcards to birdhouses and tabletop sculptures. There's also work by Mi'kmaq artisans. 1723 Hollis St. www.artgalleryofnovascotia.ca. © **902/424-4303.**

Atlantic News ★★ NEWSPAPERS You'd think the Internet would have sunk this popular newspaper and magazine shop. But Atlantic News is still going, partly because of the enormous selection of titles it stocks and partly because it can print any of over 700 newspapers from 74 countries in 40 languages on the date of publication. How cool is that? Corner of Morris and Queen sts. www.atlanticnews.ns.ca. © **902/429-5468.**

Drala Books & Gifts ★ GIFTS This shop claims to be "the destination for supplies for the contemplative lifestyle." You'll find crystal balls, incense, calligraphy and ikebana materials, paper screens, chopsticks, teas, teapots, books on design and philosophy, pillows, meditation cushions, and more. Instructors sometimes teach meditation, tea ceremony, and the like. 1567 Grafton St. www.drala.ca. © **877/422-2504** or 902/422-2504.

Newfoundland Grocery Store ★★ FOOD Whenever I get a craving for seal flipper pie—admittedly, that's never (and it *is* a real pie)—I head to the friendliest store in Halifax, where groceries are either basic or odd and conversation is free. Where else can you goods like Purity candies that look like they time travelled from the World War II era? 6061 Willow St. © **902/423-6209.**

Urban Cottage ★ HOMEWARES This consignment store in the middle of downtown has a sizable and eclectic selection of furniture, housewares, and collectibles, nicely displayed and reasonably priced. 1819 Granville St. © **902/423-3010.**

WHERE TO STAY

As with any urban center, Halifax has an enormous selection of accommodations, including selections through Airbnb for as low as C$33. For other budget listings, beyond those picked here, you'll find old-fashioned affordable motels like the **Stardust** ★ at 1067 Bedford Hwy. (www.stardustmotel.ca; © **902/835-3316** or 877/472-3316) and the **Esquire Motel** ★ at 771 Bedford Hwy. (www.esquiremotel.ca; © **902/835-3367**) along the Bedford Highway just a 10-minute drive from downtown. Both offer rooms starting well under C$100 a night; the Esquire has a roadside restaurant just across the street.

Expensive

Courtyard Marriott ★★ Surprisingly few Halifax hotels are actually *on* the waterfront like this one, which means stellar views of Georges Island and the harbor from many rooms. Not that you'll need a view to distract you from your digs: Rooms here are unusually pleasant and roomy, with such nice touches as cushy beds, usable work stations, and large fridges. The lobby is also quite attractive, decorated with artifacts discovered during the 2010 excavation for the foundations of the hotel, and housing a Starbucks and a bistro. You can get a quick meal at the latter, but for something special head to **Cut** ★★, the excellent on-site steakhouse. *Two tips:* Don't confuse this hotel with its sister property, the **Halifax Harbourfront Marriott,** which can be quite noisy from the late partying at Historic Properties. And though parking is valet-only here, and pricey at $25, there's a free lot across the street.

5120 Salter St. www.marriott.com. © **800/321-2211** or 902/428-1900. 125 units. C$119–C$450 double to suite. **Amenities:** Cafe, lounge, pool, whirlpool, spa, fitness center, rooftop patio, Zen garden, Wi-Fi (free).

The Halliburton ★★★
Charm is front and center at what we think is downtown Halifax's finest boutique hotel. Three townhouses—the main one dates to 1809—are combined to provide 29 unique rooms and suites, some with wood-burning fireplaces, some with balconies overlooking quiet back gardens, all with color schemes taken from a Monet watercolor, burnished antique wood furnishings, and wonderfully comfortable beds. The intimate first-floor dining room, **Stories** ★★, serves dinners nightly that demonstrate a light, creative spark with local ingredients. Looking for a romantic getaway? You've found it.

5184 Morris St. www.thehalliburton.com. © **888/512-3344** or 902/420-0658. 29 units. C$145–C$350 double; off-season discounts available. Rates include continental breakfast and free parking (limited; first-come, first-serve). **Amenities:** Restaurant, babysitting, room service, fireplace (some units), balcony (some units), Wi-Fi (free).

Hollis Hotel ★★
New management poured C$7 million into renovations of this centrally located property, making it one of the most desirable in the downtown area. Many of the units are oversized suites with kitchenettes, and such niceties as walk-in showers with rainfall showerheads. Most have views of the harbor (though some look into offices across the street; ask when booking). An exceptionally friendly, helpful staff is the cherry on top.

1649 Hollis St. www.doubletree3.hilton.com. © **800/333-3333** or 902/429-7233. 120 units. C$129–C$309 rooms and suites. **Amenities:** Restaurant, room service, pool, whirlpool, fitness center, Wi-Fi (free).

The Westin Nova Scotian ★
This historic hotel is on the same site as the VIA Rail train station and the Maritime Bus Station. It's close to the harbor, Pier 21, the Halifax Seaport Farmers' Market, and the cruise-ship docks—a long way of saying: The location can't be beat (though the building itself is removed enough to give it an urban-retreat feel). Rooms are not as spacious as the others mentioned in this category, and some feel dated. We include the Westin for the location and because it's often sold on Priceline for half the official rates.

1181 Hollis St. www.thewestinnovascotian.com. © **877/9WESTIN** [993-7846] or 902/421-1000. 310 units. C$139–C$299 double; C$395 suites. Luxury suites also available. Valet parking C$22, self-parking C$18. Pet friendly. **Amenities:** Complimentary downtown shuttle, restaurant, room service, health club, pool, whirlpool, spa; tennis courts, Internet (free).

Moderate

Hampton Inn and Suites ★★   One of the newest hotels downtown, these twin towers are near Citadel Hill, so a bit farther from the attractions of the Harbor than my other recommended hotels. But for those seeking slightly longer stays, this property is ideal, because many of the suites are equipped with full kitchens (minus ovens). And even if you don't splurge on a suite, all of the digs here are airy and spacious, with lots of light, spiffy contemporary decor and good beds. In units above the tenth floor, you get a view (over the apartment buildings opposite) of the harbor.

1990 Barrington St. www.halifaxdowntown.hamptonbyhilton.com. ℂ **855/331-0334** or 902/422-1391. 181 units. C$110–C$199 double. **Amenities:** Hot breakfast included, pool, fitness center, Wi-Fi (free).

Waverley Inn ★★★   No hotel in Halifax has more character than this little gem. The rooms are named for the famous guests—like Oscar Wilde and P. T. Barnum—who have stayed here since 1876 when the Inn opened. I think they would recognize it still today. Each room is unique, pleasingly old-fashioned and ornately furnished, with jewel-toned heavy drapes; lovely Victorian wallpapers; and beds that are (often) works of wooden art, thanks to their intricately carved headboards. A modern touch: the Jacuzzi-style bathtubs in some rooms. Free parking and a hearty breakfast is included in the rates.

1266 Barrington St. www.waverleyinn.com. ℂ **800/565-9346** or 902/423-9346. 34 units. Mid-May to Oct C$135–C$235 double; Nov to mid-May C$119–C$179 double. Free parking. **Amenities:** Breakfast, snacks, afternoon tea, Jacuzzi (some units), Wi-Fi (free).

Inexpensive

A 15-minute walk from downtown, but convenient to bus lines, are the dorm rooms at **Dalhousie University** ★ (www.conferenceservices.dal.ca; ℂ **888/271-9222** or 902/494-8840), furnished with plain single beds and each rented to the traveling public when school isn't in session (mid-May to mid-Aug). Many rooms even have private bathrooms and kitchenettes (you have to rent dishes for a small fee), making them an especially good deal for families. Rooms are C$50 single, C$77 double. Varied-size apartments cost somewhat more. Remember, summer demand is high, so book as far in advance as possible. Also note that a 2-night minimum stay is required for some units.

On the southwest corner of the Dalhousie campus, the **University of Kings College** ★ (www.ukings.ca/accommodations; ℂ **902/422-1270, ext. 132**) rents rooms in summer. Another option is **Mount Saint Vincent University** ★ (www.msvu.ca/en/home/community/conferenceservices/Accommodations) on the Bedford Hwy. Both are on par with Dalhousie, in terms of room variety, and both are slightly cheaper.

Halifax Heritage House Hostel ★★   The 75-bed Hostelling International–Maritimes is within easy walking distance to train and bus stations, many downtown attractions, and a number of convivial bars. Whether you share a room with other travelers or get one of the private rooms or family units, you'll be pleased with the level of cleanliness here and the friendliness of the staff. There are lockers in each room; charging stations for electronics; shared bathrooms for all; and a shared, fully equipped kitchen with free tea and coffee. Weekly events keep the place quite lively.

1253 Barrington St. www.hihostels.ca. *②* **902/422-3863.** 75 units. C$39/person in dormitories, C$79 for a double bed in a private room. **Amenities:** Kitchen, Wi-Fi (free)

WHERE TO EAT

Coffee emporia have cropped up throughout Halifax over the last decade, just as they have everywhere. Many also stock sandwiches, pastries, and light snacks in addition to the java. A few of the best downtown options are **Caffé Ristretto** (*②* 902/425-3087) at 1475 Lower Water St. (Bishop Landing), notable mostly for its nice harborside location; **Cabin Coffee** (*②* 902/422-8130) at 1554 Hollis St., with its bohemian feel and good espresso and cappuccino; and the dependable Canadian chains that seem to appear every few blocks, **Second Cup** and **Tim Hortons.** Down at the seaport, the **Java Factory Roasting Company** (*②* 902/468-2326) at 1113 Marginal Rd. serves mean sandwiches and samosas, along with free Wi-Fi.

Spring Garden Road and tiny side streets happily mix upscale fare with more basic grub. Nova Scotia's homegrown coffee chain, **Just Us! Coffeehouse** ★★ (*②* 902/423-0856) is in a barely renovated old house at 5896 Spring Garden Rd., as close to Dalhousie University as it is to downtown, just a 5-minute walk west of the Halifax Public Gardens (see p. 277). The coffee is topnotch, and the edibles make perfect sides.

The **Brewery** ★★ complex, on the uphill side of Lower Water Street just above the docks, is a fun one-stop shopping and dining experience. Originally the site of the Alexander Keith brewery—North America's oldest—the space has been redesigned and renovated to enclose courtyards from the weather, link the various structures of the abandoned brewery, and create an interior market of shops and restaurants. The complex houses one of the city's finest Chinese restaurants (see **Cheelin** ★, p. 285). While navigating the labyrinthine courtyards can be a bit confusing, it is a lark to see what is around the next corner.

Expensive

Haligonians and their visitors love to eat out. Restaurants here always seem to be in flux—new chefs, new trends, hot spots changing at a frenetic pace. Listing favorites is risky because they could be gone tomorrow, but those below *seem* to have staying power. These days, the most popular eateries are those that focus on local ingredients prepared and presented in innovative ways that manage to retain something of traditional cooking methods.

Several of Halifax's hotels have very good fine-dining restaurants tucked within them, among them the Prince George Hotel's **Gio** ★★ (www.giohalifax.com; *②* 902/425-1987) at 1725 Market St., which has won raves and culinary awards, especially for its *banh mi,* a Vietnamese sourdough baguette sandwich of roasted spicy pork, pickled carrot, cilantro, and ginger aioli;

Stories ★★ (www.storiesdining.com; 𝄯 **902/444-4400**) in The Haliburton for truly fine dining with mains like swordfish, elk, and tuna; and **Cut Steakhouse and Urban Grill** ★★ (www.cutsteakhouse.ca; 𝄯 **902/429-5120**) at the Courtyard Marriott, which boasts the best steak in town.

Chives Canadian Bistro ★★★ CANADIAN Local culinary celebrity Craig Flinn (he's a regular guest on the popular CBC Radio call-in show *Maritime Noon,* where he dispenses cooking advice) is infatuated with the products of Nova Scotia. And you will be, too, after dining here. The menu—it begins with a list of farms . . . a long list—changes daily, based on what's freshest in the market and what came in off the fishing boats. His signature chicken dish, for example, is named for the farm where it was raised, and the kitchen uses quark from the local Fox Hill Cheese farm to create a delicious ravioli. A summer salad could be a mighty stack of grilled local melon, apple, Dragon's Breath blue cheese (made in Nova Scotia), and house-made pancetta. Expect one main course each of lobster, scallops, chicken, beef, lamb, and vegetables. The atmosphere is casual fine dining, the decor of earth tones and textures in a space that once was a bank building on Barrington Street, the main thoroughfare through downtown.

Chef Flinn runs two other notable eateries. His **Ciboulette Café** ★★ (www.ciboulette.ca; 𝄯 **902/423-5282**), is a swell pick for breakfast or lunch; and **2 Doors Down** ★★ (www.go2doorsdown.com; 𝄯 **902/424-4224**) is a fab supper spot. Both are topnotch in their category, more affordable than the flagship restaurant, and both are next door to Chives and run by the same talent.

1537 Barrington St. www.chives.ca. 𝄯 **902/420-9626.** Daily for dinner 5–9:30pm. Reservations suggested. Main dishes C$31–C$50. Breakfast and lunch available in their Ciboulette Café next door, Mon–Fri 7:30am–4pm.

daMaurizio ★★★ ITALIAN For over 20 years, daMaurizio has been one of Halifax's signature fine-dining experiences. Service is attentive and warm, and the meals are unusually satisfying, whether the preparation is somewhat rustic (like the excellent eggplant with prosciutto baked in tomato and béchamel sauce) or downright luxe (lobster ravioli in a truffle cream sauce—the height of decadence!). You'll be awhile, so choose a wine to accompany the experience (there's a vast but well-curated selection), and travel by taxi. The restaurant is located inside a cleverly adapted former brewery, its vast space divided into a complex of intimate hives with columns, exposed brick, fresh flowers on the tables, and dim lighting. A great place to head for a celebration.

1496 Lower Water St. (in the Brewery). www.damaurizio.ca. 𝄯 **902/423-0859.** Reservations highly recommended. Main courses C$19–C$37, prix-fixe 3 courses for C$45. Mon–Sat 5–10pm.

McKelvie's Restaurant and Grill ★★ SEAFOOD It's not the first name in seafood restaurants in Halifax, but in my experience, it comes out ahead of those that jump to mind. Set in a 1906 fire station smack in the center of downtown, McKelvie's specializes in seafood with a twist, and always with the accent on bold flavors. I've never had a better calamari dish than their spicy "jump-up calamari" in jalapeño tomato sauce with a touch of honey. Another star of the menu: little fish tacos filled with light, tempura-battered haddock bits, seasoned with cilantro lime cream. If those don't tempt, know that all the usual fish dishes are also here, everything from pan-seared scallops to blackened organic salmon, but prepared with real flair.

1680 Lower Water St. www.mckelvies.ca. ✆ **902/421-6161.** Reservations recommended. Main courses C$27–C$47. Mon–Fri 11am–10pm, Sat–Sun from 4–10pm.

Moderate

The Bicycle Thief ★★★ NORTHERN ITALIAN/CANADIAN
Halifax's leading restaurateurs, husband-and-wife team Stephanie and Maurizio Bertossi (he's the son of a five-star Venetian chef) were behind the creation of this hugely popular, trendy restaurant. They've since sold it, but it retains their stamp, which is lively fusion fare (they call it "North American food with an Italian soul") in a setting that feels like the hippest place in the city. Dishes are divided into "1st Gear," "2nd Gear," and "High Gear," but be careful: Often the 2nd gear offerings are as large as the High Gear ones, so it's not unusual to over-order. Not that that would be a tragedy: The menu is awash in winning dishes like lobster raviolini, seared Nova Scotia halibut wrapped in pancetta and topped with whipped lobster mascarpone sauce, and a creamy fish soup that's swimming with seafood of all sorts. You'll know the place by the old bicycles out front and the din of happy diners.

1475 Lower Water St. (in Bishop's Landing, entrance at end of Bishop St.). www.bicy clethief.ca. ✆ **902/425-7993.** Reservations highly recommended. Mains C$20–C$35. Daily starting 11:30am.

Bistro Le Coq ★★ FRENCH
At the heart of Argyle Street, where it's wall to wall restaurants and bars, this Bistro stands out by its French accent. Quite simply, this place transports guests to Paris with both its looks (a classic zinc bar, pressed tin ceiling, red leather banquettes) and the food, which is classically Gallic. I'm talking straightforward but delicious *steak frites;* excellent tuna tartare; crepes; and a charcuterie board with smoky beef sausage, whipped pork belly, and blueberry preserve, among other tasty bits.

1584 Argyle St. www.bistrocoq.ca. ✆ **902/407-4564.** Main dishes C$19–C$28. Mon–Thurs noon–10pm, Fri noon–midnight, Sat 11:30am–midnight, Sun 11.30am–10pm.

The Stubborn Goat ★★★ GASTROPUB
You know you're in a different sort of pub when the fish and chips arrives and there's a whole, head-and-tail-on fish next to your home fries, with tzatziki and caper vinaigrette for dipping. That kind of bold inventiveness permeates an excitingly eclectic menu on which everything, from the sausage to the risotto croquettes, is house-made and delicious. The pizza oven turns out fantastic thin-crust pizzas, and the burgers are flavorful and generous. Even the side dishes are outstanding, like the roasted Brussels sprouts topped with local bacon and sriracha-spiked mayo. The extraordinary menu; the two-floor, casual layout;

and well-stocked bars (with some 75 different types of beer, many from Nova Scotia) guarantee this place is hopping at all hours—reserve a table.

1579 Grafton St. www.stubborngoat.ca. ℭ **902/405-4554.** Reservations highly recommended. Main courses C$16–C$30. Mon–Fri 11:30am–2am; Sat–Sun 10:30am–2am.

Inexpensive

Cheelin ★ CHINESE   For being one of this city's best Chinese restaurants, the prices here are surprisingly low—almost everything is under C$20. Cheelin specializes in both Szechuan and Beijing cuisine, meaning the chef doesn't shy away from spiciness in dishes like Hunan haddock in chile-tomato sauce or eggplant stuffed with shrimp and pork. I recommend starting with the fresh, house-made spring rolls and the gingery pan-fried dumplings. On Fridays there's an impressive lunch buffet. Cheelin offers takeout, as well as delivery to your hotel.

1496 Lower Water St. (inside the Brewery). www.cheelinrestaurant.ca. ℭ **902/422-2252.** Most items C$13–C$19. Mon–Sat 11:30am–2:30pm; daily 5–10pm.

The Chickenburger ★★ FAST FOOD   Time travel to a 1950s-style burger joint at the Chickenburger in Bedford, Canada's oldest drive-in diner. This is fast food, but it's also entirely handmade—simple but delicious burgers and fries, onion rings and shakes. The big draw (and a favorite that makes this place really stand out) is the chickenburger—juicy shredded chicken in a bun—simple and delicious since 1940. Enjoy a nostalgic meal inside on the shiny chrome tables and stools under neon lights or in your car outside.

1531 Bedford Hwy. www.chickenburger.com. ℭ **902/835-6565.** Hamburger C$2.85; chickenburger C$3.75. Sun–Thurs 9am–10pm; Fri–Sat 9am–11pm.

enVie: A Vegan Kitchen ★★ VEGAN   It's a joy to dine at a place where the staff are clearly having a blast and the food is as creative as it is at enVie. Everything is made from scratch using only organic ingredients sourced locally (as often as possible) in the creation of mains like "The Doug Burger" named for the neighborhood cat. It's a black-bean patty with greens, caramelized onion, and pickles with tangy mayo inside a sesame-seed bun. For a pasta choice, the roasted-squash tortellini with artichoke and cashew puree, sherry gel, and parsnip milk is a standout. The desserts are especially tempting. The baklava is phyllo-wrapped cheesecake with orange blossom pistachios and candied lime. On weekends, there's a special brunch menu.

5775 Charles St. www.enviehalifax.com. ℭ **902/492-4077.** Mains about C$15. Tues–Wed 11am–9pm; Thurs–Fri 11am–10pm; Sat 10am–10pm; Sun 10am–9pm.

Henry House ★★ BREWPUB   Old Peculiar—it's both the name of the best beer made on the premises (since it opened as Atlantic Canada's first brewpub in the mid-1980s) and an apt description of the place. From the outside, the 1834 ironstone building is austere and more than a bit foreboding. Inside it's, well, the same, especially in the downstairs pub where the walls are also stone. Still, the place is a local landmark, meaning that it's possible to find a wedding party in for a celebratory pint on the way from the chapel. Both the beers, ale, stout, and the pub grub (like chicken-and-leek pie, bread pudding, or fishcakes) honor British classics.

1222 Barrington St. www.henryhouse.ca. ℗ **902/423-5660.** Main courses C$12–C$19. Daily 11:30am–12:45am.

Salvatore's Pizzaiola Trattoria ★★★ PIZZA   Salvatore's makes the best thin crust pizza in the city, nearly all flavors and sizes for under C$20. Among the top picks is Pizza Miguel, a thin crust brushed with garlic-infused olive oil and layered with Spanish onion, mushrooms, and Romano cheese under a blanket of smoked mozzarella, finished with Parmesan, basil, and roasted garlic.

5541 Young St. (near Isleville St.). www.salvatorespizza.ca. ℗**902/455-1133.** Small pizzas start at C$9.45, heroes C$4.45. Tues–Sat 11:30am–11pm, Sun 4pm–10pm, Mon 11:30am–10pm.

HALIFAX BY NIGHT

Where Halifax (www.where.ca/nova-scotia/halifax.com), which will likely be given out at your hotel, is an excellent and comprehensive monthly guide to the city's entertainment and events. You'll also find live music performances listed in *The Coast* (www.thecoast.ca), a free newspaper widely available around Halifax

Among the city's premier venues for shows is the downtown **Scotiabank Centre**, 1800 Argyle St. (www.scotiabank-centre.com; ℗ **902/421-8000**), which hosts sporting events (figure skating, pro hockey) as well as concerts by a variety of big-name artists. Note that tickets are sold by the Ticket Atlantic Box Office (www.ticketatlantic.com; ℗ **902/451-1221**).

Performing Arts

Shakespeare by the Sea ★ (www.shakespearebythesea.ca; ℗ **902/422-0295**) stages both plays by the bard and works by other masters from July through Labour Day at several alfresco venues around the city. Most performances are held at Point Pleasant Park, where the ruins of old forts and buildings are used as stage settings, with the audience sprawled on the grass, many enjoying picnic dinners with their *Midsummer Night's Dream.* The company also operates an 82-seat black box theater called The Park Place Theatre for rainy days and off-season productions.

The **Neptune Theatre,** 1593 Argyle St. (www.neptunetheatre.com; ℗ **800/565-7345** or 902/429-7070), benefited from a multimillion-dollar renovation and now also runs an intimate 200-seat studio theater. Top-notch dramatic productions including musicals and dramas by Canadian and international playwrights are offered throughout the year. (The main season runs Sept–May, with a summer season filling in the gap with eclectic performances.) Mainstage tickets generally range from around C$15 to C$45.

A Road Trip to Peggy's Cove

About 42km (26 miles) southwest of Halifax is the fishing village of **Peggy's Cove** ★★★ (pop. 120), perhaps Nova Scotia's most recognizable icon. It offers postcard-perfect tableaus: An octagonal lighthouse (surely one of the most photographed in the world) is perched on wave-carved rock. Tiny fishing shacks line the harbor where graceful fishing boats bob.

The bonsai-like perfection hasn't gone unnoticed by the big tour operators, however, so it's a rare summer day when you're not sharing the experience with a few hundred of your close, personal bus-tour friends who swarm the rocks, restaurant, and gift shops. Here's another caution—be aware of sudden and surprisingly powerful waves. A tourist or two is swept away from time to time from these rocks, so enjoy the scenery well back from the water line.

While there, be sure to stop at the touching **Swissair Flight 111 Memorial** ★ among the rocks just before the turn-off to the cove; this site memorializes the passengers of that flight, which crashed into the Atlantic just off the coast.

The **Bus Stop Theater,** 2203 Gottingen St. (www.thebusstoptheatre.org; ✆ **888/639-1169**) is a multi-use space with about 70 events a year, many of them live theater, but including music, dance, book launches, craft fairs, and more. Productions are typically more challenging, political, or experimental than those in the larger theaters.

The Club & Bar Scene

Nightlife in Halifax is heavily concentrated in the downtown, from Historic Properties on the waterfront up to Citadel Hill, and from Scotia Square to Spring Garden Road with spill over up Spring Garden to the Public Gardens. Walk these streets and you'll find a bar, nightclub, or pub every few doors. In the case of Argyle Street, nightlife is even more concentrated. Sidewalk patios, rooftops, and the dark, labyrinthine interiors of some bars positively throb with music, reveling every weekend and many weeknights, particularly in summer.

One of the coolest places to hang out is **Economy Shoe Shop** ★★ (www.economyshoeshop.ca; ✆ **902/423-8845**), at 1663 Argyle St., not a shop but rather a cafe/bar that runs like a rabbit warren through historic buildings, with decor that has the feel of a film set. The Economy serves food from 11am all the way until 2am from an eclectic mix of menus; its wine list is impressive. **Obladee** ★★ (www.obladee.ca; ✆ **902/405-4505**) at 1600 Barrington St. is set in a former bookstore—you can sit in the display windows with your drink and people watch. This wine bar is co-owned by Heather Rankin of Cape Breton's best known Celtic music group, the Rankin Family. Because she is now a sommelier, the wine selection is excellent, as are the cheese and charcuterie boards. And **The Maxwell's Plum** ★ at 1600 Grafton St. (www.themaxwellsplum.com; ✆ **902/423-5090**) is an English pub where peanut shells litter the floor and patrons quaff from a list of 150 imported and Canadian draft and bottled beers. The nightly happy-hour and pitcher specials can considerably cut your cost.

An impressive roster of the hottest singer-songwriters in the region and across the land appear every weekend at **The Carleton** ★★ (www.thecarleton.ca; © **902/422-6335**) at 1685 Argyle St. In the evening (and late afternoons on Sat), you'll find lively Maritime music and cheap beer at the **Lower Deck Pub** ★ (www.lowerdeck.ca; © **902/425-1501**), a longstanding popular pub on three floors of the Historic Properties complex on the waterfront. If you love the blues, head to **Bearlys House of Blues and Ribs** ★★ (www.bearlys.ca; © **902/423-2526**) at 1269 Barrington St., a gritty, working-class bar with split levels so you can shoot a game of pool while watching the best blues musicians on the East Coast. There's entertainment here pretty well every night of the week, and a blues jam every Sunday evening. The top local rock bar is **Marquee Ballroom** ★★ at 2037 Gottingen St. (www.facebook.com/marqueeballroom; © **902/429-3020**).

PLANNING YOUR TRIP

The three eastern provinces of Canada (also known as the Maritimes) are safe and scenic yet stretched out, with limited travel options. And the tourist season here is short, with many seasonal operations in rural areas that only open for the 2 to 4 months of summer. As such, the region requires some care when planning if you want to be sure about getting maximum value for your travel expenditures, and find available accommodations that fit both your budget and your needs.

On the other hand, you won't need to worry at all about things that vex travelers to some destinations: violent crime, snakes, sharks, inoculations against disease. All in all, this is one of the easiest, most comfortable places to travel with a family or as a lone traveler. If you dislike long drives, then pick one area and concentrate on enjoying that rather than trying to squeeze three provinces (or even one very large province—we're talking to you New Brunswick) into one short vacation. Plan realistically, allowing yourself time to enjoy the places you want to experience rather than trying to cram it all into a few days.

In these pages, you'll get the nuts and bolts of travel in the provinces: when to come, the documentation you'll need, where to get more info, how to keep connected with the office or family, on-the-ground resources, and more. These basics just might make the difference between a smooth trip and a bumpy one.

GETTING THERE

By Plane

Airports around Atlantic Canada offer access via scheduled flights. Halifax, Nova Scotia (YHZ), the region's major air hub, has frequent flights in and out of the region, as well as onward connections to local airports. Other major airports include Moncton, New Brunswick (YQM) and Charlottetown, Prince Edward Island (YYG). All offer direct flights to and from airports outside of the region.

The main air carriers serving Atlantic Canada are: **Air Canada** (www.air-canada.com; ℭ **888/422-7533**); **WestJet** (www.westjet.com; ℭ **877/929-8646**), which connects Halifax, Moncton, and Charlottetown with other airports in Canada; and **Porter Airlines** (www.flyporter.com; ℭ **888/619-8622**) which flies into Halifax and Moncton from Toronto. Several American carriers including **United** (www.united.com; ℭ **800/864-8331**) are also jumping into the Eastern Canada fray.

See the individual "Getting There" sections at the beginning of each chapter for more information on direct connections into specific cities.

By Car

Overland access to Atlantic Canada from the United States is through Maine. The most direct route to New Brunswick is to drive to Bangor (about 4½ hr. from Boston), then head east on Route 9 to Calais, Maine (about 2½ hr.). Here you can cross into St. Stephen, New Brunswick and pick up Route 1 to Saint John and beyond. If you don't plan to stop until you hit Moncton or points east of Moncton, a slightly faster alternative is to continue northeast on the **Maine Turnpike**—which is the northernmost end of the Eastern seaboard's famous Interstate 95—to Houlton, then cross the border and pick up the Trans-Canada Highway. Remember that the turnpike is a toll road for a stretch (the toll is US$5 maximum one-way for a passenger car), although it becomes completely toll-free past exit 113 at Augusta.

New Brunswick can be accessed from other parts of Canada via Québec using the Trans-Canada Highway, which enters the province near Edmundston. Route 20 east from Montréal or Québec to Riviere-du-Loup links with Route 185, which becomes Route 2 at the border with New Brunswick; or the less-traveled route 132 enters New Brunswick at Campbellton.

By Ferry

A year-round ferry connects Saint John, New Brunswick (about a 4-hr. drive from either Bangor or Bar Harbor, Maine), with Nova Scotia. See "Getting Around," below for details. A seasonal service from Maine to Yarmouth, Nova Scotia has been in flux for a number of years; check with Tourism Nova Scotia (www.novascotia.com; ℭ **800/565-0000**) before you leave home, if you would like to cross directly to Nova Scotia. Reservations are advised during the peak summer season.

By Train

Inter-provincial rail service is now but a pale shadow of its former self. Prince Edward Island lacks rail service completely, as does southern New Brunswick (you can no longer travel by train to either Fredericton or Saint John).

There's just one train line: **VIA Rail** (www.viarail.ca; ℭ **888/842-7245**), the national rail carrier, which stops in a handful of towns along its single overnight route between Montréal and Halifax. The train runs three times weekly. In New Brunswick, VIA trains stop at Campbellton, Charlo, Jacquet

River, Petit Rocher, Bathurst, Miramichi, Rogersville, Moncton, and Sackville. In Nova Scotia, you can get on or off the train at Amherst, Springhill Junction, Truro, or Halifax.

Fares for the trip depend on which class of seat you buy, from an economy seat (sleep sitting up) to various configurations of cabins. A non-discounted economy seat will run you about C$200 each way from Montréal to Halifax or back. Sleeping berths and private cabins are available at extra cost—the cheapest bed in a double-bunked cabin is about twice the cost of the no-bed fare—and VIA has even added a higher level of summer service on its overnight run (known as Sleeper Touring class) which includes better beds, presentations from an onboard guide, and a dome car. Discounts for those buying tickets in advance are sometimes available.

The entire trip takes between 18 and 21 hours, depending on direction.

By Bus

Bus service into and out of this region tends to be slow and cumbersome. To get from New York to Halifax, for instance, you'd have to take one bus to Montréal (8–10 hr.), then connect to another bus line to Halifax (something like 18 hr.)—not my idea of a fun start to a vacation week.

Greyhound (www.greyhound.com; © **844/477-8747**) offers service from diverse points around the United States to Montréal's bus station (© **800/661-8747**), where you can connect directly to Atlantic Canada–bound buses. There is a bus service, the **Maritime Bus** (www.maritimebus.com; © **800/575-1807**), making it possible to travel from Montréal and other Québec centers to locations around the Maritimes.

Many local transit companies pick up the ball from there, such as **Kings Transit** (www.kingstransit.ns.ca; © **888/546-4442** or 902/678-7310), which can shuttle you cheaply among Wolfville, Kentville, and Digby.

GETTING AROUND

By Plane

There's a serious lack of competition for air routes in Eastern Canada, which can mean you'll pay high fares for even a short hop to or around the region. **Air Canada, WestJet,** and **Porter** are the only options; see "Getting There" above for contact information.

Note that smaller airports throughout the region such as Sydney are starting to offer connections to the three main provincial hubs of Halifax, Moncton, and Charlottetown. Contact the local tourism authority in advance about such connections if you're interested.

By Car

Atlantic Canada's road network is extensive and generally well maintained. But travelers expecting to find six-lane highways with high-speed on- and off-ramps will be in for a surprise. With few exceptions, the highway system here is on a far smaller scale. Although there are now long sections of divided highway in New Brunswick and Nova Scotia, many of the main arteries are still two lanes (one coming, one going). The Trans-Canada Highway is the main road running through this region. It enters north of Edmundston, New Brunswick, and continues some 1,800km (1,120 miles) to St. John's, Newfoundland—taking a break at the Atlantic Ocean, of course. Numerous feeder roads connect to the Trans-Canada.

A few rules of the road: As in the United States and continental Europe, **drive on the right.** You may **make a right turn at a red light,** provided that you first stop fully and confirm that no one is coming from the left. (At some intersections, signs prohibit such a turn.) **Radar detectors are prohibited in all the Atlantic Provinces.** Drivers and passengers are required to wear seat belts.

If you're arriving by plane, the usual suspects offer **car rentals** at major airports. Despite the number of rental outfits, however, it can be difficult to reserve a car during the short summer season, when demand soars. It's best to reserve ahead. Cars can be rented in any major center, most easily at airports. But be aware that it will be less expensive to pick up a car in town than at an airport. Most major car rental firms are represented in the region. The best rates for rental can usually be obtained by booking ahead through a travel agent; the Internet; or in tandem with air, train or accommodations. Rates depend on the season, type of car, and points of pickup and drop-off. Be sure to investigate car insurance carefully. You may be able to save substantial dollars by having rental cars included on your own car insurance or via your credit-card coverage rather than buying it at a daily rate at the time of renting. Be sure to investigate carefully about **car-rental insurance** before setting out on your trip.

Remember that Canadian gas prices are higher than those in the U.S., though lower than they are in Europe. See "Gasoline" in "Fast Facts: The Maritimes" later in this chapter for more information.

By Ferry

To shorten the long drive around the Bay of Fundy, look into taking the ferry across the bay (operated by Bay Ferries) that links **Saint John, New Brunswick,** with **Digby, Nova Scotia.** Remarkably, this ferry sails daily year-round, with two sailings per day during peak travel periods.

The peak season one-way fare (June–Oct) was C$45 for adults, C$30 for children age 6 to 13, C$5 per child under age 6, and C$35 for students and seniors. A car costs an additional C$90 (more for motor homes, trucks, vans, and buses), plus a C$20 fuel surcharge. Fares are a bit cheaper outside the peak travel months. Complete up-to-the-minute schedules and fares for this route can be found at www.nfl-bay.com or by calling ✆ **877/762-7245.**

Another ferry service from **Maine** to **Yarmouth, Nova Scotia** has been an on-again, off-again option for many years now. Because the situation changes so often with this route, check with Tourism Nova Scotia (www.novascotia. com; ✆ **800/565-0000**) to see if there is a ship on the route; if so, ask for fee and schedule information.

A **second inter-provincial car ferry** links Prince Edward Island with Nova Scotia, though it doesn't save you time or money. You can also connect with Québec's Magdalen Islands by ferry from Souris in Prince Edward Island (www.ctma.ca), and with Newfoundland via a ferry from Sydney, Nova Scotia (www.marine-atlantic.ca).

By Train

Once again, there's just one train in Eastern Canada, **VIA Rail** (www.viarail. ca; ✆ **888/842-7245**), which runs three times weekly on an overnight route between Montréal and Halifax. If you're serious about taking this train, see "Getting There," above, for more information, and consult the VIA website for fares and schedules.

By Bus

Decent bus service is offered between major cities and many smaller towns by **Maritime Bus** (www.maritimebus.com; ✆ **800/575-1807**).

TIPS ON ACCOMMODATIONS

Eastern Canada is a unique region, with a unique set of lodgings to match. You won't find many five-star hotels outside of the main cities, but rather a more homey hospitality—a patchwork of B&Bs, simple country inns, motels, and chain and business hotels. Please note that Frommer's ratings, the stars that you'll see in this book, are NOT the star ratings given to properties by the Canadian government (called **Canada Select**). Since we take value into account, a really wonderful campground might get three stars from our author, and a more expensive, but less character-full and well-maintained luxury resort could only get one.

Please note that when you're looking at the **Canada Select** rating, you're not getting all of the hotels in the region. Properties have to pay a fee to be rated. The majority of hotels join because it's tremendously useful as a marketing tool, so a Relais & Châteaux–affiliated property in New Brunswick, for example—a five-star experience by every possible measure—wouldn't join, because they don't need the marketing boost. Second, it sometimes seems hotel inspectors are looking for inclusion (of breakfast, dinner, alarm clocks, parking lots, and so on) first, quality second. A place missing one thing on a long checklist might be demoted a star or two, even if it's great.

Types of Accommodations

Here are the various categories of lodgings you'll find in Eastern Canada, as defined and classified by Canada Select.

BED & BREAKFASTS Very common in Eastern Canada, B&Bs will have rooms in a private home with en-suite, private, or shared bathrooms with a common living room and breakfast. If something is listed as a "tourist home" that means it may not supply breakfast. "Farmhouse" B&Bs must be located on fully operating farms, by law. Everyone has dreamed of staying in a cute

TURNING TO THE internet FOR A LODGINGS DISCOUNT

Before going online, it's important that you know what "flavor" of discount you're seeking. Currently, there are three types of online reductions:

1. **Extreme discounts on sites where you bid for lodgings without knowing which hotel you'll get.** You'll find these on such sites as Priceline.com and Hotwire.com, and they can be real money-savers, particularly if you're booking within a week of travel (that's when the hotels get nervous and resort to deep discounts to get beds filled). As these companies use only major chains and well-known hotels, you can rest assured that you won't be put up in a dump. For more reassurance, visit the website BetterBidding.com or BiddingTraveler.com. On it, actual travelers spill the beans about what they bid on Priceline.com and which hotels they got. We've also found that if you go to Priceline's "Express Deals," look at the amenities listed for the hotels, and then plug in those amenities into the filter on the non-blind bidding part of the site, you can figure out pretty quickly which hotel you'll likely be getting. Prices we've seen recently shave the cost of a night by as much as 50% off the rates you'll see on other sites. I think you'll be pleasantly surprised by the quality of many of the hotels that are offering these "secret" discounts.

2. **Discounts on the hotel's website itself.** Sometimes these can be great values, as they'll often include such nice perks as free breakfast or parking privileges. Before biting, though, be sure to look at the discounter sites below.

3. **Discounts on online travel agencies as Hotels.com, Booking. com, Expedia.com, and the like.** Some of these sites reserve rooms in bulk and at a discount, passing

B&B on vacation, and indeed many of the places listed in this book fall into this category. They range from three-star experiences to very simple places, but every one has been visited by our author and is personally recommended.

COTTAGES There are numerous cottages for rent in Canada's eastern provinces, at all price levels, and these can be one of the very best ways to see the region, especially for a family. You save money because you can cook, and the cottages are usually set in a lovely natural setting (beside the sea, overlooking fields or a golf course, and so on). And, a big plus for parents, there is always the option of putting the kids to bed and having some comfortable private time for Mom and Dad.

On the downside, they can vary wildly in quality because most will be decorated and maintained by private owners. Beyond those listed in this guide, you'll find a plethora of cottages on such sites as FlipKey.com, VRBO. com, AirBnB.com, and Homeaway.com. Always look to see what extra fees are added on to a rental. All of the above companies charge travelers a booking fee, and there are also often cleaning fees.

along the savings to their customers. But instead of going to them directly, I'd recommend looking at such dedicated travel search engines as **HotelsCombined.com** and **Trivago.com.** These sites list prices from all the discount sites as well as the hotels directly, meaning you have a better chance of finding a deal. On a recent test of all the hotel websites (which you can find full details about on Frommers.com under the name "The 10 Worst and Best Booking Sites for Hotels", we found that HotelsCombined came up with the lowest rates in almost all of our searches. Trivago came in second, though, annoyingly, it often floated the rates of its parent company Expedia to the top of search, even when those weren't the lowest rates. *Note:* Sometimes the discounts these sites find require advance payment for a room (and draconian cancellation policies), so think carefully about how definite your plans are before committing, because cancellation fees have been climbing recently.

4. **Rental websites.** Amazingly, cottage rentals can often be on a par, price-wise, with hotel rooms, despite the fact that they give you much more room and a kitchen. Be aware that in early 2016, a number of sites—such as Homeaway.com and VRBO.com—started charging 5% to 15% booking fees (AirBnB.com already had those costs). So make sure you add up all fees before inputting your credit card information. In addition to booking fees, these could include fees for cleaning and/or electricity. Beyond the two sites listed above, also take a look at FlipKey.com and Rentalo.com

It's a lot of surfing, I know, but when high season is short, as it is in the Maritimes, prices can rise precipitously and this sort of diligence can pay off.

HOTELS & MOTELS In practice, these vary so much that one hardly knows where to begin. Check our rankings closely. Also be aware that, at some point, you might end up in a chain hotel that's boring as bread. It happens, especially in smaller cities and towns, when the few good options (those cute B&Bs are often pretty small) are all filled up.

INNS According to Canada Select, the only difference between a B&B and an inn is that the latter offers dinner. In practice, inns tend to be larger and more luxurious than B&Bs. There are plenty of inns in the eastern provinces, and they are often the highest-end accommodations in their areas.

RESORTS According to Canada Select, a "resort" must have four or more rooms in a main building, a full-service dining room, and extensive on site recreational facility (sports equipment, a pool, a spa, a fitness club, and so on). Resorts are destination properties and can include resort hotels, spas, ranches, condo hotels, and lodges, with rooms or housekeeping units.

Once again, while many resorts offer extensive services and exceptional location or amenities—a world-class golf course, for example—there's sometimes a gap between appearance and reality. We've seen many a place in

Eastern Canada describe itself as a "resort," when in fact it is that in name only. Read reviews carefully before booking.

HOSTELS There are very few hostels in Eastern Canada, but those that are here are generally pretty decent. If you don't mind the communal atmosphere and possibly doing a few chores before checkout, budget-conscious travelers should give them a look. Most come with shared kitchens, so saving money on meals is possible. Note that youth hostels once imposed an age limit on their guests, but they no longer do in all except a few European countries.

For more info on hostels go to: www.hihostels.ca.

There are also some very good hostels affiliated with Backpackers Hostels (www.backpackers.ca) like the one in Digby, Nova Scotia.

UNIVERSITY DORMITORIES In summer, when Canada's universities and colleges are (mostly) on break, many institutions open up their dorm rooms and communal spaces to traveling families for daily or weekly rentals. These rooms are almost uniformly spartan and inexpensive, but you often get the use of a private or shared kitchen in the deal. Some universities offer higher-end accommodations like apartments with full kitchens. We've listed a number of these options in Halifax.

HOUSE RENTALS Renting a house or condo apartment is an option in the Maritimes, though it's far, far easier to rent a cottage. Once again, check out the major rental sites listed above to get the lay of the land. Occasionally, you can find an independent vacation-home rental agency that rents out the homes of part-time residents such as Sandy Lane Vacation Rentals in Shelburne, Nova Scotia at www.sandylanevacations.com that manages over 40 properties.

CAMPGROUNDS & CAMPING CABINS Campgrounds are easy to find throughout the region, both private and government-run in provincial and national parks. Many, such as KOAs, offer camping cabins. Rustic (they provide a roof, walls, and basic beds but no linens), they keep you dry and sometimes warm. Recently, Parks Canada has added to many of its campgrounds two new options—yurts and oTENTiks. Yurts usually come with a wooden floor, bed frame, tables, and chairs inside a round, canvas-covered frame, while oTENTiks are a hybrid of a cabin and a tent (imagine a cabin with flexible walls made of canvas or very thick plastic and you've got it). You need your own sleeping bags and pillows. These are excellent options if you like the outdoor experience but don't like tenting, and a good way to save money.

SPECIAL-INTEREST TRIPS & TOURS

In addition to the tours listed in the destination chapters, here are some others that are well worth consideration.

Adventure Trips

In New Brunswick, **Gaston Adventure Tours** ★★ (www.facebook.com/GastonAdventureTours; ✆ **506/365-7787**) out of Doaktown offers a guided trip along the great Miramichi River deep into the forest via off-road vehicle to see old-growth forest and the province's highest waterfall. The company also offers guided canoe trips and salmon-fishing excursions on the river. Rates range from C$60 to CC$180.

In Nova Scotia, **Great Earth Expeditions** ★★★ (www.greatearthexpedi tions.com/index.html; ☎ 902/223-2409) offers a serious eco-adventure tour of Cape Breton Island—hiking the highlands, sea kayaking, whale and wildlife watching, and a boat tour to bird islands, all in 4 days. In addition, the company offers half-day trips from Halifax to the South Shore, the Eastern Shore, and the Annapolis Valley. They also offer cruise-ship passengers arriving in Halifax excursions around the city and to Peggy's Cove. Great Earth operates May through October. Rates range from C$90 to C$495.

Backroads ★ (www.backroads.com; ☎ 800/462-2848 or 510/527-1555) is one of North America's largest adventure travel companies, and it offers multi-day walking and biking trips through southeast Nova Scotia, among other programs in the eastern provinces.

Food & Wine Tours

In New Brunswick, **Uncorked Tours** ★★ (www.uncorkednb.com; ☎ 506/324-4644) offers walking tours in St. Andrews, Saint John, Moncton, and Fredericton, as well as tours by van of places in between. Their wine tours stop at several of New Brunswick's wineries and come with cheese tastings, lunch, or dinner. Rates range from C$50 to CC$150.

Aboard the pink British double-decker **Wolfville Magic Winery Bus** ★★ (www.wolfvillemagicwinerybus.ca; ☎ 902/542-4093) in Nova Scotia, you'll travel to four local wineries for tastings and tours. Guides speak about the human and natural history of the area and how they contribute to the terroir. The company will arrange for group pickup in Halifax, if requested. Tours run three times daily from July to mid-September, Thursday to Sunday. Rates range from C$20 to C$25.

Learning Vacations

The **Gaelic College of Celtic Arts and Crafts** ★★, St. Ann's, NS (www.gaeliccollege.edu; ☎ 902/295-3411), offers programs for children and adults that specialize in local culture—such as Highland bagpiping, dancing, drumming, and Cape Breton fiddling—on its campus near Baddeck.

Sunbury Shores Arts & Nature Centre ★, St. Andrews, NB (www.sunburyshores.org; ☎ 506/529-3386), offers day- and weeklong trips and classes on various topics: plant dyes, printmaking, mosaic work, raku pottery, and watercolor and oil painting. Some summer classes and programs are specially geared toward children and teenagers. The center is located on the water in St. Andrews; lodging can be arranged locally, as well.

At **Village Historique Acadien** ★★, near Caraquet, NB (www.village historiqueacadien.com; ☎ 877/721-2200 or 506/726-2600), the lives and arts of early Acadian settlers are the focus of programs held at a re-created historic village. Children and adults can learn to spin wool and hook rugs. The historic village is open from early June through mid-September.

Bus Tours

Prince Edward Tours ★★ (www.princeedwardtours.com; ℂ **877/286-6532**) offers tours of Charlottetown on a blue double-decker British bus, as well as several excursions beyond. One called "Island's Finest" includes stops at a fishing village, lighthouses, Green Gables National Historic Site, and the PEI Preserve Company. Private tours can be arranged for deep-sea fishing, golf, distilleries, and other themed trips. Tours depart Charlottetown daily. Rates range from C$16 to C$70 for set tours, but you'll pay more for private tours.

    Nova Scotia Ambassatours ★★ (www.ambassatours.com; ℂ **800/565-9662** or 902/423-6242) is the province's premier bus tour company. Besides a fleet of pink British double-decker busses for hop-on, hop-off tours of Halifax, they offer a deluxe city tour that takes you to sites important to the history of the *Titanic,* landmarks like the Citadel National Historic Site and the Public Gardens. Tours outside the city run to Peggy's Cove and to the Town of Lunenburg, a UNESCO World Heritage Site. Tours run from mid-June to mid-October and cost between C$46 and C$86.

    In New Brunswick, **Roads to Sea** ★★ (www.roadstosea.com; ℂ **877/850-7623** or 506/850-7623) focuses on guided tours along the Bay of Fundy to experience the best of the region, like Hopewell Rocks, Cape Enrage, and Fundy National Park. Along the way, local guides speak off the cuff about the history and culture (no rehearsed monologues here!). Full day tours by 14-person van run daily in summer and cost C$167 per person and include all entrance fees. They also offer half-day excursions from Moncton, as well as cruise-ship excursions in Saint John.

Multi-Day, All-Inclusive Tours

Some travelers enjoy the structure offered by tours that predetermine all your hotels, restaurants, and itineraries. Basically, you sit back and enjoy the trip without having to worry about planning (or local transportation). Be aware that such tours usually bring groups to a large number of famous sights in a short time, without lingering much. They're especially convenient for people with limited mobility and can be a way to make new friends. On the downside, you get little opportunity for spontaneous interactions with locals; the tours tend to leave little room for individual sightseeing; you won't see "off the beaten track" spots; and heaven help you if there's a crank on the tour with you.

    Also see our description of **Road Scholar,** an excellent guided tour company for travelers over 55. You'll find it under "Senior Travelers" in the "Fast Facts" section below. These two firms offer especially good escorted tours of Eastern Canada:

○ **Maxxim Vacations** ★★ (www.maxximvacations.com; ℂ **800/567-6666** or 709/754-6666): Newfoundland's largest travel provider has a top-rate reputation and offers a huge range of trips throughout the four Atlantic

Provinces, including plenty of both guided and unguided excursions. From a "PEI Golf Getaway" to a "Romantic New Brunswick" (thankfully unescorted) tour, Scott and Judy Sparkes' family-owned company offers it all, professionally and well. Tour prices helpfully come with airfare from your home city already factored into the equation.

○ **Collette Vacations** ★ (www.collettevacations.com; *©* **800/340-5158**): Collette offers a number of excellent tours of Eastern Canada (about 10 days each, on average) that range from fly/drive packages to the escorted everything's-done-for-you variety throughout the Maritimes. Top-rated offerings include "Canada's Atlantic Coast Featuring the Cabot Trail" (touching three provinces), and "Hidden Treasures of the Maritimes" (which *does* bring in some lesser-known sights). Additional side trips are even possible on Collette tours for an extra fee, but note that your airfare isn't included in the quoted base package prices.

[Fast FACTS] THE MARITIMES

Area Codes The area code for New Brunswick is 506. The area code for Nova Scotia and Prince Edward Island is 902.

Business Hours Bank, government, and business hours are generally 9am to 5pm in winter and, for some, 8am to 4pm in summer, Monday to Friday. Retail shops are generally open 10am to 10pm, every day except holidays; however, regulations differ from province to province, community, or time of the year, so check locally. Some retail shops, especially seasonal operations, may be open shorter hours.

Customs International visitors can expect at least a probing question or two at the border or airport. Normal baggage and personal possessions should be no problem, but plants, animals, and weapons are among the items that may be prohibited or require

additional documents for admittance. For specific information about Canadian rules, check with the **Canada Border Services Agency** (www.cbsa-asfc.gc.ca).

Tobacco and alcoholic beverages face strict import restrictions: Individuals 18 years or older are allowed to bring in 200 cigarettes, 50 cigars, or 200 grams of tobacco; and only one of the following amounts of alcohol: 1.14 liters of liquor, 1.5 liters of wine, or 24 cans or bottles of beer. Additional amounts face hefty taxes. Alcohol must accompany you, and you must be legal drinking age (19).

Possession of a car radar detector is prohibited, whether or not it is connected. Police officers can confiscate it and fines may run as high as C$1,000. A car driven into Canada can stay for the duration allowed the visitor, which is up to 6 months unless the

visitor has arranged permission for a longer stay. Visitors can temporarily bring recreational vehicles, such as snowmobiles, boats, and trailers, as well as outboard motors, for personal use. If you do not declare goods or falsely declare them, they can be seized along with the vehicle in which you brought them.

Doctors Walk-in clinics are found in most communities, except small villages. If you have an emergency, call **911** for immediate attention or go to the emergency or "out patients" section of the nearest hospital. Check the yellow pages in the telephone book for the hospital or clinic near to you, and its hours of operation.

Drinking Laws In Nova Scotia, New Brunswick, and Prince Edward Island, the legal drinking age (the minimum age at which a person is allowed to buy and/or drink alcohol) is 19. With a few exceptions (a specialty wine shop, an outlet in a rural store far from government outlets, and so on) liquor (including beer) can only be purchased at government-operated Liquor Commission stores or producing distillers or wineries. For a listing of locations go to www.mynslc.ca (Nova Scotia), www.peilcc.ca (PEI), and www.nbliquor.com (New Brunswick).

Drinking and driving laws are tough, and enforced with extremely serious penalties. Don't drink and drive. Also do not carry open containers of alcohol in your car or on your person unless in an area where drinking alcohol is permitted. National and Provincial Parks have alcohol regulations. Check when entering the park.

Drugstores & Pharmacies

Chain drugstores and independent pharmacies are located throughout Atlantic Canada. Stores in larger cities and towns are likely to be open later than those in more remote villages. One of the larger national chains is **Shoppers Drug Mart** (www.shoppersdrugmart.ca), which has a store locator on its website. Most independents belong to one of two large associations, PharmaSave (www.pharmasave.com) and PharmaChoice (www.pharmachoice.com).

Electricity

All Canadian hotels, inns, and private homes use the same electrical current as the United States: 110–115 volts, 60 cycles. If you're traveling from the U.S., you won't need adapters for your plugs. Coming from anywhere else, you probably will.

Embassies & Consulates

All foreign embassies are located in Ottawa, Ontario, as follows:

Australian High Commission, Ste. 710–50 O'Connor St., Ottawa, Ontario K1P 6L2; www.canada.embassy.gov.au; ℂ **613/236-0841.**

New Zealand High Commission, Ste. 727, 99 Bank St., Ottawa, Ontario K1P 6G3; www.nzembassy.com; ℂ **613/238-5991.**

United Kingdom, British High Commission, 80 Elgin St., Ottawa, Ontario K1P 5K7; www.gov.uk; ℂ **613/237-1530.**

Embassy of the United States of America, 490 Sussex Dr., Ottawa, Ontario K1N 1G8; http://canada.usembassy.gov; ℂ **613/238-5335.**

U.S. Consulate General Halifax, Ste. 904, Purdy's Wharf Tower II, 1969 Upper Water St., Halifax, Nova Scotia B3J 3R7; http://halifax.usconsulate.gov; ℂ **902/429-2480.**

Emergencies

The emergency number for Eastern Canada is ℂ **911** throughout.

Family Travel

Atlantic Canada is simply a great place to take the kids: It's safe, clean, and sprinkled with just enough amusements and outdoor jaunts to keep them engaged. The provinces vary, though, in their ability to entertain the young 'uns.

Prince Edward Island is the best destination for young girls, simply due to the proliferation of attractions related to *Anne of Green Gables*. For the whole family there are miles of sandy beaches and many lighthouses to explore. **New Brunswick** abounds with easy adventuring (golfing, biking, kayaking, big-tide sightseeing, and so on), living historic villages, and it throws in a handful of amusement parks and museums for good measure. **Nova Scotia** holds great appeal for the 6-and-up set: dinosaurs and fossils, forts with wonderful programs (check out Fortress Louisbourg), and one of the best interactive museum programs, with locations around the province, which is simply wonderful for kids.

Gasoline

Gas stations are basically the same as in the U.S., but gasoline is sold by the liter, not by the gallon. (3.8L equal 1 U.S. gal.). Gas prices in Nova Scotia are set weekly by a government agency, so you are always guaranteed to pay pretty well the same (within a range of two cents per liter) for gas and diesel across the province. See http://nsuarb.novascotia.ca for current prices. The same is the case in PEI; check current prices there at http://irac.pe.ca. New Brunswick sets maximum prices for gas and diesel which are found at www.nbeub.ca.

Health Canada is one of the safest, cleanest countries in the world; as such, traveling in Eastern Canada doesn't pose any special health threats. Poisonous snakes? Sharks? Tropical diseases? Not here. And the food and water are very clean and safe to consume.

Canada's healthcare system is excellent; you shouldn't ever have trouble finding English-speaking medical help, unless you're in very remote areas of, for example, Northern New Brunswick (away from the coastal towns) or wilderness Cape Breton. It is advisable to always obtain good travel insurance to cover the time you are away from home. Such sites as **SquareMouth.com** and **InsureMyTrip.com** act as clearinghouses for travel insurance with healthcare included.

Insurance Canadians are covered when traveling within their own province, but may not be when travelling to other Canadian provinces; check with your province's healthcare insurance provider for details. Most U.S. health plans (including Medicare and Medicaid) do *not* provide coverage for travel to Canada, and the ones that do often require you to pay for services upfront and reimburse you only after you return home. Those from other countries need to check out the situation in their country well before leaving home.

As a safety net, you may want to buy **travel medical insurance.** See above for our advice on insurance.

Pharmacies are easy to find in Eastern Canada (see above). Still, if you suffer from a chronic illness, consult your doctor before your departure. Pack **prescription medications** in your carry-on luggage, and carry them in their original containers, with pharmacy labels—otherwise they won't make it through airport security. Carry the generic name of prescription medicines, in case a local pharmacist is unfamiliar with the brand name. It is wise to make a list of *all* medications and carry it with you at all times. Either e-mail the info to yourself or ask your pharmacy for a printout.

Internet & Wi-Fi Free Wi-Fi is now widely available across the Maritimes. Cities like Halifax and Charlottetown are rife with Internet cafes; anywhere else, it's catch-as-catch-can—but many towns in Eastern Canada now sport at least one cybercafe. It might double as the town laundry/coffee shop, but it'll be there somewhere. So ask. Even some coffee chains like Tim Hortons offer free Wi-Fi.

Most airports have free Wi-Fi. Many **public and university libraries** in Canada offer free Wi-Fi, as well as public use computers. Most **youth hostels** in Canada have at least one computer with Internet access, though there is just a thimbleful of hostels in the Maritimes. Nearly all **hotels and motels** now offer free Wi-Fi. Sometimes an entire community will be blanketed by coverage—the city of **Fredericton,** New Brunswick, for instance, has won national awards for its free citywide Wi-Fi network—but that's rare.

Language English is spoken throughout the region. In some areas of all three provinces, Acadian French is also spoken.

Legal Aid Legal Aid offices located across Canada can be sourced at www.canlaw.com/legal-aid/legal-aid-offices.html or contact the following:

Legal Information Society of Nova Scotia, 5523 B Young St., Halifax, Nova Scotia, B3K 1Z7; www.legalinfo.org; ℂ **800/665-9779** or 902/455-3135.

New Brunswick Legal Aid Services Commission, 2-403 Regent St., Fredericton, New Brunswick E3B 3X6; www.legalaid.nb.ca; or ℂ **506/444-2776.**

Community Legal Information Association of Prince Edward Island, P.O. Box 1207, 1st Floor Sullivan Building, Fitzroy St., Charlottetown, Prince Edward Island; www.cliapei.ca; ℂ **800/240-9798** or 902/892-0853.

LGBT Travelers Canada as a whole is considered extremely friendly to gay travelers. No accommodation or other service in Eastern Canada will turn away or otherwise discourage LGBT travelers, but some establishments are openly and explicitly welcoming, particularly in the cities.

LGBT travelers to PEI are welcomed by the Tourism PEI website and referred to the **PEI Gay Tourism Association** at www.gaytourismpei.ca for specialized info. The other two Maritime provinces do not provide information specific to LGBT travelers, but **GayHalifax** (http://gay.hfxns.org) is a good online starting point to help you find out what's going on locally. **Destination Halifax** (www.destinationhalifax.com/experience-halifax/lgbt) is the best online guide to the city's gay events and services.

Mail Canada Post offers a reliable international postal service. Postage for letters or postcards within Canada is approximately C85¢, to the United States C$1.20, and international C$2.50. You can determine costs with a rate calculator at www.canadapost.ca. Postage stamps and mailboxes are readily available throughout the Maritime provinces. If you require fast shipment of parcels or letter packets, FedEx and other courier services are available in most towns and cities. Some office supply stores and hotels offer pickup points for couriers.

Medical Requirements Unless you're arriving from an area known to be suffering from an epidemic (such as cholera or yellow fever), inoculations or vaccinations are not required for entry into Canada.

Mobile Phones Yes, foreign cellphones work in Canada. However, depending on your phone plan, you may have to pay roaming and long-distance charges that can push call costs up to very expensive. Some large U.S. carriers offer tack on Canadian calling plans that reduce these charges while making calls from within Canada. Check with your carrier about switching on to one such plan for the duration of your trip—without any penalties for switching it back off after you get back home, making sure they understand that you will be calling back to the U.S. from Canada and making calls within Canada.

You should be able to make and receive calls in all the populated areas of Eastern Canada, assuming your cellphone works on a GSM (Global System for Mobile Communications) system or you have a world-capable multiband phone. In the U.S., T-Mobile and AT&T Wireless use the quasi-universal GSM system; Sprint and Verizon don't. All European and most Australian phones come GSM-ready. GSM phones function with a removable plastic SIM card, encoded with your phone number and account information.

FYI, Canada has three national wireless providers, Bell Mobility, Rogers Wireless, and Telus Mobility. Rogers is GSM, Bell uses LTE and Telus uses CDMA technology.

To use the phone in Canada, simply call

your wireless carrier before leaving home and ask if "international roaming" needs to be activated on your account and the cost. Again, per-minute charges can be high, even if you do subscribe to some form of extended calling plan or international add-on plan that includes Canadian minutes.

Buying a disposable Canadian cellphone is another option, and might be economically attractive if you can locate an inexpensive prepaid phone system. Local calls might be as low as C10¢ or C20¢ per minute; do a quick Internet search for options in your arrival city.

All Canadian cellphones should work in the Maritimes, although some of the "discount" brands with smaller coverage areas may only work in major centers. Although you will not incur roaming charges if you are traveling out of province, long-distance charges may apply. These provinces are thinly populated in some regions and as a result cell towers, especially Rogers, can be few and far between. You may not be able to use your cellphone everywhere; even driving the Trans-Canada Highway, you can pop in and out of service. In the major cities, you will always be reliably connected; in the smaller towns, most of the time; and, in the wilderness of the big national and provincial parks, probably only in hotspots or not at all. Definitely ask park wardens about cell coverage before you venture into the backcountry.

If you have access to the Web while traveling, you might consider a broadband-based telephone service (in technical terms, **Voice over Internet Protocol,** or **VoIP**) such as **Skype** (www.skype.com) or **Vonage** (www.vonage.com), which allows you to make free international calls if you use their services from your smart phone or laptop.

Money & Costs Frommer's lists prices in the local currency. Smart travelers watch the exchange rates and buy money for their destination when advantageous.

Frommer's lists exact prices in the local currency. The currency conversions quoted below were correct at press time. However, rates fluctuate, so before departing, go to XE.com for current rates.

Cost-wise, the eastern provinces of Canada are **incredibly affordable—** among the most affordable such places in North America. You'll pay normal prices for food and gas, because those things are generally imported to the provinces, but hotel, restaurant, and transit rates are middling to lower than average. And shopping is a downright bargain.

Canadian currency, like U.S. currency, is denominated in **dollars and cents,** though there are some differences. Canada has no C$1 bill, for example. Instead, Canadians use a C$1 coin (nicknamed a *loonie* because it depicts a loon) and a C$2 coin (sometimes called a *toonie* because it rhymes with *loonie*).

To get the best exchange rate, simply head to the nearest **ATM** machine. You'll find these widely available. At the airport, make sure that the ATM is from a bank and *not* an exchange service, to avoid extra fees. Avoid exchanging money at commercial exchange bureaus and hotels, which usually have the highest transaction fees. If your card uses the **Cirrus** (www.mastercard.com) or **PLUS** (www.visa.com) networks, you'll be able to find ATMs throughout Eastern Canada that connect to your bank.

If you're driving into Canada, you needn't worry about stocking up on Canadian dollars before or immediately upon entry into Canada. That's because **U.S. currency is widely accepted** here, especially in border towns, and you'll often see signs at cash registers announcing current exchange rates. These are not always the best rates, however, so it's best to

visit an ATM as soon as you're able.

Remember that **many banks impose a fee** every time you use a card at another bank's ATM, and that fee can be higher for international transactions (up to US$5 or more) than for domestic ones. Members of the Global ATM Alliance usually charge *no* transaction fees for cash withdrawals at fellow Alliance member ATMs; these include Bank of America in the U.S. and Scotiabank in Eastern Canada, as well as BNP Paribas, Barclays, Deutsche Bank 24, and Westpac. So, if you have a BoA account, seek out Scotiabank ATMs.

Finally, **credit cards** are one last safe way to get or spend money. They provide a convenient record of your expenses and generally offer relatively good exchange rates. Do *not,* however, withdraw cash advances from your credit cards at banks or ATMs, as high fees will make these credit-card cash advances a very pricey way to get cash (the bank counts these transactions as a loan). Credit cards that are more or less universally accepted in Eastern Canada include Visa, MasterCard, and American Express. Diners Club and Discover cards are accepted by a few

THE VALUE OF THE CANADIAN DOLLAR VS. OTHER POPULAR CURRENCIES

C$	A$	€	NZ$	£	US$
1.00	0.99	0.66	1.06	0.49	0.72

WHAT THINGS COST IN THE MARITIMES

	C$
Taxi to/from Charlottetown airport to downtown	14.00
or to/from Halifax airport to downtown	63.00
Bus fare in Halifax	2.50
Cup of coffee	2.00
Pint of beer at a bar	6.00
Moderate hotel room	100.00–150.00
Comfortable bed-and-breakfast	80.00–110.00
Takeout fish and chips	14.00
Expensive 3-course dinner without wine	50.00–85.00

merchants, but not many. Interac or debit cards are almost as widely accepted as cash.

One good habit to get into is to call your credit-card company before you leave and advise them of your destination and dates of travel. It may save an embarrassing and upsetting delay in transactions while the credit card company checks for possible thefts. Remember to bring some cash, in any case: Although even some farmers' market vendors accept debit and credit cards, some small businesses cannot afford the fees.

Newspapers & Magazines
Along with local newspapers, Canada's national newspaper, the *Globe and Mail,* is readily accessible, as are magazines. For foreign newspapers, check public or university libraries or newsstands in larger communities.

Packing
Dress style in Eastern Canada is basically casual unless attending a formal event. Summer days can be hot, but it cools nicely in the evenings. In winter, you will need winter footwear, winter coats, hats, and gloves. The watchword for comfort here is "layers." Dress in layers, say the locals, to adjust according to weather.

Passports
It is no longer possible to enter Canada by showing a government-issued photo ID (such as a driver's license) or proof of U.S. citizenship (such as a birth or naturalization certificate). The **Western Hemisphere Travel Initiative (WHTI)** requires all U.S. citizens returning to the U.S. from Canada to have a U.S. passport (this includes children 17 and under). In other words, if you are a U.S. citizen traveling to Canada by air, sea, or land, you must have a valid U.S. passport or a new passport card (see www.getyouhome.gov for details) in order to get back into the U.S. Citizens of other countries will also need a passport to enter and exit Canada.

Police
Large communities usually have their own police forces in Canada, while smaller communities and rural areas are policed by the RCMP (Royal Canadian Mounted Police). Dialing 911 will connect you with the appropriate police force in the event of an emergency.

Safety
The towns and cities of Atlantic Canada are small, well policed, and generally safe. Partygoers and those who have over-imbibed may occasionally be annoying or even a bit threatening, especially late on weekend nights in downtown neighborhoods, but serious crime is extremely rare in Eastern Canada. A stranger is more likely to return your dropped wallet than to steal it.

Nonetheless, whenever you're traveling in an unfamiliar place in this region, stay alert, be aware of your immediate surroundings, and take precautions, such as locking your car and hotel room and not walking alone in dark, unpopulated urban areas late at night. Try not to drive late at night when there's likely to be no one else out on the road if you run into trouble. And **carry a cellphone** at all times if you have one; coverage in Eastern Canada certainly isn't complete, but it is improving year by year.

The emergency number for Eastern Canada is ☏ **911** throughout.

Senior Travel Few countries are as attentive to the needs of seniors as Canada. Discounts are extended to people 60 and over (sometimes 55 and over) for everything from public transportation to museum and movie admissions. Even many hotels, tour operators, and restaurants offer discounts, so don't be bashful about inquiring, and always carry identification that shows your date of birth. (It's always best to inquire before checking in or ordering.) This discount varies widely; in practice, the gap between senior prices and full price seems to be narrowing in recent years. Members of the **AARP** (www.aarp.org; ☏ **888/687-2277**) get discounts when traveling to or in Eastern Canada at some hotels, airfares, and car rentals. **CARP,** the Canadian Association of Retired Persons (www.carp.ca; ☏ **888/363-2279**) has chapters in Prince Edward Island, Nova Scotia, and New Brunswick, and a similar range of benefits.

Elderhostel now calls its programs **Road Scholar**

(www.roadscholar.org; ☏ **800/454-5768**), which encompasses worldwide educational adventures and study programs for those 55 and over. They manage several excellent tours of the Maritimes, including a Nova Scotia, New Brunswick, PEI combo (10 days).

Single Travel Many reputable tour companies offer singles-only trips, and some of them dip into the Maritimes. The popular outfitter **Backroads** (www.backroads.com; ☏ **800/462-2848**) offers active-travel trips to destinations worldwide, including several hiking and biking tours in Nova Scotia.

One of the best bets for singles is to enroll in a program such as the culinary or artisan educational sessions or learning vacations (see "Tours" p. 296) that bring you together with like-minded folk. Check out the arts, music, and performing arts for example, or college or university offerings.

Remember that on some package vacations to Canada, as a single traveler you might be hit with the dreaded "single supplement" to the base price. To avoid it, agree to room with other single travelers or find a compatible roommate before you go from a specialized roommate-locator agency.

Smoking All three Maritime provinces have banned smoking in public places and workplaces. Basically, smokers are relegated to the outdoors, well away from entranceways.

As well, most (if not all) hotel rooms are designated nonsmoking. If you smoke, check when reserving or checking in to ensure you get a smoking room, otherwise you may face surcharges if you light up.

Taxes Sales tax is added onto most purchases and services. In Prince Edward Island the federal GST of 5% is added, then a 9% provincial sales tax (PST) is added, creating the harmonized sales tax (HST) of 14%. PST is not charged on clothing or footwear (sports or protective equipment and accessories are not exempt). In Nova Scotia an HST (harmonized sales tax) of 15% is added. In New Brunswick an HST of 13% is added.

Telephones The United States and Canada are on the same long-distance system. To make a long-distance call between the United States and Canada (in either direction), simply dial ☏ **1** first, then the area code and number. Callers to other countries will need to check the country code in the phone book or with the long distance operator.

Remember that numbers beginning with **800, 888,** and **866** in Canada are toll-free—so some of these numbers won't work if they're dialed from outside Canada. Just the same, some toll-free numbers in the U.S. won't work if they're dialed from Canada.

Time The three provinces in the Maritimes are in the

Atlantic Time Zone. Change your clocks when crossing the border from the United States or Québec. Daylight saving time begins at 2am local time on the second Sunday in March when clocks are turned ahead 1 hour. Clocks are turned back at the end of daylight saving time on the first Sunday in November.

Tipping In hotels, tip **bellhops** at least C$2 per bag (up to C$5 if you have a lot of luggage) and tip the **chamber staff** C$2 to C$5 per day (more if you've left a big mess for him or her to clean up). Tip the **doorman** or **concierge** C$2 only if he or she has provided you with some specific service (for example, calling a cab for you or obtaining difficult-to-get theater tickets). Tip the **valet-parking attendant** C$2 to C$5 every time you get your car.

In restaurants, bars, and nightclubs, tip **service staff** and **bartenders** 15% of the check, tip **checkroom attendants** C$2 per garment, and tip **valet-parking attendants** C$2 per vehicle.

As for other service personnel, tip **cabdrivers** 10% to 20% of the fare; tip **skycaps** at airports at least C$2 per bag (up to C$5 if you have a lot of luggage); and tip **hairdressers** and **barbers** 15% to 20%.

Toilets Washrooms are generally very clean and readily available. You won't find public washrooms on the street very often, but they are in malls, large retail stores, and government

buildings. If you're stuck, a coffee shop or fast-food restaurant is your best bet.

Travelers with Limited Mobility Canada has made tremendous efforts toward eliminating barriers to mobility for its citizens and, by extension, its tourist visitors. City pavements feature curb cuts for wheelchair travel, and larger hotels and airports have wheelchair-accessible washrooms. A growing number of restaurants and tourist attractions are now designed for wheelchair accessibility as well, although room for improvement remains. National and provincial parks are almost always accessible, at least to a degree.

The Canadian Paraplegic Association (aka **The Spinal Cord Injury Association**) maintains an office in each of the three Maritime provinces. In New Brunswick, visit www.cpanb.ca or call ℰ **506/462-9555;** in Nova Scotia, visit www.the spine.ca or call ℰ **902/423-1277;** and in Prince Edward Island, visit www.sci-pei.ca or call ℰ **902/370-9523.**

Travelers with disabilities headed for Nova Scotia can also ask locally about accessible transportation and recreational opportunities by contacting the **Nova Scotia League for Equal Opportunities** (www.novascotia leo.org; ℰ **866/696-7536** or 902/455-6942). The organization maintains a useful network of contacts throughout the province.

Some travel agencies offer customized tours and itineraries for travelers with disabilities. One of the best is **Accessible Journeys** (www.disabilitytravel.com; ℰ **800/846-4537** or 610/521-0339). Check with them for the latest tours to the Maritimes.

Avis Rent a Car (www. avis.com/access; ℰ **800/669-9585**) has a good "Avis Access" program that offers services for customers with special travel needs. These include specially outfitted vehicles with swivel seats, spinner knobs, panoramic mirrors, and hand controls; mobility scooter rentals; and accessible bus service. Be sure to reserve well in advance.

Visas American travelers to Canada do not require visas and neither do residents of many other countries, including citizens of most European countries, Australia, New Zealand, Japan, and some present and former British territories in the Caribbean—this includes anyone holding a green card in the U.S. or anyone who is a British overseas citizen of the U.K. Starting in 2016, visitors flying into or passing through Canada from countries other than the U.S. that are visa exempt will need Electronic Travel Authorization, which may be obtained from www.cic.gc.ca/english/visit/visas.asp for C$7. Visit the same site to find out if you need a visa.

Visitor Information It's well worth a toll-free call

in advance of your trip to stock up on the free literature and maps that provincial authorities mail out. Here's how to reach the official tourism folks who dispense these goodies:

Tourism Nova Scotia: www.novascotia.com; ℂ **800/565-0000.**

Tourism New Brunswick: www.tourismnewbrunswick. ca; ℂ **800/561-0123.**

Tourism PEI: www.tourism pei.com; ℂ **800/463-4734.**

All three provinces staff helpful **visitor centers** at key access points, including the main roadways running into the provinces and in their major cities. Expect cordial staff and exceptionally well-stocked racks overflowing with menus, brochures, and booklets. Excellent **road maps** are also available from all three provincial tourism authorities—ask at the welcome centers. These maps are free.

Water   Water for consumption is monitored and safe throughout the Maritimes.

Women Travelers   This destination is popular with women travelers who appreciate the safety and ease of travel. A caution about being careful where you go late at night is the same as would be offered anywhere. Common sense and attention to your surroundings is always wise.

Index

GENERAL INDEX

Accommodations

Restaurants